CHRISTIAN FANTASY

Also by Colin Manlove

MODERN FANTASY: Five Studies
LITERATURE AND REALITY 1600–1800
THE GAP IN SHAKESPEARE: The Motif of Division From
  Richard II To *The Tempest*
THE IMPULSE OF FANTASY LITERATURE
SCIENCE FICTION: Ten Explorations
C. S. LEWIS: His Literary Achievement
CRITICAL THINKING: A Guide to Interpreting
  Literary Texts

Christian Fantasy

From 1200 to the Present

Colin Manlove
Reader in English Literature
University of Edinburgh

University of Notre Dame Press
Notre Dame, Indiana

First published in the United States in 1992 by
University of Notre Dame Press
Notre Dame, Indiana 46556

Published in Great Britain by
The Macmillan Press Ltd

ISBN 0–268–00790–X

Printed in Hong Kong

Library of Congress Cataloging-in-Publication Data
Manlove, C. N. (Colin Nicholas), 1942–
    Christian fantasy : from 1200 to the present / Colin Manlove.
      p.   cm.
    Includes index.
    ISBN 0–268–00790–X
    1. Christian literature, English—History and criticism.
  2. Fantastic literature, English—History and criticism.
  3. Literature, Medieval—History and criticism.   4. Fantastic
  literature—History and criticism.   5. Christianity and literature.
  6. Supernatural in literature.   7. Fantasy in literature.
  I. Title.
  PR145.M36   1992
  820.9'382—dc20   91–47494
                                                              CIP

For Jill

With this ambiguous earth
His dealings have been told us. These abide:
The signal to a maid, the human birth,
The lesson, and the young Man crucified.

But not a star of all
The innumerable host of stars has heard
How He administered this terrestrial ball.
Our race have kept their Lord's entrusted Word.

Of His earth-visiting feet
None knows the secret, cherished, perilous,
The terrible, shamefast, frightened, whispered, sweet,
Heart-shattering secret of His way with us.

No planet knows that this
Our wayside planet, carrying land and wave,
Love and life multiplied, and pain and bliss,
Bears, as chief treasure, one forsaken grave.

Nor, in our little day,
May His devices with the heavens be guessed,
His pilgrimage to thread the Milky Way,
Or His bestowals there be manifest.

But in the eternities,
Doubtless we shall compare together, hear
A million alien Gospels, in what guise
He trod the Pleiades, the Lyre, the Bear.

O, be prepared, my soul!
To read the inconceivable, to scan
The myriad forms of God those stars unroll
When, in our turn, we show to them a Man.

Alice Meynell, 'Christ in the Universe'

Contents

Preface

I wrote this book out of two wishes. First I wanted to find out the variety of fictions dealing in some way with the Christian supernatural, particularly those concerning journeys to a paradise or heaven. The rarity of such works intrigued me. I had been struck, for example, by the way modern science-fiction writers awaken wonder at their suggestion of worlds wholly other from our own, and then reduce them within the parameters of our universe of space and time. The kind of world I wanted to explore is well described by C. S. Lewis:

> No merely physical strangeness or merely spatial distance will realise that idea of otherness which is what we are always trying to grasp in a story about voyaging through space: you must go into another dimension. To construct plausible and moving 'other worlds' you must draw on the only real 'other world' we know, that of the spirit.

The infrequency with which such worlds are portrayed is marked, and I was drawn to explore them.

I also wanted to trace the origin of modern Christian fantasy, to show how, far from being some isolated outgrowth, it is part of a wider pre-Romantic 'kind', which, while infrequently written, was then the highest type of fiction imaginable. But there were obvious differences in the character of modern Christian fantasy, and I began to see that a larger story could be told, involving not only analysis of the major works, but also an account of their changing character from the time of the first significant such fiction, the French *Queste del Saint Graal* in about 1200, to the present day.

I leave this book with a sense that the story has many more elements than I have covered, and also with regret, because it has been so enriching an experience to explore these works and their changes. There will doubtless be authors I have missed out – I have attempted only a survey of the main figures – and a restricted knowledge of theology may have made me miss a number of possible insights. But if this book can convey afresh some of the pleasure and wonder of these texts, and surprise its readers with some of the connections it discovers, it will have done all that could be wished.

I would like here to thank Eileen Crerar-Gilbert, who gave me so much of her enthusiasm, and made so many helpful suggestions, from her love for the subject. I am also indebted, as ever, to Sheila Campbell, for a monumental labour in deciphering and flawlessly typing the manuscript. I would like to acknowledge my special appreciation for the care and precision of the copy-editor, Graham Eyre. I was glad too that the subject of this book so matched his own interests, and it is sad that his recent tragic death has lost for us the power to share it further.

C. N. M.

1

Introduction

Many people, faced by the term 'Christian fantasy', will feel a slight sense of surprise. What has Christianity, which is supposed to be concerned with what is true about the universe, got to do with works founded on invention? Christianity is not fantasy; it is meant to be fact. Surely, if one turns it into a work of imagination, one is suggesting the very thing the atheists maintain – that the Bible story itself may be a fable, created by man to assuage his own uncertainties?

One answer to this is that it is not at all impossible to see the Bible itself as a Christian fantasy. There are few apart from fundamentalists now who would take the Bible as the direct word of God; few who would maintain with the Victorian John William Burgon, Fellow of Oriel College Oxford and vicar of the University church after the intellectually 'dangerous' J. H. Newman,

> The BIBLE is none other than the *Voice of Him that sitteth upon the Throne*! Every book of it – every chapter of it – every verse of it – every word of it – every syllable of it – (where are we to stop?) every letter of it – is the direct utterance of the Most High! The Bible is none other than the word of God – not some part of it more, some part of it less, but all alike, the utterance of Him, who sitteth upon the Throne – absolute – faultless – unerring – supreme.[1]

Such literalism has been challenged not only in our time, but in allegorical interpretation since the earliest days of biblical commentary. But over the last two centuries it has become possible also to see the Bible as in part at least a collection of myths, themselves based on the imagery of other myths.[2] It is now well established, for instance, that the apocalyptic book of Revelation is founded on earlier Jewish accounts of the Last Things. Additional factors, particularly the theory of human evolution propounded by Darwin, have made the picture of man and the fall in Genesis untenable.

1

The miracles of Christ have been questioned. Indeed Christ's supernatural existence has been emphasised less than His human life on earth, and His example. The tendency has been towards desupernaturalising the Bible: but also towards remythologising it – towards showing that its narratives are part inventions, not necessarily to be taken at face value, to be experienced even as literature rather than as literal.[3] No claim is made here that this approach to the Bible as a collection of myths is any more valid or valuable than the approach that says that every word of it is divine truth: the point is only that 'truth' is almost as problematic a word for the Christian as 'fantasy', and that, where the one is not settled, nor can the other be.

Another point, related to this, is that the Bible is often written in the form of a fantasy. It has a mythic paradise, talking beasts, gods, dragons, angels, visions, many miracles, accounts of other worlds. J. R. R. Tolkien says, 'The Gospels contain a fairy-story, or a story of a larger kind which embraces all the essence of fairy-stories. They contain many marvels – peculiarly artistic, beautiful, and moving: "mythical" in their perfect, self-contained significance; and among the marvels is the greatest and most complete conceivable eucatastrophe ["happy ending"]'.[4] In the seventeenth century, when the use of the supernatural and the free imagination were under attack in England from philosophers and critics such as Hobbes and Locke, Cowley and Dryden, the permitted exclusion from such censure was work dealing with the Christian supernatural; but it was clear that this was under licence from faith, for in all other respects such works contained the same elements as were present in the proscribed secular ones.

> But there remaineth yet another use of POESY PARABOLICAL opposite to that which we last mentioned; for that tendeth to demonstrate and illustrate that which is taught or delivered, and this other to retire and obscure it: That is, when the Secrets and Misteries of Religion, Pollicy, or Philosophy, are involved in Fables or Parables. Of this in divine Poesie wee see the use is authorised.[5]

On the whole, though, the kind of 'divine Poesie' that was most approved was that which stayed close to biblical narrative: one finds Davenant complaining of Tasso's use of fantastic fictions and pagan fables in *Gerusalemme Liberata* to embody divine truths, for 'a Christian Poet, whose Religion little needs the aid of Invention, hath less occasion to imitate such Fables';[6] and Cowley asking, 'Can all the *Transformations* of the *Gods* give such copious hints to flourish and expatiate on as the true *Miracles of Christ*, or of his *Prophets* and *Apostles?*'[7] In these censures we see a typically neo-classical dislike of the mixing of modes, but it is clear that they recognised both the similarity of genre, if not of objective, of Christian and pagan 'fantasy', and the temptation for writers to use the one to figure the other.

If this might seem to argue too much in the direction of Christian and biblical narrative being potentially *mere* fantasy, the balance can be redressed by considering those Christian writers from Dante to Milton who have insisted that their creations are in part divinely inspired – in Dante's case that he was given a direct vision of the worlds beyond death. Here we are dealing not with the authority of biblical narrative, but with the more or less immediate inspiration by the deity of narratives which may be quite other than scriptural in appearance. It is this that makes it possible to talk of 'fantasy' in the same breath as truth. God's imagery is often wholly different from ours, or may be quite other from our capacity to represent it except through fantastical imagery: therefore, if He speaks to men, they can only represent His truth through images that will look strange to us.

> 'Tis not ev'ry day, that I
> Fitted am to prophesie:
> No, but when the Spirit fils
> The fantastick Pannicles:
> Full of fier; then I write
> As the Godhead doth indite.
> (Herrick, 'Not every day fit for Verse')

Sidney relates the divine and human imaginations thus: 'Giue right honor to the heauenly Maker of that maker, who, hauing made man to his owne likenes, set him beyond and ouer all the workers of that second nature, which in nothing he sheweth so much as in Poetrie, when with the force of a diuine breath he bringeth things forth far surpassing her dooings.'[8] Here the relation is not immediate divine inspiration, but rather man' imagination working as it was created to do, in the image of God's. But still it can be felt that even an imagination operating in such freedom returns divine truth from its fictive creations. Thus Tolkien suggests that all fantasy is hallowed, because the story of the Gospels is in the mode of a fantasy, and a fantasy which entered history and became true: 'Art has been verified. God is the Lord, of angels, and of men – and of elves. Legend and History have met and fused.' For this reason it is conceivable that in 'Fantasy' the Christian 'may actually assist in the effoliation and multiple enrichment of creation. All tales may come true; and yet, at the last, redeemed, they may be as like and as unlike the forms that we give them as Man, finally redeemed, will be like and unlike the fallen that we know.'[9] Tolkien is here suggesting that all fantasy truly written, even where it is not Christian in intent, may be grounded in divine truth. It is rather like a reversal of the kind of anticipation of Christian truth present in Virgil's Fourth Eclogue.

The believed truth of their fantastic worlds is an issue with many of the writers we shall consider. The dream given to the mortal man in *Pearl* is a 'veray avysyoun', at the same time as it is a dream re-created by the writer of the poem. The image of the New Jerusalem therein is close to the believed reality of St John the Divine. Dante's other worlds are meant to be believed by his readers, for their better amendment of life. Spenser's Fairy Land is an image of a reality, the human soul. Marlowe's Faustus, who wants to have divine powers and be a god, arguably enacts at a human level the 'aspiring insolence' of Lucifer, for which he was thrown from the face of heaven. Milton's Bible-based account of the temptation and fall of man in *Paradise Lost* was one in which he could be said literally to have believed. Modern Christian fantasy, while its fictions are at a greater distance from their underlying biblical and divine realities, is also much concerned to prove itself 'true', from Kingsley trying in *The Water-Babies* to demonstrate the presence of God in nature, or MacDonald maintaining that the productions of his unconscious imagination come from God, to Lewis suggesting that what is myth in one world may be fact in another, and that certain images that awaken profound longings in us are sent into our minds by God. Nor should we as modern readers forget that the 'reality' of a fantastic work can change through time: that for example we now read Dante's pictures of Hell, Purgatory and Heaven for enjoyment and edification, but not with that quickening of fear and desire that must have beset his contemporaries as they read of worlds in whose ultimate reality they believed, and in which meetings are reported with persons who had recently walked in their Italian cities: at one sweep Dante opened the door between this and the next worlds, and showed the terrifying continuance and familiarity of the souls of the dead, souls whose otherness is never more starkly realised than when they are presented in the lineaments of the personalities they had while on earth.

The differences between Christian 'truth' and 'fantasy', and vice versa, are not therefore so great at all, from whatever angle one considers it. Even if we say that the Athanasian Creed commands belief, and fantasy only the willing suspension of disbelief, there still nowadays remains the issue of what exactly is meant when we speak of Christ incarnated or risen. Equally we may see the other worlds of Dante's *Commedia* as invention, but what are we to do with the spiritual truths they embody? or what with his assertion that they were a vision given to Dante direct by God?

Nevertheless it remains the case that, whatever truth a fantasy may contain, it is only an image of the real. To Dante's image of Heaven we might reply with Swedenborg's different one, also 'divinely given'. That is witnessed to by the very variety of the worlds and images of Christian fantasy: each author filters 'the truth' in a different way.

It is also the case that each author has somewhat different concerns: and here we had better come to matters of definition and description. By 'Christian fantasy' is meant 'a fiction dealing with the Christian supernatural, often in an imagined world'. This at once distinguishes such works from those which deal with Christian conduct – these range from *Piers Plowman* to Newman's *Loss and Gain*, and form decidedly the vast bulk of Christian literature. What we are concerned with are works which give substantial and unambiguous place to other worlds, angels, devils, Christ figures, miraculous or supernatural events (biblical or otherwise), objects of numinous power, and mystical relationship with some approximation of the deity; and all under the aegis of Christian belief.[10] Thus in Dante we find the other worlds of Hell, Purgatory and Heaven, meet devils, angels and even God himself. In Spenser, Bunyan and George MacDonald we travel into a Fairy Land of the soul which is imbued with the supernatural. Marlowe's *Dr Faustus* depicts a man who bargains away his soul to the devil. Milton's *Paradise Lost* re-creates the story of man's fall in Genesis. Blake's 'Little Black Boy' pictures a heaven where he will be consoled for the miseries he has suffered on earth. Kingsley looks for 'absolute divine miracle' within created nature. They are all

extraordinarily different, and all have different Christian intent –
some to admire, some to warn, some to explain, some to educate.
Some of them are not obviously Christian. Spenser's Legend of
Holiness scarcely mentions God or Christ, and the same goes for
most modern Christian fantasy, which comes as it were heavily
disguised: C. S. Lewis, for instance, invites us to perceive a Christ
story in the slaying of his lion Aslan in *The Lion, the Witch and the
Wardrobe*, and the Christian truth in his retelling of the Cupid and
Psyche myth, *Till We Have Faces* (1956), is still more deeply hidden.
There is a certain amount of mutual indebtedness: Dante's
Commedia may be a source for the Middle English *Pearl*, and Milton,
Blake and particularly Charles Williams owe much to the poem.
Spenser may be indebted to the French *Queste*; Bunyan has much
in common with Spenser, Blake looks often to Swedenborg;
MacDonald to both these and to Spenser and Milton; Lewis to all,
but particularly to MacDonald. Of them all, only Marlowe, the
metaphysical poets and Kingsley seem to stand alone, and the first
two of these owe much to the Bible, as do all the others. We may
then speak of a certain sense of 'genre' in these writers: they know
those with whom they have most kinship. It still has to be said,
though, that this 'genre' is composed of works of very diverse
character and purpose.

Perhaps this explains why there has been so far no book about
this literature and its development. Yet in another way it is extraordinary, for this literature is about the central supernatural concerns of the Christian faith. Precious little has been written about
Christian literature as a form in any case: only where it can be
limited to a specific area of interest, or where a marked 'craze' for
writing Christian novels occurred as in the nineteenth century, are
there books devoted to it, as in David C. Fowler's *The Bible in Early
English Literature* (1976), Margaret M. Maison's *Search Your Soul,
Eustace: A Survey of the Religious Novel in the Victorian Age* (1961), or
Robert Lee Wolff's *Gains and Losses: Novels of Faith and Doubt in
Victorian* England (1977). On Christian fantasy there is Martha
Sammons' *'A Better Country': The Worlds of Religious Fantasy and
Science Fiction* (1988), but this is confined to mainly American and
post-war fantasy for children; and there is also Malcolm Scott's *The
Struggle for the Soul of the French Novel: French Catholic and Realist
Novelists, 1850–1970* (1989), which shows the devices used by such
writers as Barbey d'Aurevilly and Georges Bernanos in disguising
works using the Christian supernatural as naturalistic novels. There

are books on religion in literature, but that is another matter: examples range from Patrick Grant's *Six Modern Authors and Problems of Belief* (1979) or T. R. Wright's *Theology and Literature* (1988) to *The Transcendent Adventure: Studies of Religion in Science Fiction/Fantasy*, edited by Robert Reilly (1985), or Robert Detweiler's *Breaking the Fall: Religious Readings of Contemporary Fiction* (1989).

So far we have talked about how these books are fantasy, but the question remains of the ways in which they are Christian. If by 'Christian' we meant 'that which in some form contains or re-creates the acts of Christ', not all our works would answer. Dante, yes; but Milton and the fall of man? or Marlowe and the pact with the devil? To that we have to say that such works suppose, even while they do not dramatise it in specific terms, a Christian context for their actions. Faustus damns himself continually by refusing and finally being unable to recognise the grace offered to him through Christ's sacrifice for man. Milton's heaven is full of Christ and the promise of redemption for man after his fall. Even Blake, who reverses the traditional categories of 'Messiah' and 'Satan', still creates an inverted Christian universe. And it is fair to say that most of these works seek to persuade us of the supernatural reality of Christ and of heaven: their object is to open our eyes to the larger dimension of divine reality that surrounds us. They are there to teach us conduct often within this world; but most frequently that conduct is directed to the reaching of another world in Christ, where, as Bunyan's Christian has it, 'We shall be with *Seraphims* and *Cherubins*, Creatures that will dazle your eyes to look on them: There also you shall meet with thousands, and ten thousands that have gone before us to that place; none of them are hurtful, but loving and holy; every one walking in the sight of God; and standing in his presence with acceptance for ever.'

Works of the kind that we shall be discussing are, it must be said, rather rare. A certain shyness or modesty perhaps often overcame the more sophisticated Christian confronted with the possibility of dramatising heaven. Only ambitious spirits such as Dante or Milton would so dare; Swedenborg would not have uttered if he did not think he had authority from God and angels. There is certainly a reticence. Part of it is to be accounted for by the authority of the Bible: if that story is true, no other version will be readily acceptable. Part of it also arises from the mystics' sense that we cannot know God, and the Christian's belief that we must first know ourselves. At any rate, several of the works we shall be considering are very much more concerned with human conduct on earth – Spenser's Legend of Holiness in *The Faerie Queene*, Bunyan's *The Pilgrim's Progress*, Kingsley's *The Water-Babies*. There have been periods when Christian fantasies have been particularly rare, such as the time from Bunyan to Blake, and it is fair to say that at present, too, they are in eclipse. (By this is meant 'dramatised' works, fictions: there are plenty of visions of the afterworld or near-death experiences up to 1400, as there are in modern times, but they are intended as reports of the truth, not as literature.[11]) It is a curious fact, too, that most of the best-known of them are of British provenance; and, since our objective here is not to recount a history but to consider the most significant, a certain national bias may seem to appear. Yet, rare though they are, these works set out to re-create what is for the Christian the deepest reality of all.

'Re-create' is of course the word. For many Christians past and present, as we have partly seen, the route to faith is through the Bible alone, and not through any alternative fiction, which may be a form of blasphemy. There has in history been a strong vein of belief, Platonic and later Puritan, that literature is lies; and, since lying is the distinctive ability of the devil, the making of any Christian stories but the biblically authorised ones could constitute a wandering from the true spiritual path. Therefore the writing of Christian fantasy has from the first been closely bound up with that faculty most involved in its creation – the human imagination. Every time the writer of Christian fantasy creates a Fairy Land in which to explore the supernatural world of the spirit; every time he describes the search for Christ in terms of a knightly quest for a Grail, or the way to heaven in terms of a pilgrim's journey along a road: every time he invents metaphoric pictures or mythic re-creations of spiritual truth, his imagination, whether or not 'under licence' from God, is at work, and is open to challenge for impiety. No matter that Christ used parables to put over truths Himself – indeed, still more matter – since Christ's imagination is far superior to ours and we have no earthly right to exchange His hallowed pictures for those of our own making. To Tolkien's 'we make still by the law in which we're made',[12] a whole line of Christian thought would reply with Aquinas, 'The poet employs figurative modes of expression for the sake of visible representation. But Holy Scripture employs images and parables because it is needful and profitable.'[13] The imagination is often attacked as free and self-indulgent. And that danger was often felt just as strongly by its practitioners. They know the dangers of invention: they know that new images may divert the mind from the truth contained in them. But they believe also that through such new images the faith can be revitalised; and that the very act of 'going away' from truth may bring one nearer to it.

Our concern for much of this book will be with the treatment of the imagination in Christian fantasy. How much freedom of invention does the Christian allow himself? What is his attitude to the workings of the imagination? We shall find writers who are at pains to translate their imagery directly into instruction, others who assign their creations not to their own wits but to divine inspiration, others who contrast the divine and human imaginations to the disfavour of the latter, others still who let their imagination range as wide as God's universe precisely in order to show the far greater magnitude of that divine imagination which creates not just pictures but realities. Against all such apologies, allegories and translations we shall have to set the fact that all those authors nevertheless chose to create fantastic worlds, beings, objects or events with which to render their Christian visions.

This investigation will be no static thing. Attitudes to the Christian use of the imagination shifted from the early Christian period, through the 'Middle Ages', the Renaissance, the period of the Enlightenment and Romanticism: this has been well portrayed in a recent collection of essays edited by James P. Mackey, *Religious Imagination* (Edinburgh University Press, 1987). We shall be showing how the changing theories of the role of the imagination portrayed in this book are reflected in Christian fantasies themselves. After the Romantics, for reasons which may be guessed at but which will be explained later, the imagination is no longer such an issue, and different problems and questions affect Christian fantasy.

But for now the point to remember is that all these writers want to put over a vision of supernatural reality, and that they chose to do so through fantastic inventions. They have all of them set out to render a new picture of Christian truth. The novelty of that picture remains even where they draw heavily on Scripture for imagery, allegories of Christian patterns, or textual reference. They are all of them voyagers. As if in keeping with this, many of their works are founded on journeys – whether in quest of the Holy Grail, in search of other worlds in Dante, *Pearl* or C. S. Lewis, between Heaven, Hell and Earth in *Paradise Lost*, though Fairy Land in Spenser and

MacDonald, on pilgrimage to the Celestial City in Bunyan, or downstream to the ocean in Kingsley's *The Water-Babies*. For many of them, perhaps – for often we cannot know their intentions – their direct object in using such fantasy would be to 'get through' to readers as the scriptural accounts of Christianity, through long familiarity, might not be able to do. How would it not shake them awake to be reading of a man dreaming of making his way through a strange landscape of jewelled cliffs till he comes to a river, with a beautiful young girl covered with pearls standing on the other side of it, and beyond her a golden, four-walled city which is gradually seen to be identical with the New Jerusalem of Revelation? Would that not surprise them with God better than any other means? and would it not show too how God is present in all things, even in the seemingly strangest of worlds? But there is another implicit reason behind this continual choosing by each writer of new fantastic worlds – even, in the case of say C. S. Lewis, the choosing of a new world from work to work: a Narnia, a Malacandra, a heavenly borderland, a Perelandra, the inside of a mind.[14] However much Scripture must have authority, and however (varyingly) those writers look back to it, they sense that divine truth is not to be caught by one image, not even if that image is given direct by God, as they sometimes claim. For God, as the mystics know, is beyond all images, even if for some He is also in them: 'This also is Thou; neither is this Thou', says Charles Williams,[15] and in that aphorism is contained the dialectic of the imagination that must fill its creations with life, being and reality at the same time as knowing they are but 'an image, not the very real'.[16] That is the point at which it becomes fully legitimate to speak as we did at the beginning of this chapter of a gap between Christian fantasy and Christian reality. Even so, the very existence of so many worlds and modes in which to render the divine testifies to its reality within them even while it remains also utterly beyond them.

Today Christian fantasy seems a dying form, not because of any loss in believers – a recent survey, for instance, suggested that almost all Americans believe in God[17] – but because Scripture has lost authority, and the Church political power. Christian fantasy, previously the greatest literature that could be written, is now often seen as quaint and peripheral. Many of the impulses that directed it have been taken over and translated into secular terms by the new mode of science fiction – a longing for God rendered into a hunger for the infinite, the moral questioning of man into inquiries into the metaphysical foundations of the universe, the Last Things into thermonuclear war, the God who comes down into the man who goes up, the numinous reality in fantastic worlds into amazed wonder. Of this a good image is Olaf Stapledon's *Star Maker* (1937) in which the hero's journey is ever outwards to larger dimensions and discoveries, from intelligences in stars to intelligences in whole galaxies, and finally to the Star Maker himself, a cosmic scientist.

The loss is great. While there are outward journeys to the planetary spheres in Dante and C. S. Lewis, the universe they portray is an ultimately bounded and circular one: and that sense of a bounded universe is, more and less, behind all Christian fantasy. It is concomitant with the dialectic of the imagination, at once expansive and controlled, that the universe in Christian fantasy should be of such a character. Yet it is fair to say that never is our sense of the infinite and the utterly beyond so strong as it is in these works with their comparatively enclosed cosmoses; and that is not just on the principle of infinite riches in a little room, but comes from their presentation of spiritual rather than material distances, in which a far greater gulf yawns between Dante and the entombed shade of Farinata sitting up in front of him than from here to the dimmest receding point of light in the universe.

This book then, besides recording the existence of the literary genre of Christian fantasy, must at the same time admit its disappearance – like a star whose light reaches us while its source is gone. Even while it is in part intended as a celebration of the variety of this genre, it must also be something of an elegy. And yet for this writer there has always been a stubborn wonder that great works of this type are no longer written, and unwillingness to believe that they can no longer be created. There does not seem, given the theology of a Kierkegaard or a Rudolf Otto, any reason to suppose it impossible any longer to sustain the notion of a theocentric heaven; so why not create an image of it? The peoples of developed nations sometimes forget that the Christian faith is still very strong in the world. Perhaps before long there will be another great 'Christian fantasy', from Bolivia or Zaire or Beirut. Perhaps we ourselves should not wait.

2

The French *Queste del Saint Graal*

In the first millennium of Christian history, particularly from the fifth to the eleventh centuries, the Church was generally hostile to any form of the supernatural which was not *miraculosus* – that is, issuing from God and Christ. All pagan imagery was suspect and usually suppressed.[1] For that reason alone there is little 'Christian fantasy' in the whole of that period: what supernaturalist Christian literature there is is almost always either a retelling of biblical narrative, as in Avitus's *Poematum de Mosaicae Historiae Gestis* (AD 507) or 'Caedmonian' *Genesis* (*c.* 700–850),[2] or else in the mode of a vision of heaven or hell.[3] The use of the 'marvellous' or *mirabilis* – stories of monsters, fairies, enchanters and magic, for instance – was more or less outlawed.[4]

In the so-called 'renaissance' of the twelfth century, however, 'the marvelous suddenly makes an appearance in high culture'.[5] Bernardus Silvestris, in his *Cosmographia* (*c.* 1150), for example, takes us on a tour through and beyond the planetary spheres to seek out Urania, queen of the stars; Alanus ab Insulis, following Bernardus in his *Anticlaudianus* (*c.* 1183), describes a journey by celestial chariot to secure from God a soul for the creation of man. Thomas of Britain, Béroul and Gottfried von Strassburg popularise the story of Tristan and Isolde, with its central episodes of a dragon-slaying and a magic love potion (*c.* 1160–1210).

Perhaps the most striking mode in which the new cult of the marvellous manifests itself is in Arthurian romance. At first legend, this is soon elaborated into a half-believed fictive history of Arthur and his knights. For many these narratives were an unconscious rebellion against the shackling of the imagination by the Church. But the Church itself was by now less antagonistic to the use of the marvellous, which it felt it could tame and use for its own purposes.[6] Thus, Arthur and his knights need not be left to joust beyond the pale: they and their deeds could be caught up within the Christian scheme, and thus the secular impulse they embodied would be 'converted'. The most striking form of this conversion is seen in the treatment of the legend of the Grail, and its climax in the pivotal book of the French Vulgate Cycle (1215–30), the *Queste del Saint Graal*.

The story of the search for the Grail exists in many forms, and took its origin in Celtic legend, when the Grail was not associated with Christ at all, but rather with the healing of a wasted land. The Arthurian connection was probably made early, through Welsh tales, but the Grail still has its largely pagan connections in Chrétien de Troyes's *Le Conte del Graal* (1190); only gradually, through Wolfram von Eschenbach's *Parzival* (1200–12) and possibly the French prose romance *Perlesvaus* (1191–1212), did it take on its Christian application.[7] In *Parzival*, achievement of the Grail, together with ability to ask a previously neglected question of its wounded keeper, is more a sign that Parzival has developed spiritually into divine favour rather than a holy and mystic event in itself: in that great poem there is more emphasis on God's approval of good secular knighthood than a critique of the wordly limitations of chivalry. In *Perlesvaus*, however the achievement of the Grail is directly linked to the movement of Arthur's court from sickness and spiritual decay under the Old Law to health under the New, and to the marriage of the temporal to the eternal.

The *Queste del Saint Graal*, under probable Cistercian influence, is far more world-renouncing than any of its predecessors:[8] here achievement of the Grail is directly related to purity of soul, a criterion which the natures of all but three knights of the Round Table fail to meet, and one which condemns the relation of Lancelot and Guinevere, and with it the corruption of Arthur's court. Here, at perhaps the highest point of the Arthurian story, absolute rejection of all worldly knightly urges is most prominent: the Arthurian world is at once understood and transcended. In catching up the wonder and excitement of chivalry and romance and yet translating them into something wholly 'other', the *Queste* represents a remarkable Christian creative triumph; yet this triumph is achieved at the price of a certain narrowness.

The story it tells is of the brief appearance of the Grail at Arthur's court and then of the departure of a large part of the knights in search of a true vision of it. Lancelot, repentant for his sinfulness with Guinevere, is eventually granted a partial sight of it which he forfeits through the impetuosity of his desire; Gawain and Hector fail utterly in the Quest; Bors's brother Lionel goes insane with evil rage; and Sir Owein and King Bagdemagus are killed. Only

Galahad, Perceval and Bors achieve the full vision of the Grail, and of these only Galahad has a sight of the mysteries in the Grail, after which he is granted the death he has sought. Thereupon he is borne to heaven, and a hand comes down from thence and removes the Grail from the world also.

Despite obvious debts, and allowing for the existence of a lost original, the author of the *Queste* has invented numerous episodes and characters. It is he who puts Galahad at the centre, in place of Perceval as in previous versions. He is responsible for the whole idea of the Grail as a *test* of the chivalry of Arthur's court; he has created, in whole or in part, many of the episodes, such as the islanding and temptation of Perceval, the trial of Bors, the castle with the leprous lady or the miraculous ship and its journey; and more than all he has welded all his materials into a narrative full of Christian patterns, with Galahad ('Gilead') as a Christ figure who mediates a transition from the spiritual condition of man under the Old Law to that of the Gospels and the New.

Our concern is most directly with his attitude to fantasy. And here we find that, while he can produce episodes of extraordinary supernatural occurrence, he is at pains often at once to reduce them to doctrine. 'One can fairly say', declares his most recent translator, 'that he did not write a single paragraph for the pleasure of story-telling.'[9] When a lady invites Perceval to lie down with her in a tent, and only his 'chance' blessing of himself reveals her for the devil she is, the scene is afterwards glossed, as are so many, by a passing 'good man'. He takes as his 'text' the words of the woman, 'Perceval, come and rest yourself and sit here until nightfall out of the sun, for I fear it is too hot for you':

> These words of hers were far from trivial, inasmuch as she construed them differently from you. The tent, round in shape like the earth's environment, quite plainly signifies the world, which will never be free from sin; and sin being ever present in the world, she did not want you to stay outside the tent: that was the reason for its setting up. And when she called to you she said: 'Perceval, come and rest yourself and sit down until nightfall.' By sitting and resting she meant that you should be idle and give your body its fill of earthly cheer and gluttony. She did not exhort you to work in this life and sow your seed against the day when good men reap their harvest, the day of eternal judgment. She entreated you to rest until night came, which is to say till you

were snatched by death, which is termed night most aptly whenever it catches unawares a man in mortal sin. She called you in lest the heat of the sun should be too much for you, and it was no wonder that she feared its strength. For when the sun, for which we must read Jesus Christ, the one true light, warms the sinner with the fire of the Holy Ghost, the chill and ice of the enemy can do him little hurt if he has fixed his heart on the heavenly sun. (p. 132)[10]

This certainly has the effect of evacuating the story of its literal context. No action or object is left merely itself: a tent is much more than a tent. Indeed it is mortal blindness to all but the literal or physical level of the world that is a prime source of sin in the *Queste*. We might think that it is the simple fact of being unchaste that would constitute Perceval's sin, but it is also blindness to the full horror of that sin that defines it. The issue is at least as much one of perception as of action, which is why there are so many wandering literary critics in the *Queste*. The whole work is studded with long passages of explication in spiritual terms of almost every event. Above all, we are made directly aware of the fact that it is made to be the re-creation in chivalric terms of Christian patterns of salvation: it is, as it were, inverted typology.

The obvious effect of this is that the sequence of events is continually being checked while a hermit or passing good knight goes over recent happenings to explain their meaning. The jolt to awareness is admitted at times by the text: 'And now, said the monk, he had told him the whole truth: to which Galahad answered that he had never thought the adventure held so high a meaning' (p. 65); 'This explanation left Gawain at a loss for words' (p. 80). The object is to deny freedom to the imagination, which in Augustinian and Cistercian terms would be felt to be the potential dupe of man's corrupted senses. Indeed the interpretations of each episode could be seen as corrective reminders to any strayings and excitements of our imaginations by the events themselves. At times even the surface level of the story may be obscured: when Perceval disenchants the demonic black horse on which he is riding, he is beside a river, but next morning he finds himself on an island surrounded by a vast ocean; this island is said to be a huge peak jutting out from the sea, but then we learn of 'a strange and beetling crag' in the middle of the island (p. 114), which certainly obscures the topography.

It is true that there are areas of the *Queste* which are not so explained, and patterns which the spiritually sophisticated reader is left to perceive. Such are the Grail as a symbol of divine grace; Lancelot as Adam, and Galahad as the risen Christ; and the whole quest as a journey from the Old Law to the New. Such less 'evident' symbolism becomes more marked as the story shifts from moral analysis to mystical vision in the approach to Corbenic.[11] Nevertheless, while we are not explicitly told, for example, of the significance of the miraculous ship (the Church) with its terrible sword and its three joined posts of white, green and red wood, we know that each item has a definite and 'limited' significance, and in an explicatory chapter on 'The Legend of the Tree of Life' we are given a good idea of what that significance might be. And, while numbers of scriptural and typological patterns may be detected within the story, these are discovered not through freedom of the imagination but by a trained spiritual perception that sees how all phenomena, even in a secular-seeming romance, bespeak the things of God. Indeed the author's very choice of Arthurian romance as his medium may in great part have been to show this; certainly, given the enormous popularity of stories of the Round Table in his day, he was exploiting the market, drawing people to read his work while turning it to an intensity of spiritual purpose which would not have been anticipated. The Arthurian fiction is continually 'violated' by the divine presence and by overt Christian doctrine – an image in itself of God's immanence within His creation.

With all this, the story remains extraordinarily vital, not least because of the vividness with which it has differentiated the knights, both personally and spiritually – Perceval's modesty, Lancelot's courtly reserve and restraint (as much as constriction at the various merciless analyses of his morals by sundry squires and hermits), Gawain's boredom and hearty blasphemies, Arthur's sorrow at the parting of them all from Camelot. At the same time the author's account is clear and economical: he uses just a few knights to give us a spectrum of the spirit, and he does not over-embellish with details and spiritual minutiae; even his frequent biblical references are not given chapter and verse. The result is that he achieves a degree of focus and attention that enables his meaning to come over forcefully. Such is the degree of sophistication that one is tempted to credit the work with more organisation than it admits – to argue, for example, that the form of the whole narrative may be seen to imitate that of the circular Grail vessel itself, by giving us a series of actions circling inwards about the Grail, a tapered line of knights who seek the Grail and a further tapering in the degree of sight of it given to those who reach it, and an increasing depth of spiritual awareness in those who approach nearest to the centre where it is. But such a reading is not evidently intended: indeed it is precisely against the liberty of imagination implied in such a reading that much of the *Queste* is written, however welcome it might be in this instance.

The Christian vision of the *Queste* is a narrow one, and one that moves continually away from the world. Anything human is to be transcended, anything connected with the flesh or the senses is to be rejected. Gawain and Hector fail because they regard the quest as a mere adventure. Lancelot must utterly renounce Guinevere. Sir Perceval must overcome the blandishments of women. Sir Bors must choose to rescue an unknown woman rather than his own brother. Those who succeed are the 'knights of heaven'; those who fail are 'the earthly knights' (p. 159). As for narrowness, there is first the exclusiveness of the Arthurian context itself and the question of its relation to the lives of readers. We have to remember though that, at the time the *Queste* was written, its readership would have been solely among the upper classes, and that those classes themselves lived lives not altogether removed from the mores of Arthur's court: indeed that they themselves often tried to imitate the way of life of knights of the Round Table; certainly Wolfram's *Parzival* is a striking reflection of the social mores of the aristocracy in medieval Germany. Nevertheless as an account of Christian life the *Queste* must remain socially very restricted – and, in contrast to the 'democracy' implicit in Christ's descent from on high for all men, it suggests a hierarchy whereby only the highest and most sinless may succeed. We may also note that unlike in Wolfram's *Parzival* we here move steadily away from the specifically Arthurian context with which we start, dropping more or less 'corrupt' knights as we go until we are left with the human gold that may attain the Grail.

The application of the *Queste* is further restricted by the frequency with which human sinfulness is seen in terms of unchastity. The condemnation of the Round Table centres largely on Lancelot's adultery with Guinevere rather than on the failure of secular chivalry itself. Lancelot's fatherhood of Galahad is implicitly an example of God creating good out of human corruption; certainly the sheer spiritual gulf between the two is only occasionally bridged. Much of the trial of Sir Perceval relates to chastity. Sir Bors is marked by a youthful failure of chastity, albeit repented. There are certainly other virtues required for the achievement of the Grail; and the moral grading of the various knightly participants in the *Queste* could be said to give a kind of spiritual cross-section of humanity, with Galahad the highest and Gawain or Lionel the lowest: and yet somehow the virtues involved do not carry far back into human life.

One of the reasons for this is that the *Queste* does not really set out to teach conduct, but rather to offer judgements. The situations encountered by the knights are often so strange, however much they may be allegorised, that they could not be applied to ordinary human life. How often does one come across a collection of succubae, a castle where every passing maiden has to give a bowlful of blood, or a situation in which one has to choose between rescuing a distressed damsel and rescuing one's own brother? And, while we do have an instance of someone who develops spiritually, in Lancelot (though he reverts again), the qualifications for attaining the Grail are a pre-existing purity and faith in God which are demonstrated variously by Perceval, Bors and above all Galahad. From the beginning Galahad is marked out from all around him: a special Seat of Danger is prepared for him, in which no one but he may sit; he alone may wield a magic sword in a stone; and much is made of his being the long-awaited ninth of the line from Joseph of Arimathea who will after more than four centuries be the one to heal the Wounded King and thus return the Grail to its heavenly place. What is done in the Grail quest effectively depletes the Round Table of many of its best knights, as Arthur sorrowfully foresaw at the outset; and the spiritual purity required to achieve the Grail is effectively an analysis of the impurity of Arthur's court. Then there is the Grail itself. While the approach to it is obviously a sign of holiness and a mystical act, not to mention a symbol of Communion, the Grail is also a highly individual object, and one that must be removed from the world: nowhere perhaps is the extent to which the *Queste* turns its back on the concerns of fallen men more evident than in this, and in Galahad's death and ascent into heaven.[12] The whole spiritual direction of the story is upwards and away from the earth, which is left to the impending disaster it merits. The story is not harsh in tone, indeed it is often sorrowful and compassionate, but this is still the effect.

Nevertheless it is still the case that the author of the *Queste* has chosen the Arthurian matter in which to set his story: we cannot set it aside *entirely* for allegorical readings or renunciation. And here we should perhaps consider the story rather as a marvellous legend describing a wonder of God and of divine action. We must take the story of the dish from which Christ ate with his disciples at the Last Supper, its being brought to Britain by Joseph of Arimathea and its subsequent guardianship by a line of Fisher Kings for four centuries until the arrival of Galahad, as in one sense 'literally intended': it is too specific to be simply allegorised. Since he considerably reworked the story, the author of the *Queste* could not entirely have believed it, but he would have believed that it was the sort of wonder that could be accomplished by God and a particularly holy relic, and he wanted his readers at least to admire if not believe the miracle of God's workings that it portrays. That is the kind of imagination, if we like, that he will permit in his story. There may have been a Grail. The world for him is such that angels and devils walk up and down in it, guiding or hindering men. There may be a realm which one eventually reaches – it matters not that it could also be allegorised as the deepest part of the soul – where one may come across a magic ship which will take one to the holy castle of Corbenic.[13] If the 'natural' is a delusion to be seen through, the supernatural is often all too real. The whole of the *Queste* is scattered with demonic illusions that must be penetrated, with dreams that must be interpreted aright in every detail, set in a world whose sensuous blandishments must continually be set aside; yet, while the world is seen as a hollow fraud, and while truth is frequently seen as spiritual and allegorical rather than physical and literal, the spiritual things are not mere abstractions but realities, and within and beyond all is the reality of the Christian supernatural.[14] Put aside the delusions of the world, and there is nothing; put aside the frauds of Satan and they reveal his reality. When Perceval blesses himself as he reaches a river on a black horse given to him by a damsel,

the enemy felt himself weighed down with the burden of the cross, which was exceedingly heavy and hateful to him, [and] he gave a great shake, and freeing himself of Perceval, rushed into the water howling and shrieking and making a yammer such as

was never heard. And it came about then that bright sheaves of
fire and flame shot up from the river in several places, so that the
water itself appeared to burn.   (p. 113)

For those who will see, the world is not sufficient to itself, but is
permeated by supernatural beings and events that demonstrate the
eternal realities surrounding man in his cocoon of mortal illusion.

3

Dante: The *Commedia*

If we set aside the Bible, and perhaps the *Queste*, Dante's *Commedia* (1307–21) may be called the first great work of Christian fantasy. The Bible is different: the 'fantastic' accounts there, whether of the Garden of Eden, the vision of Ezekiel, the birth, life, death and resurrection of Christ or the Revelation of St John, are intended to be believed, even while they may also be allegorised. The events surrounding the fall may not, if such an event really occurred, have been those of the myth in Genesis; but that myth was intended as truth, in so far as the Bible was the revealed word of God, and was taken as truth in countless artifacts and writings at least for most of the 2000 years from the life of Christ – as, of course, was every detail of Christ's life. The vision of the Last Things granted to St John in Revelation may have been tailored to his mortal capacity and remoulded in his own memory, but his imagery has conditioned the way we think of such events: 'The Revelation of Jesus Christ, which God gave unto him, to shew unto his servants things which must shortly come to pass; and he sent and signified it by his angel unto his servant John: who bare record of the Word of God, and of the testimony of Jesus Christ, and of all things that he saw.'[1]

But with Dante it is different. While it is true that he both maintained and at least partly believed that the *Commedia* was a vision of the truth granted him by God, he did not intend that his images of the worlds beyond death should usurp the place of scriptural certainties, nor did he wholly believe in them himself in the way of a Swedenborg. He described them, and God described them through him, to persuade a materialist world of the eternal destiny of the soul. He knew his Hell, Purgatory and Heaven to be fictions at the same time as he believed in their reality;[2] and his readers are often persuaded of their reality even while knowing them to be fiction. How many of us, when reading, have not felt that Ugolino really is in the frozen lake of Cocytus in Hell, that Statius really has been liberated from Purgatory during Dante's visit, that Beatrice verily does sit in the last Heaven near to the feet of Mary? Yet, 'in reality' Dante has to some extent put all these figures there: he has 'played

God' in his fiction and assigned these people by his own judgement to those places.

To the extent that he knows his work is a fiction, to the extent that he invents, Dante is a fantasist. We may in this connection speak of him as having invented Purgatory, for instance: no one before had pictured it as a huge and many-tiered mountain in the midst of a vast ocean in the southern hemisphere;[3] and in its creation Dante provided an answer to another, equally vexing problem of theological geography, by locating Paradise at the summit of the purgatorial mountain.[4] For his other worlds of Hell and Heaven he was 'indebted' – to speak at the literary and fictive level of creation – to Virgil, the Muslim picture of Hell, the *Celestial Hierarchies* of Pseudo-Dionysius and the Islamic *Mi'raj*; but even those indebtednesses he so transforms and elaborates that it is better to speak of them as re-creations.[5]

It is perhaps strange that Dante was the first writer to explore the Christian universe in this way. There had been numerous legendary journeys to Hell, Purgatory and Heaven before Dante, but these are brief visions, not really narratives, and there is little that foreshadows his fullness and subtlety of treatment.[6] To a large extent this is simply the result of Dante's genius: no one of his literary stature had appeared in all that time. Another and important factor is the new status given to the human imagination in his time, particularly by Aquinas.[7] And it is of course the case that circumstances were peculiarly propitious in Dante's time for the success of such genius as his. The culture of northern Italy was approaching the high point of renaissance. The new universities were flourishing. The confidence of the Christian faith had perhaps never been so great, nor its influence so pervasively felt in every aspect of life: no more was it the Church embattled, as in the first thousand years of its history, nor the Church militant, as in its crusades against Islam, but was nearer the Church triumphant; the danger was rather that it might become the Church corrupt. For a time Dante nourished hopes that through the Emperor Henry VII the time of universal peace and of a world state was near. The fuse of Dante's genius appears to have been lit by his childhood vision of the girl Beatrice Portinari, who turned his soul with an intense desire at once human and divine, a desire cast into permanence by her death.[8]

Yet Dante's life was to be the reverse of secure or happy. He wrote the *Commedia* in exile from his beloved Florence. Along with other White Guelphs he had been banished from Florence when

Charles of Valois and the Black Guelphs seized it in 1301; subsequently he broke with his fellow exiles and left them, and for years he was a wanderer, and poor. His wife Gemma was left in Florence; and later (1314) his sons too were banished on pain of death. But the fact that he was thus made an outsider must have given Dante a rare vantage point. He was perhaps able to see further into the nature of man than he might otherwise have done. And, which concerns us, he was able to be novel with less inhibition. In writing Christian poetry at all he went against the theological disapproval of it as a somehow inferior and inaccurate mode of religious communication.[9] Moreover, he wrote it in the vernacular of Italian rather than in the accepted literary language of Latin;[10] and he put contemporaries or near-contemporaries from his own society into his poetry, instead of only imaginary, historically remote or biblical figures. Last, and most important for us, he chose what, curiously for his age (and despite much extant, if usually brief and rather stereotyped, visionary literature), is a relatively underdeveloped topic: a systematic exploration of the worlds beyond death and of the posthumous destinies of human souls. Yet perhaps we can understand the choice of this subject; for what else, on this level, is it, but his own exile from the world and a journey through pain to a society that will not betray him and a love that cannot die? The journey through Hell is one where further gulfs continually open beneath one's feet: it is a landscape of uncertainty. But thereafter there is a gradual ascent to assurance. This is not the meaning of the poem as created, and it is only a small and mortal part of what it becomes; but it may well have been a strong, if unacknowledged motive in its making.

Much of Dante's originality in the *Commedia* arises from his treatment of the classics – the *auctores* as they were known in his day. These authors – who include writers from the pseudo-Homer, Juvenal, Ovid and Virgil to Augustine, Prudentius, Martianus Capella and even Bernardus Silvestris – were used as storehouses of wisdom in such disciplines as law, science, medicine, philosophy, music, astronomy and even theology. Their sayings were often learnt by heart. As contributors to the body of human knowledge the pagan writers among them were not radically distinguished from the Christians: even the new texts of Aristotle which were discovered in the twelfth century and banned by the Church were eventually assimilated into Aquinas's *Summa Theologica* (1266–74). But the fact is that their work was not much attended to as 'litera-

ture' until quite late. Prior to the thirteenth century, when schools
of grammar and rhetoric began to be established in universities,
they were treated largely as repositories of knowledge.[11] Nor will
one find much that is Ovidian or Virgilian in terms of creativity in
the *Psychomachia* of Prudentius or the *Anticlaudianus* of Alanus ab
Insulis: few metamorphoses owing anything to Ovid's, few wanderings owing anything to the *Aeneid*.[12] But Dante is one of the first,
and certainly the first great writer, to value the invention and
originality in the earlier writers, to respond to them as creators, and
to attempt to re-create their visions in works of his own. He is, in a
way, ready to use the *difference* of Virgil from him as earlier writers
had not been.[13] The interest of most literature prior to Dante had
been doctrinal, concerned with the establishment of the Christian
world view and with the dramatisation of the spiritual values on
which it depended: Dante's age, with the Church secure, allowed
the exploration of other modes. Dante is the first great narrative
poet of Christian culture: he knows the enormous potency of fable,
of simply telling a story in the furtherance of a Christian purpose.
Beyond that, he knows the power of invention, of the imagination,
as few before him. So he puts a frail human being, a figure of
himself, in a series of strange landscapes and through a sequence of
encounters which, however allegorical, are still literal; and he has
him move across a mapped terrain to a definite goal. And this is
possible not only because he is Dante, but because he has entered
into a unique relationship with classical narrative, a relation made
flesh in his accompaniment by a dramatised Virgil throughout his
Hell and Purgatory.

While Dante's poem is supremely original, it is also written at the
summit of the allegorical and symbolic tradition. Looking back
from our more secular culture today, the 'solid' features – the
exciting narrative, the novelty, the exploration of the whole
spiritual universe, the meetings with souls in Hell or Heaven, the
speeches with the shades of great men – are the ones that draw us,
possibly to the exclusion of much of the Christian significance
contained in them. We are inclined to attend, to put it in medieval
terms, to the literal rather than the allegoric levels. Nor can it be
denied that for Dante himself the voyage was not only one to
Heaven, but also one of discovery, by which the whole nature of
the universe could be explored and, as it were, colonised by mind.
This exploring spirit, this expansion outwards to know all, seems a
central drive of the poem:

Io veggio ben che già mai non si sazia
   nostro intelletto, se'l ver non lo illustra
   di fuor dal qual nessun vero si spazia.
Posasi in esso, come fera in lustra,
   tosto che giunto l'ha; e giugner puollo:
   se non, ciascun disio sarebbe *frustra*.
Nasce per quello, a guisa di rampollo,
   a piè del vero il dubbio; ed è natura
   ch'al sommo pinge noi di collo in collo.

Well do I see that never can our intellect be wholly satisfied unless that Truth shine on it, beyond which no truth has range. Therein it rests, as a wild beast in his lair, so soon as it has reached it; and reach it it can, else every desire would be in vain. Because of this, questioning springs up like a shoot, at the foot of the truth; and this is nature which urges us to the summit, from height to height.   (*Par.* IV.124–32)[14]

Yet we do Dante wrong if we see him as a Renaissance scientific imagination pushing outwards without restraint: more still if we see his exploring and innovative urges as at war with his faith in God. Rather his new – and 'given' rather more than self-derived – knowledge is used as a way of bringing home to us the holy nature of reality. Nowhere more than in Heaven, where it is least able to go astray, is this impulse of scientific inquiry more nakedly seen and openly satisfied, than in Dante's continual questionings concerning the operations of the spheres, in his discovery of his own future history, in his instruction in the nature of predestination or the hierarchy of the angels. Dante's journey reveals more and more of the harmony of a universe that man but for his sin and mortality would know as his true home. It reveals a total and fully explained system for every single human being and action. Aquinas – and Dante himself in the *Convivio* – had described that system theoretically; here Dante gives it in pictured and narrative form. What he is attempting to provide is an image of the whole universe as an extraordinarily detailed and subtle spiritual body, composed of innumerable closely interrelated members.[15]

   To attend to the individual, or the 'physical', at the expense of its larger spiritual reality was a mistake that Dante learnt all too painfully in his experience of the loss of Beatrice. Thus his poem, while giving great imaginative excitement, does not remain with the blandishments of the image alone. That is one meaning of Dante's meeting in *Purgatorio* xix with the Siren who turned Ulysses out of his way with her singing 'qual meco s'ausa, / rado sen parte; sì tutto l'appago!' ('whosoever abides with me rarely departs, so wholly do I satisfy him'): Dante, 'gazing on the ground', confesses to Virgil that 'In such apprehension I am made to go by a new vision, which bends me to itself so that I cannot leave off thinking on it' (ll. 23–4, 55–7); to which Virgil bids him turn his eyes upwards from the earth, 'to the lure which the eternal King spins with the mighty spheres'. So, in the *Paradiso*, Dante condemns all fables which are not grounded in the Scriptures and divine truth, but exist merely to show the maker's ingenuity (xxix.85–126): Beatrice tells Dante, 'Christ did not say to his first company, "Go and preach idle stories to the world", but he gave to them the true foundation' (ll. 109–11). As for the workings of the creative imagination, or 'invention', Dante did not suppose them to be wholly self-begotten means of praising the Almighty: rather they were at least in part for him the products of inspiration from God. It is not true, he says, that such things derive as Aristotle maintains only from the recombination of images derived from perception of the world:

> O imaginativa che ne rube
>   talvolta sì di fuor, ch'om non s'accorge
>   perché dintorno suonin mille tube,
> chi move te, se'l senso non ti porge?
>   Moveti lume che nel ciel s'informa,
>   per sé o per voler che giù lo scorge.

O imagination, that do sometimes so snatch us from outward things that we give no heed, though a thousand trumpets sound around us, who moves you if the sense affords you naught? A light moves you which takes form in heaven, of itself, or by a will that downwards guides it.   (*Purg.* xvii.13–18)

Thus this invention is not a self-governing adventurer, nor is it insulated from spiritual truths.

In order to direct us to this light from Heaven, Dante has so organised the images of his poem that we will not be seduced by them, but will constantly see their spiritual significance or the larger pattern to which they belong – and this without direct authorial pointing. But in doing so, as we have said, Dante does not negate the literal level of reading: the images are to be appreciated for themselves so that the truths they contain may be more fully realised. In his letter on the *Commedia* to his friend Can Grande, Dante speaks of four levels of meaning in the poem – literal, moral, allegorical and anagogical: here, it appears, he wrote an 'allegory of theologians', in which all four levels of understanding were operative.[16] One can see the difference from the French *Queste del Saint Graal*, where an 'allegory of poets' seems to have operated; for there the literal level is continually undermined by translation into explicit doctrinal content: the *Queste* is at pains to evacuate much of its fictiveness. Dante lets his story say what it means without ceasing to be itself, through patterns of structure, imagery, narrative, character and even number. That is the double way his Beatrice exists too, both as herself and as God imprinted in flesh. Thus the *Commedia* can be at once a journey from this world to the next, a vision of Hell, Purgatory and Heaven, an exploration of the inner worlds of the soul, a recapitulation of Christian history to the Last Things, a political and moral commentary on Dante's contemporaries and a rewriting of Virgil's *Aeneid* as a journey to an eternal city.[17]

There is scarcely a single feature of Dante's landscape which does not owe its configuration to some special meaning while still remaining itself. In the third Bolge of the eighth circle (Malbolges) of Hell, Dante sees the figures of the simoniacs planted head-first in holes in the rock, with only their legs visible and waving with the torment of their burning feet. Shortly after this, in the Fifth Bolge, Dante sees the barrators, who made money by trafficking in public rather than ecclesiastical offices, plunged entirely in boiling pitch. The simoniacs are placed upside-down because they put earthly before divine values; they inverted the order to which they belonged. The barrators are immersed because they abandoned all principle to worldly greed. The priests are shut in rocks because they mishandled the unbinding keys of St Peter (*petros* = a rock) entrusted to them. The rock holes also remind Dante of the font in the baptistery of the Church of St John Baptist at Florence, which had holes in the stone in which the priests could stand in order not to be knocked over by the press of people while carrying out baptisms (XIX.16–18); these priests are now inverted in their stone holes, and, because they have turned God's gift of baptism to gifts of worldly preferment, the water that they dropped on the heads of the baptised is now changed to fire on their feet. None of this significance prevents us from seeing the fact of the stone potholed like cheese, with the legs sticking out and waving under almost ludicrous torment from the agony of their burning extremities: in a way it could be said that, the more meaningful this emblematic scene, the more solid it is. And of course it is fantasy, as all such emblems are: they use distortions or grotesque extrapolations from what we take as the 'normal', in order to highlight its true nature. As for the barrators, we have already seen some significant contrast with the simoniacs in their immersion: they did not even have the knowledge of God to invert. Further, as the devils say who with their pitchforks keep them from surfacing, they are hidden in the pitch because their dealings were secret (XXI.52–4). Of the pitch we may say, with Dorothy L. Sayers in her gloss, that 'Money stuck to their fingers: so now the defilement of the pitch sticks fast to them.'[18] And, as for the liquid nature of the element in which they are placed, that may symbolise the absence of any secure trust that could be reposed on them: they were shifting and slimy, like pitch itself.

Thus our imagination is not allowed scope to ramble and dilate by Dante. He is always exact, always tying us to a significance. One of the ways in which he differs from writers of modern fantasy is in his refusal of a simply 'other' world, a 'sub-created world' as Tolkien called it, 'into which both designer and spectator can enter, to the satisfaction of their senses while they are inside'.[19] Tolkien wants us imaginatively to enter and live in Middle-earth; and Mervyn Peake puts us so fully into his world of Gormenghast that we may come to feel, as the Countess of the castle says to her son, 'There is nowhere else'.[20] Dante's Hell, Purgatory and Heaven are, however, *de facto* connected to this world inasmuch as the souls of formerly living people go there. And Dante has them all, like Virgil's shades, acutely – and in the case of the infernal shades obsessively – aware of their lives or of politics on earth. His other worlds do not exist on their own but continually look back to this one – a fact which the presence of a figure of Dante himself within them only reinforces.[21] We are further detached from them and placed in an assessing role by the fact that the journeying Dante is most commonly an observer rather than a participant – in contrast to George MacDonald's Anodos, say, in Fairy Land, or C. S. Lewis's Ransom on Venus, both of whom have to become direct actors in the worlds they enter and mediate. Again, while we do have a strong sense of the overall form of each of Hell, Purgatory and Heaven, they are all so subdivided into units, into deepening or expanding circles of graded sin or spiritual renewal, that we are not allowed to rest in any one vision but are continually shifted from one context to another, as part of a regulated investigation of each world. Most of all there is the fact that these are not simply geographical places, but graded assemblages of human souls, souls that fill the whole *Commedia* with their different voices and conditions. At the surface level, the stages travelled are stages of people, not locations. And the whole element of desire in the poem, the thrust of the journey, is not just towards a place, but towards the person that is the place – Beatrice, Christ, God. Thus Dante's 'fantastic world' is not self-contained, nor does it give us a chance to luxuriate in any settled assumption.

And that is what Dante is taught and teaches within the poem. The self is to be exact; and, while in a final sense selfhood matters, mere self is to be transcended. The transcendence, the burning-out, of the egoistic self is enjoined by what we see in Hell, and performed in Purgatory. Thereafter, with Purgatory come to a point, but a point which, unlike that of Hell, is directed upwards and outwards, we move into the progressively wider freedom of the concentric Heavens until we step out of the frame of creation altogether. Any illusion we might have, when Dante reaches the lost Paradise at the summit of Mount Purgatory, that he is spiritually fit to be there is stripped from us, and we reminded that he is there in his normal 'sinful' self by special dispensation, when on seeing Beatrice he is shamed for his betrayal of the Good in her at her death (*Purg.* xxx–xxxi). Only by thus addressing Dante can Beatrice push him beyond knowledge of her only as a person to knowledge of her as incarnate Charity, when by free gift she shows him Paradise and the Heavens. But first he must be transformed by drinking the water of oblivion, or Lethe. And in the *Paradiso* Dante turns direct to the reader, to tell him that, if he has been reading the story in a merely worldly and narrative and superficial manner, he will not comprehend at all what follows; only those who hunger and thirst for righteousness will be able to understand anything of Heaven (ii.1ff.).

Thirty-four cantos to Hell; thirty-three each to Purgatory and Heaven. Five circles of sin in Upper Hell; two, the inner having three rings, in the first part of Nether Hell; one, divided into ten Bolges, in the second part of Nether Hell; then one, comprising four

circles of traitors, ending with the traitors to their lords in the
frozen lake of Cocytus; and last, at the centre, Dis. Purgatory is
made up of two ante-purgatorial terraces, the second having three
groups; and then seven levels, or cornices, before the arrival in
Paradise. In the *Paradiso* we move first to the Heaven of the Moon,
and then, in order outwards, to the Heavens of Mercury, Venus, the
Sun, Mars, Jupiter and Saturn; thereafter we ascend to the eighth
level, the Starry Heaven of the zodiac, and thence to the Primum
Mobile, or Crystalline Heaven, before the final approach to the
Sempiternal Rose, which is of no place and all places. Each book
thus has nine marked stages; and, if we add Dis, Paradise and God,
these come to ten. It need hardly be said that not only is the
fantastic world of each book highly organised and classified, but
each is made in parallel order with the others. And each level of
course corresponds to a graded series of sins, whether committed
or repented, or of bliss. This scheme makes us conscious of both
numbers and degree as much as of the stage itself for its own sake:
when we see the Heaven of the Just on Jupiter we attend to what
happens there no more than we think of the Heaven of the
Warriors of the Cross which preceded and the Heaven of the
Contemplatives on Saturn which will follow it; and no more than
we think of this as the sixth stage on our journey towards a
terminal point, here of very Heaven itself. At the same time we are
aware of all sorts of other patterns: of the fact that Dante's whole
journey takes place in Easter week of 1300, his time in Hell
representing the descent into death (and Christ's own harrowing of
Hell), and thereafter the continued life on earth followed by the
Ascension. The effect as a whole of all this number and order is
to demonstrate the highly patterned character of the universe,
in which each item takes its meaning from its place in a larger
totality.[22]

Throughout the *Commedia* Dante progressively removes the
element of the sensuous and the visual. One paradox is that we see
most in Hell, which is dark, and least in the Heavens, which are
flooded with light. The journey through Hell is very strongly felt.
The first we know of the place is the noise that issues forth from the
dark gateway: we expect the cries, groans and curses, but not the
constant clapping of hands we also hear, and we suddenly sense
that Dante is in part describing a medieval madhouse. We see the
vast funnel of the pit, going down into unfathomable darkness;
shrink at the taloned monster Cerberus as it approaches across the

rain-soaked field of the mangled gluttonous; pause at the red iron walls of the moated City of Dis when the devils slam the door in the faces of the travellers. Thence we swim on the back of the three-formed monster Geryon down into the void below the Great Barrier to the second level of Nether Hell; struggle up over the rockfall of the broken bridge from the bottom of the sixth Bolge; pass the frozen lake of Cocytus in which the traitors are sunk, some of them only to the neck; and finally arrive at Dis (Satan) himself, who with his three heads is preoccupied in continually rending and devouring Judas, Brutus and Cassius, traitors to their lords. From here we are taken with the travellers down the shaggy and rime-covered body of Dis till at its midpoint they are at the centre of the world; whereafter gravity is reversed and they must ascend by way of his feet to reach the tunnel that leads eventually out to Mount Purgatory on the surface of the southern hemisphere.

There is much less of this kind of physical detail in the *Purgatorio*. For one thing, we see only the human form: no monsters here. For another, topography is relatively uniform. Each cornice, or ledge, around the conical mountain is physically much the same as the last, except that at times it may be narrow enough to cause Dante fear of falling. Again, the figures in Purgatory are not often in such active and often rebellious relation to their pains as those in Hell: they accept them without question, which makes them less sensuously immediate; and this is increased by the fact that the physical pains are here more perfunctorily and emblematically described, whether it be the proud going about weighed down by stones, or the covetous fettered face down to the rock, or the wrathful embroiled in thick dark smoke. The exception, so far as detail and immediacy are concerned, is the lost Paradise we find on the summit of Mount Purgatory: a paradise made unusual in that it is wooded, being based on the pineta near Ravenna where Dante wrote the latter part of the *Commedia*; but this is a special case, to which we will return. All the 'humans' that Dante meets in Hell and Purgatory are 'shades' of humans but it is in Purgatory that we feel them the more insubstantial, ghost-like. In Hell the wrathful batter one another with their fists in the mire, or attempt, in the form of Filippo Argenti, to attack Dante by clutching at his boat, and have to be thrust off by the boatman. Even when Dante and Virgil walk through the bodiless shades of the gluttonous in the cold sleety hail of their circle, we still feel the squelch of the rain-sodden souls, 'we were setting our feet/upon their emptiness, which seems real bodies' (*Inf.* vi.35–6). In Hell of course the physicality of the tortures expresses the materialism of the sinners, who have put aside the spirit for the body and the world. But it does also give some scope for that 'lower' faculty of the imagination to pause and wonder at oddities.

In Purgatory the shades, after some brief account of their pains, talk with Dante and Virgil: there is no attempt at physical interaction. Here, of course we see the shades in sunlight, which shines through them (*Purg.* v.4–9, 25–35). And yet, by typically Dantean paradox, it is in Purgatory that Dante asks why it is that the bodies of the shades seem so solid, so substantial (xxv). What we do feel in Purgatory is the difficulty of the ascent (though this is a mountain that reverses nature, in that the lower reaches feel most tiring and it becomes progressively easier to climb, despite the uniform gradient – iv.88–90). We feel the strain as Dante and Virgil force themselves up the rock chimney on to the second terrace of Ante-Purgatory (vi) or weave from side to side up the tortuous rocky path from St Peter's Gate (x), or walk carefully in single file along the outer edge of the seventh cornice, where a refining fire shoots out and up from the inner bank (xxvi). We feel too, in the extraordinarily vivid suspended syntax of xvii.64–78 the slow freezing of motion, as, with sunset, their feet are brought to a halt at the top of the stair leading to the fourth cornice. We sense with Dante the huge horizon and the vast cope of the stars after sunset on the seventh cornice (xxvii.70–2, 88–90). But the primary journey of the *Purgatorio* is the emotional one for Dante, crowned by his searing encounter with Beatrice; and a spiritual one for all the shades on the mountain, who, unlike those in Hell, are not stuck in their particular zone of punishment, but endure each stage for a time longer or shorter depending on their worldly adherence to a particular vice, and then move on. This is the world of the divine *Bildungsroman*, of becoming, rather than being.

Hell is full of great discontinuities and barriers to progress – the forbidding door itself, the river Acheron, Minos the judge of Hell, the three-headed dog Cerberus, Pluto, the City of Dis, the Minotaur, the precipice to the seventh circle, the river Phlegethon, the Great Barrier, the broken bridge over the sixth Bolge. In Hell Dante is continually being told to go back. But in Purgatory he is continually encouraged forward, and he and Virgil are assisted and advised by the shades they meet. Here too there are no abrupt-nesses apart from St Peter's Gate and the fire above the seventh cornice, and one ascends by regular steps towards God. Hell could be said to portray progressive loss of motion, though this is not a clear-cut pattern. The damned are rather more at liberty in Upper Hell: certainly they are not continually overseen by devils. In the Bolges we have flatterers plunged in filth, simoniacs embedded head-down in rock, barrators sunk in boiling pitch, hypocrites walking in gilded cloaks lined with lead, thieves stung to dissolution by serpents and reconstituted, sowers of discord being continually cut to pieces, falsifiers stricken with disease, and finally all motion reduced to at most a mere gnawing in the frozen lake of Cocytus. By contrast, in Purgatory motion becomes more easy and swift the further up the mountain one progresses. In Hell a day and a night pass, but we do not know what time it is, cut off from the clock of the sky. But Purgatory is a place of time, of times of punishment measured by numbers of lifetimes, of simple day and night measured by the rising and setting of the sun across the great southern ocean; and here Dante travels for three days and sleeps three nights.

The great power of the *Purgatorio* is in its mixing of natural and supernatural, physical and transphysical concerns. So far as emotion goes, it is certainly the most *moving* – in every sense – book of the *Commedia*; but then we are to learn, in Paradise, that emotion both is and is not enough. Again, we all of us know the sense of elemental purity that climbing an ordinary mountain can give us, and Dante has exploited this: unlike in Hell, we are on the *outside* of a cone pointing upwards, with the world about us visible, and for a time its winds felt; and above us wheel the heavenly bodies of sun, moon and stars. Yet at the same time we are not to see this simply in terms of an earthly mountain. Above the level of St Peter's Gate there is no rain, hail, snow, dew, wind, cloud or thunder (XXI); and this is more than just a matter of physical elevation. The natural-seeming sleeps that Dante and Virgil have are in fact 'supernaturally' induced in them. As seen, the way up the mountain becomes less, not more, tiring the higher one goes. And of course we have the more 'natural' inversions of west and east regarding sunrise and sunset, and the different constellations in the night sky, not to mention that the southern hemisphere is opposite to the northern in being covered with water rather than land. Similarly the beings met on the ascent are both identities and identities-in-transit: they have a spiritual nature that places them on the cornice of the covetous, or of the watchful, or of the lustful, for the time, but that nature is simultaneously being eroded so that they may, as the soul of Statius does while Dante and Virgil pass, break free and ascend to become free citizens of the Heavens. Thus their apparent stasis is played against by their spiritual motion. And in the same way the muted solidity of the mountain both hints at and is juxtaposed with its existence as a metaphysical construct, an artifact with a purpose.

It is this sense of being always shading into something else which gives the *Purgatorio* its unique allegorical force and at the same time its great poignancy. Our affections are engaged, if they are to be transcended; our desires for the Paradise we have lost are aroused, even if they are also to be set aside. Although the *Purgatorio* so often transcends while it marries nature, it can be said to enthrone nature, if by that term we understand 'innocent nature, what we were made to be' – that union of flesh and spirit, natural and supernatural, perfect being and becoming, represented in Paradise. At the top of Purgatory sits the lost garden of Eden, a garden we once inhabited, a garden to which all aspire on Mount Purgatory. It is a natural, as much as a supernatural, garden: below it is all variously *corrupted* nature. So in a sense the summit of Purgatory is nature herself; though Dante goes far beyond Bernardus or Alanus, prime exponents before him of nature's immanent wonder, in giving us a nature transfigured by divine presence. If we look forward and back from this point, it can be seen that Hell is sub-natural (which accounts for its being beneath the earth, its monsters and the reduction of man to physically tormented thing therein); and Heaven, both by virtue of the fact that it ascends above this world, and through its transcendence of our Paradise, is truly super-natural.

Correspondingly, what we could be said to have in the *Commedia* is an ascent of the imagination, or fantasy-making faculty, itself. In Hell the appeal of the violent and vivid images and figures is to the most earthbound and sensationalist level of the imagination: this is it at its lowest, to match the lowness of its context. In Purgatory this materialism begins to be transcended, in a mountain which is both a physical and a spiritual climb, and the laws of which are at once natural and inverted. Here too we are outside, symbolising a steady move out of self and into the clear air, eventually towards the divine source of all beyond the widest universe. And we may too see Hell, the dark interior madhouse, as an image of the sub-conscious, of the wild and dangerous operation of corrupt *fantasia* as the medievals saw it: here again we move out of that dark self into the growing light of true spiritual being and so to the super-conscious. The endpoint of the journey is a vision of God in which the imagination is lost – and yet found, in that only its operations over the whole journey of the poem have led us to Him.[23] Further, while the journey of the imagination is thus serial, the final vision serves to remind us that, however obfuscated, divine vision has been at the root of the creation of the poem from the outset, from the first moment where Dante has lost his way in a wood and will encounter Virgil and the way to Hell.

What then of the *Paradiso*? Here there are hardly any physical details. Images of fire, light, stars and circles are pervasive. All being is mobile in the sense that the intelligences that meet Dante and Beatrice in the various planetary heavens have come there by heavenly courtesy to meet them: they 'belong' to their particular spheres, depending on their particular spiritual natures (for instance, those formerly inconstant to their vows to the Heaven of the Moon, those who were warriors of God in the Heaven of Mars), but they do not have to stay or be confined there (the confinements of Hell and Purgatory have now gone). We hardly see them: at first, in the Heavens of the Moon, Mercury and Venus, still within the cone of Earth's shadow, they are known as 'shades', and dimly seen as human faces and shapes; then, in the further planets they are 'spirits' which manifest themselves as stars and voices; within the furthest Heavens their forms would be quite uncapturable to human sight, and therefore they appear to Dante in the human shape they will wear at the Last Judgement. These spirits group themselves in the forms of circles (the Sun), a cross (Mars), the head of an eagle (Jupiter), or are themselves shaped about God in the form of a rose. It may seem to us mathematical, dry, intellectual. The whole of the *Paradiso* is studded with discussions, on the nature of universal gravitation 'upwards' to the source of being (I), the reason for the markings on the moon (II), whether Plato was right on the stellar location of souls after death, whether good works can make up for unfulfilled religious vows (IV, V), the necessity for the incarnation (VII), the diversity of natural attributes (VIII); even amid the petals of the Sempiternal Rose there is still discussion between Dante and St Bernard on the nature of predestination and of elective grace (XXXII). Heaven is 'pure light: / light intellectual full of love, / love of true good full of joy, / joy that transcends every sweetness' (XXX.39–42).

That point concerning 'sweetness' is precisely what Dante is about here. God and the blessed are for him far beyond the point of human longing and desire. 'Desire', in the sense of an obsession with a particular object or person, is burnt out of Dante by Beatrice at the end of the *Purgatorio*, in her terrifying rebukes of him. The images of the Heavens and the beings therein must not be definite, nor they themselves static and locatable, lest our passional imagination catch at them with its mass of hooks – or, to use another and perhaps more appropriate metaphor, lest it be caught in the gravitational pull of one of the spheres and stop that universal gravitational motion outwards which alone drives us to God. The refusal of affective images, such as a fantastic presentation of Venus (as C. S. Lewis gives it in his *Perelandra*), the mathematics, and the emphasis on intellectual love are meant to be chilling to our fallen ardours. But they do more than this. For one thing they express the incapacity of language and imagination to capture the Heavens in solid images, as Dante frequently acknowledges. Secondly, they convey to us by how much Heaven transcends our notion of it (for example, *Par.* x.43–8). Thirdly, they express the fact that we have now reached the highest level of human being, the intellectual, by which alone we may ascend to contemplate the divine nature. Finally, the mode of the *Paradiso* expresses a sense of the utter transcendence of God, beyond all our conceivings of Him. Only such cool imagery can take us near enough to Him for us to know how much further beyond it He still is. The *Paradiso* is not a cold picture of God: it is the only vehicle by which we may come near to knowing our ignorance of Him.

No one before Dante had ever tried to depict Heaven at such length.[24] It is perhaps a strange fact. But in a sense no one could create such an account who had not been made ready for it by writing the *Inferno* and the *Purgatorio*. If we were to define a fantasy as a work which tries to imagine a supernaturally 'other' world, then Dante's *Paradiso* is the most fantastic of all fantasies, as no world is so 'other' as the one he has presented. And yet he has done it precisely by *not* creating a fantastic world, by refusing all but mathematical structures and schematic images. For he is not attempting to portray an image, but the Real; and to find that the most accurate means of approach is by the refusal of pictures. But the denial of images is not complete: far from it. Rather what Dante is giving us is an image of precision and clarity: these are not abstractions but living ideas, much more real than any 'physical' realities. In other words, the image of the mathematical universe is infinitely more 'concrete' than any solid image of a wonderful world of bliss. At the same time, of course, Dante is saying that such imagery is itself inadequate: after all, at the most common-sense level, and even allowing for mystic vision, he has in part made it up himself. But this point about the higher 'solidity' of ideas is one key to the *Paradiso*. For all it may feel like it to our fallen gaze, we are not in a world of empty abstractions, but rather one like a gigantic brain, where ideas flash to and for in full expression of their being. And the same goes for the souls of the redeemed that we meet, presented as stars, flames or bolts of light: they are so presented not because they are more 'ghostly' or 'insubstantial' than the shades we saw more clearly in Hell or Purgatory, but because their substantiality is of a different order from our notions of it.

The further achievement of Dante's Christian imagination is in realising the incarnational nature of reality at the same time as he so stresses divine transcendence. For God is 'not only' the being who is the centre of the Sempiternal Rose: He is also manifested in all the beings and doings of His creation. He is not only the being 'up there', but also the Christ who came 'down here' and was made man out of love; and to mirror that the poem must take the form not only of an ascending ladder, as we have so far, but also of a reconciling circle. The very circularity of every aspect of Dante's universe from the beginning has figured this. We have been with God in the workings of Hell and Purgatory, and in the forms of the redeemed and the angelic intelligences he has created in the circling spheres of the Heavens. We first see the light of God as a reflection in the eyes of Beatrice (*Par.* XXVIII). Nor, while we are in Heaven, do we forget the Earth.[25] In the Heaven of the Moon, Piccarda dei Donata tells the story of her being forced by her brother from a convent into marriage; in the Heaven of Mars, Dante meets his ancestor Cacciaguida, who speaks of the virtues of old Florence and foretells Dante's exile from the city; in the Heaven of Saturn, the souls of the contemplatives roar in concerted execration of the behaviour of contemporary monastic life and the priesthood, an attack continued in the Empyrean itself (XXVII, XXIX); in the Empyrean, St Peter pronounces Pope Boniface VIII dethroned (XXVII) and Beatrice shows Dante the throne awaiting the emperor Henry VII (XXX).

Nor should we forget that Dante's vision is no lonely one: out of Heaven's generosity and love Beatrice has come down to meet Dante and escort him through the Heavens; and his whole journey

through Hell, Purgatory and Heaven has been presented as accomplished through God's gift, and for the better illumination of
man. Man and the body are redeemed in Christ. And the spirits in
Heaven, presently without flesh, will on the day of the Last Judgement put on the redeemed and incorruptible body and their light
become transfigured (VII.145–8; XIV.37–60). Nothing is sufficient
only to itself. Hell has been harrowed and blasted by Christ. The
refusal of the devils to admit Dante and Virgil to the City of Dis
is countermanded by a heavenly messenger who drives back
the Furies with which they are threatened (*Inf.* VIII, IX). The very
appearance of Dante and Virgil in Hell and Purgatory is a violation
of the norm, for Dante is a living being, not a shade, and neither he
nor Virgil is in these places to suffer any torment. Planes of being
shift and intermingle: Hell as readily contains Pier della Vigne (XIII)
as Brutus or the Minotaur; Purgatory mingles Hugh Capet and
Statius, angels and sinners. Hell, Purgatory and Heaven are organised in circular structures, with roughly the same number of circles
in each; and each is allotted almost the same number of cantos. At
the point where we are apparently furthest from the Earth, in the
Heavens, we are most told of the incarnated Christ (*Par.* VII, XIII, XIV,
XXIII).

The greatest 'incarnational' personage within the poem is
Beatrice herself. Formerly the Florentine girl with whom Dante fell
in love, she is here a part of Christ's nature. And yet she mainly
meant that to Dante while he was still in Florence, even though his
fallen nature continually obscured the image of Heaven that she
presented to him: so it is described in the *Vita Nuova*. We see the
remnants of that misunderstanding in Dante's meeting with her at
the end of the *Purgatorio*.[26] It is not that she has stopped being
Beatrice: she tells Dante in her first words, 'Look at me well: indeed
I am, indeed I am Beatrice!' (*Purg.* XXX.73). Rather it is that, having
become truly herself, she can be more than herself. The cantos at
the end of the *Purgatorio* are justly celebrated for their unique
power in conveying different layers of reality simultaneously.
Literally, our emotions are engaged with Dante as he is led by
Matelda through the wooded Paradise to a stream on the other side
of which, in an open space, appears a Pageant of the Sacrament,
with Beatrice in the midst of it, on a triumph-car drawn by a
gryphon. It is, at this level, an exciting narrative moment, with
images which fire our imaginations. And on the same level, as
Dante begins to speak with Beatrice, our own human nature leads

us to think of it partly as rather like the scolding of a foolish child by a mother. But we know also that much more is going on. There are allegorical figures and significances in the Pageant, with its seven gifts of the spirit represented in the seven candlesticks, and the twenty-four books of St Jerome's Old Testament figured in the twenty-four elders, the three theological and the four cardinal virtues seen in the three and four ladies to right and left of the chariot. Then the four six-winged and many-eyed creatures and the gryphon are symbolic. The figure of Beatrice does not *represent*, however: it is Beatrice and it is Christ together.[27] What we have is a situation in which any level on which we attempt to read is interpenetrated with another. That is the nature of the whole *Commedia*, where while we are in Hell, for example, we constantly discuss worldly matters with the damned whom we meet; but it is most poignantly seen here. It is a denial of *fictional* certainty, even of the grounds of fantasy itself. No one image is enough: the ground is always breaking beneath us. The process of reading on more than one level is of course native to allegory, and is often accomplished by a form of translation: thus, 'This man finding a key with which to escape from the Giant's dungeon is a Christian escaping from the vortex of despair through renewed hope.' But in Dante we do not need to translate: we *feel* them both at once, feel the 'real' world turn into something quite other as we read. This is because Dante puts us continually close to his emotions. Not only that, but, unlike the protagonists of most extended allegories, Dante does not insist on any spiritual development on his part, so that we are never alienated from him: he visits some very remote places, but his business is to take us with him, not to show a fictional spiritual evolution we cannot share. (He may become more confident and more questioning as he proceeds, but that is another matter.) So we are very close to him as he speaks with Beatrice, and that makes us the more powerfully aware that Beatrice is both herself and much more. And, to the extent that we apprehend both levels simultaneously, we experience not allegory but incarnation. Dante had wondered how the twofold nature of Christ, as God and as man, might be experienced: here he has realised it in his poetry, as Beatrice, girl and risen Christ, speaks to him as lover and errant earthbound soul (XXXI.37–75).

Today we are perhaps inclined to exaggerate Dante's qualities as a fantasist and as a human being at the expense of his Christian vision. We are sometimes too ready to identify his adventurous

Ulysses, who is in any case wrecked on Mount Purgatory and damned (*Inf.* XXVI), with the flights of his own imagination. We may sometimes see his Hell less as itself than as a kind of medieval *Dunciad*, in which Dante could create a fictional final indictment for his enemies. The *Commedia* has such mortal impulses, doubtless, as it has imaginative ones which we have seen. But we do Dante wrong to see him in our terms. His ensphered universe may seem perhaps to us a small and enclosed affair, in contrast to the one we know of boundless space and time; but distances within it are as said measured not by light years but by advances of the spirit – and in this connection we have to remember that his Hell, Purgatory and Heaven are 'here' in us, as much as out there, and that in neither case are they simply material. In Dante's *Commedia* we have a union of opposites expressing the nature of Christian reality – a poem whose source is both divine truth and human invention, whose impulse is at once to inflame and freeze the imagination, whose characters and events exist simultaneously as literal and allegorical realities, whose structure depends on forward movement and recapitulation, time and eternity, whose very verse form, *terza rima*, unites both the line and the circle;[28] a poem which, as it reaches its consummation in God, founds itself on an inexpressible paradox of poignant nearness and utter and enrapturing distance:

> Qual è'l geomètra che tutto s'affige
>   per misurar lo cerchio, e non ritrova,
>   pensando, quel principio ond'elli indige,
> tal era io a quella vista nova:
>   veder volèva come si convenne
>   l'imago al cerchio e come vi s'indova;
> ma non eran da ciò le proprie penne:
>   se non che la mia mente fu percossa
>   da un fulgore in che sua voglia venne.
> A l'alta fantasia qui mancò possa;
>   ma già volgeva il mio disio e'l *velle*,
>   sì come rota ch'igualmente è mossa,
> l'amor che move il sole e l'altre stelle.

As is the geometer who wholly applies himself to measure the circle, and finds not, in pondering, the principle of which he is in need, such was I at that new sight. I wished to see how the image conformed to the circle and how it has its place therein; but my own wings were not sufficient for that, save that my mind was smitten by a flash wherein its wish came to it. Here power failed the lofty phantasy; but already my desire and my will were revolved, like a wheel that is evenly moved, by the Love that moves the sun and the other stars.   (*Par.* xxx.133–45)

4

The Middle English *Pearl*

Strictly speaking *Pearl* (1375–95) is not a narrative but a visionary and consolatory episode,[1] in which a man, lamenting the loss of a precious pearl – in part perhaps his daughter – is granted a vision of his pearl among the blessed in heaven, and bid to grieve no more. But as a piece of Christian supernaturalism, as a peculiar picture of the strong current of otherworldliness in medieval Christian literature already glimpsed in the *Queste*, and as a poem of rare beauty in its own right, it demands some consideration here.

Pearl opens with a speaker describing himself as a jeweller who has lost his most precious pearl in a garden. Wretched with despair, he falls asleep in the garden and has a dream in which he is taken to a rich country of forests, glades and cliffs, with a land divided from him by a stream he cannot cross. On the other side of the stream, at the foot of a crystal cliff, he eventually observes a little girl whom he recognises; she looks like a pearl, her gleaming clothes are covered with pearls, and she has a great pearl set in the midst of her breast. The jeweller now asks her if she is the pearl he has lost (ll. 241–3). She can be seen as a child who died young, and he has just told us that 'Ho watʒ me nerre þen aunte or nece' (l. 233):[2] there are other clear hints that he stands in relation to her as father to daughter as much as any other (ll. 411–2, 483–5). He bemoans his loss to her, tells of his misery and asks her to return with him. She tells him he is ignorant of where he is and what she is. She tells him that when she died she was taken to heaven and now lives as a queen in the company of 144,000 innocents with her bridegroom the Lamb, and that she cannot return. When he finds it hard that she should be made a queen in heaven when she had never lived long enough on earth to do good, she replies with Christ's pledge to save the innocent 'by right', and with the parable of the vineyard (Matthew 20.1–16), whereby the labourers who came late in the day for employment were paid as much as those who had worked since first light. The jeweller now wishes to be with her, to join her in heaven: she answers that this is impossible, but that by special dispensation he may have a sight of the heavenly city and herself in the company of the Lamb. When he thus sees her he is eventually filled with such longing that he tries (like Lancelot at his sight of the Grail) to reach her by crossing the stream, only to be cast out of the dream and to find himself once more lying in the garden where he fell asleep. Rebuking himself, he vows a new life in the service of the Lamb.

The poem is clearly intended to be read as an allegory. As in Dante's *Commedia* the dreamer's vision of heaven is both literal and spiritual (an 'allegory of theologians'):[3] heaven is the place where the souls of the saved go after death, but it is also the place that Christ has made in the human heart for those who can realise it. The pearl that was lost in the garden may be allegorised as man's loss of innocence in the Garden of Eden, and its recovery in heaven may be seen as expressing the redemption of man through Christ; more generally, however, it can be seen as an image of man's soul.[4] The dreamer cannot reach the pearl, cannot recover innocence as it were, except by returning to earth and living out his life, by which means he may come to the 'jeweller', Christ. In larger and more anagogical terms we may see his living his life on earth is mankind in general working out its salvation until the Last Things (imaged in the account of the New Jerusalem taken from Revelation 21 (ll. 917–1092).

If we set aside its allegorical aspects for the moment, however, the whole poem is an exposure, often quite harsh-seeming, of the gap between earthly and heavenly understanding. The dreamer judges with his senses only, not with any spiritual imagination. He thinks the girl is his former pearl, and cannot fully comprehend the gulf between himself and her, still trying to go over to her at the end. This is condemned as worldly possessiveness, a refusal to yield up the pearl to her true jeweller, Christ Himself. The dreamer is variously rebuked for his misery, his ignorance of where he is and his refusal to comprehend how one so young has become a queen in heaven. He thinks the Jerusalem before him is an image of that in the world:

> Þou telleʒ me of Jerusalem þe ryche ryalle,
> Þer David dere watʒ dyʒt on trone,
> Bot by þyse holteʒ hit con not hone,
> Bot in Judee hit is, þat noble note.
>
> (ll. 919–22)

Certainly his vision of her and her place is inadequate: even near the end he still thinks to take her back home with him.

But such severance of earth from heaven comes not just from him but from the pearl also. As Dante did in the *Paradiso*, but with even more rigour, the ways of heaven are separated from those of earth. The dreamer cannot understand how the pearl–girl, who died in infancy, can be taken to heaven immediately and promoted to one of its highest places, while those who have the 'misfortune' to live longer and thus be more exposed to sin have a much greater struggle if they are to reach heaven. It is certainly a theological 'problem', and one the poem by its subject matter has thrust into prominence. And it is one that is not helped for mere mortal understanding by the pearl's citation of the parable of the vineyard: for that is precisely a parable that flies against our notion of 'right', with those who come late to work being given the same as those who have worked long.[5] But, the pearl insists, 'Þe innosent is ay saf by ryȝt' (ll. 672–720): she imposes another and heavenly notion of 'right' on our earthly one. Dante devoted attention to a related issue in the *Paradiso* when he asked why the heathen who happened by ill chance to live before Christ had to languish, Virgil included, in Limbo in Hell; but, while he too is told that the ways of heaven are different from those of earth, he is allowed to discuss the issue fully with the Just Rulers and reach a measure of satisfaction (*Par.* XIX, XX), and there is also the promise in the redemption of the pagan emperor Trajan (*Par.* XX.43ff.). Further division in *Pearl* between earth and heaven occurs where the pearl maintains that, where she is, hierarchy can coexist with equality; that each of the 144,000 innocent of which she is one is also 'Queen of Heaven'.[6]

To a large extent all is owing to the ignorance of the dreamer. He has been given a vision, itself probably to be seen as a piece of supernatural grace (ll. 967–8, 1184).[7] His imagination, we should recall, as in much Christian fantasy, is the medium of the poem. Yet, instead of moving towards the truly 'fantastic', he retreats to the merely worldly level of understanding, judging only with his senses. Therefore we may say that what he sees becomes to him harsher and more uncompromising in appearance than it really is.[8] Certainly he is no Dante, who by the time he has reached the Heavens is receptive to what they are. This may explain the often cold treatment administered to him by the pearl: this at once expresses his distance from what she is, and is a necessarily corrosive remedy.[9] He has no knowledge of the symbolic character of the pearl: its loss for him parallel to man's loss of his young innocence; its beauty, purity and roundness expressing the 'pearl of great price' of Matthew 13.45–6 which is heaven; its promotion to heaven expressing the rescue of the soul through Christ. Instead he talks of her only as his daughter, and also sometimes in the materialist analogy of a favourite pearl lost by himself as jeweller. So, when he speaks of taking her home with him, she retorts, 'Wy borde ȝe men? So madde ȝe be!' and 'Þou ne woste in worlde quat on dotȝ mene; / Þy worde byfore þy witte con fle' (ll. 290, 293–4). Hard from a lost daughter, hard too from a soul saved through Christ's compassionate incarnation; but on this reading necessary. We might wish to compare the dreamer's meeting with the pearl with that of Dante with Beatrice in the *Purgatorio*, where Beatrice is similarly quite harsh, telling Dante to 'lay aside the seed of tears and listen' (*Purg.* XXXI.46), when he speaks of her as his former Florentine beloved: indeed it is possible that the poet of *Pearl* drew his idea for the visionary meeting of a mortal with his former beloved on either side of a stream from Dante's poem.[10] Nevertheless there is a plea made for mercy for Dante by Beatrice's attendants, which we may assume expresses in part the fact that he is more spiritually enlightened than the dreamer of *Pearl*; and certainly Dante is enabled to cross the stream to Beatrice, and eventually under her conduct enter the Heavens, as this dreamer is not.

Also perhaps expressing the unenlightened state of the dreamer in *Pearl* is the peculiar sense of enclosure that attends the portrayal of heavenly things.[11] The dreamer in his ignorance reaches out, tries to become a part of this other world, tries to continue his old and earthly relation with his 'pearl', and eventually even to take her back; but the whole 'resultant' imagery of the pearl so smooth, so round, so singular and unique conveys the sense of a sphere of wealth sufficient to itself and cut off from all else. The same impression comes from the portrayal of the New Jerusalem, descending from heaven like some medieval Laputa, with its foundation of precious stones, its moat, walls and platform of stairs: all that the dreamer sees of the Lamb's procession goes on within it, and is lit by the lamp of the Lord, for the light of the sun or moon would be quite inadequate; it is apparently wholly independent, divided from the external world. It may be a re-creation of the New Jerusalem as described in the Book of Revelation, but this emphasis on its isolation is peculiar to this poem. In Revelation there is stress rather on the city as God's dwelling among men (21.3), and on its accessibility to all nations rather than its exclusiveness (21.24, 26). All this separation of the two worlds may be taken as an expression of the divine transcendence; but equally it can be seen as a picture of the dreamer's worldliness, his inability to move in any great degree from natural to supernatural vision. He cannot key himself into that vision, and it therefore must remain aloof from him. Thus a poem which so much insists on Christ's sacrifice for man does not portray a bridge between the two realms, remains apparently non-incarnational, non-Christian even, in the sense of Christ's specific acts for man. But the whole poem is filled by the need for that bridge: mistakenly apprehended by the dreamer, sought through spiritual awakening of him by the pearl. In that sense the very absence of the spark between heaven and earth portrays the need for it; and the poem can thus be said to be a supernatural vision of the absence of true connection – in short, a Christian fantasy, in a special mode.

Such a perspective on the dreamer's worldliness is not, it should be said, easily reached by us. We too feel some sympathy for him as he expresses his desire for her, for it seems genuine love rather than mere possessiveness:

> Now rech I neuer for to declyne,
> Ne how fer of folde þat man me fleme.
> When I am partleʒ of perle myne.
> (ll. 333–5)

Like him we may well think that the pearl is a lost daughter, and sympathise with his grief and longing to renew that relation and have her back; and we may find almost cruel her rejection of his human feelings. But, if we feel so, we too are being tested and found wanting; and that is in large part the power of the poem.[12] Only at the end, when the dreamer has lost all, does he accept enough of the truth to begin to gain. He gives away his pearl to Christ, and as he does so Christ comes down to him and enters and strengthens him; the poem ends with the incarnational imagery it has so long sought:

> To pay þe Prince oþer sete saʒte
> Hit is ful eþe to þe god Krystyin;
> For I haf founden hym, boþe day and naʒte,

A God, a Lorde, a frende ful fyin.
Ouer þis hyul þis lote I laȝte,
For pyty of my perle enclyin,
And syþen to God I hit bytaȝte
In Krysteȝ dere blessyng and myn,
þat in þe forme of bred and wyn
þe preste vus scheweȝ vch a daye,
He gef vus to be his homly hyne
Ande precious perleȝ vnto his pay.

(ll. 1201–12)

With that last line the dreamer gives himself as pearl into the hands of a far greater jeweller: he will seek no longer to possess, but to be possessed.

As we have said, the poem has much in common with Dante's, particularly the encounter with Beatrice in the *Purgatorio*. This is seen also at the level of the fantastic landscape. The dreamer finds himself, as his vision begins, among cliffs, beyond which is a forest towards which he makes his way. The shining leaves of the forest let through occasional bright gleams from the sky and the woods are filled with beautiful birds in harmonious song. A stream, its bed covered with precious stones, runs through the forest, and he follows it up; but by no means can he cross it. Eventually he sees on the opposite bank a maiden sitting beneath a cliff, whom he knows well. This is very close to the description in Dante. But in *Pearl* there is one striking difference. The landscape is one continually described in terms of precious stones. The cliffs are rich-hued, dazzlingly adorned and crystalline. The trees are like gems with boles of indigo and shimmering leaves of silver. The birds are a further 'adubbement' (adornment) – the word recurs throughout this part of the poem. The gravel the dreamer walks on is of pearl. The banks of the stream are as brilliant in appearance as threads of gold, and made of beryl; and dazzling stones – emeralds, sapphires and other gems – cover the bed of the stream. All this fills the dreamer with bliss and with longing to get to the Paradise which he feels must be at the centre here; but he cannot cross the stream, though he struggles long (as Dante did not).[13] The only mention of gems in Dante is in relation to the emerald eyes of Beatrice, and this reference to precious stones is not so much literal as adjectival or even symbolic (*Purg.* xxxi.116–17). Dante's description is all organic, where that of the dreamer is much harder, more mineral.

The difference comes partly from the fact that *Pearl's* very subject is a precious stone or pearl; and that part of its theme concerns the nature of true preciousness. From the outset the dreamer speaks of his loss in terms of a jeweller's loss of a precious gem:

> Perle, plesaunte to prynces paye
> To clanly clos in golde so clere,
> Oute of oryent, I hardyly saye,
> Ne proued I neuer her precios pere.
> So rounde, so reken in vche araye,
> So smal, so smoþe her sydeȝ were,
> Quere-so-euer I jugged gemmeȝ gaye,
> I sette hyr sengeley in synglere.
> Allas! I leste hyr in on erbere;
> Þurȝ gresse to grounde hit fro me yot ....
>
> (ll. 1–10)

The rest of this first part of the poem has as the refrain to each stanza his 'precios [*or* pryuy] perle wythouten spot', by which 'spot' the dreamer means material, rather than spiritual blemish. When he meets her in his vision (part IV) she is again his 'precios perle'. She appears to him covered with pearls: her clothes are adorned with them, she has a crown made of pearls, and in the midst of her breast is set a flawless pearl which in particular awakens his wonder. In part V of the poem the dreamer addresses the girl as the pearl he lost in the grass of the 'erber', and talks of himself as one who since her loss has been 'a joyleȝ juelere' (l. 252); now, he says, he has found her again and will stay with her, as a 'ioyful jueler' (l. 288). The pearl-girl seeks to change his notion of her. What he loved and lost on earth was not a pearl but a mere rose 'þat flowred and fayled as kynde hyt gef' (l. 270). Through redemption it has been changed to a pearl indeed, but a pearl which is no mere material gem but one 'of prys', of spiritual excellence symbolised in its form (Matthew. 13.45–6). She goes on to rebuke the dreamer for materialism, for judging everything by mere eyesight, thinking he sees her in this valley and can pass over the water to dwell with her (ll. 289–300). Later, in parts XIII–XV, she elevates the notion of the true pearl further to Christ Himself, who is her jeweller in the spiritual sense. As we see the New Jerusalem, it is described with much mention of precious stones, drawn from Revelation 21–2 – jasper, sapphire, chalcedony, emerald, sardonyx, ruby, chrysolite, beryl, topaz, chrysoprase, jacinth and amethyst; and twelve gates of pearl (ll. 985–1038). But now the stones are evidently symbolic: they are of spiritual, not material value.[14]

Arguably the landscapes of the poem take the form that they do because of this theme. Because the jeweller is blinded by the material value of things, the landscape during his approach to the girl–pearl is seen in terms of gems and wealth as it is not in Dante's *Purgatorio*. The pearl he meets is a 'transitional' mixture of 'material' and symbolic pearls; and thereafter in the poem we deal much with gems of spiritual value. Clearly the theme is the difference between earthly and heavenly wealth; and there is also the issue of who is the girl–pearl's true 'jeweller', and in what sense. If, as we are supposed to do, we see the whole dream as a vision granted by God to the dreamer, the first part of it, while he is still alone, is seen in his idiom; but then, when he encounters the maiden and is subsequently given a vision of the New Jerusalem, the dream is in God's spiritual terms, which he must understand. The transition from 'self' to 'other', from material to spiritual vision, is helped for him by the fact that the value of gems is made a continuous issue in heaven. Thus it could be said that the landscape of the dreamer before he meets the maiden is in part one coloured by his own earthly nature; and gradually we are moved, through the intercession of the maiden, away from this subjective vision to the much more objective, scripturally 'given' landscape of the New Jerusalem as described in Revelation, which expresses the nature of God. In other words, in landscape terms the poem enacts a kind of fantastic ascent, from the partly self-begotten to the wholly bestowed, from human fantasy to divine imagination.[15] How far the dreamer or any of us is capable of following that ascent is then for us to determine and live.

For all the harmony that we have thus traced between imagery and Christian meaning in *Pearl*, it must be said that the position of the imagination in this poem is rather different from that which it held in the *Queste* or the *Commedia*. There it was either subordinated or harnessed to 'meaning'. Here the meaning *is* its lack of sub-ordination – at least in so far as it is the human imagination. The whole poem, as we have seen, dramatises a conflict between the refractory and shallow mortal imagination and the spiritual imagination of the great Maker of all. Thus, while the poem integrates this conflict within a larger purpose, the conflict is at least admitted. And from now on we are going to see the 'rebellious' human imagination playing a larger and often less readily controlled part in Christian fantasy.

5

Spenser: *The Faerie Queene,* Book I

In many ways *The Faerie Queene* (1590–6) seems similar to the French *Queste*. The context is one of knights and knightly contest; we move through a landscape of forests, valleys and plains with occasional castles; there is a quest; there are apparently random encounters with knights, damsels, demons and succubae; and above all there is allegory, whereby we are invited to see spiritual significance in or under the narrative. It is hard indeed to believe that Spenser was not as indebted to the *Queste* as to Ariosto.

Yet the differences are marked, and some of them point to fundamental shifts in the character of fantasy over the close on four centuries that separate the two works. The first book of *The Faerie Queene* is, like the *Queste*, a legend of holiness, but its orientation is towards being holy in this world. The Redcrosse knight has to learn how to be truly pure in spirit so that he can live aright. The virtue of holiness he learns does not stand alone: it is meant to be joined to other virtues, among them temperance, justice and courtesy, portrayed in later books, and all brought together in the recurrent figure of Arthur, or Magnificence. When the Redcrosse knight has succeeded in his quest and released Una's parents from their thraldom to the dragon, he marries Una and returns to the world. Not so Sir Galahad in the *Queste*: he is there to demonstrate by his life the perfection of Christ and the imperfection of the Round Table. His perfection implies that he cannot be imitated by us, just as he cannot be matched by any other knight (or demon for that matter) in the story; whereas Spenser's Redcrosse is a fallible figure, who stumbles and has to be helped towards grace. And at the end Sir Galahad leaves the world, taking the Grail with him. The entire story is directed towards a gradual removal from this world, in the shift away from Arthur's court and the steady increase of holy supernatural events, just as it is directed to a condemnation of all earthliness. In the same way its allegory continually evacuates the literal level of understanding, reducing the story to explicit spiritual content.

This 'otherworldly' emphasis is present in various degrees in all the works we have considered so far. Dante of course puts us in the worlds of the afterlife, as does *Pearl*: both invite mortal men to direct their behaviour with regard to what will happen to them after death. That regard is basic to all Christian behaviour, but with greater or less emphasis. We could find it also later, in Bunyan's *The Pilgrim's Progress*, where the ideas of renunciation of the world and the quest for a spiritual prize are very reminiscent of the *Queste*. What is different in the writers earlier than Spenser is the proximity of the other world to the here and now, even while the two are often utterly opposed spiritually. The Grail enters Camelot. Dante enters Hell, Purgatory and Heaven. The man in *Pearl* has an interview with the pearl–girl outside heaven. The mortal and immortal worlds are shown as readily interconversant. But in later works this kind of communication is reduced.[1] The world may for the late sixteenth and seventeenth centuries be packed full of evil spirits, so full that, as Thomas Nashe charmingly says, 'Infinite millions of them will hang swarming about a worm-eaten nose',[2] but encounters with them are rare, and negotiations with them, like that of Faustus, of course forbidden. In *Paradise Lost* we see man and God separating from one another, and this world and heaven becoming partially disjoined. Emphasis begins increasingly to fall on human conduct within this world as a means of reaching the next: there is something of a division of the two realms. The incarnational vision which, for all its asceticism, characterises medieval Christian fantasy becomes rather eroded and infrequent. Thus in the faërian landscape of Spenser's Legend of Holiness we will not find quite so much in the way of supernatural presence as we did in the *Queste*.

Another difference with *The Faerie Queene* is that its narrative is much more a fiction. Spenser did not believe in the Matter of Britain, or in the existence of the world of his poem, or his knights, or their quests. Nor do the knights and tourneys any longer reflect the character of actual society, which has long since seen the last of all knights slow his charger to an amble with the weight of his over-elaborated armour. This is a romance in the full sense of the word so far as the literal story goes. As Spenser himself puts it,

The generall end ... of all the booke is to fashion a gentleman or noble person in vertuous and gentle discipline: Which for that I conceiued shoulde be most plausible and pleasing, being coloured with an historicall fiction, the which the most part of men delight to read, rather for variety of matter, then for profite of the ensample: I chose the historye of king Arthure, as most fitte for the excellency of his person, being made famous by many mens former workes, and also furthest from the daunger of enuy, and suspition of present time.[3]

Because the world of knightly romance and chivalry no longer reflects society, it can curiously be more generally applicable: the reader must relate the fiction to his own life rather than his life to the knightly mores portrayed. The intention is to be at once more democratic and more effectively educational, 'to fashion a gentleman or noble person in vertuous and gentle discipline'.[4]

But how is this relation of the fiction to our lives to be achieved? For Spenser clearly sees a danger that people will prefer to read his semi-Arthurian material for delight rather than instruction, 'rather for variety of matter, then for profite of the ensample'. Faced by a similar problem, the author of the *Queste* often made overt translation of the story into significance. There is still much unstated spiritual patterning in his narrative, but his method makes us alert to its presence. In Dante's *Commedia*, merely the fact that we are in Hell, Purgatory and Heaven provides a climate for reading allegorically. Always the religious dimension is in some sense overt: 'depend upon it, whatever you saw was but as it were a figuration of Jesus Christ'.[5] The extreme in this connection is a morality play such as *Everyman* (1485), where all the characters have allegorical names and the play labours to make its significance obvious. God is angry at man's delinquency and instructs his servant Death to call Everyman to account. Everyman, terrified by the approach of Death, calls all his attributes, such as Goods, Strength, Five Wits and Discretion, about him to be his defence; but all, apart from Knowledge (who instructs him), his Good Deeds (which will speak for him) and Confession (who shrives him), desert him before the end, because they are of the world only. The drama is a kind of allegorical filtration process, until Everyman is left with the true gold of those values that are eternal. The play's achievement is that, for all this stress on meaning and moral content, its labelled figures are extraordinarily vivid.

Spenser, however, has chosen to go in almost the opposite direction from *Everyman*. 'Knowing how doubtfully all Allegories may be construed', he still writes his *Faerie Queene* as 'a continued

Allegory, or darke conceit', the moral intent of which he feels constrained to outline in his letter or 1589 to Raleigh with the publication of the first three books. Instead of restricting the reader's imagination, he has given it more freedom, and more fiction.

> To some I know this Methode will seeme displeasaunt, which had rather haue good discipline deliuered plainly in way of precepts, or sermoned at large, as they vse, then thus clowdily enwrapped in Allegoricall deuises. But such, me seeme, should be satisfide with the vse of these dayes, seeing all things accounted by their showes, and nothing esteemed of, that is not delightfull and pleasing to commune sence. For this cause is Xenophon preferred before Plato, for that the one in the exquisite depth of his iudgement, formed a Commune welth such as it should be, but the other in the person of Cyrus and the Persians fashioned a gouernement such as might best be: So much more profitable and gratious is doctrine by ensample, then by rule.[6]

Again there is hint of doubt on Spenser's part as to the efficacy of his method when 'all things [are] accounted by their showes, and nothing esteemed of, that is not delightfull and pleasing to commune sense'. He has accommodated his poem to this outlook, but he registers a sense of the risk too.

How is this reflected in *The Faerie Queene*? We have seen already how Spenser chooses a faërian and semi-Arthurian context of knights, damsels, wizards, giants and monsters, set in a romance landscape of forest and plain. Actually the story is not directly Arthurian at all, using none of the narratives of the Round Table, particularly that of the Grail Quest; and this as it were does away with the significances more or less latent in those narratives. No knight save Sir Tristram (VI.ii) has an Arthurian name, despite the presence of 'Arthur' himself in a rather untraditional errant role in every book. It seems that – leaving aside the historical role of Arthur himself in relation to the Tudors – the story is more fictive than the Arthurian fiction itself: Spenser has, it seems, set us in a Fairy Land and left us to find our own bearings.

What then of his characters? Here we find Spenser giving rather more help, though it varies considerably. Some of the characters are given directly allegorical names. In book I there are Error, Despair and the House of Holiness. However, the knight of this book is called Redcrosse (and, for example, Sir Guyon is the knight of

Temperance in book II), the evil magician of the story is named Archimago, the evil women are called Duessa, Corceca and Lucifera; there is a giant named Orgoglio and a vast and nameless dragon with which Redcrosse has to do battle at the end of his quest. Spenser thus in part asks us to translate. 'Simple' translations are the three knights Sans Joy, Sans Foy and Sans Loy, or the ladies of the House of Holiness – Fidelia, Speranza and Charissa; Lucifera is the female version of Lucifer in her pride; Orgoglio is drawn from the Italian 'orgoglio', which became the Middle English word 'orgueil', meaning 'pride' or 'haughtiness' (OED). Others we have to translate using different methods. For example, the headnote to canto ii tells us that the Redcrosse knight's companion is 'Truth'; but her name 'Una' portrays the nature of truth – one, single and entire – and this itself is not fully clear to us until we see her in contrast to the 'recycled' sprite Duessa, or 'two-ness', who is deceptive, multiple, and always seen dependent or parasitic on others.[7] The seven-headed monster on which Duessa rides at Orgoglio's castle requires biblical and other explanation: on it she represents the Whore of Babylon or the evil of the Roman Catholic Church; and the dragon itself is drawn from the scarlet-coloured beast of Revelation 17. As for the dragon at the end of the book, which has for long held Una's parents prisoner in a tower, it may be seen as a form of Satan, who engineered the fall of man, and its destruction by Redcrosse may be seen as apocalyptic. But these identifications are often fluid or partial. At times Redcrosse represents the ordinary Christian, learning through errors the way to holiness; at times his history could be said to figure that of the Church since the death of Christ, made triumphant in the time of Elizabeth; at times, especially in the latter part of the book, he comes to partake in the nature of Christ Himself, restoring man through three days of sacrificial battle with the devil. And a similar range of interpretations and levels of reading is possible with the episodic actions – for they are often a series of imagistic episodes – as much as with the various characters.

Why has Spenser so often thus obscured, or forced us to work for, his meaning? It seems almost as though he has chosen a story and a setting that will take him as far away from the real world and its concerns as possible; and yet it is to that real world that his poem is addressed. How could a work written in an estranged, pseudo-archaic language, and discussing the doings of knights in a remote Fairy Land, speak to an Elizabethan audience?[8] Certainly Spenser poses the problem directly himself:

Right well I wote most mighty Soueraine,
That all this famous antique history,
Of some th' aboundance of an idle braine
Will iudged be, and painted forgery,
Rather then matter of iust memory,
Sith none, that breatheth liuing aire, does know,
Where is that happy land of Faery,
Which I so much do vaunt, yet no where show,
But vouch antiquities, which no body can know.

(II. proem 1)[9]

In presenting this Fairy Land he has chosen to go even further than his romantic sources, Ariosto's *Orlando Furioso* (1532) and Tasso's *Gerusalemme Liberata* (1581). These are centrally accounts of real-life or else quasi-historical events: the one describes a besieging of Charlemagne in Paris by a Saracen army, and the other the siege of Jerusalem under Godefroi de Bouillon in 1099. Both of them, particularly Ariosto, show a delight in fabulous events and places also; and this and the episodic method of Ariosto particularly drew Spenser to them. But neither, not even Tasso (who may have imposed its meaning on his story retrospectively), shows anything quite like the allegorical tendency of Spenser, or his consistent remoteness from the real or historical world. It looks as though Spenser wanted to make his poem both 'escapist' as regards the fantasy in it, and 'responsible' as regards its allegory, and the two impulses do not seem to sit well together. Ever since the appearance of his poem there has been a sense of both sides, and an attempt to square them. 'All recent critics', observes Paul Alpers, 'define Spenser's technique by the poles of narrative and allegory'; and he goes on to show that the two poles cannot be reconciled.[10]

The first and most simple answer is that Spenser has chosen his episodic mode and his faërian context because they provide the most effective image of the fluid landscape of the soul. The abrupt changes and discontinuities that characterise the story thus mirror changes in the soul that could not be portrayed in a normal mode of sequential narrative. Thus too the monsters, fairies and marvels are images native to the mind, and the magic and metamorphoses express the swift and often abrupt transformations of the spirit. So too we are started off *in medias res* ('A Gentle Knight was pricking on the plaine...'), without any introduction or sense of who the characters are or where they are going, in order precisely to dislocate our normal mode of consciousness and to make us more open to a spiritual level of comprehension. In that sense Spenser's Fairy Land becomes a way of talking about a level of reality more real than that of the mere outside world we know. By contrast *Everyman*, for instance, is not a picture of man's spirit or soul: it is a typical account, in allegorical shorthand, of the experience of any Christian faced by death. Spenser's work, thus seen, has its allegorical links rather with the genre of the psychomachia.

The second answer is that Spenser intends *The Faerie Queene* to work precisely by being 'a darke conceit'. On this view the reader is, allowing for some help, to do much of the work for himself. Thus only if he has biblical knowledge and some understanding of, not to say involvement in, the Christian faith and its practice, will he begin to comprehend the full meaning of Lucifera, the significance of Archimago or the several layers of meaning present in the final great battle with the dragon. This is quite different from *Everyman*, which labours to be absolutely clear. It is not that Spenser wishes to give us licence to improvise, to be as free as we please. Rather, as much 'precision' as we wish is there, if we bring to the poem the right equipment. If we think it arrogant of Spenser to demand this, we should recall that Dante and Bunyan do so too, and that such matters, if they are to be talked about at all, will make demands on us to be understood. On those terms, if we read *The Faerie Queene* for its wonders and have some faint glimmerings of significance now and then, there is a cruel truth that says we will have learnt only about our own materialism. And yet it is typical of Spenser's complexity that, if we read *The Faerie Queene* solely in order to comprehend its deep significance, we run the risk of spiritual pride. Seen thus, whichever way we read, the poem becomes a test of us, demands both more and less.

Nevertheless it must be said that Spenser's method with his narrative does help the reader towards a contemplative approach to his fiction. Explaining in his letter why he starts his poem *in medias res* Spenser says,

the Methode of a Poet historical is not such, as of an Historio-grapher. For an Historiographer discourseth of affayres orderly as they were donne, accounting as well the times as the actions, but a Poet thrusteth into the middest, euen where it most concerneth him, and there recoursing to the thinges forepaste, and diuining of thinges to come, maketh a pleasing Analysis of all.

The poet does not need to follow a narrative sequence, and he may thus remove from the reader the kind of narrative excitement which might otherwise blind him to the spiritual dimension of the work. Thus we do not find much suspense or anticipation of events in the poem: things simply 'happen' in this faërian world, and the end of a story may be given to us before its beginning, as with the story of Amoret and Scudamore in books III and IV. And, although there is a quest, a final objective in view, it is rarely mentioned, and we are not strongly aware of it. At a merely narrative level the final dragon with which Redcrosse does battle comes more or less unheralded, as just one more episode.

The third explanation for Spenser's frequent disguising of his meaning is that a given personage or action is often not simply to be summed up or conceptualised, but can only be understood in its total embodiment in the poem. This is even true of the labelled figures themselves. The figure of Despair may seem obvious enough, but it is not till we have seen the full articulation and subtlety of his temptation of Redcrosse to make away with himself that we begin to understand something of the network of routes and even philosophies that can lead to Despair's cave. Fidelia in the House of Holiness seems clear enough; but Spenser is intent on taking us away from the mere concept to the profundity of the spiritual condition in which this Faith lives:

> She was araied all in lilly white,
> And in her right hand bore a cup of gold,
> With wine and water fild vp to the hight,
> In which a Serpent did himselfe enfold,
> That horrour made to all, that did behold;
> But she no whit did chaunge her constant mood:
> And in her other hand she fast did hold
> A booke, that was both signd and seald with blood,
> Wherein darke things were writ, hard to be vnderstood.
>
> (I.x.13)

Doubtless much of this can be explicated,[11] but the effect depends on an apprehension of the stanza as a whole. Similarly with a figure such as the wizard Archimago, where what he is is a complex of what he does and the guises under which he appears. Again, with Duessa, we do not know all of her until we have seen her as the false Una, the lady Fidessa looked after by Sans Foy, the paramour of Orgoglio on her many-headed monster, and the stripped and repulsive thing that crawls away after her and Orgoglio's defeat by Prince Arthur. To say that Duessa's final exposure reveals her for what she is is certainly true; but she has also been, and in the world exists as, the other shapes with which she covers herself. She is as it were a composite of all her apparitions, including the reality itself. And the same can be said of all the other characters and actions, in all their appearances and aspects. Indeed, this is in part a key to understanding the nature of the poem itself. The 'story', the mere narrative, may be in part only an appearance, but it is part of our total experience of the work, and cannot be set aside entirely for the significance it masks.[12]

So far we have discussed the poem generally. Our particular concern here is with book I, the Legend of Holiness, which we may call an example of Christian fantasy. Some of the 'fantastic' element we have already explored. But it is worth adding that this book is distinctive in texture in several ways. First, it has more monsters than any other. Redcrosse's first encounter is with the monster Error in its woodland den, a beast of female body and serpentine tail; Duessa is mounted on a huge hydra; and the dragon at the end is as big as a hill. There are also far more specifically magical episodes and transformations. There is Fradubio, transformed to a tree; Archimago, magician and shape-shifter; Lucifera, pulled in her chariot by her extraordinary team of the Seven Deadly Sins; the figure of Night herself; the repair of the dead Sans Joy by Aesculapius in Hell; Duessa's magic cup; Arthur's magic shield; the Well and the Tree of Life that sustain Redcrosse in his final battle. In the other books of *The Faerie Queene* there are not nearly so many fabulous creatures and events: most of what we see has a human face. This may be because the virtues described in those books relate more specifically to secular conduct – to temperance, love, justice or courtesy. But there may be another reason still.

For Spenser has made one of the recurrent motifs of this first book that of illusion.[13] In such a context the presence of numerous fantastical beings would be appropriate. The first adventure of the book involves a *de*lusion, a losing of one's way, in a wood, before the monster Error is met and overthrown. That monster may well represent the various perversions or turnings aside of the True Faith into theological speculation and heresy. In her struggle with Redcrosse, Error vomits forth (not very happily for the allegory, perhaps) a mass of books and papers: we can see these as tracts and papers arguing over and misinterpreting Scripture, thrown in

Redcrosse's way to divert him from his path.[14] The fact that Una is with the knight will then be significant, for she figures Truth, and her presence, we may therefore suppose, helps him to overthrow Error. For, divided from her for the next eight cantos, he is continually overcome. After the defeat of Error, the path leads Una and Redcrosse, as it did not before, out of the wood. We may therefore call this illusion an illusion of direction.

The next illusion of falsehood comes in the person of Archimago, who appears to the pair as a humble and devout hermit who invites them to stay in his cell for the night. Both Una and Redcrosse are deceived: the fact that this is so forces us to see Una in another way from the one we have assumed (we too are continually under illusion). For, if we thought of her as plain Truth, then presumably she would pierce through Archimago's disguise. But, if we now think of her as Redcrosse's Truth, what truth he has living in him, then the failure of sight here will be more comprehensible – we may further recall that Una is veiled and covered with a black cloak here where later she shines forth unobstructed. This reading is reinforced by the fact that when she is taken away from Redcrosse he falls into further illusion. Nevertheless there is still the problem that she and Redcrosse are *separately* deluded later. Here as elsewhere we have to be careful not to reduce the narrative to a bare scheme which it will often deny.[15] Archimago subsequently engineers a false sprite to simulate Una and tempt Redcrosse to lust; failing which, he has this apparent Una lie in the arms of an equally false squire for Redcrosse to awake and see. After this, Redcrosse quits the cell in disgust, leaving behind the true Una, who is in another room. All these illusions may be said to be illusions of identity. And there are many more during the story, especially as Redcrosse continues deluded by Duessa. There is even one more attempted after Redcrosse has defeated the dragon and been betrothed to Una by her father: a messenger comes from Fidessa, daughter of the Emperor of the West (Satan), declaring that she has prior claim on Redcrosse owing to his sinful involvement with her. It is cruel blow, but one which Una is able to see through and turn aside; she too perceives that the messenger is Archimago in disguise and has him seized. At this point the power of illusion fails, for truth has been enthroned and Redcrosse has repented and redressed his earlier turning-aside to the world.

Archimago – 'arch-imago' – we may remark, is in himself a figure of the kind of delusive imagination to which the whole character of the poem is opposed. The imagination that he represents is aimed at deceiving with shows – his guise as a hermit and later as Redcrosse, his pretty rustic cell, the dreams from the Cave of Morpheus, his manufacture of Duessa from a sprite, his deception of Una in the guise of her knight (I.iii) and as a pilgrim (vi), his appearance as a messenger at the court of Una's parents with a false letter designed to ruin the marriage of Una and Redcrosse (xii). His effect on Redcrosse, as others, is 'with false shewes [to] abuse his fantasy' (i.46): he is the imagination gone bad.[16]

Now it is quite evident that the various illusions with which Redcrosse is beset in this book are to be seen in Christian terms as a blindness to the truth and a sinful adherence to the things of this world. But it is certainly distinctive in Spenser that this theme should be put in terms of *perception*, of how things are seen rather than (more directly) what corrupt things are done. If we compare Spenser with Bunyan here, Christian's backslidings in *The Pilgrim's Progress* are clear enough. But Redcrosse, at the level of the plain narrative, is more deceived than sinning, more a victim than an obvious wrongdoer. It is true that he allows his affections to be in part seduced by Duessa, but that stems from his persuasion through Archimago's false shows that Una has been false to him. Of course, at the level of allegory, we can see his distrust of Una and her debasement in his eyes as emerging from a corruption in him as much as from without. But that still leaves the fact that at the literal level he may seem relatively innocent while at the allegorical he is sinful. Why should this be?

This is the first book of *The Faerie Queene* and we might well expect it to be the one in which Spenser sets out the terms in which his allegory works. If we attend too much to the surface level, we will either miss or find ourselves in conflict with the truth beneath. In this sense, the way in which Redcrosse is gradually trained to read 'life' is parallel to the way in which we are trained to read allegory: we are to pierce through the illusive shows to the substance. As said earlier, seeing only the literal, the surface narrative of things is equivalent to seeing only with the senses, and thereby becoming sensual, as the Redcrosse knight does. For he takes the apparition of Una in bed with the squire at face value, and thus becomes involved in the mere things of this world, from Duessa to the Palace of Lucifera and the Seven Deadly Sins; and after that involvement in the world it is not a great step to its obverse, in hatred of life and Despair. Only when he learns the things of the spirit, at the House of Holiness, can he proceed on his original, and long-abandoned, quest, against the dragon which in a sense has been the source of all the illusions that have troubled him from the outset. And we too, as readers – and this will be what will give this book its special impact – must learn to read spiritually too, as we are confronted with the deceptive-seeming narrative. Seen thus, it can be said that Spenser 'meant' his narrative to seem at variance with his meaning.

It seems so clear, so much to answer to the character of the poem, that this reading seems the 'right' one. And yet why should Spenser align his account of holiness to a form of literary criticism? More still, can we accept a reading which, as with the French *Queste*, involves the wholesale rejection of the sensible world or the literal level? After all, the succeeding books of *The Faerie Queene*, most notably those on temperance and love, are to find a sanctified place for the things of this world, treated with due moderation and purity of heart. Are we to suppose that the practice of holiness is different from the that of the other virtues, involving a rejection of the world as they do not? There may be some truth in that; but we have also to remember that what Spenser is trying to do in *The Faerie Queene*, at least so far as his explicatory letter to Raleigh is concerned, is 'to fashion a gentleman or noble person in vertuous and gentle discipline' – that is, to show all the qualities that go to make up the ideal man of Magnificence, embodied in his Arthur, who appears in every book of the poem. In other words, the ideal man will not simply be a man of holiness, but one possessed of all the other virtues also; and in that sense holiness is not to be separated from the more world-oriented virtues and impulses, for Spenser's ultimate aim is to produce a picture of the complete man. It is to this world that Redcrosse returns at the end: he does not go to heaven as does Galahad in the *Queste*, or Christian in *The Pilgrim's Progress*. He meets with Guyon in the next book and merges into a knight of temperance, as though handing over a baton in a relay race.

These issues are closely related to our concerns, for they involve the question of whether Spenser rejected the world, and thereby the world of images, in his Christian fantasy. It is certainly the case that the view of the world and of the imagination in this first book does not seem a happy one. We first take shelter from the rain in a dark and mazy wood where a peculiarly repulsive monster is encountered and reduced to a mass of stinking liquids and excremental detritus. Then we meet a seemingly pious man who turns out to be an evil magician who throws dirt on goodness. On his subsequent wanderings Redcrosse finds that he cannot even pull a twig from a tree but it turns out that the tree is a former man metamorphosed through his sensuality. Thereafter there are variously the Palace of Lucifera, sheathed in gold but built on sand and surrounded by heaps of corpses; the castle of Orgoglio, where he takes his lust of Duessa while Redcrosse languishes in prison; and the cave of Despair, in a landscape devoid of all birds save the owl of death:

> And all about old stockes and stubs of trees,
> Whereon nor fruit, nor leafe was euer seene,
> Did hang vpon the ragged rocky knees;
> On which had many wretches hanged beene,
> Whose carcases were scattered on the greene,
> And throwne about the cliffs.
>
> (I.ix.34)

Only at the House of Holiness do we begin to find any joy, and that is not so much of this world as oriented towards the next, of which Redcrosse is given brief glimpse. Even the satyrs of the forest who rescue Una from rape are bestially ignorant: when Una stops them from worshipping her they worship her mule instead; and Satyrane, the knightly paragon of the woods, helps Una escape only because he hopes to win her. Nevertheless, all this unpleasantness that seems to make up the world is arguably only the way it appears when it is either treated wrongly or seen awry.

The question is really one that comes down to the status of the imagination rather than of the world simply. The imagination of Redcrosse may be perverted in that he is subject to false dreams; but Spenser is the dreamer dreaming him. The sheer creativity and inventiveness of book I of *The Faerie Queene* are oft celebrated – not just for incessant novelty, as with Ariosto, but because each new item, however bizarre, is part of an overall design; in other and Coleridgean words, imagination rather than mere fancy is at work. Never before in English literature had there been quite such a concatenation of different pictures and adventures, at once so diverse and yet so connected. Leaving aside for the moment the issue of the apparently loving attention Spenser gives to even the most repulsive of his creations, we have the plain fact that he has created a world out of his own imagination seemingly in order to warn against the dangers of the imagination.

If we take these two points – first, that all the hideous creatures of the book are in part at least the creation of Spenser's imagination; and, second, that the landscape of the book is that of the imagination itself, which can cloud itself with bad images as much as illuminate itself with good[17] – we can see that Spenser's very subject in this book is in one way the imaginative faculty; and to that extent he has given fantasy itself an important role in the Christian scheme. He has chosen a faërian landscape, a remote genre of chivalric romance, and a mass of fantastic creatures, not to mention the motif of illusion, in order to focus more fully on the imagination itself in its relation to faith.[18]

As said, at its most simple Redcrosse's constant error is that he sees with his eyes only, and is thus subject to illusion. Because he does not see spiritually, and with the spiritual imagination, but only in material terms, he is bound to mistake. We should not forget that, real in a sense though they are, the apparitions of Fidessa, Lucifera, Orgoglio or Despair are fantastical projections of Redcrosse's own mind. In short, his imagination is diseased, and to some extent what the book describes is its healing through the purging off of these corrupting images. He meets Lucifera in the form that he does because his mind is full of bright and evil shapes through his worldliness. At this level, this is all his imagination can perceive: it is only when his spirit has been healed in the House of Holiness that it becomes capable of being helped to a vision of heaven through the assistance of an unnamed old man whom we may identify as Contemplation, and of whom we are told, 'wondrous quick and persant was his spright, / As Eagles eye, that can behold the Sunne' (I.x.47):

> far off he vnto him did shew
> A little path, that was both steepe and long,
> Which to a goodly Citie led his vew;
> Whose wals and towres were builded high and strong
> Of perle and precious stone, that earthly tong
> Cannot describe, nor wit of man can tell . . . .
>
> (I.x.55)

Having witnessed this, Redcrosse tells the old man that this city has in his mind now supplanted in excellence the city of Cleopolis (belonging to Gloriana), which he previously thought the fairest in creation: an image from the secular imagination has now been

replaced by a sacred one.[19] We should remark that this heavenly
city is that of Revelation, and is similarly portrayed in *Pearl* and in
The Pilgrim's Progress, but that there the emphasis is less particularly
on the faculty of imagination perceiving it.

But, considered more closely, the entire book, however much it is
apparently dominated by images of evil and corruption, can be said
to show the workings of Christian 'fantasy' from the outset. Against
the magic that Archimago uses to further his evil designs is
increasingly set the miracle by which, out of the operation of evil
itself, is brought a greater good. It is right to say that Redcrosse was
diverted from his true course by the deceptions of Archimago; and
yet it is also true to say that that very diversion seems to lead him
on a spiritual journey which alone could direct him to the House of
Holiness and the eventual object of his quest. Only a man who had
experienced the humbling of his pride to the point of despair, and
thence to revived hope, could be open to the grace offered to him
through the Well and the Tree of Life in his battle with the dragon.
The miracle is that all this is born out of sin; all this 'direction' out
of a series of corrupting and confusing images. We know that what
is at work in the Redcrosse knight, even in his most sinful moments,
is the indwelling spirit of Christ. Early on, when he has left Una
and has met and joined battle with Sans Foy, who in part represents
his faithlessness in leaving Una, Sans Foy explains his inability to
defeat him thus:

> Curse on that Crosse (quoth then the *Sarazin*)
> That keepes thy body from the bitter fit;
> Dead long ygoe I wote thou haddest bin,
> Had not that charme from thee forwarned it.
> (I.ii.18)

And certainly we must suppose it is by Christ's aid alone that
Redcrosse proves the victor. Another instance of operant grace
occurs a little later, when Redcrosse, now growing enamoured of
Duessa (known to him as Fidessa, or 'little faith'), stops to rest
beneath two trees. These trees turn out to be the transformed
shapes of Fradubio and his lady Fraelissa. Fradubio tells how
Duessa led him by illusion to doubt the worth of Fraelissa and come
to disaster; he warns Redcrosse against Duessa, whom he cannot
recognise as present. Even if this warning, though immediately
relevant to his case, does Redcrosse no good, as he cannot perceive

Duessa for what she is, the appearance of Fradubio at this point is sufficient indication of divine concern: it is the fault of Redcrosse that he cannot use his imagination to liken his case of doubting his own lady to that of Fradubio ('doubt'). In the Palace of Lucifera, Redcrosse has enough shame at pride, even if he has come there, to object to the discourteous way in which he is received and the 'vain' glory of the lady's attendants: upon which, with only the thought, and no voiced criticism from him, Lucifera 'suddenly' calls for her coach, to take the air. This at once shows Pride for what it is for those with eyes to see: a haughty and magnificent woman in a costly and rich vehicle, with Satan as coachman, drawn by the revolting images of six of the Seven Deadly Sins, of which, we are now reminded, she is the seventh; and beneath the wheels of the wagon the bones of men. Redcrosse at least disdains the sight (iv.37); and later his dwarf, whose shrunken size may well convey the small use made by his master of his imagination, reveals to him more of the sordid truth (v.45–52), after which Redcrosse leaves Pride's castle.

Again we are reminded of the continued working of Christ and Christian miracle in the armour and shield of Redcrosse, which Duessa fears in his contest with her beloved Sans Joy: 'he beares a charmed shield, / And eke enchaunted armes, that none can perce, / Ne none can wound the man, that does them wield' (iv.50). This Sans Joy scorns, to his cost. Later the gracious power of those arms is demonstrated when Redcrosse takes them off to rest, and is overthrown by the giant Orgoglio. Meanwhile we have had another instance of God's working in the battle between Redcrosse and Sans Joy, where Duessa, seeing Redcrosse at Sans Joy's mercy, calls out, 'Thine the shield, and I, and all' (v.11). Redcrosse wrongly thinks she is calling to him, and this false belief spurs him to rise and in turn overwhelm Sans Joy. Here again evil is made inadvertently to bring forth good. And so we may continue. Una, saved by the satyrs from rape, is saved in truth by 'Eternall prouidence exceeding thought' (vi.7). The sudden appearance of the resplendent Arthur in canto vii, himself a divine answer to Lucifera's spurious magnificence, is a piece of unexpected grace, by which alone can Orgoglio and Duessa be overthrown, and Redcrosse released from prison:

Ay me, how many perils doe enfold
The righteous man, to make him daily fall?
Were not, that heauenly grace doth him vphold,

And stedfast truth acquite him out of all.
Her loue is firme, her care continuall,
So oft as he through his owne foolish pride,
Or weaknesse is to sinful bands made thrall:
Else should this *Redcrosse* knight in bands haue dyde,
For whose deliuerance she [Una] this Prince doth thither guide.

(I.viii.1)

During this battle we have the two forms of 'magic': there is the witch's golden cup whose poisonous contents she throws over Arthur's squire to incapacitate him; but then there is the 'accidentally' unveiled shield of Arthur, which strikes Duessa's monster blind and renders Orgoglio faint with knowledge of his certain doom, and is likened to 'th'Almighties lightning brond' (viii.14, 19–21). At the end, in the battle with the dragon, Redcrosse is saved from death only by the fact that on each of the two nights he 'happens' to fall by the Well and Tree of Life respectively, which give him new strength. In the first instance the dragon itself throws him into the Well and thinks it has triumphed (xi.31): here again evil unwittingly furthers good. The miraculous and Christ-like powers of the Well, far surpassing any of the powers of magic, which can only falsify appearance, not alter reality, are stressed: it can bring the dead to life, remove sin from the guilty, heal the sick and make the old young again (ix.30). As for the Tree of Life, it grants happy and everlasting life. Spenser's emphasis here on divine fantasy, if we may call it that, is marked by comparison with Bunyan's *The Pilgrim's Progress* (doubtless part-indebted to *The Faerie Queene*); for Bunyan will not admit the direct use of such fantasy, but has Christian win his parallel battle with Apollyon with courage and sword, and only after his victory has a hand come to him with some leaves from the Tree of Life (not growing there) with which to heal his wounds.

As the narrative draws towards its climax, the *evident* instances of grace, from the appearance of Arthur onwards, become more numerous. This is not because such grace is as it were precipitated by the evil in the story: grace is, in any final sense, freely given. But there are more instances of such miracle in these latter stages because Redcrosse is nearer to it, and more open to it. Its action hitherto has been more concealed from him, as he has been ensnared by some of the delusions of the world. Now that he is broken by

Pride and Despair alike, and healed by Holiness, it may come to him more plainly. But we should not look for the operation of grace in terms of specifically supernatural workings only. It is present too in Redcrosse's very journey into evil. The Christian rhythm, embodied in Christ, is that the way to gain is through loss, the way to the light through darkness, at least for fallen man. Christ was no sinner, but He suffered vicariously. Thus the descent of Redcrosse to the dungeon of Orgoglio, and his subsequent 'resurrection' through the mediation of Arthur, partakes in a primal Christian rhythm. At another level, as seen, Redcrosse had to fall into sin and lose himself in order to be made holy enough to face the dragon: he had to be broken to be made whole. Sin is not wished for by God; but fallen man must know his sinfulness if he is to be healed of it. This more continuous pattern of action both supernatural and natural is the specifically Christian one, and is in a sense more 'fantastic' than the 'fantastic miracles' themselves. And by it, and in far wider compass, we see again how the mere magical enchantment of the evil is circumvented by Christian fantasy: how out of its very machinations evil is led to generate good.

As this happens, the landscape of the imagination which the book has figured becomes purified. The dead Orgoglio becomes a mere empty bladder. Duessa, stripped, is a miserable, hideous thing that scuttles away. After the crowds in Lucifera's palace, Orgoglio's castle is not manned and only the solitary Ignaro keeps the dungeons. Evil seems to shrink down to more isolated figures. But it gathers too. Despair is a real temptation to Redcrosse, and the last dragon is a mighty enemy. But now, with Arthur, or in the House of Holiness, or with Una's parents to save from the dragon, we seem to move in a region where the agents of goodness are more evident, and joy much nearer. The false worldly dreams of the imagination have been purged; equally the world-renouncing delusions of Despair have been refused; and now we move in a realm of holy fantasy which is also truth and substantial fact:

> A multitude of babes about her hong,
> Playing their sports, that ioyd her to behold,
> Whom still she fed, whiles they were weake and young,
> But thrust then forth still, as they wexed old:
> And on her head she wore a tyre of gold,
> Adornd with gemmes and owches wondrous faire,

Whose passing price vneath was to be told;
And by her side there sate a gentle paire
Of turtle doues, she sitting in an yuorie chaire.

(I.x.31)

This is Charissa in the House of Holiness, whose outgoing fecundity
in part answers the inward movement of the spawn of Error in the
first canto. This image is founded in divine truth where that was
the product of infernal delusion.

Throughout Spenser suggests the emptiness, the insubstantiality
of sin, even as it manifests its power. As produced by Archimago, it
can reveal itself only as show, a false picture. We, unlike Redcrosse,
are sometimes given privileged insight here. Archimago disguises
himself as Redcrosse to trick Una, but is overthrown. Duessa hides
her true nature from Redcrosse and fools him as she for long fooled
Fradubio. The palace of Lucifera looks solid and magnificent, covered
with gold; but we are told that its back parts are much decayed and
cunningly disguised with paint, and that the whole structure totters
on a hill of sand as foundation (iv.4–5). Lucifera's pride is also
undermined for us by her loathsome attendants. Evil is strong enough
for those who will let it have a hold on them; but, Spenser is saying,
truly seen it is unstable, a mere delusive fantastical image which
must be put aside for the far more wonderful and substantial truth.
Thus throughout we are reminded of the frailty and transience of
the fantasies created by evil. By the time we get to Despair, a filthy
old man surrounded by a wilderness of corpses, we are inclined to
wonder how anything so evidently repellent could attract anyone.
But here there is a subtle change: what looks repulsive actually proves
attractive, in reverse of the previous experience of evil; the temptation
now is one based not on concealment but on spurious revelation of
the truth about reality. Only the renewed presence of Una saves
Redcrosse from this temptation.

What happens towards the end of the story is a kind of stripping.
Redcrosse is stripped of his pride, his illusions and even much of
his flesh, to be new-made in the House of Holiness. The evil is
divested of shows, first via the false realism of Despair, and thence
to the true 'fact' behind all the forms of evil we have seen in the
story – indeed their source – in the mighty dragon, figure of Lucifer,
which the knight comes to defeat; a dragon which does not vanish
upon its destruction. In a sense the story has been a kind of analytic
process, a moving through a hall of mirrors until the true shape is

made manifest. And as this happens we move from what might be called a relatively contingent narrative to one founded on scriptural realities. (The process is similar to that in *Pearl*.) The Bible speaks of the Seven Deadly Sins, of the wiles of the devil, of sojourn in the wilderness and so forth; but at no time is there so consistent an adherence to scriptural fact as in the last cantos, where the figures of Una's parents, Adam and Eve, besieged in their tower of sin by Satan, are released through the Christ-like overthrow of the dragon through three days of torment. It is both an image of Christ's sacrificial act, and a vision of the apocalypse in the defeat of the dragon in Revelation 12 and 20.1–3. All the other episodes in book I are invented by Spenser as this one, apart from its guise as knightly contest, is not. The Redcrosse knight has moved from romance to myth, and to a myth which is also Christian fact. The imagery of the dragon is now no less fantastic than that of earlier dragons, but now it is also the reality. We thus move in the story, so far as evil is concerned, from its false shows to its true, if still fantastical, lineaments; and, with the good, from the operant presence of grace within the world to a vision of that pattern of action the divine imagination takes.

One other form of Christian fantasy in the story is the defeat of the apparently large and all-present by the small and inconspicuous. The Christian miracles that occur in the story are often unemphasised or seemingly engulfed by the presence and attention given to the evil. No more than two remarks, for instance, are made about the power of Redcrosse's emblem, armour, sword and shield over his opponents. It is his mere dwarf who discovers for Redcrosse the truth about Lucifera and her palace. When Arthur attacks Orgoglio and Duessa, it is as a relatively small if glorious figure against a giant that he must hew to pieces and a monster also far larger than he. Indeed it can be said that the dragons and the evil grow in size and strength throughout the book: Error is quite fearful and readily dispatched; Duessa's huge seven-headed monster overcomes Arthur's squire and is only defeated when Arthur's shield is exposed; and it takes three days to slay the last and most gigantic dragon. Meanwhile Archimago's cell 'expands' to the Palace of Pride and the castle of the giant Orgoglio, and the evil figures, first single, become more multiple. If the evil may thus dilate, the good do not. Redcrosse's battle with the dragon is that of a tiny figure against a colossus: a colossus given an enormously long description in canto xi to match his nature. The victory is largely achieved by the seemingly negligible, a well and a tree beside which Redcrosse 'happens' to fall on successive nights: even Una does not recognise them for what they are and despairs as each day ends. It is therefore all the more miraculous when these gracious actions and victories take place. But Christian truth is itself founded on disproportion. It says that out of the acts of one man all creation could fall; that out of those of a second Adam the whole world could be redeemed; and that through faith and the grace of Christ any one Christian could overthrow the blandishments of the devil and all his angels. The reverse is the case with evil: out of all its efforts, all its mighty assaults comes in the end nothingness. But there is a further point behind some of those relatively brief overt appearances of grace earlier in the narrative; for it is the case that goodness exists in modesty, partly symbolised in Una's veil, and evil in ostentation. And that in itself, quite apart from the fact that it is continually being exposed from within, or forming a pattern in its own defeat, may be why so much place is given to the evil delusions early on, sufficient almost to make us believe that the faculty of fantasy-making is itself being attacked. Goodness is single, symbolised in Una; evil is multiple, symbolised in Duessa. Evil spreads, but goodness concentrates.

Lastly, we must return to the question of why Spenser has chosen to tell this Christian story in the form of a romance of knights, ladies, dragons, magicians, castles and dungeons. We have given some answers to this already. One of those answers was that he is testing our ability to see beneath the 'show' of the narrative to the substance, in a way parallel to that by which Redcrosse must see through the illusive appearance of evil to the truth. In this sense the reader must use his imagination, to pierce beneath the mere sense impressions of things. Here again the imagination, albeit operating in a relatively ascetic mode, receives Christian validation. And certainly, when at the House of Holiness we find Redcrosse's preparation to face the dragon to involve not the body-building and knightly instruction we might at a literal level expect after his defeat and bodily wasting at the hands of Orgoglio, but rather Penance, Remorse and Repentance for 'Inward Corruption, and infected sin' (x.25–7), we are forced to that further level of understanding whether we like it or not. But we questioned whether in reading the allegory so wholesale a rejection of the literal and thus the sensible world was really required. At the time there seemed no ready answer; but, with the experience we now have of the poem, we may be able to suggest one.

Suppose that, in addition to seeing Spenser's landscape as a thin and penetrable platform of the literal below which further levels of meaning may be perceived, we see what he has made as an *alternative* world, a fantasy world in which Christian victories are really won through knightly contests with monsters, and within which the figures of Sans Foy, Duessa, Fradubio, Lucifera or Orgoglio are 'real' actors rather than only images demanding allegorical explanation.[20] In such a case *The Faerie Queene* would be, in Tolkien's phrase, a 'sub-created' imaginative world just like, say, *The Lord of the Rings*, or C. S. Lewis's *Perelandra* or his *Chronicles of Narnia*. Indeed the last is quite instructive, for in *The Lion, the Witch and the Wardrobe* Lewis has created a wholly 'other' world – though no more 'other' than our own is in relation to it – in which a series of adventures occur which closely parallel, in terms of a witch overthrown by a lion, the story of Christ's passion and resurrection. There, Lewis does not say that this story stands only in allegorical relation to our own version; but rather that the myth, which is also fact, recurs in each world in its own mode.[21] But we must not push this too far: Spenser asks a much closer concentration on the allegorical aspect than Lewis, and it is unlikely that he shared Lewis's beliefs in the possibility of similar myths occurring in alternative fantastic worlds. Nevertheless, intention is not everything. We know from our experience of book I how richly and fantastically imagined a work *The Faerie Queene* is; and we know, too, something of Spenser's delight in the fantasy-making power of Ariosto. Here then it may just be possible to see the Fairy Land of *The Faerie Queene* both as the human mind, particularly the imagination, which it is, and in part as the creation of another world in which the great truths of Christian experience are recapitulated in lineaments different from those that mark them in our own world. In this way *The Faerie Queene* would have a relation to us at once allegoric and mythic; and the poetic imagination which created it would in one way not be different from Sidney's 'Arcadian' conception of it:

Onely the Poet . . . lifted vp with the vigor of his owne inuention, dooth growe in effect another nature, in making things either better then Nature bringeth forth, or, quite a newe, formes such as neuer were in Nature, as the *Heroes, Demigods, Cyclops, Chimeras, Furies,* and such like: so as hee goeth hand in hand with Nature, not inclosed within the narrow warrant of her guifts, but freely ranging onely within the Zodiack of his owne wit.

Nature neuer set forth the earth in so rich tapistry as diuers Poets haue done, neither with plesant riuers, fruitful trees, sweet smelling flowers, nor whatsoeuer els may make the too much loued earth more louely. Her world is brasen, the Poets only deliuer a golden.[22]

6

Marlowe: *Dr Faustus*

Our soules, whose faculties can comprehend
The wondrous Architecture of the world:
And measure every wandring plannets course:
Still climing after knowledge infinite,
And alwaies mooving as the restles Spheares,
Wils us to weare our selves and never rest,
Until we reach the ripest fruit of all,
That perfect blisse and sole felicitie . . . .

(Tamburlaine Part 1, II.vii.21–8)

These remarks might just have been made by Dante, whose *Commedia* was partly the product of a desire to fathom the furthest limits of reality, while at the same time being the expression of a scientific urge to know and to chart the unexplored. Dante, however, was both more and less ambitious, in that he was exploring a more than natural universe, one in which his imagination was to be directed and educated by realities beyond it. Tamburlaine's universe has much less of the divine in it. His ruling principle is nature, not supernature; and nature gives us our aspiring minds, not God (ll. 18–20). The speech quoted ends rather strangely, for, instead of telling us that he seeks the final key to the mysteries of the world, as we might now expect, Tamburlaine says that his 'perfect blisse and sole felicitie' lies in 'The sweet fruition of an earthly crowne'. We come down to earth and vulgar reality with rather a jolt. But in this Tamburlaine becomes like all Marlowe's other aspiring heroes. For, while their spirits lift them beyond the earth, they cannot put their ultimate desires in any other but earthly terms. This is to be seen most tellingly, and with most condemnation, in Dr Faustus, Marlowe's scholar–magician, who, unlike Tamburlaine, lives in the world of intellectual conquests, and could have found best satisfaction for his thirst in theology, which would have taken him beyond the limits of the earth; but chose instead to go in search of worldly pleasures. Tamburlaine, as military conqueror, has to fall back on

73

earthly prizes as his goal. We should look back to the comment of Theridamas, Tamburlaine's chief captain, for the understanding of that last line:

> And that made me to joine with *Tamburlain*,
> For he is grosse and like the massie earth,
> That mooves not upwards, nor by princely deeds
> Doth meane to soare above the highest sort.
>   (ll.30–3)

In other words, for all his aspiration, Tamburlaine has his feet on the ground, indeed cannot leave it. Theridamas perceives that the upward spiritual urge here expresses itself as what we may call a horizontal drive outwards. He is the practical man who knows 'what it comes down to', as Tamburlaine's speech literally came down to its seeming bathos.

But, while this is what happens, there is also for us still the sense of strain in converting or reducing the spiritual impulse to a mere material satisfaction. And this is what, in greater or lesser degree, these heroes of Marlowe's register: the sense that somehow they have mistranslated. Much of Tamburlaine's speech is restless, involving continual movement towards some grand object. That the named object should be so mean, so abrupt, can only suggest its inability to satisfy; and that is what we find in the play, where no sooner has Tamburlaine gained one crown than he seeks another, and then more, until he wears himself out. Only in his vision of his queen Zenocrate does he retain something of the spiritual thirst that in part animated the speech we have quoted (Part 1, v.i.160–73; Part 2, ii.iv.15–37). And just as with Tamburlaine, but far further back in his psyche – indeed, on the evidence, long before the play in which he is the protagonist begins – we feel that Faustus had an imaginative energy more nearly associated with the life of the universe, but one which he has let dwindle to mere secular ambition.

Nevertheless there are real differences between Tamburlaine and Faustus, who makes a pact with the devil to grant him the powers his impatient imagination seeks. Where Tamburlaine's energies are directed at overthrowing mortals, Faustus challenges the authority of God himself, and seeks to violate the laws on which nature is founded. Tamburlaine portrays the energy that drives him as the same as impels the gods and nature both:

The thirst of raigne and sweetnes of a crown,
That causde the eldest sonne of heavenly *Ops*,
To thrust his doting father from his chaire,
And place himself in the Emperiall heaven,
Moov'd me to manage armes against thy state.
What better president than mightie *Jove*?
Nature that fram'd us of foure Elements,
Warring within our breasts for regiment,
Doth teach us all to have aspyring minds . . . .
(Part 1, II.vii.12–20)

Despite various blasphemies by Tamburlaine he still portrays himself, particularly in Part 2, as a scourge of God, His mortal agent, in his overthrow of heathen empires and corrupt Christian armies alike.[1] But Faustus does not go with the grain of reality like this. Initially at least he wants to be a 'Demi-god' and do as he pleases,

> Be it to make the Moone drop from her Sphere,
> Or the Ocean to overwhelme the world.
> (*Dr Faustus*, I.iii.266–7)[2]

And to do this he allies himself with God's prime enemy, Lucifer. Of course, the very fact of having a Christian moral scheme of good and evil in this play alters our attitude to him; and not just by imposition, but in truth, because we see how much Faustus, in contrast to Goethe's Faust, wants for himself. Part of the difference between Tamburlaine and Faustus lies also in the fact that Tamburlaine releases some of his ambitious energies in practical warfare and expresses them in almost limitless territorial expansion, whereas Faustus is an intellectual who can range freely only, in Sidney's phrase, 'within the Zodiack of his owne wit', and thus tends to be more extreme and inaccurate in his ambition. Therein lies much of the tragic potential of the play; but the moral edge is much keener, and involves the indictment of a man whose intellect may be vast but whose true imagination is very limited. The effect in any case is that, whereas Tamburlaine's imagination can wonder at the fabric of the universe as it is, Faustus can only become excited at the thought of changing it. For all Tamburlaine's ceaseless battles, he is the one really capable of contemplating the universe; by contrast the scholar Faustus does nothing but act and move.

Further, Tamburlaine's imagination is such that he can look beyond himself, to wonder at the heavens and 'every wandering planets course' or become lost in the contemplation of the nature of beauty through his beloved Zenocrate: he is in a way a genuine intellectual. We sense the force of Tamburlaine's imagination throughout, whether in the impulse that drives him to conquest or in his continual flights of aspiring verse. But the imagination is not so evident in *Faustus*. There is restlessness and desire for power, but the limited instances of this occur only at the beginning of the play. And all of them are directed not at going out to the world, but at bringing all things into the self:

> I'le be great Emperour of the world,
> And make a bridge, thorough the moving Aire,
> To passe the Ocean with a band of men,
> I'le joyne the Hils that bind the *Affrick* shore,
> And make that Country, continent to *Spaine*,
> And both contributary to my Crowne.
> The Emperour shall not live, but by my leave,
> Nor any Potentate of *Germany*.
> (I.iii.332–9)

'I'le . . . I'le . . . my . . . my': it is all self-directed, absorptive, centripetal; the irony is that, in contrast to Tamburlaine, Faustus can only do it in league with other powers. The syntax is chipped and broken up, a little shopping-list of greedy ambitions: this is no Michelangelo, but a Pizarro. There is only one moment in the play where the imagination of Faustus really soars like Tamburlaine's, and that is when as the end approaches he asks for Helen to be brought to him.

> O thou art fairer then the evenings aire,
> Clad in the beauty of a thousand starres:
> Brighter art thou then flaming *Jupiter*,
> When he appear'd to haplesse *Semele*:
> More lovely then the Monarch of the sky,
> In wanton Arethusa's azur'd armes,
> And none but thou shalt be my Paramour.
> (v.i.1781–7)

But, unlike Tamburlaine's Zenocrate, this Helen is an infernal succuba, copulation with whom is damnation: Faustus's wonder here is at once glorious and corrupt.[3] Further, the soaring syntax of the lines is an index not so much to a soaring soul as to one driven by terror at approaching hell-fire; the passionate lyricism here expresses the use of Helen as a respite. Indeed it is arguable that in *Faustus* the most powerful imaginative moments come not from aspiration but from desperation: not from a secular imagination but from one made helplessly aware of Christian realities.

> O I'le leape up to my God: who puls me downe?
> See see where Christs bloud streames in the firmament,
> One drop would save my soule, halfe a drop, ah my Christ.
> Rend not my heart, for naming of my Christ,
> Yet will I call on him: O spare me *Lucifer*.
> Where is it now? 'tis gone. And see where God
> Stretcheth out his Arme, and bends his irefull Browes:
> Mountaines and Hils, come, come, and fall on me,
> And hide me from the heavy wrath of God.
>
> (v.ii.1938–46)

Whereas Tamburlaine's restless spirit has always been moving towards some object, Faustus spends much of his energy in running away from one, whether God or hell: the force of his imagination is, as it were, negative.

Faustus is the only 'fantasy' Marlowe wrote, a fantasy set in a world surrounded and interpenetrated by a heaven and a hell, a devil and an incarnated Christian God. For much of the play we see present on the stage Mephostophilis, one of Lucifer's agents, as he seeks to secure Faustus's soul for his master. Just as in the play *Everyman*, and in contrast to Dante's *Commedia*, there is no fantastic world as such here, aside from the presence of Mephostophilis – unless we say that this world is made fantastic by being portrayed as so much of a platform between two supernatural realms. The presence of God, however, is more immediate and pervasive than at first appears. The play is one in which it seems that Faustus alone decides his ultimate destiny; but in fact that destiny is determined and shaped by the collision of his will with God's and the ultimately supernatural character of reality. God is as it were present by His absence: the more Faustus turns from Him, the more he activates divine opposition to him; at the end he is acutely aware of 'the heavy wrath of God' (v.ii.1946). That opposition is seen through a number of surrogates – Faustus's own extraordinary ignorance, the devils themselves, the process of erosion of the capacity to repent, and the ironies and collapsing structure of the play itself. We are told in the prologue that Faustus' 'waxen wings did mount above his reach, / And melting, heavens conspir'd his over-throw' (ll. 21–2): the natural law of melting by the sun is the means through which the heavens work. The play thus testifies to God's power; but not to His cruelty, for Faustus continues to invoke only a dark image of Him: indeed His aspect and Faustus's wretched experience are a direct reflection of Faustus's wretched soul.

Two forms of 'fantasy' are opposed in *Faustus* (as, if differently, in *Pearl* and *The Faerie Queene*). Faustus himself is a *mere* fantasist who wants to remake the world to suit with his own desires. He thinks that the universe is a composite of adjustable matter:

> All things that move betweene the quiet Poles
> Shall be at my command: Emperors and Kings,
> Are but obey'd in their severall Provinces:
> Nor can they raise the winde, or rend the cloudes:
> But his dominion that exceeds in this,
> Stretcheth as farre as doth the mind of man:
> A sound Magitian is a Demi-god,
> Here tire my braines to get a Deity.
>
> (I.i.83–90)

But, while Faustus is enjoying such limited powers as his pact with the devils gives him, it is Mephostophilis who on question tells him of the immutable character of the universe; Mephostophilis the devil who depicts for him a cosmic and spiritual 'fantasy' he cannot comprehend:

> FAUSTUS. Think'st thou that *Faustus*, is so fond to imagine,
>   That after this life there is any paine?
>   Tush, these are trifles, and meere old wives Tales.
> MEPHOSTOPHILIS. But I am an instance to prove the contrary:
>   For I tell thee I am damn'd, and now in hell.
> FAUSTUS. Nay, and this be hell, I'le willingly be damn'd.
>   What, sleeping, eating, walking and disputing?
>
> (II.i.522–8)

The materialism of Faustus here is of a piece with his conception of the soul as a solid commodity: 'Had I as many soules, as there be Starres, / I'de give them all for *Mephostophilis*' (I.iii.330–1).[4] Faustus is condemned through the failure of his own fantasy, the fact that his earthly imaginings blind him to the far more miraculous and here terrible truths of the universe. In effect the play becomes a critique of that fantasy which tries to exist in opposition to Christianity.

For all the glorying by Faustus in the pictures created by his impatient imagination, one of the central ironies of this play is precisely how *lacking* in imagination this ambitious wizard is. The devils 'do their best' to tell Faustus of the true nature of what he is doing, even appear to warn him against it:

> FAUSTUS. Where are you damn'd?
> MEPHOSTOPHILIS. In hell.
> FAUSTUS. How comes it then that thou art out of hell?
> MEPHOSTOPHILIS. Why this is hell: nor am I out of it.
>   Think'st thou that I who saw the face of God,
>   And tasted the eternall Joyes of heaven,
>   Am not tormented with ten thousand hels,
>   In being depriv'd of everlasting blisse?
>   O *Faustus* leave these frivolous demandes,
>   Which strike a terror to my fainting soule.
> FAUSTUS. What, is great *Mephostophilis* so passionate
>   For being deprived of the Joyes of heaven?
>   Learne thou of *Faustus* manly fortitude,
>   And scorne those Joyes thou never shalt possesse.
>   (I.iii.301–14)

This 'ubiquitarian' notion, whereby 'Hell hath no limits, nor is circumscrib'd, / In one selfe place: but where we are is hell' (II.i.510–12), could be said to be a means of further heightening Faustus's materialism: he thinks of hell as a solid place of physical torments if it exists at all (and he is eventually given his own image of it); he does not understand the notion of hell as separation from God.[5]

At least, he does not understand it *yet*: he has come very close to realising and experiencing this truth by the time of his last, agonised soliloquy. It is here that we encounter one of the organising principles of the play: the spiritual law of action and reaction by which, the nearer to his end Faustus comes, the more he comes to believe in the reality of a God whom his refusals have made him unable to serve, and of a hell which he cannot avoid. At first he thinks of Mephostophilis as some sort of a genie he has called out of a bottle, and does not believe the devil when he tells him that it was not his supposed necromantic powers that called him up, but the peril into which he had placed his soul, 'For when we heare one racke the name of God, / Abjure the Scriptures, and his Saviour Christ; / We flye in hope to get his glorious soule' (I.iii.275–7). Gradually, however, he becomes more nervously aware of the possible reality of the divine system he has so scorned. And, as he does so, the fantastic powers he has derived from his league with Lucifer are increasingly used not to satisfy his ambition but as anodyne or diversion, to shut out the disturbing thoughts that begin to plague him. It is, to say the least, ironic that Faustus should be reduced to using the powers granted to him by the devils simply to wall off the dawning knowledge of what he has done; whenever he suffers anything like an attack of repentance, he is glad to have his mind entertained by a pageant of the devils, the Seven Deadly Sins or a succuba of Helen, 'That heavenly Hellen, which I saw of late, / Whose sweet embraces may extinguish cleare, / Those thoughts that do disswade me from my vow, / And keepe mine oath I made to *Lucifer*' (v.i.1762–5). It is not surprising, therefore, to find that pleasures used for the avoidance of pain rather than for their own sake should be often trivial or absurd: anything, even a pageant of Seven Deadly Sins or playing silly tricks on a horse-courser, will serve to divert.

The other spiritual law in the play is the Christian one by which Faustus's frequent refusals of God make him ultimately unable to repent – the law of despair. The man who had all freedom of choice ends with none, out of his own heart. At first he would have spirits 'Performe what desperate enterprise I will' (I.i.108): that word 'desperate' takes on an aspect of mordant anticipatory humour when seen in the light of its usage later in the play; as again when, during his bargain with the devils, Faustus uses what is to him theological gibberish in saying that he has 'incur'd eternall death, / By desperate thoughts against *Joves* Deity' (I.iii.316–17). Later, after the Good and Evil Angels have vied for attention in his soul, he begins to sense that

> My heart is hardned, I cannot repent:
> Scarce can I name salvation, faith, or heaven,
> But fearefull ecchoes thunder in mine eares,
> *Faustus*, thou art damn'd ....
>
> (II.ii.569–72)

After this and some bullying by Lucifer, Faustus is almost unable to use his will at all, and the pattern of his behaviour switches from thoughts of repentance to despair at his inability to repent: the apparently active mind of the first scenes becomes wholly passive. Typical is his reflection during his pranks with the Horse-courser:

> What art thou *Faustus* but a man condemn'd to die?
> Thy fatall time drawes to a finall end;
> Despaire doth drive distrust into my thoughts.
> Confound these passions with a quiet sleepe:
> Tush, Christ did call the Theefe upon the Crosse,
> Then rest thee *Faustus* quiet in conceit.
>
> (IV.iv.1478–83)

After a last-minute visit by a good Old Man, who still bids him 'call for mercy, and avoyd despaire', Faustus is powerless: 'I do repent, and yet I doe despaire' (V.i.1733,1740). Though he desires to repent he can no longer will it. He asks for grace, here and later, and yet despairs of receiving it. This psychic hell is brought to a pitch of immediacy in the last speech and hour of his life. And, throughout, the growing confinement of his will is imaged: first in the fact that the devils give him powers far narrower than he had expected; then in the gradual reduction of the time available to him; and then in the place of final constriction which he reaches simultaneously with the paralysis of his will.[6]

These two processes – the growing awareness of the reality of heaven and hell, simultaneous with an increasing inability to do anything with this knowledge – give the play an extraordinary symmetry and ironic intensity. These ironies and principles are activated rather then generated by Faustus: his behaviour and his psychological development become means of throwing into relief the divine realities which ultimately govern them. Certainly if one continually chooses in one direction, habit if nothing else makes it impossible to choose in the opposite; but despair, the belief that God is hostile, is another matter. God is no humorist here: the ironic neatness of the psychic inversions does not reflect His local choices, but rather the action of the universal order, the symmetry of the spiritual cosmos, that Faustus has persistently ignored and sought to violate with his chaotic greeds.

It is, we may add, in that stoppage of the will at the moment of maximum perception of what it will cost not to be able to use it that what there is of tragic effect in *Dr Faustus* lies – not in any frustration of a supposedly adventurous intellect by a jealous God and the snares of hell. There is little about Faustus for much of the play to awaken our sympathy or admiration. Our involvement with him grows to the extent that he grows in the spiritual awareness of his position. And our sense of waste comes from the loss of this growth of soul in his inability to do anything with it. It is a sense which as said is keenly edged with irony, but it is not the less tragic for that.

A remarkably complex network of ironies and structures governs the entire play – a play which has often been seen as lacking in organisation. If Tamburlaine's imagination and mind could be said to dilate through the play, the process in Faustus's case is one of shrinkage, in conflict with divine reality. As said, the devils give him less than he asked for: indeed the man who expected to have the power to make 'the Moone drop from her Sphere, / Or the Ocean to overwhelme the world' (I.iii.266–7) is allowed only to play tricks with fireworks on the Pope or to call up a succuba or enjoy practical jokes with a stupid horse-courser or a rude knight. The great and swelling necromancer of the early scenes turns into an obsequious household conjurer, amusing the Emperor by calling up a shade of Alexander, or fetching grapes from the other side of the world for the pregnant Duchess of Vanholt.[7] Even more remarkable is the fact that Faustus never repines at these limitations: indeed he derives much pleasure and a certain Lilliputian pride from his trivial exploits.[8] And 'Lilliputian' may be the apposite word; for perhaps we are to picture his ambition as having been shrunk to pygmy size during the play. These middle scenes of the play are often poorly written, without much creative intensity; and on those grounds they have been argued to leave the play without a dramatic centre. It may be, however, that at a deeper level that is, in effect, the point. The void in the play might be said to express the void that is in Faustus. Alternatively, we may see these scenes as simply random and disconnected episodes of delusive pleasure thrust by Faustus between his initial act and its consequence – this serving to collapse the two ends of the play together.

This notion of a spiritual vacuum, a hollowing-out of a centre so that the peripheries collapse in on one another, is evident from the first. The prologue begins with negatives, 'Not marching in the fields of *Thrasimen* . . . Nor sporting in the dalliance of love . . . Nor in the pompe of proud audacious deeds, / Intends our Muse to vaunt his heavenly verse': we learn about Faustus by way of what he is not. The starveling announcement of the play's subject comes as anticlimax:

Onely this, Gentles: we must now performe
The forme of *Faustus* fortunes, good or bad,
And now to patient judgments we appeale,
And speake for *Faustus* in his infancie.

The suspense created by the previous lines and the grand pause
with which they end suddenly give way to stumbling rhythm and
banal, repetitive-sounding diction ('per*forme* / The *forme* of *Faustus*
fortunes'). Now we are warned that this figure will tax our patient
judgments. We are told that the prologue will speak for Faustus 'in
his infancie': in fact it does no more than tell us that he was born of
base parents in the German town of Rhode. The rest of the speech is
a remarkable piece of temporal telescoping.

At riper years to *Wittenberg* he went,
Whereas his kinsmen chiefly brought him up;
So much he profits in Divinitie,
The fruitfull plot of Scholerisme grac'd,
That shortly he was grac'd with Doctors name,
Excelling all, whose sweet delight's dispute
In th'heavenly matters of Theologie,
Till swolne with cunning of a selfe conceit,
His waxen wings did mount above his reach,
And melting, heavens conspir'd his over-throw:
For falling to a divellish exercise,
And glutted now with learnings golden gifts,
He surfets upon cursed Necromancie:
Nothing so sweet as Magicke is to him,
Which he preferres before his chiefest blisse;
And this the man that in his study sits.

We are given an account of Faustus's total history in advance (this
is quite in contrast to Marlowe's other plays): 'swolne with cunning
of a selfe conceit, / His waxen wings did mount above his reach, /
And melting, heavens conspir'd his over-throw'. The sequence of
events is distorted, for the speech then returns to talk of Faustus's
growing fascination for necromancy: one feels his beginning and
end come together.[9] This is also conveyed by frequent switches of
tense: 'Now is he borne', 'to *Wittenberg* he went', 'his kinsmen chiefly
brought him up', 'he profits in Divinitie', 'shortly he was grac'd with
Doctors name', 'His waxen wings did mount above his reach', 'heavens

conspir'd', 'glutted now', 'He surfets', 'Nothing so sweet as Magicke is to him', 'he preferres', 'this the man that in his study sits'. The whole is a microcosm of the temporal shrinkage that we are to witness throughout the play.

This kind of depiction of the 'hollowing-out' of Faustus is done with such extraordinary subtlety that it seems fair to speak of a magical use of words that far outmatches his own use of spells. The magic that is the play is used for a spiritual end, the instruction of other souls; but that of Faustus is used only for himself. The one expands outwards; the other contracts. 'Of course' Marlowe wrote the play; but who wrote Marlowe writing it? The vatic notion of creation was one particularly prominent in the Renaissance:[10] it was the period's rendering-down of the literature of granted vision to the literature of ventriloquism. At any rate, we need not suppose this far just now: it is sufficient that the evacuation of Faustus's soul shows the existence and the workings of spiritual law in the universe of the play.

The same process is at work in Faustus's opening speech, where he reviews all branches of learning and opts for necromancy. This speech might appear a condensed history of Faustus's deliberations over a number of years, or as a review of the current state of his intellectual life before he selects magic. But in fact we have already been told that Faustus is a necromancer:

> For falling to a divellish exercise,
> And glutted now with learnings golden gifts,
> He surfets upon cursed Necromancie:
> Nothing so sweet as Magicke is to him,
> Which he preferres before his chiefest blisse;
> And this the man that in his study sits.
>
> (Prologue, ll. 23–8)

The whole of Faustus's soliloquy thus becomes redundant. While he looks as though he is choosing, he has already made his choice. Then what is the soliloquy for? It is a way of giving spurious rationalisation to a predetermined choice – a choice made not from any love of superior learning, but out of greed for power. The soliloquy, with its apparently careful weighing of the arguments for each discipline before moving on to the next, is in fact a sham, a skin of rationality over a void of power-lust and materialism, so that Faustus may persuade himself that the process by which he arrived at necromancy was inevitable. The central instance of this twisting of evidence is Faustus's summary dismissal of divinity as he flicks through the Bible:

> *Stipendium peccati mors est*: ha, *Stipendium*, & c.
> The reward of sin is death? that's hard:
> *Si peccasse negamus, fallimur, et nulla est in nobis veritas*:
> If we say that we have no sinne we deceive our selves,
>   and there is no truth in us.
> Why then belike
> We must sinne, and so consequently die,
> I, we must die, an everlasting death.
> What doctrine call you this? *Che sera, sera*:
> What will be, shall be; *Divinitie* adeiw.
>
> (I.i.74–83)

Faustus here omits the saving clauses concerning Christ's grace and mercy to repentant sinners: 'but the gift of God is eternal life through Jesus Christ our Lord' (Romans 6.23); 'If we confess our sins, he is faithful and just to forgive us our sins, and to cleanse us from all unrighteousness' (1 John 1.9). It is unlikely that Marlowe intended to portray Faustus here as ignorant of the very theology of which we have just been told he is a master (Prologue, ll. 15–19).[11] Unless we are prepared to accept at face value and apply retrospectively Mephostophilis's claim near the end of the play (v.ii.1886–9, not in the A text) that he directed Faustus's reading of the Bible, it is clear that sense is made of the scene only when we view it in terms of Faustus directing and limiting his own reading. And certainly Mephostophilis did not claim responsibility for the earlier distortion of texts from logic by Faustus,[12] or his contemptuous citation from law (I.i.34–8, 55–63). Thus what seems to be a consideration is not really a consideration at all: even as Faustus appears to treat law or divinity as if they could matter to him, he is intent on proving them worthless, nonentities, by any means. The very mention of other disciplines before they are dismissed increases the sense of shrinkage.[13] As we follow the speech it shrivels away to nothing, a perverted conjuring-trick. Faustus presents us with apparent substance only to reduce it to shadow; the irony of the play is that he himself is to turn from substance to shadow, under the spiritual laws of a magician

far greater than he. It is certainly interesting that we first see Faustus
at work perverting words, and in particular the Word: as suggested
earlier, far greater Words that have become flesh, not to mention
the true-speaking spell that is the play, are to conjure with him.

This greater conjuring is evident throughout the first soliloquy,
where we are always aware of larger truths which make nonsense
of what Faustus is doing. Indeed the very existence of irony suggests
an intellectual perspective of which he is incapable. He is himself
already a hollow man: an intellectual with no real wisdom, a man
involved with creations of mind whose only interest is in personal
and physical gratification, a theologian who knows neither truth
nor virtue. He tells himself to 'sound the depth of that thou wilt
professe' (he often thus addresses himself as someone else): he does
not know to what depths that will lead him. He bids himself apply
his selected branch of learning to being 'a Divine in shew': this
rejection of the spiritual for the material and external recurs on
Mephostophilis's first arrival, when Faustus, finding him too ugly,
tells him to assume the garb of a Franciscan friar, since 'That holy
shape becomes a devill best' (I.iii.254). (Incidentally, since the devils
portray themselves as relatively helpless beside God's power,
Mephostophilis's holy disguise, worn throughout the play, may
become other than a mere blasphemous joke, and he appear to us
as the agent of God he may in fact be construed indirectly to be.)
Faustus takes leave of analytics, saying, 'Bid *on kai me on* farewell',
but it is precisely not farewell that he is taking of the issue of being
and not being: he may turn away from metaphysics, but it will not
release him. Moving on in distaste from medicine, because it can do
no more than repair the body, Faustus asks, 'Couldst thou make
men to live eternally, / Or being dead, raise them to life againe, / Then
this profession were to be esteem'd': we are suddenly aware that
this fantastic power is at the centre of the Christian religion,[14] and
that it is God's power not man's; and to this ignorant blasphemy is
added further irony, for Faustus will experience the fact of eternal
resurrection, and it will not be the joy he thinks it. The latter of his
legal quotations – '*Exhereditare filium non potest pater, nisi* – ' ('A father
cannot disinherit his son, except – ') – is also ironic, for it can obviously
be applied to Faustus's relation to God and the reasons for his own
disinheritance.[15] Turning in revulsion from the discipline of law
Faustus tells us,

This study fits a Mercenarie drudge,
Who aimes at nothing but externall trash,
Too servile and illiberall for mee.

(I.i. 61–3)

From someone who has just bid himself 'be a Divine in shew', and
who is about to gloat over the material gain and applause he will
derive from the practice of magic, this can only be crushingly
ironic; less directly so is the 'servile and illiberall', which describes
precisely the imprisoned condition of Faustus's spirit during the
exercise of that magic power designed to free it. With truth beyond
his wit Faustus now says, 'When all is done, *Divinitie* is best'. And,
when he moves on to consider necromancy, his spiritual stupidity
is strikingly caught in his assertion, 'Negromantick bookes are
heavenly'.[16] His complete ignorance of spiritual matters, his allegiance
to nothing but the physical, is in large part to be his undoing in his
relations with the devils.

It would be a mistake to see Faustus only as a remarkably obtuse
scholar. It would be fairer to say that, just as he limits his reading
here, so he limits and reduces himself by going against the grain of
spiritual reality. The ironies show that he is out of touch with true
value, or they would not be operative. His poverties of mind and
spirit are in part the product of his belief that he can be a god altering
reality as he will – in short, the consequence of a megalomaniac
imagination which, meeting with divine fact, erodes the faculties of
its owner.

Other ironies scatter the play. Faustus calls men's souls 'vaine
trifles' (I.ii.289), but it is he who is the vain trifler, he too who pursues
trifles through necromancy. He tells Mephostophilis not to be so
gloomy about hell but to cheer up (I.iii.311–14). He enters into the
bond with Lucifer, 'Seeing *Faustus* hath incur'd eternall death, / By
desperate thoughts against Joves Deity' (I.l. 317): it is a mere formula
to him here, but is later to become all too real, especially the 'desperate
thoughts'. It is ironic that throughout the play Faustus should show
more terror of God than of the devils. His belief that Mephostophilis
will protect him from God shows him approaching the kind of
'doom of Nonsense' that has been seen in Milton's Satan;[17] the
process goes one stage further when, seeing the inscription '*Homo
fuge*' on his arm after he has signed the bond with Lucifer in his

own blood, he asks, 'whether should I flye? / If unto God, hee'le throw me downe to hell' (II.i.466–7).[18] Nor are the scenes in which the clowns try to use Faustus's magic books for their own purposes without an element of satire. Their triviality reflects on that of Faustus; and their poverty makes their need for magic more real. Wagner, Faustus's servant, says of Robin, 'I know the Villaines out of service, and so hungry, that he would give his soule to the devill, for a shoulder of Mutton, tho it were bloud raw' (I.iv.349–51). When Robin replies, 'Not so neither; I had need to have it well rosted, and good sauce to it, if I pay so deere, I can tell you', we are left in no doubt how much more practical, and aware of the reality of hell, this supposedly ignorant man is.[19]

The last scene of the play is full of dramatic inversions of the first,[20] which collapse the two ends of the play together. The man who'surfeited' upon necromancy is now himself eaten – 'The jawes of hell are open to receive thee' – and will be fed with 'soppes of flaming fire'.[21] The man who sat restlessly in his chair at the outset of the play is now shown a burning chair in hell on which he will sit writhing for all eternity. The 'Demi-god' who said, 'All things that move betweene the quiet Poles / Shall be at my command', now finds himself the victim of their inexorable movement:

> Stand still you ever moving Spheares of heaven,
> That time may cease, and midnight never come.

The man who has tried to live beyond the bounds of nature is now at nature's mercy:

> Faire nature's eye, rise, rise againe and make
> Perpetuall day: or let this houre be but
> A yeare, a month, a weeke, a naturall day,
> That *Faustus* may repent, and save his soule.

The third line parallels the shrinkage of time to this point in the play itself, and also, analogously, the shrinkage of Faustus's desires throughout. This is also seen in the way that Faustus, who once asked to be a god, now asks to be less than a beast or even an object, a mere gas (ll. 1952–6); and in his crazed haggling for the blood of Christ which he sees as streaming in the firmament – 'One drop would save my soule, halfe a drop, ah my Christ'. Now Faustus realises only too immediately the full natures of hell, heaven and the immortality of the soul which he treated as a mere commodity. Earlier, when his blood became too thick for him to sign the bond with Lucifer in the words *'Faustus* gives to thee his soule', he asked, 'Why shouldst thou not? is not thy soule thine owne?' (II.i.456–7); now he finds how truly it is his own.

> Why wert thou not a creature wanting soule?
> Or why is this immortall that thou hast?

The question of who is 'running the show' is one that is continually present in this play. The very subject of learning that Faustus chooses to permit him to change the world is the one that offers that urge least scope. For a necromancer helped by devils, every change in the world, every metamorphosis or magical being, is an illusion constructed by demons. Faustus's fantasy is built on the phantasmal, the unreal: it is literally a lie, not even a fiction. What he becomes he becomes in show only; and this adds to the sense of a void at the centre of the play. Further, it is a show stage-managed by Lucifer, Mephostophilis and the other devils, who are the most evident 'playwrights' within the play. In their play, it is not Faustus who controls them but they who control Faustus: he has the chief part in their 'fantasy'; and their fantasy will grasp reality in the shape of Faustus's soul. In their greed and ambition they are in a sense another version of Faustus; in their cool insight into the true issues at stake, however, they differ from his self-deluding imagination. As said earlier, it is all a matter of perspective to some degree. Who is writing this play, this fantasy? Is it Marlowe? Faustus? Mephostophilis? Or is it God? (Even Marlowe's actual authorship of parts of the play is in doubt.) Faustus is a magician; the clowns of the play practise magic too; and there is larger magic beyond both, in Marlowe as the creator of the play, and in God as the maker of the universe. This tapering, and the constant ironic perspective, give the play its 'ripple effect' outwards. For, as for Mephostophilis himself, he may have power over Faustus through Faustus's assent, but he can himself be viewed as an agent of God's justice. As said, even his ironic guise of Franciscan friar can be seen as hell itself in the habit of heaven. Nor are the devils free agents. They cannot accomplish the dramatic upsets of nature that Faustus first asks of them (I.iii.264–70). They cannot name who made the world. They cannot give Faustus a wife. Nor can they tell Faustus much more of the planets, stars and heavens than is already familiar knowledge to him.[22] And the strange thing about these devils, or at least about Mephostophilis, is that they apparently cannot lie.[23] They make no attempt to conceal from Faustus what they are, or the nature of hell, or the fate of his soul.

The fantasy of this drama may as we have suggested be conceived as one engineered by the deity. It is a fantasy in which a supernatural creation, a soul, is seen to shrivel and shrink before our eyes, under the direct action of its collision with divine laws it has sought to negate. Through the destruction of a perverted man the play then becomes a picture of God's power in action. It might appear that that picture is a harsh one, involving as it does the casting of a human soul into endless torment; but it can equally be argued that it is a picture of divine love, both because Faustus was offered every chance possible to repent, and because heaven thereby asserts itself to be a place which only love and those who love could understand or enter. Further, we have suggested that the darkened nature of Faustus's soul determines the nature of what he sees, and that the frowning God and the apparently inaccessible Christ of the play are the only forms of them that Faustus could understand. In this light their seeming remoteness from him expresses his from them; and the much greater presence of hell than of heaven in the play depicts his refusals. In the same way it can be said that the self-enclosure and blinkering in Faustus's mind as we see it in the opening soliloquy is extended in his bargain with Mephostophilis, and even in the enclosed aspect of the Christian universe of sin and punishment that comes to surround him.

Marlowe has often been seen in *Dr Faustus* as torn between sympathy with the ambitious imagination in Faustus and the need to judge it as damnable. Faustus is viewed as a product of the expansive Renaissance spirit, which from the evidence of most of his other plays, particularly *Tamburlaine*, Marlowe is said to have admired. It is certainly true that an impatience with knowledge based on bookish and outdated authority is a feature of many Renaissance thinkers, not least the Swiss doctor Paracelsus, on whom the Faustus story was founded.[24] It is true too that in the Renaissance the freedom given to the creative imagination (as we now call it) was far greater than before, so that, for example, Pico della Mirandola in his *Oration on the Dignity of Man* (1486) could have God tell man that

The nature of all other beings is limited and constrained within the bounds of laws prescribed by Us. Thou, constrained by no limits, in accordance with thine own free will, in whose hand We have placed thee, shalt ordain for thyself the limits of thy nature. We have set thee at the world's centre that thou mayest from thence more easily observe whatever is in the world. We have made thee neither of heaven nor of earth, neither mortal nor immortal, so that with freedom of choice and with honour, as though the maker and moulder of thyself, thou mayest fashion thyself in whatever shape thou shalt prefer. Thou shalt have the power to degenerate into the lower forms of life, which are brutish. Thou shalt have the power out of thy soul's judgment, to be reborn into the higher forms, which are divine.[25]

One should observe, however, that Pico was fully aware of how one who abused this freedom could find himself a path downwards to the bestial. There is not one Renaissance thinker of moment who allows complete licence to the imagination: all at some point demand that its flights be constrained within the bounds of good doctrine or sense. Faustus, of course, flies against those prescriptions. For him there is to be no limit, and no moral directive to his mind's ambition; and for this very reason, in the divine medium of the play, his imagination is shrunken and damned. Moreover, it is difficult even to see Faustus as a Renaissance seeker after knowledge. He is impatient with his existing knowledge, but does not seek to extend it; rather, what he wants is more power: 'O what a world of profite and delight, / Of power, of honour, and omnipotence, / Is promised to the Studious Artisan?' He has the bookish scholar's desire to be the centre of the world's attention, even so far as being a 'Demi-god', a 'Deity' (I.i.80–2, 89–90). In this, it may be remarked, he contrasts strikingly with Goethe's more intellectually inquiring Faust, who seeks for true experiential knowledge of nature's essence through magic, and who helps others rather than himself. For these reasons, while there is sympathy for Faustus's sufferings, the waste of his talents and his inability to repent, the play seems to cast him far more as a moral example than as a fully tragic figure. And the moral analysis is set partly in terms of Faustus's failure to comprehend the Christian fantasy that is the universe, and his preference for a materialist and selfish fantasy which proves no more than empty illusion – indeed turns literally into illusion in the form of the fraudulent pleasures given to him by the devils. The theme of a materialist and selfish fantasy was also seen in *Pearl*, but there the dreamer came to a truer understanding of spiritual things and the beginnings of an approach to heaven; *Faustus* portrays the opposite movement, the refusal and then the inability to absorb spiritual truths, and a steady journey towards a materialistic hell.

The Christian fantasy of *Faustus* lies precisely in the clash between the corrupt imagination of the protagonist and the spiritual frame of the universe. It is a Christian vision which for the first time in our survey exists in terms of a continued and unresolved struggle. While in *Faustus* the corrupt imagination is judged and put in its place (which here is hell), the conflict of the two sides is not overcome. That, we may say, marks the play as a Renaissance work: it registers the pull of the renegade human imagination against the divine. More important for our purposes, we will find that the issue of how far the imagination should be restrained or liberated is behind Christian fantasy from now until the nineteenth century.

7

The Metaphysical Poets

While it is true that Dante gives scope to his imagination, in that he invents the topography of Purgatory, and through his pictorial genius creates an unforgettable Hell, that imagination is highly ordered and restrained within the patterning given to these places, and the devotion with which they are explored. Dante's universe is a unique blend of imaginative freedom and theological doctrine. Other medieval Christian fantasies tend to be slightly reductive in tone. The *Queste del Saint Graal* removes all value from the worldly chivalry of the Round Table, insisting on a steady self-renunciation as the route to God; *Pearl* refuses the dreamer the licence of human feeling and any place for merely human understanding; the medieval mystics often find God through negation; *Everyman* portrays the reduction or stripping of the individual to meet death and God in the anonymity the title of the play suggests.

While there is often just as much renunciation of the self and the world in religious and neo-Platonic thought of the sixteenth and seventeenth centuries, the new scope, even licence, given to the imagination in the depiction of reality is marked. Jacopo Mazzoni writes, defending Dante, that 'phantasy is the true power over poetic fables, since she alone is capable of those fictions which we of ourselves are able to feign and put together'; and that in the *Paradiso* Dante is a model for poets in his use of 'marvelous and noble artifice' to represent 'with idols and beautiful images before the eyes of everyone all intellectual being and the intelligible world itself'.[1] Spenser, in the face of the defenders of 'divine poetry', particularly Du Bartas, is able to use the materials of secular and often faërian romance to convey religious experience and retell the facts of fall and redemption in a new mode.[2] So too, in his romances *The Winter's Tale* and *The Tempest*, which dramatise the themes of the lost being found, the apparently dead being resurrected and the regeneration of the kingdom, is Shakespeare. Marlowe re-creates the story from the *Faustbook* to show the primal nature of the deity through the particular and fantastical behaviour of an individual. Others, of course, are not so devotional – Rabelais for one, even

Malory, in his ultimate championing of the values of the Round
Table, for another; and Cyrano de Bergerac in his *L'Autre Monde*
(1657) mocks both Christian doctrine and biblical mythology. The
potential gap between imaginative creation and evident doctrine
becomes greater. There is not a step we take in the *Commedia* in
which we do not feel the pressure of Christian meaning, the evidence
of God's immediate working. But Spenser leaves the significance
veiled, asks us to look for his meanings through and beyond his
images. Paradoxically the greater stress of the Renaissance on the
imagination is accompanied by a sense of its contingency – 'This is
one image by which to perceive Christian working, but there are
others': the emphasis is on 'invention', on finding matter.[3] Dante's
imaginings, by contrast, are portrayed as *given* to him by Virgil, are
presented as *visions* of the truth itself, not to be gainsaid. Another
form of the gap between 'creation' and 'Significance' in the
Renaissance is seen in the very fact that it has been possible for
numbers of commentators to read *Dr Faustus* as a picture of the
omnipotence of hell rather than of heaven: there is a creative
tension which admits of both possibilities, even if, as we have
argued, the devotional one seems much nearer to the truth.

This potential gap between imagination and devotion is most
strikingly seen in the metaphysical poets – particularly in Donne,
who puts a form of his own personality squarely at the centre of
interest:

> At the round earths imagin'd corners, blow
> Your trumpets, Angells, and arise, arise
> From death, you numberlesse infinities
> Of soules, and to your scattred bodies goe,
> All whom the flood did, and fire shall o'erthrow,
> All whom warre, dearth, age, agues, tyrannies,
> Despaire, law, chance, hath slaine, and you whose eyes,
> Shall behold God, and never tast deaths woe.
> But let them sleepe, Lord, and mee mourne a space,
> For, if above all these, my sinnes abound,
> 'Tis late to ask abundance of thy grace,
> When wee are there; here on this lowly ground,
> Teach mee how to repent; for that's as good
> As if thou'hadst seal'd my pardon, with thy blood.
>
> (Holy Sonnet 7)

The great blast of syntax that spreads through the whole octet shrinks suddenly to the solitary murmurs of the sestet, with its brief chips of grammar. Looked at one way, the poem seems fundamentally dialectical: it seems to play one kind of vision against another. Thus the vastness of eternity and of the infinity of souls, pouring across line ends, collecting all creation in its flow, dwindles back to 'me', and 'here' and now. As the poem first strikes us, the octet describes a longing for the great consummation of apocalypse, expressed in sublime imagery which at once follows and itself dilates on Revelation: it is the end that all await, the terminus to all doubt, the final grand meeting with God. It seems almost an invocation; and yet, as we read into the sestet, all the raised figures are abruptly bid back into the ground, and we come to see that this is because the poet has realised that he would be included in the numbers he has raised, and that the Last Judgement is not just a wonder, but a terror to those whose sins are still black, and that he is such a one. The suddenness with which the tone changes stresses the delusional flights of an imaginative picture that becomes caught up with itself: the sestet, if we like, has all the 'sense'. And this division between imagination and sense is real, if Donne has comprehended it. It is even there in the other aspect under which the whole poem may be viewed: as a meditation, in which the sinner deliberately calls up a picture of the Last Things or of Christ, in order to heighten for him now the terrifying reality of his own sin and the immediacy of his need for repentance and absolution.[4] For, even if the poem might be seen that way, it strikes us as much less deliberate in its way of doing it: rather, as a picture of an ignorant sinner caught out in the indulgence of the 'sensuous appetite' of the imagination. And that he remains ignorant is sufficiently underlined by his concluding, 'As if thou'hadst seal'd my pardon, with thy blood', which is of course precisely what Christ *has* done for him.

But beyond this it is possible to see the imagination as it were authenticated in one way. For what the speaker has done is first to have imagined God in His transcendent and infinite majesty, calling all His vast creation together at the Last Things; and then to have portrayed God 'contracted to a span', brought down from immensity to this lowly ground to help save this single sinner. It is on this view a marvellous imitation, particularly in the apparent shock of its transition, of a transcendent deity, surrounded by His angels, becoming incarnate, and mere lonely man. And that is of course precisely the Christian picture of the twofold aspect of God, as both above us all and intimately with each of us. As the speaker calls a halt to the Last Judgement here, so God called a halt to the first judgement on fallen man, in His gift of Himself in Christ. The reversal of the poem, seen thus, symbolises God's apparent reversal of Himself. In this way the violence of 'metaphysical conceit', yoking together opposite ideas, could be viewed as exactly matching the inmost character of the Christian faith. Nevertheless there remains some strain in this reading, not least in the fact that all the imaginative force of the poem in the octet has to be set aside for the speaker's development in the sestet.

There are thus several different directions in which the workings of the fantastic imagination may be viewed here. Another quite different reading can be derived from a 'psychological' approach. The fantastic event – the arrival of God in all His glory and the calling to judgement of all souls – may be seen as at first desired by the speaker, desired perhaps because it will bring him to behold the God he longs for: it will end all struggle, and all doubt. Beyond this it might be seen as a way of abdicating from personal responsibility: by imagining the end of time, the speaker projects a situation in which he need do no more, for God will be doing it all. That this is so is further suggested in the sestet. For, even when the speaker realises that, with all the abundance of creativity he has imagined in the Last Judgement, the one thing there will not be is abundance of grace and mercy for the unrepentant, he still sees, as he returns to his own sins and his need for repentance, God doing most of the work for him: 'Teach mee how to repent'. And a glance at Donne's other divine poems will show the same stress on divine grace rather than human will: 'Except thou rise and for thine owne worke fight, / Oh I shall soone despaire' (Holy Sonnet 2); 'Batter my heart, three person'd God; for you / As yet but knocke, breathe, shine and seeke to mend' (Holy Sonnet 14); 'Burne off my rusts, and my deformity, / Restore mine Image, so much, by thy grace, / That thou may'st know mee, and I'll turne my face' ('Good Friday, 1613. Riding Westward'); 'thou lov'st not, till from loving more, thou free / My soule' ('A Hymn to Christ, at the Authors last going into Germany').[5]

And yet, however we make sense of the workings of the imagination in the poem, beyond all these lies as said a sense of unbridgeable duality. For that picture of the end of the world can be seen also as an exploration, a bursting of the imagination beyond its limits in time and space to investigate the greatest immensities of the universe. For what could be more immense than an event so wholly 'other' and so cosmically final? This is the same kind of imagination as operates in those science-fiction writers who go beyond this earth to try to comprehend the universe and its direction. In one view it is Faustian, but here it is a true curiosity. Here it becomes significant that the speaker should be so specific, even so scientific. 'At the round earths imagin'd corners, blow / Your trumpets, Angells': the scientific rotundity of the world plays against the flat, cornered earth pictured in Revelation 7.1 to produce paradox. Then there is the careful construction of the picture, with the holocaustic flood and fire, again opposites, as termini; and, in between, the exploration of the particular modes of death at a more individual level. The scene is thoroughly built up for its own sake, without reference to any argument or theme, which only becomes apparent in the sestet. Thus there is a gap between the free visualisation and its application. The imagination operates with some licence, and the image amasses to itself an interest not wholly absorbed by the rest of the poem.

This is true in another way of poems where the sense seems more closely integrated with the (still violent) imagery.

> Batter my heart, three person'd God; for, you
> As yet but knocke, breathe, shine, and seeke to mend;
> That I may rise, and stand, o'erthrow mee, and bend
> Your force, to breake, blowe, burn and make me new.
> I, like an usurpt towne, t'another due,
> Labour to admit you, but Oh, to no end,
> Reason your viceroy in mee, mee should defend,
> But is captiv'd, and proves weake or untrue,
> Yet dearely ' I love you, and would be lov'd faine,
> But am betroth'd unto your enemie,
> Divorce mee, ' untie, or breake that knot againe,
> Take mee to you, imprison mee, for I
> Except you ' enthrall mee, never shall be free,
> Nor ever chast, except you ravish mee.
>
> (Holy Sonnet 14)

The first image appears to blame God for the weakness of His assault on the speaker. It seems designed to shock in its potential blasphemy – 'You, God, are not doing enough.' The next two images say that the fault is not just God's but also the devil's. None of them blames the speaker himself. *He* wants to admit God to his town, but God's own 'viceroy' in him, his reason, has given itself away to the enemy. *He* wants God as his lover but has been betrothed outwith his choice to the devil. It is theologically orthodox that only God's grace may rescue us from our mortality and sin; theologically most unorthodox to blame God for failure to penetrate the wicked soul: Donne dances on the edge of the permissible, delighting in it.[6] He offers three images describing God's relation to the speaker – first that of a tinker or blacksmith who is trying patchwork rather than radical restructuring, then that of a besieger of a castle, and last that of a lover. There is no need for three images rather than one, unless we relate them (rather far-fetched) to the 'three-person'd God' of the first line[7] – each simply asks God to do more. Clearly the speaker likes the ingenuity involved in thinking up three different pictures which convey the same meaning. Particularly he likes the potential for paradox that they carry. 'Knock me down so that I may rise and stand'; 'Imprison me so that I may be free'; 'Rape me so that I may be chaste'. A further toying on the edge of blasphemy is seen in the picture of a loving God acting by violence in all three images. These paradoxes may be possible within a faith where opposites come together; but it is clear that the poem is a picture not so much of the nature of God as of the needs of man. The daring is that of a poet on a theological high wire, attempting a triple somersault. The fantastic imagery, loosely tethered to the sense, is like the very town the speaker describes, invested by God and yet surrendered to another. It is not truly reason, but imagination, that is God's enemy here, an imagination which has so delighted in various images for the speaker's plight that the gravity of that plight has been lost.

It would be idle to pretend that this gap between imagination and sense is to be found in all 'metaphysical' poetry. What we are dealing with is a tendency, a tendency which surfaces sometimes more and sometimes less: less in Herbert, more in Crashaw, more in Cleveland, less in Marvell. Herbert faces the issue plainly in his 'Jordan' poems. In 'Jordan (I)' he asks, 'Who sayes that fictions onely and false hair / Become a verse? Is there in truth no beautie?' and depicts himself as a plain speaker, while in 'Jordan (II)' he describes himself as once a poet of ornament in theological matters who has now learnt better:

> When first my lines of heav'nly joyes made mention,
> Such was their lustre, they did so excell,

That I sought out quaint words, and trim invention;
My thoughts began to burnish, sprout, and swell,
Curling with metaphors a plain intention,
Decking the sense, as if it were to sell.

This is not to say that Herbert does not use imagery in his poems: far from it. But it is usually one 'image' and, however strange, closely fused to the sense – 'The Flower', 'The Pulley', 'The Collar', 'The Church-floore', 'The Bunch of Grapes'. Nevertheless, Herbert shows in the 'Jordan' poems the tendency inherent in metaphysical poetry towards divorce between imagination and doctrinal content.

Later metaphysical poetry, that of Vaughan and Traherne, often overcomes the antinomy by taking for its subject not doctrine but mystical experience. Here the 'imagination' is not separable from the 'content', for it is the guise in which the material chooses to appear:

> I saw Eternity the other night
> Like a great *Ring* of pure and endless light,
> All calm, as it was bright . . . .
> (Vaughan, 'The World')

Here Christianity becomes felt only through a dissolution of the solid world and its plastic reformations within the soul: God is apprehended only within a fantastic vision that transmutes all things in the light of His felt presence.

> News from a foreign country came,
> As if my treasure and my wealth lay there;
> So much it did my heart enflame!
> 'Twas wont to call my soul into mine ear
> Which thither went to meet
> Th'approaching sweet,
> And on the threshold stood
> To entertain the unknown good.
> It hovered there
> As if 'twould leave mine ear,
> And was so eager to embrace
> The joyful tidings as they came,
> 'Twould almost leave its dwelling place
> To entertain the same.
> (Traherne, 'News')

Here the image of news from a foreign country (Proverbs 25.25) is part of the truth itself: this is no mere likeness here, no posed mutation of reality, but the very real. The stress is on the experience of hinted bliss. The news comes from a far country, but the heart feels kinship with it as with nothing else. The news is sudden, like all news, as first described; then we learn that it is recurrent – ''Twas wont', ''Twould': such news is never old, and each experience of it is unique, for it is of the nature of heaven. It need tell of nothing specific: it is enough that it comes. Thus, when we are told that it came, the syntax suddenly shifts to 'As if my treasure and my wealth lay there, / So much it did my heart enflame!' The news itself did not come 'As if ...': what is registered in the abrupt transition and twisted grammar is the excitement of the soul as it feels it come. The coming of the news is no completed act, but something that goes on through the stanza (and the poem), pervading it. Thus we follow the heart as it is inflamed, then the soul as it is called into the speaker's ear, goes to meet the news, stands waiting at the ear's threshold to welcome it as a guest, hovers, then almost would leave its bodily mansion to entertain the comer. This is conveyed through the alterations of the figured soul as host, and the growing joy of the news as it comes nearer. The imagery is as fused to the experience as the soul is to the news.

Not all Traherne's poetry is like this, and less so Vaughan's. The poetry of Richard Crashaw attempts a different form of mysticism, one not so much of the soul directly as of transfigured sensuous bliss, as in his 'Hymn to ... Saint Teresa'. Here, though, the poetry is more deliberate, the effects more highly wrought, and we are asked to admire rather than love the baroque fantasy that reveals the workings of God and His realm.

> Upwards thou dost weep.
> Heav'n's bosom drinks the gentle stream.
> Where th'milky rivers creep,
> Thine floats above; and is the cream.
> Waters above th'Heav'ns, what they be
> We'are taught best by thy *Tears* and thee.
>   ('The Weeper', stanza 4)

But the impulse of this later metaphysical poetry is clear. It shows an ability to move away from depicting moral relationships with God, and the need for personal repentance, into direct experience of heavenly things.[8] Here the fantasy becomes fully underwritten by the fantastic truth of God, because it expresses it. These poems deal directly with the 'wholly other' (to use Rudolf Otto's phrase), which is at the same time the closest and most intimate thing to us in the universe. But Donne is not concerned with God's otherness; and neither, finally, is Herbert. Each in his different way speaks with God as a person: either, in Donne's case, as someone who has not been doing enough, or, in the case of Herbert, as someone whose doings have been frustrated by the recalcitrant soul. It is God in His human and incarnate form, rather than in His transcendent and heavenly being that tends to claim their attention. They debate issues, where the later poets more often relay experiences. The fantasy they use in their poems is a means to an end rather than the end itself. The later metaphysical poets are, as they have often been called, Christian pre-Romantics. Their poetry shows that the way to reunite imagination and sense can only lie through the rendering of immediate mystic experience.

But this experience, far from being the sort that could make the vision of a Dante universally relevant and applicable, must now be individual and idiosyncratic, even bizarre – the sudden presence of a strange image that becomes luminous, the peculiarities of distorted proportion and syntax, the obsessive devotional concentration on physical images of tears, blood or wounded flesh. The authentication of Christian experience has here begun to move away from the authority of the Scriptures into the locality of the individual imagination of truth. The standard truths of Christian history – creation, fall, redemption and apocalypse – are here set aside for a mystic concern with being reunited with God or heaven. The scope for a multiplicity of Christian visions has here been opened up, even if it has to wait more than a century to be fully explored; and even if, in the end, such freedom from the restraints of orthodox and biblical imagery can be a symptom of the eventual decay of Christianity itself. It is against such individualistic threats among others that Dryden and Pope, and the sceptical and conservative age they represent, close down on the free speculations of the religious imagination in *Religio Laici* (1682) and *An Essay on Man* (1732–4).

8

Milton: *Paradise Lost*

Milton's *Paradise Lost* (1667, 1674) is a late representative of a long tradition of biblical epic, beginning with Gaius Juvencus's *Evangeliorum libri quatuor* of around AD 330 and ending with Friedrich Klopstock's *Messias* (1751–73). Very little of this considerable literature is strikingly original at an individual level: over the centuries there was a gradual accretion of new episodes, whether invented or from apocryphal, mythological or classical epic sources, until narratives of the creation, the fall, the Passion of Christ or the apocalypse were substantially longer and fuller than the biblical originals.[1] If the motive in such re-creations must involve a certain independence, a desire to explore, expand and explain materials which are often terse or opaque within the holy text, the core narratives themselves remained sacrosanct. These retellings are thus on the whole not fantasies, both because they do not exhibit great invention, and because they partake directly in the believed truth of the biblical narratives they reproduce: they are less fiction than 'fact'. So far as invention itself was concerned, one of the prime areas of debate concerning these works in the sixteenth and seventeenth centuries (when indeed the bulk of them were produced) was how far they should admit profane or classical materials at all to figure forth Christian truth:[2] the status of the Bible as revealed Word was used continually to challenge the use of less hallowed language in its furtherance. This is not to deny that among the pre-Miltonic biblical epics are great and moving works – for instance Marcus Hieronymus Vida's *Christiad* (1535) and Diego de Hojeda's *La Christiada* (1611), both of which are highly indebted to previous literature and yet by the fervour of their conviction and their poetic power breathe new force into their narratives.[3] But Milton's work stands alone amid the rest: it is the exception which at once crowns and transforms the tradition. With all its participation in a genre, its indebtednesses and analogues, *Paradise Lost* so re-creates the story of man's fall amid a newly imagined universe that it may be considered as much fantasy as holy fact.

Paradise Lost has indeed some claim to be called the most ambitious poem in English literature. It not only portrays the fall of man, but describes, with unexampled force and spatial sense, heaven, the war of the angels in heaven, the casting-out of Lucifer and his followers, the nature of vast hell, the journey of Satan out of hell and chaos into the immense realms of God's creation, and the creation of the earth and of all on it.[4] The imaginative thrust and energy of the poem are colossal. Milton's purpose as he tells us is to 'justify the ways of God to men', but this did not at all necessarily involve the presentation of the whole cosmic scheme as he has so energetically given it. Pope's *Essay on Man* is in part a direct answer to Milton's poem: he tells us that he will 'vindicate the ways of God to men', and proceeds to do so by showing how man is made capable of realising happiness on earth, if he will only school the passions given to him to make this possible. In other words, Pope looks at existence from a human and earthbound point of view, even largely ignoring the concept of original sin, which would more directly involve consideration of divine action: as though addressing Milton, he declares,

> Know then thyself, presume not God to scan;
> The proper study of Mankind is Man.
> (*Essay on Man*, II.1–2)

Some of the irony in this is that the greatest epic poem in English literature is written by a Nonconformist, a Puritan, while those late-seventeenth- and early-eighteenth-century poets, including Dryden and Pope, who spent much of their critical time lauding the epic as the highest literary form never wrote one.

Milton had approached his topic through the consideration of other epic possibilities, from a new Arthuriad to a history of Britain (if we are to believe reports), but none offered as did this one so wide a scope to his imagination. (It is instructive to contrast this development towards a subject with that of Wordsworth as recounted in book I of *The Prelude*, 1805; for Wordsworth, having considered various epic subjects, in the end by mere seeming chance came to write about himself alone: the one widened his range, the other seemingly contracted it.) Of course Milton wanted as universal a subject as possible, such as would enable him to reach and teach all men, as he had been trying for years to instruct them through pamphlets and other prose works. But beyond that we have the Milton of the ambitious imagination, of the soul excited by infinity and the unknown, who wished to create 'Things unattempted yet in prose or rhyme'. That Milton is at one with the new scientific impulse of his day, where the mind began to move out of settled assumptions into considering the world under entirely different aspects. This is the world of late-Renaissance excitement and terror at the new infinitude of the universe, where the fixed stars are no longer fixed, but lie at varyingly huge distances, and in uncountable numbers scattered over a cosmos which can no longer be seen as an ordered set of concentric spheres. This is also, incidentally, the world in which the imagination of the science-fiction writer is at home. The mind behind *Paradise Lost* is as much an exploratory as a celebratory one.

Milton's poem is not only one of the most ambitious Christian supernatural works in English or any literature: it is also perhaps the last major work of its kind. The distrust of the use of the supernatural in literature after Milton is particularly marked in the eighteenth century, but extended into nineteenth-century realism and twentieth-century modernism. We may well ask why Milton chose to write his major poem on the subject of the loss of Paradise. Did he feel that something was finally passing away in his own time? In one way the whole poem reads as a titanic farewell. We start with directly presented divine beings – Satan, God and Christ; then, having met man, we hear by way of an angelic visitor to him, Raphael, of the rebellion and war in heaven, and of the subsequent new creation; then later, after the fall, we become increasingly confined to man and human history, as direct contact between the human and the divine is steadily withdrawn. Here it is instructive to compare Milton with Dante; for Dante steadily widens our purview, from the shut-in Hell of still very world-oriented figures, to the upward-pointing purgatory of aspiring souls, to the ever-widening Heavens above which is God. Where Dante works out, Milton works in. In part this is because Dante is revealing a state, whereas Milton is telling a particular story; but Milton could as readily have told a more 'expanding' narrative, say of the Passion or of the Last Days. When we leave Milton's poem with Adam and Eve, as they uncertainly enter the world and through Eden take 'their solitary way', it is not just the gates of Paradise that close behind them; nor is it 'merely' sin, but in some senses scientific inquiry, that sends them forth and still lies ahead of them. 'The world was all before them': now it will be *this* world, a world to be examined, altered, improved. The world behind them rings with elegy. The old Ptolemaic concentric universe, just holding its shape as a tiny ball hanging amid the vast and more Keplerian abyss of the heavens, trembles on the verge of final disappearance.

It is part of the individuality and the strength of *Paradise Lost* that it looks both ways. It looks in its narrative right back to the very beginnings of time, and then ends by leaving the human pair with their eyes directed forward to futurity. It looks back itself, with a strange mixture of excitement at catching all the heavens for one last time, and sadness at their loss, 'imaged' here in the sin of man. It holds together two opposed pictures of the nature of the universe: the earth-centred one and the new scientific one, imaged respectively in the spheres and the expanses of the heavens. It manages at once to regret, and yet at the same time somehow to see as necessary to 'progress', the fall of man. It has an enormous evolutionary force, and yet it frustrates time too, by starting with Satan's fall and subsequent voyage to earth, and then only later giving us the account of the war in heaven and the creation of the world which respectively preceded them. It manages to be both old and new: old in its relative orthodoxy, in its picture of the primal creation and of Paradise; new in the universe it has made in which to set them, in its pictures of hell and of heaven.

Let us linger on that last novelty for a moment. How much Milton owed to the Baroque style of art, or to Michelangelo or Bernini in particular,[5] or to the quickening of the spatial sense of his own imagination under the impact of his own blindness, we cannot say. Certainly there are analogues for his energetic use of space. But no one before him had imagined the heavens and hell quite as he does.[6] He is like a Renaissance traveller bringing back news of some new country. We can see the change if again we compare him to Dante. Dante puts his hell under the earth, as do nearly all significant accounts of it, from Homer's Hades to the Jewish Sheol. For Dante the whole universe is encompassed within the Ptolemaic scheme. At the centre is the earth, with Mount Purgatory on its unknown and oceanic side; and outside that are the concentric spheres of the planets, each of which is depicted as a heaven. There is no real 'outside': beyond the region of the fixed stars and the Primum Mobile lies God, who is conceived as being all-pervasive, even while He is imaged in the shape of the multifoliate rose surrounded by the nine orders of angels. But Milton has removed heaven wholly from the context of the concentric spheres. It lies outside, like a great translucent continent from which the entire system of the spheres is hung on a golden chain, somehow small and frail. Thus Satan beholds it as he pauses in the void after his long journey up from hell:

> Far off the empyreal heaven, extended wide
> In circuit, undetermined square or round,
> With opal towers and battlements adorned
> Of living sapphire, once his native seat;
> And fast by hanging in a golden chain
> This pendent world, in bigness as a star
> Of smallest magnitude close by the moon.
>
> (II.1047–53)

Milton's skill here lies in the way he can make us see heaven far off, and then, by having it 'extended wide' across the line end, make it dilate over towards us, as later he moves in the opposite direction with our world, giving it the bigness of a star before making that star of 'smallest magnitude'. Thus he at once gives and refuses us a determinate view of heaven; and also makes heaven grow and the world diminish, a proper placing of significance. For us here the main point is Milton's interest in 'the outside', where half the action of the poem takes place. The image – and Milton would say that that is all it can be – is of a universe of verticality, with heaven at the top and hell at the bottom, and in between, before the new creation, the abyss of chaos. The creation of the world drives chaos 'downwards' towards hell, and in the clearance thus made light is established and the making of the new world goes forward. So far as distances are concerned, hell is conceived as being at an immense depth away from heaven; and scope is left for the theological view of hell as so much the opposite of heaven as necessarily to be at an infinite remove from it.[7] Nevertheless Satan's journey upwards from hell through chaos towards the light, and the description of the bridge eventually to be constructed from hell to the new-made world, suggests something of horizontal travel also. As for hell itself, it has to gape wide to receive all the fallen angels when they are cast from heaven, and then slams shut, leaving only one way out, through a locked and guarded door. Inside, hell is vast and deep, like a colossal cavern. It takes Satan considerable time to fly to its roof (though we have to recall that once in hell the devils have been literally belittled by God); and his legions pass their time organising expeditions to explore its extent. It is, conventionally, a place of darkness, of fire and also of ice and cold; but Milton, in contrast to Dante, pictures not a graded but a flat and continental hell, in which the fire and ice seem as much geographical as spiritual: there is a burning lake and barren land, which suggests a volcanic region,[8] and the portrayal of the colder regions of hell could have been taken by Milton direct from travellers' accounts of voyages to Russia or in search of the North-East Passage.[9]

> Beyond this flood a frozen continent
> Lies dark and wild, beat with perpetual storms
> Of whirlwind and dire hail, which on firm land
> Thaws not, but gathers heap, and ruin seems
> Of ancient pile; all else deep snow and ice ....
> (II.587–91)

Much of this is not only original, but has a quasi-scientific ambience. Whereas in Dante distance is spiritual (the gap between the bottom and the top of Mount Purgatory being measured in terms of the soul's health), in Milton it is at least partly physical. Satan's very vividly described voyage from hell to the purlieux of heaven – for which there is no clear precedent in previous literature[10] – gives an extraordinary sense of the bodily struggle involved, as he is battered by the winds of chaos, or dropped by them when they give way, or has to make his way through a medium like sludge:

> Quenched in a boggy Syrtis, neither sea,
> Nor good dry land: nigh foundered on he fares,
> Treading the crude consistence, half on foot,
> Half flying: behoves him now both oar and sail.
> (II.939–42)

This Satan is one of the first space-travellers.[11] Certainly he is in marked contrast to Dante's Satan, who stays still, locked in ice, and plugging the centre of the world. But then Dante gives us a tour around the universe as it is, considered as a constant, whereas Milton gives us a universe in a state of continual evolution. Milton portrays Satan falling and regrouping, war in heaven, the creation of the world and man, man's temptation by Satan and his fall, man's loss of Paradise and his future. Where Dante gives us eternity, Milton gives us history. For Milton God's ways are seen and justified dynamically, through action; for Dante they are glorified through revelation.

The novelty, solidity and energy of Milton's universe are al
factors in its ability to affect us powerfully. Milton has not only
invented: he has invented with enormous confidence and force. A:
already stated, this is no rehearsal of religious truths in stock o:
biblical imagery alone, such as could be found in Milton's predecessors
this is effectively a new universe in which such truths are to be re-
created. Milton has let his imagination off the leash, has let it roam
amid immensity. This is certainly in keeping with the new nature o
the universe as it was then being scientifically revealed, but it i:
also in keeping with the enormous ambition of his own mind, a
mind as much Renaissance and even Faustian as devoted *ad majorem*
Dei gloriam through the revelation of God's boundlessness in space
and time.

It would be false to claim that these motives necessarily complicate
the poem. It is perfectly reasonable to argue, as has frequently been
done, that Milton's giant imagination is harnessed only to depic
the giant power and creative force of God Himself, and that any
more secular drives are swallowed in this. Thus seen, his own
imagination is a mortal mirror of that spirit which from the first

> Was [ ] present, and with mighty wings outspread
> Dove-like sat [   ] brooding on the vast abyss
> And made [   ] it pregnant . . . .
>
>   (I.20–2)[12]

Nevertheless, it is as possible that where the imagination has roamed
into novelty its products may lack the controlling doctrinal force o
more orthodox imagery; may indeed be capable even of hitting on
imagistic suggestions which run not just outwith but counter to the
official direction of the poem. This line of argument is not wholly
unfamiliar: it has frequently been applied to Milton's energetic and
vital depiction of Satan – the feeling being that his presentation ha
simply run away with his creator to the point where Milton is more
excited by Satan than by the official heroes of his poem: God, Chris
and even man. But it has not been directed at the imagery o
Milton's cosmos itself, and at the specific nature of Satan's voyage
and the temptation of man within it. No one has considered the
extra-theological suggestiveness potentially present in almost the
entire imagery of the poem.

Suppose we start here with a particularly suggestive image, that
of the world hung by a golden chain in space from the heavens

Thus seen, it is capable of awakening connections we might not otherwise have considered. The 'connection' it can suggest, if not necessarily consciously, is that of an ovum or egg suspended from within a womb (and Milton several times refers to the abyss in which the world hangs as a womb). We have all heard of the 'world egg': here it seems to be symbolised.

Of course, such an implication is not consciously thought of by Milton. In any case, by itself it in no way alters our understanding of the poem. It is only when we begin to put it together with Satan, who is there seeing it, that it begins to take on significance. Bring into play with it the account of Satan's voyage, and the description of his journey into the world, to Paradise, and it becomes resonant. The account of the voyage was not evidently necessary to the poem, except perhaps to demonstrate the tenacity of evil and increase our sense of horror. But the imagery it conjures up is highly significant. Satan, from outer darkness, flies up through hell and breaks back into the universe via the temporarily resistant door guarded by Sin, with whom he has coupled to beget Death (II.746–67). Within Chaos he is seen as a tiny figure, buffeted this way and that by mighty winds, or choked and impeded by the density of the medium through which he has to force his way:

> so eagerly the fiend
> O'er bog or steep, through straight, rough, dense, or rare,
> With head, hands, wings or feet pursues his way,
> And swims or sinks, or wades, or creeps, or flies . . . .
> (II.947–50)

Add to this the fact that Satan is one from a myriad, and already we have enough, taken together with the 'ovum' image of the world, to think of him as a kind of spermatozoon.[13]

Of course, when Milton wrote the poem the microscope had yet (1677) to be invented and knowledge of spermatozoa, let alone of the true mechanics of fertilisation, was non-existent. But this need in no way affect the issue if we allow for the time that what we may have here is some sort of primal or archetypal image of the sort that C. G. Jung has described, which is independent of conscious knowledge. Certainly the imagery itself is further buttressed as other aspects of the poem present themselves. When Satan alights and walks on the outer surface of the 'world egg', he eventually finds that, just next to a stairway let down from heaven, there

                              opened from beneath,
              Just o'er the blissful seat of Paradise,
              A passage down to the earth, a passage wide.
                                                      (III.526–8)

He then 'Down right into the world's first region throws / His flight
precipitant' (ll. 562–3). When he reaches the earth and approaches
Paradise, the garden, typically of the *locus amoenus*, or 'pleasant spot',
includes the suggestion of the female genitals:

                              delicious Paradise,
              Now nearer, crowns with her enclosure green,
              As with a rural mound the champaign head
              Of a steep wilderness, whose hairy sides
              With thicket overgrown, grotesque and wild,
              Access denied.
                                                      (IV.132–7)

The fecund interior of Paradise can be seen, too, as a womb – 'a
circling row / Of goodliest trees loaden with fairest fruit, / Blossoms
and fruits at once of golden hue / Appeared' (ll. 146–9); it is a small
protected place, 'In narrow room nature's whole wealth, yea more'
(l. 207). Satan first enters by leaping over the wall, and perhaps this
may be one reason for his failure at this point. His next attempt is
more 'natural' in that he enters by the river that goes under the hill
of Paradise and comes up as a fountain in the middle to water the
garden; and here too the irrigating fountain is a resonant image.
But most striking of all, suddenly adding further validity to these
impressions, is the fact that the form which Satan assumes in order
successfully to tempt Eve is that of a serpent, the express image of a
spermatozoon.
    Satan's temptation of Eve is we find described in terms which
suggest seduction.[14] This at first comes over in the image of him as
a city-dweller taking a day trip to the country and suddenly being
allured:

              If chance with nymph-like step fair virgin pass,
              What pleasing seemed, for her now pleases more,
              She most, and in her look sums all delight.
              Such pleasure took the serpent to behold
              This flowery plat, the sweet recess of Eve

Thus early, thus alone; her heavenly form
Angelic, but more soft, and feminine . . . .

(ix.452–8)

The whole account of the temptation is packed full of images relating
to sex and seduction. Eve is compared to the pursued virgins Pales,
Pomona and Ceres (ll. 393–6). Satan's serpentine shape is described
as being lovely and alluring (ll. 503–5); he approaches Eve, we are
told, with 'tract oblique', like a ship entering the mouth of a river
(ll. 513–16); he 'Curled many a wanton wreath in sight of Eve, / To
lure her eye' (ll. 517–18), and 'Fawning . . . licked the ground whereon
she trod' (l. 526). Satan is 'erect / Amidst his circling spires' (ll. 501–2);
later, 'He bolder now, uncalled before her stood' (l. 523); and, before
his final speech of temptation, he 'Fluctuates disturbed, yet comely
and in act / Raised, as of some great matter to begin' (ll. 668–9). His
speech itself, we might even say, is not so much an argument as a
rhetorical rape. His words are described as penetrating her: 'Into
the heart of Eve his words made way' (l. 550); and, when she is
persuaded to eat of the tree, 'his words replete with guile / Into her
heart too easy entrance won' (ll. 733–4). Frequently in the poem
man is directly described as having been 'seduced' by Satan (i.219;
ii.368; vi.901; ix.287, 901; x.41, 332, 485, 577); even allowing for the
Latinate sense of the word, 'lead away', the other meaning is also
present. In a sense, therefore, we can say that hell or evil has
fertilised mankind with itself. Indeed, looking at the whole series of
images we can say that Satan has fertilised first the 'universe' (in
breaking out of hell into it), then the world of the concentric spheres,
then the earth, Paradise and man. The process is one of increasing
penetration inwards. We can even see the falling myriads of angels
at the start of the poem as a kind of seminal emission; but, since
that so evidently goes against the drift of the poem by suggesting
some junction or link between heaven and hell, it seems best to put
it to one side for the moment.

There is another area in which the image has or will have resonance.
The consequence of Satan's activities will be the Christ who will be
the Second Adam. And Christ will be born of a woman, through
the 'male' agency of God. In other words God will fertilise man
with Himself just as Satan did. Indeed in John 3.14 Christ Himself
is described as a serpent: 'And as Moses lifted up the serpent in the
wilderness, even so must the Son of man be lifted up.' God will 'have
to' carry out the same essential action as Satan, to reply to him.

It is thus evident that some pretty strange implications are presen
within the invented imagery of *Paradise Lost*. But what can we mak
of them? Clearly, at the level of Milton's conscious intention, littl
at the level of any knowledge he may have had of the actua
biological facts concerning fertilisation, still less. As said, microscope
had not yet been invented; and, while most accepted that th
woman's body contained an egg, the process of fertilisation wa
attributed to a quasi-magnetic force exerted by the seminal fluic
the composition of which was not known.[15] Telescopes had lon
been in use; and it is ironic that Milton's poem should portray o
the macrocosmic scale, against the background of an imagine
universe, a process which finds its reality at the then-unknow
microcosmic level.

It is ironic so long as we attend only to the sexual significance c
the image. But, if we know anything of C. G. Jung's famous *Th
Archetypes and the Collective Unconscious*, then we will know too c
mandalas and their origins.[16] Mandalas are one form of archetypa
image, recurrent in art, culture and dreams from the earliest record
of man, and recording in pictured form some of the deepest intuition
of the mind and spirit. They are circular in form: the image i
frequently a dynamic one in that a serpent figure is associated witl
it, penetrating the circle and fusing with its contents, which thereupo
often divide into four segments, still bound within the sphere.[17] Fo
Jung this fusion of the serpent figure with the circle, and th
subsequent fourness, is an archetypal image of psychic or cosmi
wholeness and completion.[18] In this image are subsumed th
mechanics of fertilisation, the approach of the spermatozoon to th
egg and the subsequent fusion and cellular subdivision: the biologica
facts are part of a larger imagery applicable to every level of being
physical and mental, individual and social, local and universal. Th
mandala archetype images the process of fertilisation long befor
that process is known to man consciously through science an
observation. In this sense it is possible, in describing Milton's imagery
to make a transference from the terminology of fertilisation to tha
of the mandala.

By making this transference we will be able to find strikin
significance in the image, rather than be forced to leave it as a
interesting and suggestive pattern. For, if, as Jung says, the mandal
archetype, particularly as penetrated by the serpent, is a symbol o
psychic wholeness, then it follows that, as far as the deeper levels o
the poem are concerned, Satan is shown to be essential to th

continued health of the universe. And this notion of the serpent or the shadow as the dark side of the self with which the rest of the mind must be integrated is recurrent in the archetypal images described throughout Jung's work.

What we have in *Paradise Lost*, then, is a situation where Milton's imagination, in part let loose from traditional imagery and modes of presentation, unconsciously creates a pattern of imagery which delivers a message clean counter to the official moral doctrine of the poem, whereby Satan and evil are abhorrent and to be shut out both from heaven and man's soul. The unconscious drift of the poem is towards a marriage of heaven and hell – not a divorce, as is proposed. And if we now look we may find other features of the poem which further this: the continual movement in it, which suggests that change and dynamism are good; the condition whereby Eve if not Adam can be seen as partly fallen before they fall; and the idea that out of evil comes a greater good than otherwise might have been, and a 'paradise within thee, happier far'. These points do not require pursuit here.[19] It is sufficient for our purposes to have shown how in the seventeenth-century poem which tries for one last time to celebrate the Christian order the human imagination is now so independent of the traditional materials, so exultantly inventive, as to beget at its own level a chain of imagery which goes against all that the poem officially tries to do. Milton tried, in an age when it was no longer possible, to make the freed imagination the handmaid of truth. From this time on integration of the two would only be possible where the imaginative vision carried the truth, and not the other way round. This is what we find in Blake.

Meanwhile, for over a century, the imagination, particularly that side of it dealing with the supernatural, was to languish under an ethic and aesthetic of restraint. Attacks on the unfettered use of 'wit' or 'invention' had been common in literary criticism since 1650. Empiricist philosophy regarded it as a perversion of truth. Political, social and religious thinkers saw it as undermining authority – indeed as partly responsible for the Civil War and the threat of rebellion that lingered thereafter. Imagination and fiction were attacked by Puritan and Dissenting writers throughout the seventeenth century, because they detracted from the authority of scriptural imagery and narrative, and because their sensuous shows diverted the mind from the apprehension of doctrine and truth. There was a very strong feeling that it was better not to ask too many questions, lest settled assumptions about the Bible, or accepted values, or the harmonious structure of the universe might come into question – feeling particularly sharpened by the growth of the scientif investigation of the world. Milton did not intend that his high imaginative poem should return with awkward questions abo the Christian scheme in which he believed, but on the eviden here it does. The Earl of Rochester might have been thinking of th author of *Paradise Lost* when eight years later he wrote in his *Saty Against Reason and Mankind* of his detestation of that aspiring facul 'that makes a mite / Think he's the image of the infinite, ... Borne c whose wings, each heavy sot can pierce / The limits of the boundle: universe'.

9

Bunyan: *The Pilgrim's Progress*

The Pilgrim's Progress (1678, 1684) could be said in some ways to be the reverse of *Paradise Lost*: where Milton seeks to liberate the imagination, Bunyan seeks to confine and curb it. Every step of his Christian's path towards the New Jerusalem is to be significant, every item is to be glossed, whether with biblical references or with clear allegorical significance or overt explanation. Symbolic of Bunyan's difference from Milton is the way his world is one with a single narrow path through it towards a goal, whereas Milton's is the whole range of the universe. Satan makes his own passage, while the path in *The Pilgrim's Progress* is already there. As a Puritan, Bunyan was acutely conscious of the seductive dangers of allegory, the way the reader might be tempted to stay with the literal picture rather than apprehend its significance: '*Take heed*', he says, '*that thou be not extream , / In playing with the* outside *of my Dream . . . .*'

> *Put by the Curtains, look within my Vail;*
> *Turn up my Metaphors and do not fail:*
> *There, if thou seekest them, such things to find,*
> *As will be helpful to an honest mind.*
>
> (Conclusion to Part 1)[1]

In this aim Bunyan is much more in harmony with his age than his fellow Nonconformist Milton, even while he had little kinship with the established thinkers of the time. Bacon, Davenant, Hobbes and Sprat before him, and Dryden and Locke after, all condemned the irresponsible use of wit and imagination, particularly as displayed in the metaphysical poets. For them, it has to be said, however, Bunyan himself would have been seen as a prime votary of the imagination in another sense, in preferring his individual and often idiosyncratic Dissenting vision to that of the established Church.

For all Bunyan's doctrinal intent, *The Pilgrim's Progress* was a work that had come extremely naturally to him: he describes it as a dream, and as though given. He had not intended to write thus, he tells us in his Apology: he was one day *'writing of the Way / And Race of Saints in this our Gospel-Day'* when he *'Fell suddenly into an Allegory / About their Journey, and the way to Glory'*. His thoughts *'began to multiply, / Like sparks that from the coals of Fire do flie'*; and, as he went on,

> *Still as I pull'd, it came; and so I penn'd*
> *It down, until it came at last to be*
> *For length and breadth the bigness which you see.*

He resolved with some trepidation to publish it;[2] but nevertheless defended his method of using an imagined picture to convey truth by referring to Christ's teaching by means of parable in the Gospels. So we might say that there are two sides to Bunyan's view of allegory: there is the expansive side, which gives scope to the way the story developed naturally, and then the contractive side which insists that it is pierced through and even rejected for the truths it contains.

If we consider the work at a literal level, it is the story of a man who reads in a book that the city in which he lives is doomed to destruction by fire, and, seeking to be saved, is directed across a plain outside the city to a small gate leading to a path, which, after a number of obstacles, from hills or ditches to giants or fiends, will deliver the traveller who wins through all these to a new and eternal city of joy. If we see it at the level of its meaning, the book is the story of a soul suddenly struck with knowledge of its sinfulness, and journeying further and further within itself to find assurance of grace. At this level *The Pilgrim's Progress* is Bunyan's more direct *Grace Abounding to the Chief of Sinners* (1666) retold:[3] there he describes in detail not his 'real' life but his spiritual life, and his torments of doubt and sense of exclusion until he feels himself accepted and forgiven. At the literal level in *The Pilgrim's Progress* Christian goes on an actual journey, away from one city and through a dangerous landscape towards another. At the allegorical level he may not physically have left the City of Destruction at all, only separated himself from it spiritually.

There is no reason why we should not be able to make the continuous allegorical readings which will resolve this antinomy, as in other allegories such as Spenser's *The Faerie Queene*, where we know that the landscape is most truly that of the spirit even while we are permitted to entertain ourselves with the fiction. It has to be said that there is, however, an even sharper divorce, or even contradiction, between the literal and the spiritual in Bunyan's work. This may be owing to his Puritan rejection of all earthly things in their entirety, whereby here in order to read aright we have to set aside the 'physical' journey altogether. When Charity at Palace Beautiful asks Christian whether he tried to persuade his wife and family to go on pilgrimage with him and he replies that he did but that they would not come (pp. 50–2), we are disposed to forget that he may physically still be at home with them.[4] Similarly, when Christian and Faithful come to Vanity Fair we have a definite sense of their coming to it from another place – a wilderness they have just left on their path (p. 88) – even though Vanity Fair is to be seen as conterminous with the city from which Christian 'set out' (though now seen in a new mode), if we are to read aright. That is, we have continually to cancel the impression we are given of distance, or of Vanity Fair and every other thing encountered on the journey as being separated from the city with which we begin. Such wholesale rejection of the literal narrative is hard. Certainly Bunyan's injunctions to us to see through his metaphors to the spiritual truths that they contain have in this light an added and perhaps desperate urgency. He himself sometimes forgets to do this, as when he has Christian ask after news of the City of Destruction and its inhabitants when he meets up with Faithful.

The whole notion of a 'progress' is problematic here too. Bunyan's Calvinist view is that man cannot progress, only find out whether or not he is graciously saved through Christ: because he is absolutely corrupt and reprobate, he can do no good, only open his heart for Christ to do it. Yet Bunyan has written an allegory in which the central character is shown steadily moving forward through acts of courage and resolution which do not invite us to look for a divine source.[5] Christian struggles through the Slough of Despond when Pliable gives up; Christian climbs Hill Difficulty when Formalist and Hypocrisy will not; he faces the lions before Palace Beautiful; he fights the fiend Apollyon and trudges his dangerous way through the Valley of the Shadow of Death; and so on until the end of his journey. Were this work a mirror of Bunyan's theology, then the title of his other great book, *Grace Abounding to the Chief of Sinners*, would also be applicable to this one; but, as though in unconscious admission of the different impression

produced by the later book, Bunyan has called it *The Pilgrim*
Progress.[6] The fact is that the image of a journey towards a go⟨
works against the theology of human reprobation and stasis.

These are problems arising out of Bunyan's particular form ⟨
Christianity. And there are others of a different kind stemming fro⟩
his special treatment of the pilgrimage motif itself – a motif lon⟩
domiciled in Christian literature. For what is remarkable and qui⟨
new in Bunyan's presentation of Christian pilgrimage is the degre
of intensity and focus he has given to it. We not only have just on⟩
pilgrim (at least in the first part), but one path and one goal. Th⟩
path Christian follows may have variable characters on it dependin⟩
on the natures of different pilgrims, but it is still the same cours⟩
through much the same landscape, for whoever enters on it: fir⟨
the Slough, then the Wicket-gate, Interpreter's House, the Sepulchr⟨
Hill Difficulty, the lions at Palace Beautiful, the way down to th⟩
Valley of Humiliation, the Valley of the Shadow of Death, Giar⟩
Despair and Doubting Castle, the Delectable Mountains, Enchante⟩
Ground, the River and the Celestial City beyond it (pp. 262–⟨
307–8).[7] No pilgrimage literature before Bunyan's had either th⟨
sense of a fixed path, or of a landscape which it followed. Wheth⟨
in Guillaume de Deguileville's *The Pilgrimage of the Life of Ma⟩*
(1330, 1350; tr. Lydgate, 1426), or in Langland's *Piers Plowma⟩*
Spenser's *Faerie Queene* or Simon Patrick's *The Parable of the Pilgri⟩*
(1664), the pilgrim simply wanders over an uncertain landscap⟨
and, if he has a goal, it is not insisted upon: for much of the time ⟨
Spenser's account of Redcrosse, we may forget his ultimate objectiv⟨
the rescue of Una's parents; and in Patrick's *Parable* the goal ⟨
Jerusalem is eventually dropped. Landscape is vague and indefinit⟨
and the connections between any one feature and another ar⟩
unresolved: thus Spenser mentions the odd wood, cave, castle, palac
or spring, but where they are placed in relation to one another remair
obscure; indeed the emphasis could be said to be upon the varyin⟩
characters Redcrosse encounters, rather than on any geograph⟩
Other writers, such as Deguileville or Patrick, fill their account
with long discourses, and only occasionally pay even lip-service t⟩
the journey: typical of Patrick are such rare interjections as 'In suc⟩
delightful and useful talk as this they beguiled the time, an⟩
shortened the length of the wayes', or 'In such discourse as th⟨
they passed with pleasure a long stage of their journey'.[8]

In all these works where there is not a central drive and directio⟩
to the narrative, their meanings may come across the more directl⟩

if at times more tediously, either through the direct didacticism of a
Patrick, or through the leisure we are given to contemplate as scenes
dilate their significance in Spenser. Indeed it could be said that,
where these earlier works present fictions, it tends to be in the form
of encounters, scenes and great images, rather than in connected
sequences. What happens with Bunyan, however, is that the vitality
and drive of the story and the journey together work to dispel all
but the most rudimentary forms of overt significance. The trouble is
that Bunyan thought his story could still deliver meaning in
separable form. He thought he was writing an allegory; in a sense
what he succeeded in writing was a myth.[9] It was as a myth of
heavenly promise that the Victorians took *The Pilgrim's Progress* to
heart. It would certainly be strange if an age which valued the
family so much could have admired the book for a doctrine which
starts by portraying its hero running away for good from the
entreaties of his wife and children. At the centre of Bunyan's book
is the idea of a treasure-hunt over an obstacle race. The first motive
propelling the pilgrim into action may be fear of damnation and
destruction, but looking ahead to salvation quickly becomes the
dominant impulse. Before he reaches the Slough of Despond,
Christian tells Pliable how they are going to a place of everlasting
life, joy and glory where

> we shall be with *Seraphims*, and *Cherubins*, Creatures that will
> dazle your eyes to look on them: There also you shall meet with
> thousands, and ten thousands that have gone before us to that
> place; none of them are hurtful, but loving, and holy; every one
> walking in the sight of God; and standing in his presence with
> acceptance for ever: In a word, there we shall see the Elders with
> their Golden Crowns: There we shall see the Holy Virgins with
> their Golden Harps. There we shall see Men that by the World
> were cut in pieces, burnt in flames, eaten of Beasts, drownded in
> the Seas, for the love that they bare to the Lord of the place; all
> well, and cloathed with Immortality, as with a Garment.
>
> (pp. 13–14)

Throughout the story the sense of this place of bliss as the goal is
pervasive, drawing Christian on through the darkest places. And
desire for it intensifies, as Christian is given a distant view of the
Delectable Mountains from the Palace Beautiful, and from the
Delectable Mountains can receive only a very blurred impression of

the Celestial City because his hand shakes as he holds the perspective glass; by the time he and Hopeful reach the land of Beulah, this side of the River, they are almost faint with desire. Throughout the story we are acutely aware of how Christian, through his possession of his roll and his adherence to the path, has an entry to heaven which others are without; and yet at the same time we are made continuously aware of his insecurity, of the difficulty of the way and of the penalties of digression from the path. Right in the middle of his journey, in Vanity Fair, when his companion Faithful is killed by the people there, heaven comes right forward to us as Faithful is caught up from his destruction by a chariot 'the nearest way to the Cœlestial Gate' (p. 97). In this emphasis on *Sehnsucht*, or spiritual yearning, Bunyan is at one with numbers of writers on the desire of heaven and immortality in the late seventeenth century, among them Patrick and Traherne. But, while in Traherne we saw a move away from the concern of previous metaphysical poetry with doctrine to a poetry of revelation, in Bunyan we find both impulses at variance, the urge to realise moral significance being at odds with the desire for the object of such behaviour.

It is a paradox that Bunyan should have increased the imaginative power of his work over its significance precisely by the means that he might have expected to restrict the licence of the imagination. Puritan thinkers before him had frequently condemned the free action of the mind and demanded that it be kept to one undeviating purpose. Writing in 1638, Thomas Goodwin condemned 'that unsetled wantonnesse and unstayednesse of the minde in thinking, that like quick-silver it cannot fixe . . . ; our thoughts at best are as wanton Spaniels, who though indeed they goe with and accompany their Master, and come to their journeys end with him in the end, yet doe run after every Bird, and wildly pursue every flock of sheepe they see'; and in 1681 John Owen declared, 'There is nothing so unaccountable as *the multiplicity of thoughts* in the minds of men.' One can relate these strictures to the contemporary attacks by Hobbes, Sprat and Dryden on the use of unrestrained 'fancy' in literature; but the emphasis on keeping to the path is peculiar. Goodwin declares that God requires of us 'a steady directing [of] all our thoughts straight on to his glory, our owne salvation, and the good of others', and that 'As we are to walk in God's wayes hee calls us to, so every thought, as well as every action, is a step: and therefore ought to bee steady.'[10] It begins to be clear why the pilgrimage metaphor would seem so natural for Bunyan, as a means in part of symbolising that singleness of spiritual purpose which was to direct his Christian. But the problem for him was that that very act of concentrating and directing his story brought in with it an imaginative vividness he could have done without.

Let us consider first the facts of 'concentration'. Our sense of the singleness of the path in *The Pilgrim's Progress* is increased by the way we start with Christian running across a wide plain of infinite possibility towards a gate, which powerfully brings home the feeling of spiritual focus. Then Christian has to move along a narrow track, beset by various obstacles. The isolation of that track is assured by mentioning scarcely any place outside it. By-ends comes from the town of Fair Speech, but we know no more of it; Formalist and Hypocrisy climb over a wall to get on to the path, and Ignorance enters it via 'a little crooked Lane' (p. 123), but of their places of origin we know nothing. There is, as it were, 'nowhere else'. Those who leave the path do not go to another place, but suffer instant disaster, such as Formalist and Hypocrisy lost in the wood and the field of mountains, By-ends destroyed by Demas, the blind men lost among the tombs of Giant Despair, or Heedless and Too-Bold in the slumber of spiritual death by the side of the road (Part 2, pp. 297–9). All temptations and obstacles are related to the path itself and to stopping, going back, or diverging from it. The Slough of Despond, Hill Difficulty, Apollyon, Vanity Fair – all these act as obstacles to progress; while the likes of Demas's mine or By-path Meadow, Doubting Castle and the black man represent temptations to digress from the way. Christian sees through and is not tempted by Talkative, By-ends and Ignorance, whose solicitations are not directly concerned with keeping to the path (pp. 77, 99, 123–4). For Bunyan, 'the way is the way, and there's an end' (p. 237).

The imagination of the reader is also kept to the path by virtue of the fact that the journey image is simple, strongly presented and able to be grasped with one act of mind. The movement is directly from A to B, and both A and B, the City of Destruction and Celestial City, are clearly marked. We have added sense of those termini as a frame from the fact that at the beginning Christian leaves a city and crosses a field with a slough to a gate, while at the end he comes out of the narrow path into the open land of Beulah and thence across another slough (the river) and through a gate into another city. Besides having a distinct beginning and end, the journey has a well-defined middle. The number of features and figures encountered is limited, and we have a clear picture of them and of the connections from one to the other. We are, as hinted earlier, with Christian as he runs up the highway to the Cross, and thence down to 'a bottom' and along to Hill Difficulty with the plateau and Palace Beautiful beyond it and the descent to the Valleys of Humiliation and the Shadow of Death after that. Further, we gain a strong sense of the way from the fact that its character is often drawn from Bunyan's own experience of contemporary roads in his native Bedfordshire, with its mires, ditches, fords, footpads, inns and fairs.[11]

The strength of the presentation of the journey, the path and the goal works against the detailed effectiveness of the allegory. For instance, because of the image of the journey, we naturally tend to think of the movement as one to greater and greater trials. However, Christian's contest with Apollyon, who is a form of the devil and thus the ultimate in evil, occurs in the middle of the story; and the faintly ludicrous disabilities of Giant Despair, who comes later, would make it difficult, objectively, to see him as so terrible an antagonist. Nor do we have evidence that Christian suffers more in Doubting Castle than he did in the Valley of the Shadow of Death. Yet the drive of the story makes us think in terms of increasing difficulty even where it may not in truth exist. Similar is the way in which the journey causes us to feel that each stage of the course marks a spiritual advance on the part of Christian. It is true that there is some advance: in the latter stages of his pilgrimage Christian is more experienced, and, instead of his being instructed by others, he himself now does the instructing, whether of By-ends, Hopeful or Ignorance; further, he is more perceptive, as when he sees through Talkative before Faithful (p. 77), or By-ends before Hopeful (p. 99). But when he falls a victim to Giant Despair, or sinks with terror in the last river, he arguably shows himself just as doubting and unsteady as when he fell into the Slough of Despond at the beginning of his journey. And yet such is the force and vigour of the narrative that it prevents us from making the point here, which is presumably that we remain hopelessly depraved and that our righteousness is but rags.[12]

This problem of allegorical effectiveness is also evident at the level of individual scenes. The difficulty of Hill Difficulty is very subtly and powerfully put over, but the difficulty that is conveyed is in the end more physical than spiritual. We do begin with a fairly direct moral and conceptual account:

I believe then, that they all went on till they came to the foot of an Hill, at the bottom of which was a Spring. There was also in the same place two other ways besides that which came straight from the Gate; one turned to the left hand, and the other to the right, at the bottom of the Hill: but the narrow way lay right up the Hill, (and the name of the going up the side of the Hill, is called *Difficulty*.) *Christian* now went to the Spring and drank thereof to refresh himself, and then began to go up the Hill; saying,

> *This Hill, though high, I covet to ascend,*
> *The difficulty will not me offend:*
> *For I perceive the way to life lies here;*
> *Come, pluck up, Heart; lets neither faint nor fear:*
> *Better, tho difficult, th'right way to go,*
> *Then wrong, though easie, where the end is wo.*
>
> (pp. 41–2)

The moral difficulty that is being stressed here remains general. It is hard to see how it is in any way distinguished from the difficulty of struggling across the Slough of Despond or facing up to Apollyon or the Valley of the Shadow of Death, or of not diverging into By-path Meadow: Bunyan does not specify, leaving it simply as 'Difficulty'.[13] All these obstacles require the same resolution to go straight forward: every time the pilgrim overcomes an impediment the same virtue is exercised, as enshrined in the verse '*Who would true Valour see / Let him come hither; / One here will Constant be, / Come Wind, come Weather*' (p. 295). The real energy and particularity of the account are directed to the realisation of the hill as a physical obstacle.[14] First we are told that Christian arrived at 'the foot of an Hill, at the bottom of which was a Spring': no sooner are we at 'the foot' than we have to drop our gaze lower to 'the bottom'. Then we have to look from side to side at the two possibly alternative ways round the obstacle of the hill; then straight ahead and up: 'but the narrow way lay right up the Hill, (and the name of the going up the side of the Hill, is called *Difficulty*)' – here we take a quick view of the difficulty of the path, and then in what seems slow and laboured syntax we traverse the path yet again. We then return to Christian coming to the spring, refreshing himself, and starting upward. Then,

The other two [Formalist and Hypocrisy] also came to the foot of the Hill. But when they saw that the Hill was steep and high, and that there was two other ways to go; and supposing also that these two ways might meet again, with that up which *Christian* went, on the other side of the Hill: Therefore they were resolved to go in those ways; (now the name of one of those ways was *Danger*, and the name of the other *Destruction*). So the one took the way which is called *Danger*, which led him into a great Wood; and the other took directly up the way to *Destruction*, which led him into a wide field full of dark Mountains, where he stumbled and fell, and rose no more.

I looked then after *Christian*, to see him go up the Hill, where I perceived he fell from running to going, and from going to clambering upon his hands and his knees, because of the steepness of the place.

We look back down to survey Formalist and Hypocrisy coming to the foot of the hill: then we are with them as they consider; then we move mentally round the hill with them, their avoidance of the obstacle being imitated in the way the sentence anticipates their action before they take it. The suspended syntax in 'these two ways might meet again, with that up which *Christian* went, on the other side of the Hill' neatly enacts the sense, and at the same time throws us out of horizontal views to look up now to Christian on the steep side of the hill. We have thus moved vantage point from looking upwards to looking downwards and then back again, and from Christian back to the two others at the foot of the hill before returning to Christian: here also the physical resistance of the hill is powerfully put over. We stay with Formalist and Hypocrisy for a while, watching them severally come to grief, and realising that the easy way leads to destruction – this conveys that Hill Difficulty is the way to safety, but immediately the hill removes comfort from this: 'I looked then after *Christian*, to see him go up the Hill, where I perceived he fell from running to going, and from going to clambering upon his hands and his knees, because of the steepness of the place.' The syntax and rhythm of the second half of the sentence get as it were on their own hands and knees. 'Fell' has just been used to describe the end of Hypocrisy; used again of Christian, therefore, it first suggests a lapse, before we realise it is only a slowing pace, so that the downward movement we first intuit is denied. Energy is generated, as throughout the passage, by the interaction of upward and downward movements. This is continued later when, having gained the summit of the hill, Christian realises that he has left his roll in the arbour and has to return for it. In this way the physical gradient of the hill and the exertion it requires of the climber are strongly put over.

While this mode of description gives *Pilgrim's Progress* considerable power, it does reduce its effect as allegory. It becomes hard to translate physical into spiritual travelling where the journey and experience of it are realised in such concrete detail, and where the allegory is left so general. Certainly there is a continued background sense that climbing the hill is an act of moral choice, but we do not for long think of the hill itself as a metaphysical obstacle, because our impression of its steepness and of the effort involved in climbing it are so vividly felt in terms of sight and strain. In *The Faerie Queene*, by contrast, Spenser always either keeps the literal level of action quite vague and general, or else makes any peculiarities meaningful ones, so that we apprehend literal and allegorical as near as possible in fusion; this means that the literal level is less 'gripping', but for the allegory to work this has to be so. Knightly contests are described in the set form and often clichéd romance language of jousting and subsequent swordplay that one finds throughout Malory, so that as description it makes small imprint on the mind, and one can pay attention to the fact of the allegorical contest behind it. Where there is variation, as for example in the account (IV.iii) of the battle between Cambell and Priamond, Diamond and Triamond, in which Cambell comes to fight with the strength of three, the allegory of, variously, friendship, the mundane, celestial and supercelestial worlds, and the Trinity is both clear and directly embodied in the action. Similarly, the general landscape of woods, glades and plains is not striking or individual, and therefore more readily suggests the terrain of the spirit. Such peculiarities as there are in the scenery of the poem usually relate to places rather than items on a journey, and then most commonly to constructs rather than natural features – the Palace of Pride, the Bower of Acrasia, the House of Busirane, the Temple of Venus, Isis's Church – and always the visual details of these places are directly significant, as with the Palace of Pride on its hill of sand, or the fire in the porch of Busirane's house. It is true that much successful allegory does ask attention to the literal as well as the allegorical level, and therefore runs the risk of our stopping at the former; and in this light, 'knowing how doubtfully all Allegories may be construed', Spenser sets forth his expository letter to *The Faerie Queene* – but, as we have seen with that work, there are methods of driving our experience further.

In *The Pilgrim's Progress* many items are left without specific significance or individuality.[15] Nothing in the narrative assigns a definite meaning to the Wicket-gate, more than that we feel Christian to have been so far accepted as to gain admission to the obstacle course; the biblical reference to Matthew 7.13, 'Enter ye in at the strait gate', adds no more. (It is not evidently Christ, for He comes later, when Christian loses his burden of sin.) No distinction is made between Formalist and Hypocrisy, or between the wood and the field in which each of them meets his doom (and indeed we do not know which of them went to which). An editorial footnote may tell us that the lions chained before Palace Beautiful 'symbolise civil and ecclesiastical persecution', or that their being chained refers to the fact that 'When Bunyan became a member of Bedford independent church, in 1653, penal laws against nonconformists were not enforced',[16] but the text does not; and the absence of any definite significance for the lions is further suggested in that, while in Part 1 the Porter tells Christian that they are placed there on purpose 'for trial of faith', in Part 2 they are agencies of evil, being 'backed' by the wicked Giant Grim (pp. 45–6, 218–19). And, as we have seen, we sense throughout the story that the motives and acts demonstrated by Christian are remarkably similar in character, relating only to resolution and trust, and that these are virtues required of many journeys, sacred or secular. Christian never, save in the interpolated discussions, has to display any more spiritually significant behaviour, in the way that Sir Guyon's various adventures in book II of *The Faerie Queene* build up a picture of the character of temperance, or those of Artegall in book V build up one of the nature of justice. We feel too, although we might not always be able to explain it, that the order of events in Spenser is spiritually determined; but in Bunyan, while the course is a fixed one, its order does not appear meaningful. It does not feel inevitable that, say, Hill Difficulty should have to come before By-path Meadow, or Vanity Fair after the Valleys of Humiliation and of the Shadow of Death. Often lacking, therefore, a sense of significance behind the figures and events, the motives and actions, or the order of the narrative, the conduct and the obstacles can come to seem essentially the same throughout; and thus we tend naturally read the book as a story showing how the same human resolve and trust may win to heaven through a series of difficulties which differ from one another only in so far as one is a hill, another a pair of lions, another a fiend and another a by-path. The breadth of Bunyan's appeal may be enormously increased by this, but at the expense of individuality and subtlety in the allegory.

This established, other aspects of the narrative begin to fall into place. The several digressions in which theological and moral matters are discussed, as while Christian is at Interpreter's House, or walking with By-ends and Talkative, or conversing with Hopeful as they traverse Enchanted Ground, may be seen as attempts by the author to insert into the narrative the kinds of consideration which ought to have been carried by the story as allegory, but now have to be presented directly. (The same might be said of certain of the marginal insertions also.[17]) The clash between narrative and allegory is illustrated by the account of Christian and Pliable falling into the Slough of Despond: at first we are told that they 'drew near to a very *Miry Slough* that was in the midst of the Plain, and they being heedless, did both fall suddenly into the bogg'; but later, when Help asks Christian why he did not look for the steps, moral significance is imposed on the events retrospectively: '*Fear* followed me so hard, that I fled the next way, and fell in' (p. 15).

Then the 'solidity' of Bunyan's story may be seen also in the way that the allegorical figures seem to be more outside Christian than inside his soul. For example, Christian does not meet Faithful when he becomes faithful (as, say, Spenser's Redcrosse meets Sans Foy when he has become faithless): he has exhibited faith long previously, whether in keeping to the path up Hill Difficulty or battling with Apollyon. Nor, when Faithful is executed in Vanity Fair, are we to believe that Christian has himself lost faith, since he continues on his way with courage. Many of the figures met, such as Formalist, Hypocrisy, Talkative, By-ends, Demas or Ignorance do not tempt Christian at all, and hence appear simply as 'other people'. Similarly, while Hopeful may be momentarily a part of Christian when Christian finds in himself the key by which to escape from Doubting Castle, at the crossing of the last river the two are clearly separate, the one despairing and almost sinking, the other going forward confidently on his own.

The allegory in Bunyan, where it exists, is confined to the moral level of reading. Indeed here too the path from which one must not diverge could be seen as symbolic of Bunyan's refusal of any more than one level of reading of his narrative. We witness the spiritual history of one Christian; we do not find imaged in him or his history Christ or the Last Things; the medieval levels of allegory and anagogy are absent, and with them the kind of 'freedom' and multiplicity of interpretation that we find in Langland or Spenser. Christian is a typical Christian, but not a type of Christ; his divergences from the path are individual spiritual lapses, not images of the fall;[18] and his arrival at Celestial City, though attended with apocalyptic feelings, is not a figure of the Last Things. When Christian defeats Apollyon, it is only he who does so; but the slaying of the dragon at the end of book I of *The Faerie Queene* is a type also of the victory of Christ over sin and hell in His life and death, and of God's final destruction of Satan at the Last Judgement. All the pictures in Interpreter's House relate to moral behaviour – even the image of the devil throwing water on the fire of grace while Christ sustains it with oil is concerned with the motions of the human spirit. Further, the emphasis in *Pilgrim's Progress*, as we shall see, is on doing and action rather than contemplation: the narrative and the ethic behind it are against the stillness that could be argued to be required for the perception of such further levels of meaning. And Bunyan does not usually deal with moral concepts directly: his characters are not Faith or Hope but Faithful or Hopeful; his Mr Honest insists that 'Not Honesty in the *Abstract*, but *Honest* is my Name, and I wish that my *Nature* shall agree to what I am called' (p. 247).

But, as we have seen, even the effectiveness of this level of allegory is compromised by the solidity of the image Bunyan has employed. And there is another factor at work: the tendency of the narrative often to consider items not so much on their own but as parts of a sequence of other items, so that we lose further potential to consider the significance of any one event. Apart from our own tendency to look ahead in the narrative to what is to come or the eventual goal of the journey, the story itself is internally anticipatory in the way that most of the episodes on Christian's journey are partially envisaged before they occur. Mr Evangelist points out the Wicket-gate to Christian and tells him what to do when he arrives at it (p. 10); Good Will tells Christian about the path, about his burden and how it will come off by itself at the place of deliverance, and about Interpreter's House (pp. 27–8); Mistrust and Timorous warn Christian about the lions at Palace Beautiful (p. 43); at Palace Beautiful he is given a vision of the Delectable Mountains (pp. 54–5), and learns something of the Valley of Humiliation (p. 56); the men fleeing from the Valley of the Shadow of Death describe the place and bid Christian turn back (pp. 61–2); Evangelist informs Christian and Faithful of Vanity Fair and how one of them will die there (pp. 87–8); and Bunyan tells us of the experience of previous pilgrims with Demas before we are shown Christian encountering him (p. 106). Throughout, the direct naming of the allegorical figures, as Pliable, Faithful, Talkative, By-ends or Ignorance (compare the more oblique Duessa, Acrasia, Britomart or Busirane in Spenser) serves to herald behaviour, and the name 'Christian' is a harbinger of the pilgrim's success. All this is in strong contrast, for example, to *Grace Abounding*, where each event is relatively islanded and we have no sense of what may lie ahead.

To repeat, much of the force of the story depends on the draw of heaven. The book has the appeal of a treasure-hunt, and the means and the end are seen in at least partly secular terms: Christian's resolution is rarely felt as specifically Christian resolution, and the appeal of heaven is in part to earthly desire (see for example pp. 11, 13–14, 182, 183, 199–200, 291–2, 311). In Bunyan we feel this heaven so near as to be almost round the next corner (which it is for Faithful). Thus what dominates *The Pilgrim's Progress* is the domain of ultimate 'concrete' reality: the central concern of the book is not with the allegorical but with that Real beside which our reality seems allegorical. And certainly the dominance of heaven and desire for it makes Bunyan something of a Christian Romantic: in this sense he is a writer more of fantasy than of allegory.

Thus the concentration of Bunyan's image of the journey, the sense of a goal throughout, the continual forward pressure and the solidity of the narrative can be seen as working both against the specific Calvinist theology Bunyan intended, and against the existence of allegory. At this point it becomes possible to move outwards to wider conclusions. For instance, the sheer dichotomy between *Grace Abounding* and *The Pilgrim's Progress*, the one all direct theology and the other much more physical narrative, can be seen to mirror a split between material and significance, or, more largely, 'mind' and 'body', often evident in the literature of the period. Then again, it becomes significant that Bunyan is the last writer before the Romantics to attempt an allegory of the soul's quest for heaven. Last, it may be recalled that his age was hostile to metaphor, to anything that smacked of mystery and the 'darke conceit' of allegory: in thus trying to reconcile the claims of imagination and sense Bunyan could be said to be attempting what was for his time impossible. In this respect it is instructive to contrast *The Pilgrim's*

Progress with the medieval *Queste*, for the latter is just as world-renouncing and as ruthless in its translation of fiction into allegorical significance as Bunyan intended to be in his work; but the sense of a clear landscape and a journey is far stronger with Bunyan, and one has the feeling that for the seventeenth-century writer the world and the solidity from which one must escape are far more present and real.

10

Swedenborg:
Heaven and Hell

Of the Lord's Divine Mercy it has been granted me now for several years to be constantly and uninterruptedly in company with spirits and angels, hearing them speak and in turn speaking with them. In this way it has been given me to hear and see wonderful things in the other life which have never before come to the knowledge of any man nor into his idea.... I have been instructed in regard to the different kinds of spirits, the state of souls after death, hell, or the lamentable state of the unfaithful, heaven, or the blessed state of the faithful, and especially in regard to the doctrine of faith which is acknowledged in the universal heaven.

Arcana Coelestia, I (1749) no. 5

Since the Lord cannot manifest Himself in person . . . and nevertheless has foretold that He was to come and establish a New Church, which is the New Jerusalem, it follows that He will do this by means of a man, who is able not only to receive these doctrines in his understanding, but also to publish them by the press. That the Lord manifested Himself before me, His servant, and sent me to this office, that He afterward opened the eyes of my spirit and thus introduced me into the spiritual world and granted me to see the heavens and the hells, and to talk with angels and spirits, and this now continuously for several years, I affirm in truth; as also that from the first day of that call I have not received anything whatever pertaining to the doctrines of that Church from any angel, but from the Lord alone while I have read the Word.

The True Christian Religion (1771) no. 779

This chapter may seem anomalous, for Swedenborg is not a writer of Christian fantasy in our sense of a *fiction* involving supernatural beings. Nevertheless his work is so amazingly founded on declared supernatural revelation and so detailed and 'concrete' a picture of the other worlds of heaven and hell that it demands consideration here. For thirteen years before he wrote down his *Heaven and Hell* (1758), Swedenborg soberly tells us, he was in direct communication with angels, who were pleased to give him a full account of every aspect of the heavenly and hellish realms, to the end of producing a religious revival amid the decaying Christian faith and churches of the mid eighteenth century (no. 1). In meticulous detail he therefore tells us of angelic natures, lives and occupations, of the shaping of heaven in the human form, of the network of spiritual correspondences underlying all things. If Swedenborg was deluded, his work must none the less be credited with presenting one of the most highly wrought, profound and convincing fantastic worlds ever created. If, on the other hand, he really did receive his visions from angels, then *Heaven and Hell*, to say nothing of his many other 'given' works, must be seen as the most extensive and unambiguous communication by agents of God with man that we have.

Swedenborg is more 'locally' interesting for us here too. The picture he gives of heaven does fit into an increasingly 'anthropocentric' emphasis that was appearing in other pictures of it, from Milton onwards.[1] Swedenborg did allow that his heaven was subject to change, but not that it was timebound: he would have been less than content with the idea that his was a peculiarly eighteenth-century heaven. Another factor to consider with Swedenborg is his treatment of the Bible and of biblical narrative. And he is of course important for us as being in many ways both the stimulus and the provocation of Blake, particularly in Blake's antitype to his work, *The Marriage of Heaven and Hell*. Swedenborg reasserts the divorce of heaven and hell. He gives hell but a fifth as much space as he allots to describing heaven, as if to emphasise its triviality and uninterestingness. He defines his hell as a place of those who put love of self before love of God. Blake inverts all this. Lastly Swedenborg may serve here as a representative, albeit an idiosyncratic one, of the great tradition of mysticism in the Christian faith, whereby men and women have variously reported some intuition, however oblique or ineffable, of the divine nature.

Yet at the outset we should be aware that until he reported his first contacts with angels, in 1744, Swedenborg had been an outstanding and renowned scientist and inventor, a geometer, chemist, biologist, metallurgist and applied physicist. From 1716 to 1747 he was an assessor to the Swedish Board of Mines. During the period of his assessorship he wrote almost as many books on scientific topics as he was later to write on mystical ones. Thus we have *The Motion and Position of the Earth and the Planets* (1719), *The Height of the Waters* (1719), *Chemistry* (1721), *Miscellaneous Observations* (1721–2), *Philosophical and Mineralogical Works* (1734), *On the Infinite* (1734), *The Cerebrum* (1738–40), *The Economy of the Animal Kingdom* (1740–1), *The Fibre* (written 1741), *The Rational Psychology* (written 1742), *The Brain* (written 1743–4), *The Animal Kingdom* (1743–5; parts IV and V written at this time but not published until later). Many of the works published at the time were highly regarded, and in 1740 Swedenborg was unanimously accepted to membership of the newly established Swedish Academy of Sciences on the proposal of its president, Carl Linnaeus.[2]

All Swedenborg's books, however, were increasingly directed by a religious purpose. At first this was founded on the then scientifically 'acceptable' premise that exploration of the rational order of the universe was a discovery of the wonders of God in creation: in this Swedenborg is not far from the faith known as 'deism', which is well illustrated in John Ray's *Wisdom of God Manifested in the Works of the Creation* (1691) and William Derham's *Physico-Theology* (1713) and *Astro-Theology* (1715). Later Swedenborg is to be found trying by scientific researches to expose the presence of the soul in the brain; and, in *The Rational Psychology* to investigate the existence of an immaterial world within the phenomenal one.[3] Many of the principles on which the posthumous worlds of *Heaven and Hell* are founded have analogies and anticipations in these earlier works.[4]

One of the first features that strikes us about *Heaven and Hell* is how ordered, rational and sober it is. It is constructed out of sections, much like many another eighteenth-century work built out of 'bricks' of insight into a house of vision. The architectural analogy for literary composition is common in the eighteenth century and also informs Swedenborg's notion of heaven as a house of many mansions. Thus we have chapters of a highly analytic character, each contributing one aspect of the total truth and love that makes up heaven: 'The whole heaven, viewed collectively, is in the human form'; 'There is a correspondence between all things of heaven and all things of man'; 'Time in heaven'; 'Writing in heaven'; 'Marriage in heaven', 'The immensity of heaven'; and so forth. The whole of this heaven, while founded on divine love and truth, is very rationally put together. There are innumerable cross-references from section to section, like struts, connecting the separate items.

314. That heaven is from the human race is also evident from the fact that angelic minds and human minds are similar. Both enjoy the faculties of understanding, perceiving and willing, and both are formed to receive heaven; for the human mind is just as capable of wisdom as the angelic mind, but does not become so wise in the world, because it is in an earthly body, and in that body its spiritual part thinks in a natural manner. It is different when the human mind is released from its connexion with the body, for then it no longer thinks naturally but spiritually; and when it thinks spiritually its thoughts are incomprehensible and undescribable to the natural man, and thus it becomes possessed of angelic wisdom. From this it may be seen that the internal man, which is called his spirit, is in its essence an angel (n. 57), and when released from the earthly body is like an angel in human form; (an angel is in a perfect human form n. 73–77).[5]

Swedenborg puts it directly: 'Since, therefore, man is capable of understanding truths if he is willing, I am permitted to confirm the spiritual truths of heaven and the Church by rational considerations' (no. 455). Throughout *Heaven and Hell* there is scarce a trace of the fervours we find in other mystics, none of the emotionalism of a Jakob Boehme or a St Teresa of Ávila. Indeed, as Swedenborg is conducted through the various aspects of heaven – its centre, its shape, its government, the natures of angels, their occupations, writings, dwelling-places, societies, marriages, and so forth – we may be clearly reminded of the similar procedures followed by Swift's Gulliver in each of his adventures, and particularly of his tutelage under the rational Houyhnhnms: everywhere there is the methodical, encyclopaedic approach. And Swedenborg is the detached reporter throughout: 'In order that I might know the nature and quality of heaven and heavenly joy, I have frequently, and for a long time together, been permitted by the Lord to perceive the delights of heavenly joy. I know them therefore from living experience, but I can never describe them; a few observations, however, may convey some idea' (no. 413; see also, for example, no. 174). Certainly the sobriety and rationality of Swedenborg's account partly emerge from the trained engineer in him, but they are also the expression of his age.

Dante's cosmos was also highly organised, patterned and numbered, and in a sense Swedenborg recovers something of the unique blend of faith and reason, mysticism and order, that we see in Dante. But

Dante is more inclined to use structure and symmetry as ways of giving us a bare foothold so that we may the more surely feel the unknowability of God and the heavens. Swedenborg is at pains to make everything clear and sensible to us, to give us a system of reasoning which will provide a picture of the divine world that must bring at least a sense that it has an 'inner consistency of reality', that it rings true at every point. In a way he is a philosopher, seeking to put over a world of thought which embodies the supernatural world in which he would have us believe; but of course we are asked to accept that such intellectual and spiritual worlds are not his, but have been revealed to him. He tells us that God is the Lord of heaven and of hell; that all visible and physical things correspond to or reflect divine ideas; that man will inhabit heaven or hell according to whether he puts divine love or self-love first; that there is an intermediate state after death during which tendencies evident during life become hardened and people come to choose either heaven or hell, which then open to them; that, as the human form is the highest creative idea of God, it is the form of heaven also, and that of the angels; that there is no final distinction between the sanctioned pleasures of this world and those of heaven; that heaven is now, in man's best mind, and not some far promise; that life in heaven is one of continual spiritual evolution; that the angels and devils are men who have become so. And all this leading with seemingly incontrovertible logic from point to point, so that heaven seems to grow with the argument. To contrast Swedenborg with Dante again: in the *Paradiso* Dante moves further and further out into the heavens towards God and greater mysteries, where Swedenborg starts with God as a first principle, and works inwards, to heaven and to man. Having established the universal *Urgrund*, Swedenborg explains the nature of the spiritual and material worlds it sustains: he wants us to believe through knowledge, whereas Dante wants us to approach God through an awareness of the limits of knowledge.

The emphasis on knowing in Swedenborg, on the accessibility of knowledge of heaven, marks him as a modern. In his account there is an absence of many theological absolutes. Man does not go to heaven or to hell immediately on death: there is an intermediate state in which tendencies exhibited during life are more nakedly revealed until the spirit gradually aligns itself in the direction it prefers, finding either hell or heaven hateful to it. *Prefers*: for it is not God who condemns the soul, but the spirit that chooses its habitation; here Swedenborg repudiates the Calvinist notion of a divine *fiat* of predestination. Nor are heaven and hell in every way opposed. God is the Lord of both. Both are needed, just as self and selflessness, evil and good are, for what Swedenborg calls the 'equilibrium' of the universe (nos 589–95); Blake later translates this equilibrium into 'marriage'. It is men who make hell, not God. There are no special supernatural beings called angels and devils: all the inhabitants of heaven and hell, apart from the one God (Swedenborg is Unitarian) were originally men (no. 311). Nor is heaven simply a place of delight and hell one of torture. To those who are in hell, heaven would be the most agonising place to be, and to a large extent they delight eternally in the unlimited expression of their selfish passions. Shut though they are in a coal-black burning pit which expresses by the law of correspondence their confinement to the self, they are nevertheless oblivious to it: 'I have been told that infernal spirits neither see nor feel these things, because when they are in them they are breathing their own atmosphere, and thus living in the delight of their life' (no. 585).

All is gradual, natural, reasonable: there are no absolute and 'other' breaks with what is acceptable to the human mind. Thus Swedenborg rejects the notion that anyone may be admitted to heaven by an act of unconditional mercy (no. 521). Most striking of all is his insistence throughout *Heaven and Hell* that our appearance and personalities will be little changed after death, and that though we are transfigured in heaven we shall still be in the human form, and live in houses, marriages, societies and cities just as on earth. 'Scarcely any one at this day knows what the term *spiritual* means, and still less does he understand that spiritual beings, such as angels and spirits, have a human form. Almost all, therefore, who come from the world are astounded to find that they are alive and are men just as they were before; that they see, hear and speak; and that their bodies have the sense of touch as before with no difference at all' (nos 75, 456).

> Whenever I have spoken with the angels face to face, I have been present with them in their dwellings. Their dwellings are just like the dwellings on earth called houses, but more beautiful. They contain chambers, inner rooms and bedrooms in great numbers; also courts with gardens, flower-beds and fields around them. Where they live in societies their houses adjoin one another and are arranged in the form of a city, with streets, roads and squares exactly like the cities on our earth. I have been allowed to walk

through them and to look about on every side and occasionally to enter the houses. This occurred when I was fully awake and my internal sight was opened.   (No. 184; see also nos 464–9)

Equally Swedenborg can say that where living men give themselves to divine love and charity, or where true innocence is amongst mortal flesh, then heaven may be found in our present life – though this is more an infusion from the divine sphere of the true heaven than a creation of heaven itself within the confines of our world.

What then becomes of Scripture and of biblical narrative in such a scheme? Swedenborg gives little place here to the doctrine of man's fall, to the idea of Christ's redemption of our sins through His Passion, death and resurrection, and none to the idea of the Last Things described in Revelation. His concern may be to remove the sense of human helplessness that is implicit in past doctrines and traditions relating to original sin and depravity, salvation through Christ alone, and final judgement by a righteous God. For he has man choose his otherworld destination for himself, even if, in doing so, he is choosing one of the contending forces, of God or of hell, in him. However, there is another reason. Swedenborg's cosmos is partly ahistorical, one in which divine or hellish spheres both infuse tendencies into man, the one towards love of God and heaven, the other towards love of self and hell (nos 589–92). This has always been the situation, and man's free choices of one impulse or the other are the eventual and sole determinants of his fate, no deity intervening to save or punish. There is thus no scope for any of the narrative accounts of man's history and destiny as recounted in the Bible – none, that is, so long as those narratives are taken literally. Swedenborg's application of the Bible is to read it in the spiritual and hidden sense (as Blake did after him in *The Marriage of Heaven and Hell*), which derives from his idea of the 'system of correspondences', whereby all phenomena, whether apparently physical objects or literal narratives, are the expression in matter or in art of a spiritual reality. In this he is no Platonist: for him 'matter' is less material than spirit, being the language with which to express its reality. The procedure that results with the Bible may be instanced from Swedenborg's interpretation of the account of the New Jerusalem in Revelation 21.1, 2, 16–19, 21 which portrays the four-square city descending from God, and specifies its measurements and the precious stones that make up its walls, buildings, streets and gates:

Any one who reads these words understands them merely according
to the sense of the letter, according to which the visible heaven
and earth are to perish, a new heaven is to exist, and the holy city
Jerusalem with all its dimensions as here described is to descend
upon a new earth. But the angels present with man understand
these things quite differently, for they understand spiritually what
man understands naturally. By the new heaven and new earth
they understand a new Church. By the city Jerusalem coming down
from God out of heaven, they understand its heavenly doctrine
revealed by the Lord. By its length, breadth and height which are
equal and each twelve thousand furlongs, they understand all
the various forms of good and truth contained in that doctrine
taken collectively. By the wall of the city they understand the
truths which protect it. By the measure of the wall, a hundred and
forty-four cubits, the measure of a man, that is, of the angel, they
understand the nature and quality of all those protecting truths
taken collectively. By its twelve gates of pearl they understand
introductory truths, for pearls signify such truths. By the foundations
of the wall, which were of precious stones, they understand the
kind of knowledge on which the doctrine is founded. By gold
like unto clear glass, of which the city and its street consisted,
they understand the good of love, which imparts clearness to
doctrine and its truths. Angels perceive all these things in this
way and not as men perceive them. The natural ideas of man pass
into spiritual ideas with angels, without their knowing anything
of the sense of the letter of the Word; for the angels know nothing
of a new heaven and a new earth, a new city of Jerusalem, its
wall, the foundations of the wall and the measures.   (No. 307).[6]

To repeat, these 'spiritual ideas' into which the angels translate
biblical narrative are no mere abstractions, but far more solid than
the apparently 'concrete' world which we with our lack of spiritual
sight give so much credit. 'That . . . immense power is inherent in
Divine Truth cannot be realised by those who think of truth merely
as thought or speech in which there is no inherent power except so
far as it commands obedience in others' (no. 138; see also nos 78–86
on the humanly supposed invisibility and formlessness of God).
But, while not at all reducing the Bible to mere concepts, Swedenborg's
treatment of it does evacuate locality and history from it. For our
purposes, however, the mere fact that biblical narrative is so reduced
and translated is a very significant event in the development of

Christian fantasy. To some extent it may be said that Swedenborg's treatment of the Bible fits in with his age, in which the supernatural aspects of Scripture tended to be downplayed for a more 'rational' and conduct-oriented faith; but Swedenborg's reasons for his approach can be seen to be quite the reverse, for it is his object to heighten the 'supernatural' element, to reawaken man to the afterlife of heaven and hell to which he is directed.

In thus rationalising and ordering the scheme of heaven, making it both attractive, more accessible and less sheerly 'other' to ordinary men; in testifying to a world of bliss which required neither the burden of faith nor subjection to a series of misconstrued myths; in assuring people that they would 'go on' as they are rather than be radically changed or judged; in making humanity solely responsible for the choice of heaven or hell; and in offering to the world a new church created in the heavens: in all these things Swedenborg – or God working through Swedenborg – may be seen to be as 'anthropocentric' in tendency as he has recently been portrayed as being.[7] Yet at the same time Swedenborg's heaven is still highly theocentric: the 'Divine Sphere' of the Lord constitutes heaven and the angels, who will nothing by themselves but act by direct infusion from God (nos 7, 8, 101, 143–7); in a sense it is fair to say that, beyond the intermediate state, angels, and perhaps even devils, become part of God. Further, while Swedenborg portrays the Christian behaviour required of us in basic terms of selflessness, and while in one section he tells us that 'The life which leads to heaven is not so difficult as some believe' (nos 528–35), still he insists that such selflessness be directed at and imbued by, love of the divine: 'It is heaven to know God and to be led by Him; for the first requirement of every religion is to acknowledge Him . . . . he who lives a moral life for the sake of the Divine Being is led by Him; but he who lives a moral life for the sake of men in the world is led by himself' (no. 319). And, while Swedenborg brings to us all the reality of heaven, he tells us that, unless our spiritual eyes are opened to the divine basis of reality, we cannot understand or apprehend the full nature of what he is describing: things in the spiritual world may be seen by man only 'when he is withdrawn from the sight of the body and the eyes of his spirit are opened, as can be effected instantly when it pleases the Lord that man should see spiritual things' (no. 76). Swedenborg thus presents something of a transitional figure, at once giving us a heaven and hell tailored to ordinary – and even heathen – humanity, and insisting on a

transcendent deity, an absolute supernatural figure commanding
our love and self-rejection for Him, a figure later portrayed by Blake
as Nobodaddy.

In many ways Swedenborg and his work are a meeting-place of
opposites. If God chose him as His recorder, He chose an empiricist
and an experimental scientist to relay precisely those things that are
not material or subject to experimental investigation. And yet
Swedenborg's meticulous and systematic approach serves to make
that vision more accessible and credible than it might otherwise
have been: introducing the Everyman edition of *Heaven and Hell*
J. Howard Spalding is led to ask, 'Is it possible that hallucination
could give rise to a system so complete and harmonious?'[8] In
Heaven and Hell we have an eighteenth-century built and ordered
structure in both the book and the worlds it describes, combined
with a 'Romantic' organicism whereby heaven is seen to exist in the
human form. We also have, as seen, a situation in which Swedenborg
sets out to show us quite plainly the nature of heaven and hell
while at the same time telling us we can only understand their
nature when our inner or spiritual eyes are opened. In the same
way he tells us that in heaven we shall retain our senses and
personalities, that heaven is a perfect continuation of our lives, and
yet at the same time insists that because of our involvement with
this world we can have no idea of how we shall feel in heaven. Or
in another mode, Swedenborg can tell man that his self will continue
in heaven, but that the only way to get there is to do without self.

In part these dualities in Swedenborg come from his being a
'transition', but in part also they stem from his vision of the universe
as a continuous warfare of contraries, heaven and hell. The dialectic
that is only latent in Milton is here explicit.[9] No longer is the ultimate
aim of Christian history the overthrow of hell, but hell is necessary
to universal equilibrium, and God is the Lord of both heaven and
hell. Swedenborg cannot conceive of a self-existent phenomenon or
state: 'In order that anything may exist, there must be a universal
state of equilibrium' (no. 589). His scientific mind transposes to the
spiritual realm the Newtonian law that for every action there must
be a reaction. 'Thus spiritual equilibrium or freedom, exists and
subsists between good acting on the one part, and evil re-acting on
the other; or between evil acting on one part and good re-acting on
the other' (no. 589).[10] It is this of course that adds to his attractiveness
for Blake.

Yet for all that hell is the essential opposite in Swedenborg's cosmos he gives it, as seen, scant attention. In this he is quite different from Dante and Milton, both of whom start with hell. It may be as we said that Swedenborg gave hell so little space to emphasise its meanness. But, for all his own idea of equilibrium, he is also, it would seem, registering the gradual decline in hell's theological significance. Hell figured more prominently in the seventeenth century; now it is heaven's turn, stimulated by contemporary optimism, the new interest in utopian fiction, and the millenarianism which reached its apotheosis with the apparent Christian promise of the French Revolution.[11] Thereafter, via 'Broad Church' liberalism and the growing dominance of science, the role of hell in theology steadily shrinks.[12] Nevertheless a continual strain of utopianism in the nineteenth century, together with the impulse of Romantic *Sehnsucht*, or spiritual yearning, helps to give heaven and innocence a far larger place in human thought and in literature than they have previously enjoyed. Christian fantasy from now on is far more full of states of holy joy, beauty and innocence than of pain, loss and damnation. And it is fair to say that in some sense Swedenborg stands at the beginning of this tradition.

So far our account of him might suggest that Swedenborg was 'simply' a privileged describer of the various afterworlds. But that was not all. His works are not only revelations of the spirit world, but also acts in this one. God, he said, had told him that the new heaven and earth promised in Revelation, and the Second Coming of the Messiah, would be accomplished precisely in the publication of his writings about heavenly things, and in the body of those of his readers whose internal eyes were opened to what they meant. In Swedenborg's view the old form of the Church was dead in the midst of the spiritual rottenness of the eighteenth century. Because of this death of the spirit which is the only true reality, the Last Judgement of the corrupt has taken place in the spiritual world (in 1757) and Swedenborg has witnessed it. He stands at the beginning of a new order, the restoration of a free spirit, its sole earthly herald:

It was granted me to see from the beginning to the end how the Last Judgment was accomplished; how Babylon was destroyed; how those understood by the dragon were cast into the abyss; and how the new heaven was formed and a New Church was instituted in the heavens, which is understood by the New Jerusalem. It was granted me to see all these things with my own eyes, in order that I might be able to testify of them. This Last

Judgment was commenced at the beginning of the year 1757 and
was fully accomplished at the end of that year . . . .

(The Last Judgment, no. 45)

This picture of active judgement of the evil is strangely at variance
with the account in *Heaven and Hell* of how human spirits choose
rather than are condemned to hell – strangely, given that both works
are said to come from a similar supernatural source. At any rate,
three of Swedenborg's works written in 1757 (and published in
1758) – *The Last Judgment, Heaven and Hell* and *The New Jerusalem and
its Heavenly Doctrines* – assume a special significance, particularly
Heaven and Hell, of which Swedenborg says,

> Members of the church at this day know scarcely anything of
> heaven or hell or of their life after death, although these things
> are all described in the Word . . . . Lest, therefore, such a spirit of
> denial as prevails especially among those who have much worldly
> wisdom, should also infect and corrupt the simple in heart and
> the simple in faith, it has been granted me to associate with
> angels and to talk with them as one man with another; and also
> to see what exists in the heavens and in the hells; and this for
> thirteen years; and to describe them from the evidence of my
> own eyes and ears in the hope that ignorance may be enlightened,
> and unbelief dispelled. Such direct revelation is now made, because
> this is what is meant by the coming of the Lord.
>
> (No. 1)

This is to say that, for those who can see, the Second Coming promised
in Revelation is accomplished in the publication of Swedenborg's
book *Heaven and Hell*. This seems like a megalomaniac's claim, and
questions as to Swedenborg's being deluded, or why he alone was
the chosen of the Lord, naturally occur. But of course it is precisely
because they occur naturally, and from worldly ignorance, that
they are to be mistaken – just as their wonder at Swedenborg's
powers of foreknowledge arise from lack of spiritual insight. But
the main point for us here is that Swedenborg has made his work
doubly supernatural: supernatural both in its inspiration and in the
divine event it accomplishes. He has, as it were, demythologised it
at both ends, its inception and its effect: it is neither to be seen as
mere invention, nor to be apprehended as words alone. The words
are magical, signatures both of continuing divine realities and of
immediate heavenly acts. The 'fantastic' worlds he describes in

Heaven and Hell are in his view precisely not fantastic nor fictive, but literal, and literal still more in that, as they describe heaven and hell, those places are actually brought into being: the Second Coming of the Lord, and the new heaven and earth, are achieved in the published words of this book. Of no writer of Christian fantasy that we have considered or are to consider could this be said: all their fantastic worlds are to some extent invented, to some extent fictive. Dante may in part be divinely led, but his earthly imagination also has its part; his Hell, Purgatory and Heaven may often be traditional, but he has also invented much about them, and to some extent asks us to 'suspend our disbelief' as we read.

But then Dante, like other Christian fantasists, speaks through images, using the materials of this world to try to shadow another. Swedenborg has no room for imagery or for the imagination. These words are given to him, and they are literally true while at the same time having to be understood in a spiritual mode. The fictions in the Bible are unfortunate as stories, because they have been taken at face value instead of being read spiritually. Nor is there scope for saying that this mortal world is but an image or shadow of the immortal one: in heaven we shall not be different in form and attributes, but exactly the same, so that the whole notion of 'imagery' is out of court. All phenomena are ideas in material form, a spiritual language uttered by God, to read which precisely requires only the awakening of our internal sight. This denial of a role for the imagination makes Swedenborg stand out from other Christian fantasists. It may have made him, scientist as he was, a uniquely appropriate choice for the deity to mediate His vision of an exact heaven. On the other hand, if Swedenborg was deluded as to his inspiration, then his work does, as said earlier, become a work of the imagination despite all – indeed much more fantastic and illusory a picture of the truth than any other that we have seen so far in this book. Certainly it has to be remarked that Christian fantasy from the eighteenth century onwards is founded on much more invented, imagined and fictive worlds than before: Dante and Milton in part mean their universes 'for real', but George MacDonald or C. S. Lewis know that their Fairy Lands or Narnias are only broken images of the Real. In such a context Swedenborg might seem an anomaly. And, though while reading him one may be very tempted to take him at face value, there is of course always the nagging question. It is somehow typical of Swedenborg to be the junction of such opposed promptings.

11

Blake: 'The Little Black Boy' and *The Marriage of Heaven and Hell*

For Blake, 'all deities reside in the human breast'. No vision of God or Christ or heaven is the very truth: it is at best both true and not true, a product of the imagination which, rooted in God, give promise of the final reality of our fictions. Thus the Bible is not to be taken literally, though it may be seen as a more sublime product of the imagination than any other created work: Blake thus adapts it for his purposes in *Jerusalem*. What we have in Blake is both gain and loss. Certainty is removed, particularly the certainty of truth being solely present in scriptural imagery. Yet at the same time all things may now figure God and His ways, and any image or story subsume the doings of the divine. After Blake and the Romantics we rarely find any Christian fantasy that is strongly dependent on the Bible.

Of the two works we shall be considering here, 'The Little Black Boy', one of the *Songs of Innocence* of 1789, could be said to be a critique of the use of Christian fable; while the longer *The Marriage of Heaven and Hell* (c.1790) involves a rewriting of Christianity itself. 'The Little Black Boy' portrays the use by a mother of a fantastic picture to calm the rebellious questioning of her child; *The Marriage* on the other hand, produces a series of fantastic images in support of revolution. More locally, the figure of Swedenborg stands behind both of these poems, in the case of the Song providing the imagery of the sun as divine light and heat,[1] and in, *The Marriage* being used continually, as the antagonist of the infernal vision portrayed.[2] (Blake was a member of the Swedenborgian New Jerusalem Church in London till 1789.)

'The Little Black Boy' begins with the black boy lamenting,

> My mother bore me in the southern wild,
> And I am black, but O! my soul is white;

144

> White as an angel is the English child,
> But I am black, as if bereav'd of light.

His mother takes him on her lap, kisses him, and gives him a picture of God designed to console him . She tells him that, far from being a sign of his being outcast, his black skin is the mark of God's love. God lives in the sun, 'And gives his light, and gives his heat away'. Instead of saying that blackened skin is therefore a mark of God's love, as she might have done, she produces a rather more elaborate story, whereby the black skin becomes a means given to coloured people to enable them to shade themselves from the force of God's love:

> 'And we are put on earth a little space,
> 'That we may learn to bear the beams of love;
> 'And these black bodies and this sunburnt face
> 'Is but a cloud, and like a shady grove.
>
> 'For when our souls have learn'd the heat to bear,
> 'The cloud will vanish; we shall hear his voice,
> 'Saying: "Come out from the grove, my love & care,
> 'And round my golden tent like lambs rejoice." '

As put, the mother's picture of God's relation to His creation is questionable. It is in point of fact mistaken to assert that black provides more protection from the heat than, say, white, which is the colour of the clothing worn by people in desert places. It is also unfortunate to confuse physical heat with spiritual love. There is a small problem in that the mother has just described God's heat as giving 'flowers and trees and beasts and men ... Comfort in morning, joy in the noonday': if this heat is so enjoyable – and we know that for all living things in the tropics it is not, particularly at noonday – why do we have to be taught to *bear* it, and why is the mother telling her son this while sitting beneath a tree 'before the heat of day'? But, more than this, it is simply not true to the facts of experience that we only die when we have learned to bear God's loving heat; or that old black men are spiritually better than young ones. Life defies such neat patterns. And we may also ask whether learning to bear the heat, since the physical level of this is no mere image, is the same as becoming spiritually nearer to or more aware of God. The problem is in conceiving the soul so physically, as a little grain protected by its husk.

After this picture, which the little black boy accepts, he forms certai
conclusions of his own. He turns to address the 'little English boy
envious admiration and fear of whom prompted his initial cry c
desolation. Now, he says, when I am free from my black cloud, an
he from his white one, 'And round the tent of God like lambs w
joy',

> I'll shade him from the heat, till he can bear
> To lean in joy upon our father's knee;
> And then I'll stand and stroke his silver hair,
> And be like him, and he will then love me.

Now, instead of being inferior to the white boy, the black boy wil
be able to help him in heaven. Yet the picture he has formed is a
questionable as his mother's. What is the white boy doing i
heaven if his soul has not yet learned to bear the heat? Do whit
boys, because of their skin, die when they are less prepared fo
God? Yet earlier he said that black let through less heat than white
There are certainly problems here.[3] But it would be a mis-take t
leave them simply as problems. We have to consider the ver
human situation from which they emerge, the black boy sittin
with his mother and crying because he feels left out by life. If w
look at things this way, then clearly the mother's picture of God i
not so much an objective statement as an attempt to provide
consoling myth for her child: that it is self-contradictory onl
heightens its pathos. Her son's readiness to be consoled is also ver
human, as is his need to go even beyond her terms and find himse
still better off in relation to the white boy than her picture migh
have supposed. Touchingly human too is the black boy's stil
reverential 'And then I'll stand and stroke his silver hair', and hi
need still to be loved and accepted by the white boy.

The final element here is, curiously, the first stanza, which is ir
fact in the present tense: 'I am black, as if bereav'd of light'. One
would expect it to be in the past tense, if his mother's story ha
consoled him. But maybe the frailty of the conclusions he draw
from it suggests that in his heart he knows it to be not really the
truth, but only a pleasing picture of life designed to soften hi
pain.[4] In that sense he will eventually return to the sense o
exclusion registered in the first stanza, and that is indicated by it
present tense. The poem will thus be circular.

Blake is not denying the Christian faith in this poem. He is rathe pointing out its limitations where it is used as a fixed image with which to shape experience into an ordered and 'happy' pattern. For Blake this Song of Innocence would be inadequate, for it shows an element of true 'Experience' – here pain – not accepted but denied so that Innocence may survive: such innocence is for him, however piteous, still complacency.[5] Truth is dialectical, and the tigers of wrath must go together with the doves of peace.[6] What this poem conveys is indeed a 'Christian fantasy', a fantastical picture of the truth. For Blake all visions are fantastic; but whereas some, such as those recorded in the Bible, may be said to be inspired, others, such as the present one, are manipulations of reality by man for his own purposes. Either way, however, no one fiction will do.

And that is roughly the position from which Blake starts in *The Marriage of Heaven and Hell*. The opening poem of this work is aggressively dialectical and cyclic, beginning and ending, 'Rintrah roars & shakes his fires in the burden'd air; / Hungry clouds swag on the deep'. It tells of a meek and just man who once kept his course along a perilous path, which over time grew more beautiful; but then 'the villain', who had previously inhabited the paths of ease, drove out the just man to rage in barren climes, and took the perilous paths for himself. The poem is full of shifts: from the 'meek' just man to the same man raging 'in the wilds / Where lions roam', and from the 'vale of death' to the 'perilous path', to the perilous path planted; and from the present tense to the past and back again. We are continually pulled up by the unexpected. We learn that on the perilous path 'Roses are planted where thorns grow' – *grow*, not *grew*.[7] We are told that 'Then the perilous path was planted', which is strange since, whether planted means 'made' or 'sown with flowers', both of these things have already been done. The poem is designed to upset and dislocate our normal categories. Broadly it is saying – 'enacting' would be the better word – that what was once perilous and deathly in the path the just man followed was removed, and this made the path attractive to hypocrites, who find feigning good more attractive than espousing evil, so that the just man was thrown out. But, because of the rage he feels at his expulsion, the just man will return, but now savage and not meek. The poem is both descriptive and prescriptive. In one sense it is a little history of the Christian religion, from the struggles of its early martyrs to what Blake saw as the hypocritical institutionalised religion of his own day, where the truth was shut out and in rags. In another, it is a call for revolution. But in still another sense it is a picture of how things ought to be:

for the driving-out of the just man creates the energy of tension. And in this the poem prefigures the whole work, which, while it prescribes revolution, ultimately prescribes rather the energy necessary for continual revolution. Blake in *The Marriage* is not just asking for the 'reinstatement' of the energies of the imagination in human life: he is asking that both faculties – call them 'reason' and 'imagination' – be energetically in tension with one another. Thus what he is concerned to do is not, for example, to recover the primitive form of faith, or adherence to any image, Christian or otherwise, but to demonstrate the need for a dynamic cosmology, and an imagination which never settles to any one subjective picture or story of life. 'Without Contraries is no progression. Attraction and Repulsion, Reason and Energy, Love and Hate, are necessary to Human existence.' Thus Blake sets about uprooting all categories, moral and spiritual, by turning God into devil and hell to heaven, or by arguing that all the commandments are to be broken. He tells us that, though Milton describes the devil being thrown from heaven, the devil's view of it is 'that the Messiah fell, & formed a heaven of what he stole from the Abyss'. In his poem he gives the devil a voice denied him by other writers. Thus the devil is permitted to overthrow the traditional Christian view of the authority of the soul over the body, or 'good' reason over 'evil' physicality, by offering as contraries that the soul and the body are not divisible, and that 'Energy is the only life, and is from the Body'. We, reading the poem, are ourselves thrown into dynamic tension: tempted to agree simply with the devil because of his rhetorical whip-hand, and yet at the same time seeking to detach ourselves because we know that he is the devil and is therefore bound to invert all things to fit with his image.

After the introductory poem, *The Marriage* begins with appropriately energetic abruptness: 'As a new heaven is begun, and it is now thirty-three years since its advent, the Eternal Hell revives. And lo! Swedenborg is the Angel sitting at the tomb: his writings are the linen clothes folded up.' What Blake means is that Swedenborg's account of the Second Coming, the Last Judgement and the establishment of the New Church and a new equilibrium between heaven and hell – all represented as happening in 1757 – has begotten, by the law of contraries, a revival of hell.[8] Blake uses the coincidental thirty-three years, traditionally the number of years of Christ's life, and in fact his own age at the time, as the gulf between the two visions, in order to confound hell's rise with Christ's ascension after His death (here the reference to the angel sitting at the tomb, and the folded linen clothes, has clear relation to the story in the Gospels). Typically of this poem, where opposition is to be proclaimed as true friendship, Swedenborg is to be both praised and condemned. Here he is seen as having initiated the new revolution, partly by having re-created heaven, but also because, as we are to see further later, the heaven he has described is one of control and order, of reason in charge of the passions – more simply, a heaven of the 'respectable'. Blake's poem is to be a picture of the passions breaking out.'Those who restrain desire, do so because theirs is weak enough to be restrained; and the restrainer or reason usurps its place & governs the unwilling.' Thus many of the 'Proverbs of Hell' concern the breaking of restraints: 'Drive your cart and your plow over the bones of the dead'; 'The road of excess leads to the palace of wisdom'; 'If the fool would persist in his folly he would become wise'; 'Shame is Pride's cloke'; 'The lust of the goat is the bounty of God'; 'What is now proved was once only imagin'd'; 'The cistern contains: the fountain overflows'; 'The tygers of wrath are wiser than the horses of instruction'; 'You never know what is enough unless you know what is more than enough'; 'Damn braces. Bless relaxes'; 'Exuberance is Beauty'; 'Sooner murder an infant in its cradle than nurse unacted desires.'

Yet, even while the poem so lauds the energetic breaking of restraints, it still reminds us that that truth is one uttered by only one pole of the cosmic pair, a pole we have till now called 'hell'. While Blake's object is to sterilise heaven and hell of their moral associations, he still sees them as two principles. Later he is to make this still more plain when he points out how 'one portion of being is the Prolific, the other the Devouring'. These two principles correspond to 'passion' and 'reason', or 'hell' and 'heaven', as we name them. Both are essential to existence: 'the Prolific would cease to be Prolific unless the Devourer, as a sea, received the excess of his delights'. These two principles must remain at war: 'whoever tries to reconcile them seeks to destroy existence'.

The whole poem, in keeping with this vision, must become dialectical. We have seen how it espouses the rhetoric of hell while acknowledging the dialectic of heaven and hell. The poem is there to celebrate the rebirth of hell as the other and antagonistic pole to the rebirth of heaven through Swedenborg. The marriage it describes is to be a marriage-in-divorce, with two repugnant principles locked in contest with one another. All this spills out into the very character of the poem itself. For what are words, if they do not

capture energies and reduce them to formulae? What are these dr
pages we turn while they tell of fire? This very potential for loss c
energy seems to be described within the poem, in the account of th
manner of printing books in hell for the transmission of knowledge

> In the first chamber was a Dragon-Man, clearing away the rubbis
> from a cave's mouth; within, a number of Dragons were hollowin
> the cave.
> In the second chamber was a Viper folding round the rock & th
> cave, and others adorning it with gold, silver and precious stones.
> In the third chamber was an Eagle with wings and feathers o
> air: he caused the inside of the cave to be infinite; around wer
> numbers of Eagle-like men who built palaces in the immense cliffs
> In the fourth chamber were Lions of flaming fire, raging aroun
> & melting the metals into living fluids.
> In the fifth chamber were Unnam'd forms, which cast the metal
> into the expanse.
> There they were reciev'd by Men who occupied the sixth chamber
> and took the forms of books & were arranged in libraries.

Presumably this is an analogue for the creative process itself
welling up from the unconscious: first clearing the lumber, strikin
out with glowing images, and then capturing and casting them
The last stage, necessary though it is, sounds flat and deadening
the rising rhythms of the previous stages here come down to earth
from eagles and unnamed forms to men who inhabit rather tha
belong to the sixth chamber. (But it is also true that men com
at this sixth stage because the process is in addition an analogue o
the six days of creation of the world described in Genesis, on th
last of which man was made.[9]) It may be said that the flatness of th
last statement is deliberate, reminding us of the energies that hav
gone into the books, and suggesting that, if we are to read aright
we must read not simply the end product, the book, but all th
operations going on at the same time, as of course they would in a
printing-house, so that the first stage of clearing out the cave i
contemporary with the last. This is Blake's point when he says tha
he will print 'in the infernal method, by corrosives, which in Hel
are salutary and medicinal, melting apparent surfaces away, an
displaying the infinite which was hid': in other words, he wishes t
use techniques which will drive us beyond the mere printed text t
see the infinity that feeds it. That is not the least reason why h

used the techniques of illuminated printing to supplement this poetry. But there is much that the poetry itself can do, too. For instance, Blake tells us that 'If the doors of perception were cleansed every thing would appear to man as it is, infinite. / For man has clos'd himself up, till he sees all things thro' narrow chinks of his cavern.' Yet in the very next lines, in his picture of infernal printing, he shows it going on in caverns, the very places which have just featured as symbols of myopia. Further, while the doors of perception are to be cleansed, they are still to be doors: even while one is to see beyond the dead type of a book to the energies that went to make it, the book is still essential, for it is the Devourer to the Prolific, and each is necessary to the other's existence. So the stasis of the finished product is as dialectically necessary as the flux of creation; and the conscious expression of the energies is as 'vital' as their inchoate and unconscious state.

Clearly we can extend this point to the poem as a whole. For instance, the 'Proverbs of Hell' may be seen as neat encapsulations of Blake's new truth: 'Joys impregnate. Sorrows bring forth.' Like that, it is a formula, even while it breaks formulae. Blake has chosen to enclose energetic truths in the bonds of aphorisms and definitions. In this way he enacts in miniature the tension portrayed in the poem. More largely, we may notice how much the poem as a whole is set within caves and interiors, even while it recommends the explosion outwards of energy and perception: we walk 'among the fires of hell'; dine, presumably inside, with Ezekiel and Isaiah; enter the hellish printing-house; and descend with the Angel down to an interior void, or with the poet and the Angel into a deep pit full of monkeys. And this is a poem which asks us, 'How do you know but ev'ry Bird that cuts the airy way, / Is an immense world of delight, clos'd by your senses five?'

But Blake has also used techniques within the poem to dislodge us from any complacent certainty. We have seen already how he pulls the rug from beneath us in the opening poem on the just man and the villain. The content of his poem is obviously subversive, evacuating all old moral certainties about God versus devil, or reason versus passion; at once advocating revolution and indicating that all is cycle; recommending energy yet acknowledging the role of restraint; proposing a marriage based in divorce, a friendship existing in opposition. But the poem turns rhetorically upside-down too. In the first place there is the fact that it is a poem which turns to prose, before finally reverting to poetry: it upsets genre. In the second place it mingles energetic vision, of the sort that we see in the opening poem, with direct and explicit discourse: in this way the first five chambers of the printing-house of hell oscillate with the sixth, that which transforms fiery and plastic sense into trapped and assignable discourse. And this constant shifting of the rhetorical mode, from poetry to prophecy to declaration to vision to proverbs, is part of the general displacement process. Further, within the 'Proverbs of Hell', and arguably throughout the poem, the poet repeats himself, telling us twenty times of the worth of the imagination or the energetic passions; and this itself gives a sense that the language cannot fully embody what it seeks to convey. Lastly Blake has used what one might call a technique of reversal. First Swedenborg is praised; later he is blamed. Body and soul are one, and reason is of a piece with energy, being its bound or outer circumference; and yet prolific energy and devouring reason are elsewhere not to be reconciled. Amid the proverbs on the gratification of one's own energies appears 'The most sublime act is to set another before you.' Numbers of the proverbs ask conformity with nature rather than the breaking of bounds: 'Dip him in the river who loves water'; 'The bird a nest, the spider a web, man friendship'; 'Think in the morning. Act in the noon. Eat in the evening. Sleep in the night.' In much of the poem the lion is identified with energy, and a Proverb of Hell says, 'The wrath of the lion is wisdom of God'; yet at the victorious end of the poem the lion is seen rather as a ravening predator: 'EMPIRE IS NO MORE! AND NOW THE LION & WOLF SHALL CEASE.' By these means Blake removes certainties and fixities from his own poem and its vision.[10] Everything is mobile. The energy that is good now may be evil under another mode, in the making of war, for instance. The poem does not describe apocalypse, or finality: it describes one more turning of the cycle.[11]

In a sense what is said is at once true and not true. The Ten Commandments are valid, even while the 'Devil in a flame of fire' convinces an angel that Christ broke them all and that no virtue can exist without doing so too. One of the 'Proverbs of Hell' is 'Everything possible to be believ'd is an image of truth.' In that sense Swedenborg and Milton had an image of the truth, even while the poem rejects their visions. The point is mobility: once freeze the image, and evil results. Yet even this 'statement' is questioned, as is all dogma. There are two episodes in the poem that specifically relate to the creation of biblical imagery: one a discourse with the prophets Isaiah and Ezekiel, and another a conversation with an angel. In the first the prophets are asked, 'how they dared so roundly to assert that God spoke to them'; and Isaiah admits that he spoke not out of actual experience but imaginative discernment, whereby he 'discover'd the infinite in everything', and was sufficiently persuaded by this vision to write as he did. When asked whether a firm persuasion that a thing is so makes it so, the reply is, 'All poets believe that it does, & in ages of imagination this firm perswasion has removed mountains; but many are not capable of a firm perswasion of any thing.' Here the imagination is the source of truth. Here too a vision which has been imposed on others meets with the assent of the poet.

But the opposite seems the case when the poet has a later interview with an angel, who warns him of the doom that is approaching, and on being challenged gives the poet a picture of it:

So he took me thro' a stable & thro' a church & down into the church vault, at the end of which was a mill: thro' the mill we went, and came to a cave: down the winding cavern we groped our tedious way, till a void boundless as a nether sky appear'd beneath us, & we held by the roots of trees and hung over this immensity . . . .

. . . I remain'd with him, sitting in the twisted root of an oak; he was suspended in a fungus, which hung with the head downward into the deep.

By degrees we beheld the infinite Abyss, fiery as the smoke of a burning city; beneath us, at an immense distance, was the sun, black but shining; round it were fiery tracks on which revolv'd vast spiders, crawling after their prey, which flew, or rather swum, in the infinite deep, in the most terrific shapes of animals sprung from corruption; & the air was full of them, & seem'd composed of them: these are Devils, and are called Powers of the air. I now asked my companion which was my eternal lot? he said: 'between the black & white spiders.'

But now, from between the black & white spiders, a cloud and fire burst and rolled thro' the deep, black'ning all beneath, so that the nether deep grew black as a sea, & rolled with a terrible noise; beneath us was nothing now to be seen but a black tempest, till looking east between the clouds & the waves, we saw a cataract of blood mixed with fire, and not many stones' throw from us appear'd and sunk again the scaly fold of a monstrous serpent; at last, to the east, distant about three degrees, appear'd a fiery crest

above the waves; slowly it reared like a ridge of golden rocks, till
we discover'd two globes of crimson fire, from which the sea fled
away in clouds of smoke; and now we saw it was the head of
Leviathan; his forehead was divided into streaks of green & purple
like those on a tyger's forehead: soon we saw his mouth & red
gills hang just above the raging foam, tinging the black deep with
beams of blood, advancing toward us with all the fury of a spiritual
existence.

My friend the Angel climb'd up from his station into the mill: I
remain'd alone; & then this appearance was no more, but I found
myself sitting on a pleasant bank beside a river by moonlight,
hearing a harper, who sung to the harp; & his theme was: 'The
man who never alters his opinion is like standing water, &
breeds reptiles of the mind.'

The last sentence here is the leitmotif of the entire *Marriage*. This
image of the angel's, with its amazingly vivid pictures, is one of the
most original and inventive that Blake ever created, even though it
is a reworking of images from the Book of Revelation. Here in a
sense Blake out-Swedenborgs Swedenborg. And yet this image is
wholly spurned by the poet too. He proceeds to show the angel his
own picture of *his* lot; and it is one of a mass of monkeys living in
buildings below ground, sitting chattering in chains, and from time
to time numerous enough to reach and dismember one another;
amid these creatures is a skeleton which when removed turns out
to be Aristotle's *Analytics*. The angel complains that the poet's
fantasy has imposed itself as him; to which the reply is 'we impose
on one another, & it is but lost time to converse with you whose
works are only Analytics'. In a sense this judgement is correct; but
in another it is inadequate. For, while the angel's image may constitute
an analysis of the soul of the poet, it is a supremely 'synthetic' and
vital image, full of energies. It has not reduced the poet, but magnified
his predicament in huge and dramatic symbols. Further, the angel's
picture is full of movement and colour. The poet's picture of him
seems in this way to do him an injustice, reducing the angel to a
sterile, static and repulsive brute. The angel's image expands and
dilates; that of the poet shrivels and contracts as he descends from
'the void between Saturn the fixed stars' to a church and an altar
and through a Bible to a pit where a monkey is dismembered; and
all in little dried units of syntax. Thus Blake again has it both ways.
The two images play against one another, and neither is valid. And

again, while we know that the angel does 'wrong' in so imposing his view, that view is put through the medium of the creative imagination, the same creative imagination which in Isaiah and Ezekiel made them capable of apprehending truth. And thus again the contraries play against one another, and imagination and judgement circle everlastingly about one another.

In *The Marriage of Heaven and Hell* Blake could be said to have helped to let God out of the Bible and the Church: 'For every thing that lives is Holy.' All Christian writers after him produce their own images of religious truth. It is loss and gain: it permits all men to worship Christ through their images rather than in subjection to His; yet at the same time it takes away certainty and assurance, where we know that the visionary books and Gospels are founded not on objective truth but on subjective pictures of it. Isaiah may claim that firm persuasion that a thing is true may make it true; but, as he at the same time acknowledges, 'many are not capable of a firm perswasion of any thing'.

12

Modern Christian Fantasy

While it may fairly be supposed that God did not as Nietzsche claimed, die in the nineteenth century,[1] it must be admitted that much of the 'mythology' of Christianity, the supernatural stories recounted in the Bible, became increasingly open to question.[2] The textual authority of the Bible had been in dispute long before the nineteenth century: one has only to look at Dryden's *Religio Laici* (1678), for instance, to see that. But the empirical, scientific, investigative side of the late-seventeenth- and eighteenth-century mind had long tended to practise a form of self-silencing when it came to matters of faith. It is only with the Romantics and the new 'mythophiles', with their emphasis on the creative imagination, that we begin to find systematic questioning (such as Blake's) of the visions of the prophets or apostles as subjective rather than literal,[3] or come across a pioneering attempt (J. G. Herder's *Maranatha* of 1779) to view the Book of Revelation as literature rather than a true record.[4] The new German 'liberal' theology of the late eighteenth and early nineteenth-century found its most revolutionary statement in D. F. Strauss's *Leben Jesu* (1835), in which the historical and human dimension of Christ's life began to take on significance at the expense of his divine self and his 'supernatural' actions.[5] But Darwin's theories concerning evolution constituted the greatest blow.[6] Nothing previously had so directly challenged the story of man's beginnings recorded in Genesis. For the first time there was available specific and scientific refutation of biblical narrative. Whereas previous questioning of the Bible had been founded on its textual unreliability or its possible subjectivity, there was now an external criterion of 'truth to fact' by which to assess it. And, if Genesis was open to question, so too might be many of the miraculous events described elsewhere in the Bible. Charles Kingsley, who was both a scientist and a Christian, could say that miracles are natural occurrences, not the result of overt supernatural interference, because they do not violate the true laws of nature, which 'are her invisible ones'.[7] This account is a gross simplification of highly complex and gradual changes; but certainly the Christian religion at the end of

the nineteenth century had less of a firm 'mythological' and supernatural basis than it had had at the outset.

These changes were the consequence not only of unfettered
scientific investigation, of Romantic emphasis on the individual
imagination and of liberal theology, but also of a general shift over
the centuries, through the Renaissance via the Enlightenment to
Romanticism, from a God-centred to a much more man-oriented
Christian view of the universe. This began with the destruction of
the old Ptolemaic cosmos of concentric spheres for one of infinite
numbers of stars scattered irregularly over a vast abyss: as a result
God and heaven, previously 'joined' to creation through lying in
the Empyrean beyond the ninth and last sphere, became physically
separated from it. The theology of the eighteenth century is largely
'transcendentalist' in its view of God: He heads the chain of being
scattered through all worlds, but lies at an infinite remove from us.
The eighteenth century, satirical and melancholy though it variously
was in outlook, made man the measure of things. And so, in a
different way, did Wordsworth in *The Prelude*: his imagination and
his growth are the register of nature's workings. With the Romantics
the opposite mode of making man central is found: now, instead of
'leaving' the world to man, God comes down to him democratically,
becomes humanised, immanent.[8] One can see the result in Victorian
accounts of heaven, where heaven's 'otherness' is lost for a conception
of it as continuing and refining human joys on earth – pastoral,
sexual, familial; heaven becomes a mode of utopia rather than a
place where we may meet the 'wholly other':

> What Romantic poets, Christian clergy, and pious writers all held
> in common was the belief that the eternal in the human character
> would be the substance of heavenly existence. While some notion
> of the divine might be present, the main purpose of heaven was
> to cultivate human love.... The weak barrier between heaven
> and earth permitted both the imagination of a heaven which was
> a perfected earth, and the hope that earth would imitate heavenly
> conditions.[9]

The theocentric side of Christianity, represented by such figures as
Kant, Jakob Fries, Schleiermacher, Kierkegaard, Rudolf Otto and
Karl Barth, became steadily more embattled and attenuated throughout
this period.[10] The nineteenth-century stress on God's immanence
was furthered by the emotionalising and humanising of theological

matters, as seen in F. D. Maurice and the Broad Church. Perhaps what most conditioned this sense of divine immanence was the need to give spiritual meaning to a world which might otherwise be seen in, at best, coldly scientific terms, and become nothing to man: this is the dilemma as Carlyle and Tennyson see it, and both resort to a form of 'immanentism'.[11] Where previously, in more religiously 'certain' centuries, this world was felt to be inadequate to God, now there is a real risk that God will be found inadequate to the world.

The effects of all this demythologising and desupernaturalising on Christian fantasy are stark. In the first place it ceases to be written by the dominant literary figures: it is now the product of minor, and often eccentric writers. Whatever else we say, George MacDonald, Charles Kingsley, Charles Williams and C. S. Lewis are simply not of the same order as Wordsworth, Coleridge, Tennyson, Arnold, Dickens, George Eliot, Hardy, Joyce, T. S. Eliot, Virginia Woolf, D. H. Lawrence and George Bernard Shaw.

In the second place the context for the writing of Christian fantasy is steadily narrowed. In the nineteenth century the vast bulk of Christian literature takes the form of 'real life' portrayals of the Christian life in this world – conversion, trial, charity, ministry, and so forth. This is furthered by a fastidious dislike of the use of non-Christian mythological or fantastic materials for sacred ends.[12] As we saw with Blake, one of the consequences of Romanticism was that it liberated the imagination to find all forms of discourse as potential images of the Real; and yet this was a freedom which frightened orthodoxy could not admit, lest belief be polluted or diverted by the often 'pagan' or secular materials used in its furtherance. In the twentieth century the standing of the Christian faith is no longer the central concern of intellectuals: Christianity itself, as a whole, becomes displaced and few writers evince any strong Christian leanings – T. S. Eliot in his later years; W. H. Auden, Evelyn Waugh and Graham Greene in some of their work; Flannery O'Connor and Georges Bernanos more generally. In place of Christian literature we have literature which has a 'religious' dimension in that it asks the ultimate questions, whatever answer it brings – the work of Dostoevsky, Kafka, Camus, Beckett, Bellow, Pynchon.[13]

The third effect is seen in the nature of the Christian fantasy that is written in this period. Most of it in some way celebrates 'this' world, even if 'this world' means the unconscious level of the human mind, as in the work of MacDonald, or the wider universe, as in C. S. Lewis and his followers. In earlier Christian fantasy there was much more distinction between the created world and heaven, even while the one was irretrievably dependent on the other: heaven was a place that demanded rejection of all earthly behaviour as in the *Queste* or *Pearl* or *The Pilgrim's Progress*. In such fantasy the Christian had often to journey out of the world to meet God. But now, at a time when there is an increasing feeling that the world has no connection at all with a Christian God or a heaven, modern Christian fantasy tries to put divine presence into the universe. This modern fantasy is much more determinedly 'immanentist': it finds God in nature or in certain images, whether the 'image of the city' or of 'the body' as Charles Williams conceives them, or in spiritual desire or *Sehnsucht*, as it is seen in the writings of C. S. Lewis, or in the unconscious mind as in MacDonald, or in nature itself, as in Kingsley. It takes particular pleasure in divine creativity. The Fairy Land in MacDonald's *Phantastes* is a place of extraordinary richness and plenitude; Kingsley's *The Water-Babies* celebrates all the variety of the God-created natural realm; Charles Williams' fiction portrays the complex 'pattern of the glory' in the everyday world; in the fantasies of C. S. Lewis we are invited to delight in the invented worlds of his Mars, Venus or Narnia as expressions of divine creative power, all playing their part in a great cosmic dance of being. By thus praising God's power as a maker, and portraying it through their own invented worlds, each of these writers implicitly begs the question of the status of his own fantasy: if it can portray divine creativity, then does it not take part in it itself – may each fantasy not thereby be founded on truth? Certainly, as we shall see, this issue is made explicit by George MacDonald.

Further, post-Romantic Christian fantasy is contemplative in aim. Through its narratives it always seeks to portray a state of being. For MacDonald the fairy tale exists to excite awe and wonder. Kingsley tries in *The Water-Babies* to show the 'miraculous and divine element underlying all physical nature'.[14] In the narratives of his novels and poems Williams describes how 'The pattern of the glory is a pattern of acts.'[15] Lewis tells us that fantastic stories are 'only a net for catching what is not really a process at all'.[16] Most of these fantasies follow a process of deepening insight until the divine is perceived or intuited. This concern with contemplation of the divine as it is manifested in the universe distinguishes nineteenth- and twentieth-century fantasy from that written since Dante. In *Pearl*, *Everyman*, *The Faerie Queene*, *Dr Faustus*, the works of the 'Christian metaphysicals',

Paradise Lost, The Pilgrim's Progress and even Swedenborg's *Heaven and Hell* the concern is largely with *behaviour* in a Christian super-natural context. If heaven or the divine is considered, it is more as a goal towards which the spirit draws itself and is drawn through improvement. But now, while spiritual development is also important, it is there as much to display the workings of God as to evoke imitation by man. Indeed that side of Christian fantasy has gone largely into the novel of Christian experience – such works as those by Charlotte Yonge, W. H. Mallock or Mrs Humphry Ward. Where previous Christian fantasy subsumed such moral development, now it has made a genre of its own, concerned with non-supernatural contexts which are felt to be more like 'real life'.[17]

In modern Christian fantasy we do not, as often previously, find the Bible or biblical narrative used directly. MacDonald tells a story about a young man who finds his way into Fairy Land and encounters a 'white lady' he thereafter pursues, or a tale of a princess in a castle besieged by goblins, and lets us experience the Christian significance by intuition rather than through recognisable stories. By comparing features of his *Phantastes* with his *Lilith*, we might be able to say that in some sense *Phantastes* deals with the First Things, and *Lilith* with the Last; but still this pattern bears only analogical relation to the contrast between, say, Genesis and the Gospels on the one hand, and Revelation on the other. What is happening is that MacDonald is using 'mythology' apart from that in the Bible to convey Christian truth. The idea is a post-Romantic one: God is not only in the Bible, but in every work born of the creative imagination. But the effect is that, while His 'set text' is abandoned and to that extent His presence is made less identifiable, He may now be uttered by all the texts of the world if they are aligned aright: that is, if they are 'supernaturalist' fantasies; and in this sense His potential presence in the world is extended. Effectively, though not intentionally, such an approach can give rise to a range of new, if fictive, mythologies for God's purposes, even while the sanctioned mythology in the Bible is being questioned and eventually dispelled.[18]

And one should stress the word 'fictive'; for another difference with older fantasies is that now, without the sanction of a believed primary text underlying and informing the story, the fantastic work often loses direct access to 'truth'. What Spenser portrays in the first book of *The Faerie Queene* does ultimately partake in the apocalypse-as-truth described in the Book of Revelation. But, when C. S. Lewis depicts an unfallen lady and lord on an imagined Venus, that story is not to be seen as a reworking of Genesis. Of course, there is still reference to the Bible in modern Christian fantasies; but they are less immediately oriented towards it. When they invent, they invent for the love of ultimately divine creativity as much as for any overtly referential purpose. Lewis declared that those who thought he started with a Christian purpose and then found a story to fit it were quite mistaken: 'Everything began with images; a faun carrying an umbrella, a queen on a sledge, a magnificent lion. At first there wasn't even anything Christian about them; that element pushed itself in of its own accord.'[19]

With such freedom of invention, the theme of the danger of the human imagination ceases to be the central one for Christian fantasy as we have traced it so far. Indeed, the more energetically the imagination is deployed, the more it may display the things of God. For a further feature of modern Christian fantasy is the struggle against the desupernaturalising of this world that is increasingly occurring; and here the energetic operation of the imagination becomes an instrument of revelation. MacDonald says, 'We are dwellers in a divine universe', to see which 'a wise imagination, which is the presence of the spirit of God, is the best guide'.[20] Kingsley's aim in *The Water-Babies* is to show that the universe is not a mere machine run on scientific principles alone, but that the operation of every law and the existence of every phenomenon is sustained by the immediate action of God. Charles Williams in his novels shows the ordinary world being transformed as its roots are revealed to lie in divine realities – such as the 'cosmic dance' in *The Greater Trumps* (1932):

> Imagine that everything which exists takes part in the movement of a great dance – everything, the electrons, all growing and decaying things, all that seems alive and all that doesn't seem alive, men and beasts, trees and stones, everything that changes, and there is nothing anywhere that does not change .... Imagine it – imagine it, see it all at once and in one![21]

And C. S. Lewis 'sets out' to enrich our view of reality by giving us a Narnia we might reach through a wardrobe or a picture; or a revitalised picture of an earth closely besieged by hell, with a heaven that awaits those who heed the messages it sends and has sent to the world; or a universe which, rather than the dead thing of mere matter and force to which science would reduce it, is fuller of being even in its void places than anything we know on earth. On a spaceship returning to earth one of his protagonists 'could not feel that they were an island of life journeying through an abyss of death. He felt almost the opposite – that life was waiting outside the little eggshell in which they rode, ready to break in, and that, if it killed them, it would kill them by excess of its vitality.'[22] And all these worlds are divinely based. In a sense these Christian fantasists partake in the larger Romantic desire to reanimate a dead universe, as we see it in Wordsworth or Coleridge; or in D. H. Lawrence's 'How ... are we to get back the grand orbs of the soul's heavens, that fill us with unspeakable joy?';[23] or in Tolkien's search through creative fantasy for the 'Recovery' of a fresh view of the universe in place of the boredom produced through our over-familiarity with it.[24] But in Christian fantasy the vision is to be re-established not simply for the health of our souls, but because it is the truth about our world, as these writers see it.

Finally here, what is 'Christian' and what is 'fantasy' in modern Christian fantasy? Fantasy, or 'romance' as it was often known in the nineteenth century, is a relatively new genre. Hitherto we have of course used the term 'Christian fantasy' categorically, rather than as descriptive of a genre: the works it covers have much in common with fantasy as we know it now, but each of these works is relatively isolated as a creation, and without many of the aims that we see in fantasy now. And, even while there are many similarities among modern writers of fantasy, all of whom are partaking in the Romantic licence to create new mythologies, they are not usually conscious of writing in a genre. The term 'fantasy' as we know it has to be applied retrospectively to them as, looking back, we see how their work fed into the current of literature that suddenly in the 1960s found itself a name. The name itself is perhaps more appropriately applied to works of the last two centuries in the sense that they have become more fictive, more inventive of 'other' worlds, more 'fantastic' in this sense. It is one of the seeming paradoxes of literary history that fantasy should have come into its own just when the old 'supernaturalist' view of the universe was decaying, but, if we see this as a defensive reaction, then the oddity is less.

So far as 'Christian' is concerned in relation to these works, this has to be used as variously as with those we have considered earlier. The nature of Christ Himself is far more central in Charles Williams' work than in Charles Kingsley's. There is more emphasis on Christian conduct in George MacDonald's *Phantastes* than in C. S. Lewis's

Out of the Silent Planet – though we could put it the other way round with Lewis's *The Pilgrim's Regress* and MacDonald's 'The Golden Key'. In MacDonald's work, God is found in the unconscious mind, in 'inner space'; in Kingsley's, at the root of nature; in C. S. Lewis's, in 'outer space'. So, when we say that they are all Christian, the common denominator is finally the particular sense of the numinous in the story. We are dealing now with Christian fantasies which are so not only by virtue of patterns of Christian belief and narrative in them, but also through the inculcation of a feeling, an attempt to make us thrill imaginatively to a divine reality both near and far, both with us and other. This is what we may call 'Romantic religion'.[25] It is quite new. Now it actively *invokes* our imagination, where earlier Christian fantasy questioned or confined it. 'If there be music in my reader, I would gladly wake it. Let fairytale of mine go for a firefly that now flashes, now is dark, but may flash again.'[26]

13

George MacDonald's Fairy Tales

What we shall see with MacDonald and Kingsley is something quite new in the development of Christian fantasy. We shall find both trying by literary means to show, to make us feel, that God is present in nature and this world. In earlier literature God's existence could be assumed, but now it is necessary to prove it. And, in order to do this convincingly, one must start from the apparently empirical facts of existence, not from any biblical or quasi-biblical narrative involving *a priori* assumptions. Thus each presents us with an image of the baffling character of experience, through which God or the miraculous must be apprehended. This holds good even though the reality that MacDonald presents is that of the inner world of the mind, and Kingsley's that of the physical world. The tangle of mental imagery and potential error in MacDonald's fantastic worlds is no different in terms of mundane reality from the confusing nature of the physical world in Kingsley's. Between them the two could be said to cover the whole area of mundane experience, inner and outer, in order to trace God's immanence. It is remarkable that the only Christian-fantasy writers of note in the nineteenth century should form this diptych.

Like Wordsworth, MacDonald felt the presence of God in nature, particularly among mountains, but for him this vision was only possible via the God-imbued soul. A farmer living in Fairy Land in his *Phantastes* (1858) is too much of an empiricist to believe that the country about him has any more than agricultural purpose. In *The Princess and Curdie* (1883) there is a mystic old lady who in the mines beneath her castle appears to the hero Curdie as a beautiful woman; and she tells him that her aspect to him is quite different from the one that an evil person would see: 'For instance, if a thief were to come in here just now, he would think he saw the demon of the mine, all in green flames, come to protect her treasure, and would run like a hunted wild goat. I should be all the same, but his evil eyes would see me as I was not.' When he asks her why she does not appear to him as the old lady he met in the castle the previous night, she replies, 'Shapes are only dresses, Curdie, and dresses are only names. That which is inside is the same all the time.'[1] This does not make all perception solipsistic. There is a right way of seeing, based on insight. In this sense all experience is figurative, a network of imagery through which to apprehend truth. And that truth is the more readily available to those who are in touch with the deepest impulses of the spirit, and with that which dwells in it.

For MacDonald's 'answer' to some of the issues raised by Blake was to put God into the imagination. 'God sits in that chamber of our being in which the candle of our consciousness goes out in darkness, and sends forth from thence wonderful gifts into the light of that understanding which is His candle.'[2] In a sense Blake had already put God in the imagination himself, but he conceived of the imagination as a medium in which both God and man existed together. He put the imagination first, before God: 'Imagination is eternity'; 'I know of no other Christianity and of no other Gospel than the liberty both of body & mind to exercise the Divine Arts of Imagination.'[3] MacDonald believed in an 'objective' God of the Bible and the Gospels, with whom he hoped to meet in heaven after death. This God therefore honours the imagination by His presence in it. MacDonald is at pains to remove the limitations of subjectivity from such an imagination, however fallen: 'If we ... consider the so-called creative faculty in man, we shall find that in no *primary* sense is this faculty creative. Indeed, a man is rather *being thought* than *thinking*, when a new thought arises in his mind.'[4]

The problem of determining objectivity from a God located in that faculty most commonly assumed to be the source of delusive dreams and self-begotten fantasies was of course acute. At the end of MacDonald's fantasy *Lilith* (1895), the protagonist Vane has to be reassured that his experiences in the 'region of the seven dimensions' are not mere dreams:

> In moments of doubt I cry,
> 'Could God himself create such lovely things as I dreamed?'
> 'Whence then came thy dream?' answers Hope.
> 'Out of my dark self, into the light of my consciousness.'
> 'But whence first into thy dark self?' rejoins Hope.
> 'My brain was its mother, and the fever in my blood its father.'
> 'Say rather,' suggests Hope, 'thy brain was the violin whence it issued, and the fever in thy blood the bow that drew it forth. –

But who made the violin? and who guided the bow across its strings? Say rather, again – who set the song birds each on its bough in the tree of life, and startled each in its order from its perch? Whence came the fantasia? and whence the life that danced thereto? Didst *thou* say, in the dark of thy own unconscious self, "Let beauty be; let truth seem!" and straightway beauty was, and truth but seemed?'

Man dreams and desires; God broods and wills and quickens.

When a man dreams his own dream, he is the sport of his dream; when Another gives it him, that Other is able to fulfil it.

This hardly qualifies as an ontological proof: for one metaphor of the mind's workings is substituted another which permits the inference to a Designer. MacDonald generally prefers faith and the intuitions of the heart to arguments, but at a key moment such as this he is prepared to make use of any means to hand. The dangers are obvious. As MacDonald elsewhere put it, 'If the dark portion of our own being were the origin of our imaginations, we might well fear the apparition of such monsters as would be generated in the sickness of a decay which could never feel – only declare – a slow return towards primeval chaos. But the Maker is our Light.'[5]

The object of MacDonald's fantasy is to express the inner world of the imagination, and in so doing to make available, to those spiritually open to it, something of a sense of the immanent God. Thus his fantasy takes on the character of the creative unconscious itself – mysterious, imbued with archetypal images, dream-like in its transitions from one item to another.[6] MacDonald always particularly delighted to quote Novalis: 'Our life is no dream but it should and perhaps will become one.'[7] He found in the fairy tale, particularly its German Romantic variety, the form that most suited his vision, and again quoted Novalis at the head of *Phantastes* to describe it: 'A fairy-tale is like a dream-picture without coherence, a collection of wonderful things and occurrences, e.g. a musical fantasy, the harmonic sequences of an Aeolian harp, nature itself.'[8] He wrote essays on the 'divine' imagination and on the fantastic imagination that makes the fairy tale. What we find then expressing his vision is nothing overtly Christian, but rather the imagery of the Romantic *Märchen*.

It is characteristic too of MacDonald's beliefs that the faërian forms through which the divine imagination expresses itself should themselves vary, just as shapes and dresses do. In his view, a fairy tale, never wakens the same thought in all its readers, or even a single impression in any one reader: it is continually mobile and shifting in its effects, and so too should its forms be multiple.[9] Thus there are two works of particularly dream-like structure, *Phantastes* (1858) and *Lilith* (1895), written at either end of MacDonald's creative life; and in between the 'children's' fairy tales – though MacDonald always wrote for the child-like imagination – *At the Back of the North Wind* (1871), *The Princess and the Goblin* (1872) and *The Princess and Curdie* (1883). The first of these differs from the rest in being set in Victorian London, where the North Wind from time to time visits and takes on her travels a cabman's son, Diamond; the other books are set in fairy lands, with kings, princesses and castles. Last, there is a whole range of shorter fairy tales, from the comic to the mystical. For MacDonald most of these would be different forms of the same fairy tale.

In both *Phantastes* and *Lilith* the protagonist enters a magic land by seeming accident, and undergoes a number of adventures of often uncertain significance, before attaining some spiritual growth. There is perhaps rather more direction in *Lilith*, where we know that Vane's ultimate duty will be to lie down with a sleeping multitude in a strange house of the dead in the 'region of the seven dimensions', a need beside which his other adventures are seen as a kind of truancy. In *Phantastes* the hero, Anodos, for long wanders without any aim, and only in the later stages of the narrative does he develop a certain purpose in seeking a 'white lady', who continually eludes him. Each of these stories is filled with mysterious images and significances. For instance, in *Phantastes* we have a devouring ash-tree, the white lady, a fairy palace with strange radiating halls filled with dancers, a remote planet where love is both passionate and hopeless, an old woman in a submersible cottage with four mystic doors, and a sinister church in a forest. In *Lilith* there is the figure of the strange librarian Mr Raven, a magic mirror which is the way to the region of the seven dimensions, the house of the dead, the evil but beautiful Lilith herself, a 'Bad Burrow' of hideous monsters, a mystic lady called Mara, and, at the end, a vision of the New Jerusalem (a Dantean and Bunyanesque modification of the biblical account).

The longer 'children's' fairy tales tend to focus the mystery on one particular personage, place or event rather than on many; and they tell fairly clear stories which involve direction and narrative suspense. In *At the Back of the North Wind* there are perhaps two conjoined plots – Diamond's adventures with North Wind and his

life as a poor cabman's son in London – the one informing and
sustaining the other. In *The Princess and the Goblin* the safety of the
Princess Irene is threatened by a nation of goblins who live in the
mines beneath her castle; and she is saved from them, both through
her faith in a mysterious lady of magic powers, her 'great-great-
grandmother', whom she finds living in a remote room at the top of
the house; and through the practical efforts of the miner's son Curdie,
which bring about the destruction of the goblins. *The Princess and
Curdie* continues this narrative, with Irene and her father now at the
royal city of Gwyntystorm, where the old king, now sick, has fallen
under the power of evil courtiers; Curdie, instructed by the mysterious
old lady of the castle, must set out to the rescue.

Of the shorter fairy tales, the one that is fullest of mysterious and
suggestive imagery, and thus nearest MacDonald's ideal, is
certainly 'The Golden Key' (1867), one of the most powerful and
strangely moving fantasies he ever wrote. Briefly, this describes a
boy, Mossy, who finds a golden key at the end of a rainbow, and
who with a girl called Tangle sets out to find the door the key will
open into a strange and profoundly desired land from 'whence the
shadows fall'. They meet at the cottage of an old lady, and become
parted from one another as they journey over a plain beneath a sky
alive with shadows from a country above it; then Mossy goes direct
over a sea to a mountain which he enters with the golden key,
while Tangle goes by way of three progressively younger and more
subterranean figures, the Old Men of the Sea, the Earth and the
Fire, to the same mountain. In the mountain are seven pillars of
rainbow colours, and an eighth of a wholly new colour which has a
door in it into which the key fits. Mossy and Tangle enter and climb
together with many other figures towards the country they have
longed for.

The whole story is full of extraordinary images: the air-fish that
guide the children to the old woman and then beg to be boiled in
her pot and eaten so that they may enter new life; the baths given to
Tangle by the lady and by the Old Man of the Sea; the domain of
the Old Man of the Sea, an up-ended and petrified ship; the mirror
that the Old Man of the Earth is watching; the 'oldest' man of all,
the Old Man of the Fire, who is a baby; the strange game he is playing
with various-coloured balls which he continually rearranges; the
hatched serpent that Tangle follows to the interior of the mountain;
the great blocks of stone that, falling one upon another from the side
of the mountain after Mossy has opened it, form a stairway to its

heart. If we try to translate these images we are frequently baffled, or forced to move away form mere reductive names. We may say that the land whence the shadows fall is heaven, but it is no conventional heaven and everything is subtly changed, being filled with unseen and unheard shapes, viewed only via their shadows, of not just men and beasts, but also other and unrecognisable forms.[10] We cannot allegorise the key as 'promise' or 'grace':[11] it is there in all its flashing solidity, and the tasks it accomplishes are so particular and peculiar. We might wish to say that Mossy and Tangle pass by way of the four elements (the air-fish and the three old men) and the many-coloured world (the rainbow) to a transcendence of them all in the eighth pillar in the mountain; but somehow, while these meanings or patterns are there, they exist in only dancing relation to the symbols, which seem to have a life far beyond mere 'significance'. Trying to explain why both a boy and a girl are present, we might notice that the girl goes on a journey downwards into the earth, while the boy goes upwards in his journey into the mountain; but what difference might be formulated out of this – whether of boys as 'outdoor' and aspiring, and girls as inward and contemplative – seems largely inadequate to the richness and variety of the images. MacDonald leaves his meanings much more latent and multiple than earlier Christian fantasies do.

The fact is that simply to give us significance is not MacDonald's way. For him 'The deepest of [truths] . . . are far too simple for us to understand as yet.'[12] His object is not that we should capture significances, but that they should be free and endlessly suggestive. His artistic analogies are drawn from music: 'A genuine work of art must mean many things; the truer its art, the more things it will mean . . . . It is there not so much to convey a meaning as to wake a meaning'; 'A fairy tale is not an allegory. There may be allegory in it, but it is not an allegory';[13]

The true fairytale is, to my mind, very like the sonata. We all know that a sonata means something; and where there is the faculty of talking with suitable vagueness, and choosing metaphor sufficiently loose, mind may approach mind, in the interpretation of a sonata, with the result of a more or less contenting consciousness of sympathy. But if two or three men sat down to write each what the sonata meant to him, what approximation to definite idea would be the result? Little enough – and that little more than needful. We should find it had roused related, if not identical, feelings, but probably not one common thought. Has the sonata therefore failed? Had it undertaken to convey, or ought it to be expected to impart anything defined, anything notionally recognizable?[14]

Thus MacDonald can maintain that 'The greatest forces lie in the region of the uncomprehended.'[15] His idea is not that we should be thinking about the fairy tale, but that we should be feeling it from within: that we should not have the distance that will permit us to ask questions. And all this stress on mystery, on indefiniteness of significance and on sympathetic engagement is founded on the fact of God, who is for MacDonald at the root of the true fairy tale, just as He is the author of the fairy tale we call nature:

> For in everything that God has made, there is layer upon layer of ascending significance; also he expresses the same thought in higher and higher kinds of that thought: it is God's things, his embodied thoughts, which alone a man has to use, modified and adapted to his own purposes, for the expression of his thoughts; therefore he cannot help his words and figures falling into such combinations in the mind of another as he had himself not foreseen, so many are the thoughts allied to every other thought, so many are the relations involved in every figure, so many the facts hinted in every symbol. A man may well himself discover truth in what he wrote; for he was dealing all the time with things that came from thoughts beyond his own.[16]

In this sense MacDonald is different from all the other writers we have so far considered: he asks a mystic and sympathetic response where they continually remind us of the gap between our understanding and the divine. MacDonald is much more incarnational in emphasis: his God has come down to us, made Himself part of our world.

How then does MacDonald convey a sense of God, let alone of Christian truth, through his fantasy? How can we talk about it? In *At the Back of the North Wind* it is perhaps more readily present: the North Wind who comes to the child Diamond and takes him abroad with her tells him that the often harsh things she has to do to people are her 'work', and that she can stand to do it because through all the noise of the world she can hear a far-off song, steadily coming nearer: 'I don't hear much of it, only the odour of its music, as it were, flitting across the great billows of the ocean outside this air in which I make such a storm; but what I do hear, is quite enough to make me able to bear the cry from the drowning ship.'[17] We know, not just because of the references to Dante, but because the portrait of the place draws on the archetypal desire for lost Paradise, what the country which Diamond visits at North Wind's back prefigures; and every poem in which he subsequently struggles to make words recapture it sends our minds wide with the sense of it:

> it's all in the wind
> that blows from behind
> and all in the river
> that flows for ever
> and all in the grasses
> and the white daisies
> and the merry sheep
> awake or asleep
> and the happy swallows
> skimming the shallows
> and it's all in the wind
> that blows from behind[18]

Desire for that place is a lodestar of Diamond's life, and we are to believe that North Wind under her aspect of Death takes him there when he dies at the end.

One of the motifs of *At the Back of the North Wind* is that a person or thing may be much more than we take it for; and that everything we think of as physical is also metaphysical. Thus North Wind is the wind that blows ships over and people home, but she is also a moral force, punishing people for their own good (the music that is coming closer) and a divine breath or afflatus, awakening our spirits like Diamond's to come out from sloth, or awakening our souls and imaginations to longing for the things of heaven. North Wind is at once herself and God working immanently. She is at once touchingly human in her relations with Diamond – now cross with him for hiding from her, now maternal, now confessedly unsure – and at the same time of a power and glory and beauty which seems to embody another. Similarly, within the story we are made to feel, by the use of such names as Diamond, Dives, Raymond, Ruby, Joseph and Martha, that what is going on at a human and Victorian level has taproots into larger spiritual truths; and the same effect is derived from the way Diamond's vision of North Wind is parallel to that of the heavenly visitant in Daniel 10.[19] It is always 'this, *and* this'. Diamond's experience of North Wind may be a dream, but it must be a true dream, because he loves her.[20] Diamond may see her when he is ill; may, in human terms, have 'a tile loose'; but sickness of that sort is also health, and madness sense. Diamond may seem just a little boy in London, but he is a boy for whom Christ died, and through actions as apparently banal as driving a cab or singing to babies he is performing something of the office of Christ's love to his fellows. Even a horse may turn out to be an angel in disguise.[21] Gradually, the whole story makes us feel that the world is shot through with spiritual things. Perhaps the main way in which this is achieved is through the continual juxtaposition of our apparently so solid world with the country at North Wind's back or the star or moon worlds dreamt by Diamond and his friend Nanny (chs 9, 25, 30).

But, curiously, the most doctrinally Christian feature of the story is the way that, after the initial exciting journeys with the mysterious North Wind and the mystical visit to the country at her back, we are brought back to and left in this world for a long time, until the last chapters of the book. In a sense we are shut in, just as Diamond, whose family have now lost their place and been forced to move to London, is now so hemmed in by houses that he can no longer be visited by North Wind. In thus being forced, as we are in this section, to confront human sinfulness, unbelief and mortality, Diamond is made to follow something of the self-sacrifice of Christ in coming down to this earth, eternity shut in a span, to take on its corruption and suffer under it for man's sake. *At the Back of the North Wind* is possibly the more poignantly Christian of MacDonald's fantasies in juxtaposing the real and the fantastic worlds and suggesting that experience of one without the other is not enough to know the things of Christ, and in particular the meaning of humility. It was not often that MacDonald cared to turn his attention to our mundane world in quite this way in his fantasy: generally his sense of the world as a waiting-room for heaven made him devote more attention to the construction of other worlds than of this one. However, it should be said that where a fantastic alternative was not an option, as in some of his (Scottish) novels, MacDonald could out of the landscapes, people and creatures of his childhood create images of human and spiritual pleasure.

In the 'Curdie' books, *The Princess and the Goblin* and *The Princess and Curdie*, the Christian element is even more elusive, which may explain why these stories have received readings in secular or Freudian terms. Neither story contains any direct reference to any Christian or biblical event, though there is often incidental biblical symbolism. In *The Princess and the Goblin* the princess Irene lives in a castle halfway up a mountain. In the topmost room of the castle lives her great-great-grandmother, with her pigeons, her spinning-wheel, the mystic bath she once gives Irene, and all about her on moonlight nights a great sky of whirling stars. Something of a symbolism of the different levels of mind or personality seems quite strongly suggested.[22] At least one critic has read the layers in terms of id, ego and superego;[23] others see the goblins as evils that have to be suppressed by our higher selves.[24] These are possible readings (though the latter is partly countered by the fact that the good Curdie, like the goblins, is to be found in the mines beneath the castle).[25] They go beside any schematic Christian reading in terms of the soul, the reasonable self and the passions. The real Christian or divine force of the story comes through our response to the changing images of the great lady at the top of the house; and also perhaps in our dim and not-to-be-formulated sense of some deeper truth in Irene's being sent down by that lady to rescue Curdie from his imprisonment in the mines. Typically of MacDonald, he no sooner lets us have seeming clarity at one point – as when we translate as faith the scarce-visible thread which leads Irene to Curdie in the mines, in contrast to the more secular string that fails Curdie himself – than he gives us obscurity. For elsewhere we have an episode where Irene's great-great-grandmother gives her a fire-opal ring and correctly foretells that next morning she will ask her nurse Lootie (instead of Lootie her) where she got it (chs 15, 16). Many of the symbols in the story simply resist interpretation: among them the old lady's moon-like lamp which shines through walls, the strange bath she gives Irene, the magic ointment with an odour of roses and lilies with which she heals Irene, or the fiery rose with which she cleans mud from Irene's dress. Here the symbolism seems close to being sacramental.[26]

This is even more the case in *The Princess and Curdie*. In this story the evil is much more dangerous and far-reaching, with the king and the kingdom itself under threat from evil men, and the old lady intervenes far more directly to bring about a happy issue. Curdie, who in the earlier book was able to defeat the half-comical goblins largely by his own efforts, now has to be spiritually initiated by the old lady before he can set out to save the kingdom accompanied by a collection of strange beasts; and she and her pigeons arrive to save the day in the final battle. The spiritual is thus more pervasive in this story, and the symbolism seems more certainly 'holy' or biblical, though no more definite in meaning for that: witness the purgatorial fire of roses that transforms Curdie's hand and later heals the sick king; the wilderness through which he journeys to Gwyntystorm, at one point harried by birds of prey; the bestial city of Gwyntystorm; the sick and powerless king; the final battle. And through it all comes a sense as in *At the Back of the North Wind* of music from some far source – now closer, now made more dull and faint by evil, but never silenced: it seems relayed from the old lady's spinning-wheel, symbol of the gathering of the threads of life, symbolic too of the turning circle that is the universe. That wheel is a 'great wheel of fire, turning and turning, and flashing out blue lights', and from it comes a music

> like the music of an Aeolian harp blown upon by the wind that bloweth where it listeth. Oh, the sweet sounds of that spinning wheel! Now they were gold, now silver, now grass, now palm trees, now ancient cities, now rubies, now mountain brooks, now peacock's feathers, now clouds, now snowdrops, and now mid-sea islands. But for the voice that sang through it all, about that I have no words to tell. It would make you weep if I were able to tell you what that was like, it was so beautiful and true and lovely. But this is something like the words of its song:

> > The stars are spinning their threads,
> > And the clouds are the dust that flies,
> > And the suns are weaving them up
> > For the time when the sleepers shall rise.

> > The ocean in music rolls,
> > And gems are turning to eyes,
> > And the trees are gathering souls
> > For the day when the sleepers shall rise.

> > The weepers are learning to smile.
> > And laughter to glean the sighs;
> > Burn and bury the care and guile,
> > For the day when the sleepers shall rise.

Oh the dews and the moths and the daisy red,
The larks and the glimmers and flows!
The lilies and sparrows and daily bread,
And the something that nobody knows![27]

In some ways this poem is almost a microcosm of what MacDonald is trying to put over in much of his fantasy – a sense of approaching promise: the great good coming to Anodos, the promise of the lady in the 'Princess' books, the land where the shadows fall in 'The Golden Key', the true back of the North Wind, the heaven of which Vane has been given a foretaste in *Lilith*. All evils, all conflicts, all mere narrative seem only a mode in which this vision of eternity may be realised. The poem at first describes actions, but by the end all verbs of action have gone and we are left with things themselves. In the same way MacDonald's style continually suggests its own inadequacy, pointing to a further and different language far beyond it, where words will no longer be separate from things, and the 'things' will all be alive and imbued with thought. Under that dispensation the stars will spin and the suns will weave; the trees will gather souls in the same way as the weepers will learn laughter. Not that 'style' is useless: for instance, the poem moves inwards from stars to ocean to men and moths, and as it does so the tense seems to sharpen from the vague 'time' to the 'day' when the sleepers shall rise, and finally, in the rapturous exclamations of the last stanza, to something much nearer the present, 'the something that nobody knows'.

At the same time the poem is at once excitingly rich and particular and mysteriously indefinite. Are the clouds the dust that flies up from the spinning of the star threads? Are the suns weaving these threads or the cloud dust? And what is being woven? – for it makes no sense in 'nature as we know it'. 'The ocean in music rolls': is this something it always does or is starting to do now, like the gems turning, as in Ezekiel, to eyes? Why are the gems turning to eyes? Because at the Last Things – assuming that that is what is meant by 'the day when the sleepers shall rise' – all things will be endlessly plastic and vital? In what way are the trees gathering souls? Are the souls not in some other world of heaven or purgatory after death? We may remark here how the poem surrounds the actions of man with those of the whole universe: MacDonald thus suggests that, while he (man) and the sleepers may be the centre of God's holy plan, they are a part of a living universe that looks after them. As he wrote in *Phantastes*, 'No shining belt or gleaming moon, no red and green glory in a self-encircling twin-star, but has a relation with the hidden things of a man's soul, and, it may be, with the secret history of his body as well. They are portions of the living house wherein he abides.'[28]

In the third stanza there is the kind of yoking-together we find in metaphysical poetry, of abstract and concrete, with laughter gleaning sighs and care and guile being burnt and buried; but at the same time the imagery of gleaning and of burning and burying has biblical and symbolic overtones. Here too the syntax begins to crumble as the poem fully enters the 'dream' world of eternity: 'Burn and bury' seems a new command as much as it may continue the previously indicative actions of 'laughter'.

In the last stanza everything has become fully interactive. Previously in the poem any one thing had relations with another: the stars and their threads, the ocean and music, the gems and eyes, the trees and souls, the laughter and sighs; but each pair was connected syntactically, and relatively distinguished as a unit. Now, with the loss of grammatical connectives, all items flow together and begin to exchange natures. Here 'glimmers' and 'flows' have become the same kinds of thing as 'larks'. And, as this happens, the crowded plurals seem to move together much faster and almost beget out of themselves and the kind of 'quickening of the dance' they represent a place for some further thing beyond themselves, 'the something that nobody knows'.

It is worth thus spending time on this poem, not only because it shows MacDonald's skill, but also because both in subject matter and in stylistic method it follows his aim in all his fantasy. It probably does it the better because it is poetry, which MacDonald always thought particularly apt for the expression of his vision, and which indeed he valued most of all his writing: the prose, because for him it must follow the rules of grammar and a relative attention to matters of common sense, must at times feel more discordant.

One story I will try to reproduce. But, alas! it is like trying to reconstruct a forest out of broken branches and withered leaves. In the fairy book, everything was just as it should be, though whether in words or something else, I cannot tell. It glowed and flashed the thoughts upon the soul, with such a power that the medium disappeared from the consciousness, and was occupied only with the things themselves. My representation of it must resemble a translation from a rich and powerful language, capable of embodying the thoughts of a splendidly developed people, into the meagre and half-articulate speech of a savage tribe.[29]

Thus Anodos, in *Phantastes*; and Vane in *Lilith* declares that a single thing would seem to be and mean many things, so that his own language is incapable of describing it clearly.[30] This emphasis on the multiplicity of each faërian thing we have seen registered in the poem just analysed.

If MacDonald thus creates a sense of God, Christ and heaven by the manipulation of what Ernst Curtius called an 'inexpressibility topos',[31] we may add to that his Romantic use of the motif of desire or spiritual yearning in all his fantasy. In *Phantastes*, indeed, we follow what C. S. Lewis would have called a 'dialectic of desire'.[32] It is desire that in a sense takes Anodos to Fairy Land in the first place, as he looks in the eyes of the fairy grandmother who comes to him: 'They filled me with an unknown longing. I remembered somehow that my mother died when I was a baby. I looked deeper and deeper, till they spread around me like seas.'[33] In Fairy Land he comes upon a block of alabaster, with the form of a woman in it; he becomes possessed by its beauty, 'more near the face that had been born with me in my soul, than anything I had seen before in nature of art', and is brought to sing to it, to try whether it will wake. The alabaster breaks and the lady emerges and goes off towards the woods; marking its direction, Anodos follows. In the wood he mistakes his white lady for the evil lady of the Alder, and is nearly destroyed. Later he finds her again in the fairy palace, again in statuesque form, but invisible: again he sings to her and thereby makes her first visible and then mobile. The 'point' is that only song, welling spontaneously from the divine unconscious, can turn the static and dead to the living and mobile. But, possessed by his desire, Anodos tries to seize her, and she flees him, telling him that he should never have done thus. Here again we are in discourse with the nature of the universe: to grasp it is to freeze it to a single dead thing; 'we spoil countless precious things by intellectual greed'.[34] (That is why MacDonald frequently avoids naming things in his fantasy – why he prefers the circumlocution to the label. 'What is in a Name?' is the title of the seventh chapter of *The Princess and Curdie*; and Vane in *Lilith* learns that names and personal identity are no longer important in the region of the seven dimensions.[35] A tree is better rendered through a circumlocutory riddle than a direct name in *At the Back of the North Wind*.[36])

Anodos for long pursues the white lady partially as someone he loves and wishes to possess sexually; but he is made to learn the folly of this selfish desire when he finds that she 'belongs' to another. Eventually he masters his passion to the point where he can do without self, even till death, yet still freely love the lady: 'I knew now, that it is by loving, and not by being loved, that one can come nearest the soul of another . . . . in proportion as selfishness intrudes, the love ceases, and the power which springs therefrom dies.'[37] He still wants her, but now love has become something else, and she has begun to become part of the great good that will one day come to him, part of the larger love that lights the world. In a sense Anodos's desire was for that from the beginning; but mortality and its limitations made him continually mistranslate and lower his desire: first to the level of a corpse in mere lust (the Alder maiden), then to that of a mere static thing in his urge to possess her, to seize her to himself. Yet, capable as he is of wanting to 'freeze' the lady as his own, he is equally capable of giving her life out of the forces in his unconscious, expressed in song. The person who would imprison her is likewise the one who by grace is enable to 'liberate' her. The pattern of the story is one whereby Anodos learns what true desire is, and begins to see beyond the lady to that larger love of which she is a part, a manifestation.

This pattern is not so marked in others of MacDonald's fairy tales, but the basic idea of finding the truly desirable is still very much there. Diamond in *At the Back of the North Wind* spends much of his time longing for and trying to recapture his vision of the country at North Wind's back, but is told by her that 'The real country at my real back is ever so much more beautiful than that.'[38] In 'The Golden Key' Mossy and Tangle see only the tantalising shadows cast by the land whence the shadows fall. All these stories are pervaded by a sense of *Sehnsucht*, or spiritual yearning, which defies all attempts to capture or identify it. In *Lilith* it actually expresses itself through Vane's apparent repugnance, rather than desire: he will not lie down with the sleepers in the house of the dead, and spends his time with the undead, or with the half-grown spirits of the 'Little Ones', or even with the evil Lilith herself, to avoid doing so. Eventually, to him as to Lilith, this is revealed for what it is, a truancy from the real desire of the self to be at one with the unconscious universe, and thus with the things of God. The very energy of flight from Him becomes a measure of true desire. Here desire is not perverted, or turned aside, as in *Phantastes*, but refused; yet the refusal, like the perversion, becomes a way of understanding it aright: that does not make the refusal essential, for it is still wrong in Vane, but within God's secret design it is the way by which alone he could learn. Thus not only does much MacDonald's fantasy present central images of holy desire round which the plot revolves, but his object is to sharpen our sense of it by showing it as obscured, misunderstood or refused.

The Christian content of MacDonald's fantasies is also seen in certain of their patterns; though as usual these are apprehended only indirectly through the Romantic faërian medium, and are frequently obscured. 'The Golden Key' might be said to follow the outline of a pilgrimage, and is certainly reminiscent of Bunyan's *The Pilgrim's Progress*: there is the idea of crossing the borders of the world into Fairy Land, as Christian enters through the Wicket-gate; the scheme of a fairly fixed obstacle course for Mossy at least; and the token or talisman, here the golden key, which will admit one to heaven.[39] In *At the Back of the North Wind*, as we have seen, Diamond experiences something like the immolation of Christ, shut into mortality and often isolated from heavenly assurance, as he is brought from the country at North Wind's back and set in the world with her absent from him: during the long time he is without her he lives as the humble son of a Joseph and Martha in London, acting like a little Christ among his fellow men until he grows ill and dies. There is a semi-Christian pattern in the 'Princess' books: in the first, where the action takes place in one spot and there are only a few central figures, we are involved with the purification of the self, seen in the removal of the goblins, and in the growth of true contact with the soul; in the second we are more involved with a journey, with the overthrow of a threat to a nation and generally with 'doing' in the world, in which now the old lady of the castle participates: it is rather like first the working of grace in the individual, and then the operation of grace through that individual on the world – in short, the Christian life.

In *Phantastes* and *Lilith* there is a further pairing, but with different patterns. Not for nothing do they come at the beginning and end of MacDonald's creative life, for in a sense *Phantastes* deals with the Christian First Things, and *Lilith* with the Last. In a sense Anodos as artist is parallel to the Creator, and depends on Him for whatever is of truth in his productions. His dream-like entry to Fairy Land makes that place seem much more a product of his own mind than is the case in *Lilith*, where Vane is taken into the region of the seven dimensions by the form of a long-dead librarian of the house, through a mirror in the garret room of his house. The world Anodos finds is peculiarly that of his spirit, and he must learn from it, whereas that in *Lilith* is inhabited by many other persons also, including Adam, Eve and Lilith. As a creator, Anodos wakes things to life – here represented by his power to breathe motion into two different statue forms of the white lady. *Phantastes* presents an unbroken series of new images, as Anodos pursues his journey, whereas in *Lilith* there is a set landscape with the cottage, the heath, the city of Bulika, and the place of the Little Ones and the Giants. At the same time Anodos partakes in the story of man in Paradise. Through him the divine awakens Eve from mere matter. Anodos twice disobeys prohibitions, and as a consequence gains an evil shadow and loses the lady. Here we may contrast *Lilith*, where Vane is asked not to wake things up but to lie down and go to sleep; and where he is not forbidden to act, but asked to do something. Eventually Anodos learns to do without his greedy and possessive self, and is able to re-enact something of the life of the Second Adam, or Christ, when in the evil church in the forest he attacks and slays a wolf beneath the altar so that no more of the congregation may be sacrificed to it, and in so doing is himself killed.

In *Lilith* the concern is evidently with giving an image of the Last Days when all the sleeping dead will arise and go into heaven; and that is what is anticipated throughout, even through Vane's truancies, and imaged at the close as Vane journeys with the others towards the New Jerusalem and the mount of God. Taken together, therefore, *Phantastes* and *Lilith* could be said to make up a diptych conveying the span of Christian history.[40] And perhaps it would not be going too far to see some of the 'children's' fantasies written between them – *At the Back of the North Wind*, *The Princess and the Goblin*, *The Lost Princess* and *The Princess and Curdie* – as portraying certain forms of the life occurring in the world between those two termini. Nevertheless we should not forget that all this Christian patterning occurs in fairy tales, which in MacDonalds' view would give hints enough of mystic significance if enjoyed for their own sake: indeed such hints would perhaps be the more potent for being felt rather than formulated. 'Is it nothing', MacDonald asks, 'that . . . [Nature] rouses the something deeper than the understanding – the power that underlies thoughts? . . . Nature is mood-engendering, thought-provoking: such ought the sonata, such ought the fairytale to be.'[41]

In MacDonald then we have someone who writes Christian fantasy with only intermittent reference to the standard texts and forms of Christianity. That is because of his belief that God works and lives in the unconscious mind and that the images emerging therefrom are therefore sacramental. But that belief is itself consonant with certain other features of MacDonald's outlook. He felt that no one image was sufficient to embody the mysteries of Christ and heaven. Thus, while the imagery of the Bible is recurrently implicit, so too is much archetypal imagery of the sort later to be described by C. G. Jung: as readily as he draws on St John for his mystical ideas, MacDonald draws on the more arcane Boehme or Swedenborg or Novalis; and, if he uses some of the biblical pictures of the Last Things, he also embodies them in imagery taken from Dante, Spenser or Blake. Christian though *Phantastes* is, it is Christian by way of a huge variety of literary texts, many of which are cited in chapter epigraphs: it is almost as though MacDonald's aim was to show how all literature could be seen to speak the things of God – and certainly he made this the purpose of his literary criticism in *England's Antiphon* (1874) and *A Dish of Orts* (1882). It was not just by accident or ill-luck that MacDonald had no pulpit: he was not fitted to pontificate. He was removed by his congregation from his church at Arundel precisely because he insisted on publicly undermining some of the orthodox beliefs of his hearers – particularly in his assertions that the heathen would be given a second chance in Purgatory, and animals be redeemed. His sermons thereafter were 'unspoken' in more sense than one. He revered the Bible, but would not use it to blockade the spirits of his readers. He believed in the literal truth of the born, slain and risen Christ, but felt that the story might be told in other modes. Above all he felt that what wins people to and quickens faith is not instruction or doctrine, but living truth coming from fresh images that engage the emotions and the spirit at the deepest level. And that is why he uses as a central part of his Christian fantasy not only narrative patterns re-creating those of the Bible in a new guise, but images imbued with mystery and inspiring a demanding desire which may draw us towards faith through our longing for a recovered Paradise. 'The Rose is of Paradise – the snowdrop is of the striving, hoping, longing Earth. Perhaps our highest poetry is the expression of our aspirations in the sympathetic forms of visible nature.'[42]

The emphasis in MacDonald's fantasy on desire and on the coming 'great good' may be Romantic, but it is certainly in marked contrast to the orientation of most earlier Christian fantasies. In them there

is a strong sense of the consequences of evil choice and of the hel
that awaits sinners. Indeed, it could be said that the motive to
become a Christian inculcated by those fantasies was often one of
fear as much as desire, and sometimes more so. What we have to
notice is that MacDonald is not alone in the modern period in his
different emphasis. Kingsley in *The Water-Babies* similarly finds the
universe ultimately benign, and emphasises a desirable afterlife
Charles Williams and C. S. Lewis in their fantasies stress the pattern
of the glory, or our desire for the far-off country we have in our hearts
There are those who would see this as the final loss in Christian
fantasy of a truly serious and dialectical vision of life.

The imagery through which MacDonald relays his Christian vision
in his fantasy is, as said, a mixture of the biblical, the Spenserian and
the Romantic – caves, mountains, castles, wind, moon, stars, jewels
fire, light, rivers, seas, cottages, trees, flowers, fairies, goblins, old
ladies, dragons, giants, witches. There is rarely anything sordid or
disgusting in it: it is all attractive, enchanting, at a remove usually
from the vulgar realities of life. This does not of itself make it
escapist: there is no reason why beauty should not convey at least
as much truth as ugliness. But the point is worth noting. And we
may note also that the imagery is not *contemporary*: it is drawn from
traditional modes and from the permanent forms of nature. With
Kingsley's *The Water-Babies* we shall find it otherwise, in this last
respect at least.

14

Charles Kingsley:
The Water-Babies

Kingsley has in some respects much in common with MacDonald. The two are, as said, the only two significant writers of Christian fantasy in the Victorian period. They share a number of 'Broad Church' and even heterodox theological ideas, some of them stemming from F. D. Maurice – particularly the beliefs that evil is not final, that all may ultimately be saved, and that the state of a being's soul may determine the form of its body. They are both eccentrics in relation to their age, the one often isolated or at odds with it, the other distinguished for the peculiarity of many of his views. In their Christian fantasy they both had the specially modern aim of 'showing' the existence of God in the world. In addition they were quite well acquainted, wrote at roughly the same time, and influenced one another. Kingsley's only fantasy, *The Water-Babies* (1863), probably owed something to MacDonald's *Phantastes* (1858), and MacDonald's *At the Back of the North Wind* (1871) is clearly indebted in certain features to *The Water-Babies*. And yet the remarkable thing is how at the same time they are also diametrically opposed in attitude, and how their fantasies and the aims behind them are sheerly different.

One might put the difference between them as between a 'Romantic' and a 'Victorian'. Although they were contemporaries, MacDonald's spiritual roots were, as we have seen, with the Romantics and the mystics – with Blake, Shelley, Novalis, Dante, Boehme and Swedenborg – while Kingsley is much more concerned to grapple with the movements and issues of his day in a literary mode which will do justice to their novelty: writing of the 'fragmentary and unconnected form' of his *Yeast* (1850), he said, 'Do not young men think, speak, act, just now, in this very incoherent, fragmentary way . . . ? – a very Yeasty state of mind altogether.'[1] In many ways the opposition between MacDonald's and Kingsley's ways of seeing could be viewed equally as that perennial one between the Platonist and the Aristotelian: the one with a spiritual and inward gaze, believing in innate ideas, the other directed outwards to the senses and the world, and to science.[2] But dualism was also in the very fabric of the Victorian period:

> The Cartesian divorce of mind and matter that increasingly characterised ... the Victorian sensibility results from a growing inability to accommodate the personally-perceived, experiential knowledge that the Romantics claimed as the only validly human truth, as opposed to that sought by the 'Man of Science ... as a remote and unknown benefactor'.[3]

The enormous progress of science, accompanied by the urbanisation of man in the Victorian period, posed a special challenge to that Romantic synthesis accomplished by Wordsworth through his imagination between the human mind and the external world. The two poles of naturalism and idealism, in which the former held the dominant place, came to divide the Victorian intellectual and spiritual landscape. Kingsley, as both a Christian supernaturalist and a scientist, registered the divide and the tensions it caused in himself:

> I am the strangest jumble of superstition and of a reverence for scientific induction. . . . What is a poor wretch to do . . . ? A mystic in theory, and an ultra-materialist in practice . . . what shall I do? I fear sometimes that I shall end by a desperate lunge into one extreme or the other.[4]

Kingsley's answer was to attempt to unite both sides; but whether he succeeded is another matter.

This 'Victorian' dualism manifests itself in other and sometimes more local forms. If MacDonald is all for the mysteries of the imagination, Kingsley hardly ever mentions that faculty at all: his aesthetic is one of empiricism, the exact imitation of nature as clearly as possible. If MacDonald turns away in his fantasies to look through 'other worlds' to a far world beyond ours, Kingsley seeks more immersion in this world – literally, in the form of Tom's entry into the watery world of stream, river and sea in *The Water-Babies*. If MacDonald tends to subsume nature in supernature, Kingsley does the reverse. Where Kingsley emphasises developing to more life and activity, MacDonald wants the passivity of death. Where MacDonald values night, Kingsley values day. Where Kingsley's fantasy 'spreads' horizontally over the world, there is a persistent emphasis on verticality, that which cuts through the world, in MacDonald's.[5]

Perhaps the most important point about Kingsley is that he made an attempt to square the Christian view of things with the then-new scientific discoveries about the nature of the world. Where other Christians became defensive, or shut their ears, or suffered the pains of doubt, Kingsley, who was himself an informed amateur scientist, unhesitatingly entered into debate with Charles Darwin and T. H. Huxley (with both of whom he was personally well acquainted) and tried to show them how the acceptance of their ideas could be shown to heighten rather than diminish our sense of God's presence in nature. He did not persuade them; nor did they dissuade him. But for our purposes he is the only Christian writer of fantasy who really attempts to integrate his perceptions with those of people of an opposite point of view, and truly to join his fantasy to the world 'as it was'. Others may ignore counter-arguments (MacDonald), or try to expose them (C. S. Lewis), or even try to assimilate them so that they subserve Christian purposes (Charles Williams), but Kingsley is the only modern writer of Christian fantasy to try to accept them both on their own terms and then try to put them together.

Thus, for our purposes, the first feature to concentrate on in considering Kingsley is his adherence to the scientific mode of understanding nature. MacDonald, though educated a scientist at university, came to spurn absolutely the analytic method, came to write, 'human science is but the backward undoing of the tapestry-web of God's science'.[6] Kingsley, however, who was a committed naturalist all his life, and author of several books on marine biology and geology, felt that, in investigating the physical forms of nature and the material laws which governed it, man was exploring the very methods of God, who was Himself the supreme Scientist, who made and continued to sustain all things. The work of the scientist could thus be considered to be holy. In a sense scientific investigation and deepening analysis of the world are what *The Water-Babies* portrays in the journey and discoveries of Tom, who ends in heaven as 'a great man of science, and can plan railroads, and steam-engines, and electric telegraphs, and rifled guns, and so forth; and knows everything about everything'.[7] Kingsley's view of physical nature is that it is far more filled with miracles than any fantasy. Nature is for him 'the Tale of all Tales, the true "Märchen allen Märchen" '; 'Novels and story-books are scarcely worth your reading, as long as you can read the great green book, of which every bud is a letter, and every tree a page'; fairy tales made by men are untrue 'because they are not strange and wonderful enough: far more wonderful sure than any fairy tale it is, that Madam How should make a rich and pleasant land by the brute force of ice'.[8]

All this makes Kingsley an empiricist and a 'realist' where Mac-Donald is a mystic who documents not the outer world but the inner landscape of the soul. Thus, where MacDonald takes his characters into fairy lands quite different from their 'everyday' worlds, Kingsley keeps us in this world in *The Water-Babies*. When Tom is a water-baby, the stream he lives in is very much one that might be found in the North Yorkshire Moors (even if based on one in Hampshire), and his journey down river to the sea is still in a very real river passing probably Leeds and ending in the Humber estuary. Nor is his life in the stream wholly disengaged from his previous existence as a sweep, even though for a time he has forgotten it: he meets his old master Grimes again; and Ellie, the little girl he saw sleeping when he was sweeping the chimneys of Harthover House, meets him once more (though neither knows it) when she is at a bathing-place and her companion temporarily catches him, and later again when she is herself a water-baby. True, the fairy isle of St Brandan is a little more remote, but even it is set amidst encounters with sea-creatures and places that are more evidently a part of our world. Not until we have left the great locked pool of Mother Carey near the North Pole, and descended, via the ocean floor, to the land called the Other-end-of-Nowhere, do we enter the wholly fantastical; but then it is as fantastical as that because all the people in it are in some way out of gear with reality, and must suffer for it absurdly.

As for Tom's existence as a water-baby, Kingsley is at pains to argue that there may be such creatures in nature. The argument is only in a sense flippant, for Kingsley really believes nature is far more wonderful than we know. 'You must not talk about "ain't" and "can't" when you speak of this great wonderful world round you, of which the wisest man knows only the very smallest corner, and is, as the great Sir Isaac Newton said, only a child picking up pebbles on the shore of a boundless ocean' (p. 69). So he argues that many land-creatures have their doubles in the water; or that in nature transformations as miraculous as that of a boy to a water-baby are well-known; or that the plasticity of our form is suggested by the metamorphoses we underwent while in the womb (pp. 73–5). In a similar manner he argues for the existence of fairies, using an inductive argument drawn from Paley's *A View of the Evidences of Christianity* (1794): 'There is life in you; and it is the life in you which makes you grow, and move, and think: and yet you can't see it. And there is steam in a steam-engine; and that is what makes it move: and yet you can't see it; and so there may be fairies in the world . . .' (p. 60).

Not only has Kingsley made the landscape and creatures of his fantasy fit the observed world: he has put his water-baby hero in the position of being a scientific observer. In the stream Tom is as it were a mobile magnifying-glass, seeing in great detail the sorts of tiny and 'fantastic' events normally invisible to us:

> And in the water-forest he saw the water-monkeys and water-squirrels . . . and nimbly enough they ran among the branches. There were water-flowers there too, in thousands; and Tom tried to pick them: but as soon as he touched them, they drew themselves in and turned into knots of jelly; and then Tom saw that they were all alive – bells, and stars, and wheels, and flowers, of all beautiful shapes and colours; and all alive and busy, just as Tom was. So now he found that there was a great deal more in the world than he had fancied at first sight. (p. 90)

But Tom's role as observer goes further than this. First, it spreads: as he travels downriver, and into the sea and then the Atlantic Ocean and travels north, he encounters all manner of creatures and learns of their histories, from the old 'hidalgo', the great salmon, migrating with his wife upriver, or the great lazy sunfish, 'as big as a fat pig cut in half', who has been driven off course from Delaware (pp. 140–1), to the lobster, or the last of the Gairfowl, perched in the midst of the cod-grounds-to-be around the Allalonestone (Rockall). Tom's scientific vision is thus widened metaphorically, from being within the confines of the stream, to ranging as widely as the ocean.

At the same time his vision deepens, just as does his watery medium from stream to river to sea and ocean. From seeing nature as a series of isolated phenomena and figures, he begins to have more and more of a sense of the connectives and principles that unite them. In the stream, phenomena strike him singly and he is continually surprised by them; nor do they explain themselves. The caddises, the dun-fly, the dragon-fly and the trout all live to themselves (which is doubtless what makes the lady salmon describe them as low forms). When Tom meets the otters, they are the first real family he has seen, and their appearance is a prelude to the flash flood that will drive him downstream. The salmon in the river has obvious 'connections', not just to his wife, of whom he takes honourable care, but to the noble race of salmon of which he is so proud. All these creatures have more choice: the sunfish has made a mistake, the lobster is obstinate, the Gairfowl has chosen her isolation. Many of the creatures Tom now meets explain their histories, or how they got the animal forms that they have. In short, the world begins to relate to Tom and to make much more sense to him.

His next discovery of connectives is the water-babies themselves, who help to keep the sea clean and look after the creatures in it. Before, Tom had not been able to distinguish them from the world about him, 'because his eyes and ears were not opened' (p. 186). When he has met them, he for the first time recalls his previous life with Grimes – and thus another item in drawing the world into sense is given. But, when he goes with them to their home in St Brandan's Isle he meets principles and organising-factors in nature deeper than they: these are embodied in the Fairies Bedonebyasyoudid and Doasyouwouldbedoneby, who might be said to signify the laws, both physical and moral, of action and reaction in nature. Mrs Bedonebyasyoudid is the principle behind suffering and reward. She ensures that all creatures get back what they put in. If they put in sloth, like the race of the Doasyoulikes in a story she reads to Tom, she will ensure that they devolve to apes and die out. If they are rapacious, she will make sure that a creature of greater rapacity devours them. If they will not steal to live, like one female hoodie-crow who is pecked to death by her fellows, she will ensure that they are metamorphosed to birds of paradise. The Fairy is no mere abstraction: she is as solid as anything else in creation, and is made to work on scientific and dynamic principles: 'For I work by machinery, just like an engine; and am full of wheels and springs inside; and am wound up very carefully, so that I cannot help going' (pp. 196–7). Like the soul that makes the body, or the steam that drives a piston, or the fairies that make the world turn round, she is the motor at the centre of the natural order, turning the whole into one gigantic engine. And we find that engine image recurring in accounts of nature, as when a strong wind blows Tom and the petrels north-eastward, 'for the old gentleman in the gray great-coat, who looks after the big copper boiler, in the gulf of Mexico, had got behindhand with his work; so Mother Carey had sent an electric message to him for more steam;

and now the steam was coming, as much in an hour as ought to have come in a week' (p. 260); and later, when Tom finds the hole leading to the Other-end-of-Nowhere, he sees steam rushing out of it from the great steam engine at the earth's heart (pp. 284–5).

But there is another natural principle for Tom to meet, in the shape of Mother Carey, the creative force, who sits by her Peacepool in the Arctic making the creatures make themselves. If the other fairies had to work on given creatures and acts, she is partly responsible for providing them with the materials to work on. Unlike the earlier fairies too, she does not have to do anything, no 'snipping, piecing, fitting' (p. 271): we have reached a calm, still point, remote, hidden and still as Peacepool itself. Here we have gone beyond the duality that is Mrs Bedonebyasyoudid and Mrs Doasyouwouldbedoneby: we are in the realm of paradox, of the unmoved mover. And that of course asks a further level of understanding of nature. Thus, taking the book as a whole, we may say that Tom learns, out of the initial apparent fragmentariness of nature, how it is put together, at deeper and deeper 'scientific' levels. As an explorer he has himself followed something of the course of an experimental scientist, looking beyond the seemingly chaotic sleet of phenomena and events to the laws by which they operate and come to be.

But the journey is not only that of a scientist. It is also the journey of a 'natural theologian'. For Kingsley would not have so valued the scientific and empirical method if it were not for him the way to find out the things of God. The last move of his story is a vision experienced by Tom and Ellie in which all the fairies come together to make a single person of changing aspect who says, 'My name is written in my eyes, if you have eyes to see it there.'

> And they looked into her great, deep, soft eyes, and they changed again and again into every hue, as the light changes in a diamond.
>
> 'Now read my name,' said she, at last.
>
> And her eyes flashed, for one moment, clear, white, blazing light: but the children could not read her name; for they were dazzled, and hid their faces in their hands.   (p. 326)

This seems one of the very few biblical references in *The Water-Babies*, here to the vision of Christ's transfiguration on the mount.

It was Kingsley's intention in *The Water-Babies* to follow out a process of scientific analysis which would also be a process of discovery of God and His immanent working. In a letter to Maurice in 1862 he wrote of the book, 'I have tried, in all sorts of queer ways, to make children and grown folks understand that there is a quite miraculous and divine element underlying all physical nature.' He felt that 'below all natural phenomena, we come to a transcendental – in plain English, a miraculous ground .... This belief was first forced on me by investigating the generation of certain polypes of a very low order. I found absolute Divine miracle at the bottom of all.'[9] Kingsley arrives at this sense of the divine presence by a number of means.

The first is the process of analysis itself, which by investigating further and further into nature eventually discovers a numinous source: this is the process just outlined above. But in fact, in contrast to MacDonald, Kingsley rarely reaches the kind of mystic contact with some divine source that we find in *The Princess and the Goblin* or *At the Back of the North Wind*. His God lies beneath nature, rather than on top of it like MacDonald's; and the nearer one approaches Him the more He burrows deeper away from direct notice. He is the 'absolute divine miracle at the bottom of all', an 'unknown x', 'A something nameless, invisible, imponderable, yet seemingly omnipresent and omnipotent'.[10] Kingsley himself admits, '[I] have always had the strongest faith in an unseen world, of which I never had a token, save by faith.'[11] His own instincts led him to a theology wholly integrated with scientific investigation, in which the divine becomes necessarily indistinguishable. He wished to 'accept all that Mr Darwin, all that Professor Huxley ... have so learnedly and so acutely written on physical science, and yet pre-serve our natural Theology on exactly the same basis as that on which Butler and Paley left it'.[12] Thus we find him refusing the apparent supernatural prominence in Christ's miracles: he argues that, for instance, Jesus changing the water into wine was doing 'what he does in the maturing of every grape – transformed from air and water even as that wine in Cana'.[13]

What happens to this intention in *The Water-Babies*? What we find is that Kingsley never draws our attention to this numinous *Urgrund* at all. Perhaps he may not have wanted to keep prodding the reader beyond sense experience; perhaps he simply decided to leave us, like life itself, with the fact of nature, and let us draw religious conclusions for ourselves; perhaps the tendency of his story was more towards some faint revelation of deity at the end, as a sort of reward, rather than all along the way. At any rate he presents us with nature: not nature simple, but nature made fantastic through his vision of her as an amazing machine; yet that, overtly, is as far as it goes:

> There was one wonderful little fellow, too, who peeped out of the top of a house built of round bricks. He had two big wheels, and one little one, all over teeth, spinning round and round like the wheels in a thrashing-machine; and Tom stood and stared at him, to see what he was going to make with his machinery. And what do you think he was doing? Brick-making. With his two big wheels he swept together all the mud which floated in the water: all that was nice in it he put into his stomach and ate; and all the mud he put into the little wheel on his breast, which really was a round hole set with teeth; and there he spun it into a neat hard round brick; and then he took it and stuck it on the top of his house-wall, and set to work to make another. Now was not he a clever little fellow?   (pp. 90–1)

All this is fascinating, and we are led to wonder at the amazing subtlety and miniaturism of nature, but without encouragement or more leisure – for we simply move on from this picture to another – we are unlikely to look further, particularly since the skill here is ascribed to the 'brickmaker' himself. More time might make us reflect on the design that has gone into the brickmaker's body, and the sense of purposiveness, of an immanent, conscious, shaping intent behind nature, that that might imply.

The use of argument from design is certainly another means by which Kingsley intuited God beneath nature. Marvelling in his *Glaucus: or, The Wonders of the Shore* (1855) at the multiple forms of the Sea-slug, he could ask,

> Why this prodigal variety? All these Nudibranchs live in much the same way: why would not the same mould have done for them all? And why, again . . . have not all the butterflies, at least all who feed on the same plant, the same markings? Of all unfathomable triumphs of design . . . what surpasses that by which the scales on a butterfly's wing are arranged to produce a certain pattern of artistic beauty beyond all painter's skill? What a waste of power, on any utilitarian theory of nature! . . . Inexplicable, truly, if man be the centre and the object of their existence: explicable enough to him who believes that God has created all things for Himself, and rejoices in His own handiwork, and that the material

universe is, as the wise man says, 'A platform whereon His Eternal Spirit sports and makes melody'.[14]

But this still makes God the end-point of an argument, which interposes itself, like the phenomena He has supposedly made and sustains, between us and a direct sense of Him. (Kingsley's willingness to use arguments for God's existence certainly sets him apart from MacDonald.) And Kingsley himself is sensitive enough to the limitations of arguments and inferences as means of apprehending God's presence. 'All the proving and all the arguments in the world will not make us *certain* that God made the world; they will only make us feel that it is probable, that it is reasonable to think so.'[15]

Thus, while in Kingsley's belief *The Water-Babies*, as a picture of nature, is a picture of God's working, that working is so fused with nature as to be invisible; so that what we have in the 'wonderful fairy tale' is the paradox of an absent presence. Kingsley would have 'stuck' God up above the ramparts rather more if he could, but his adherence to science and empiricism forbade it. He is left torn between his sense of the numinous and his inability to register it: 'I am the strangest jumble of superstition and of a reverence for scientific induction . . . . What is a poor wretch to do . . .? A mystic in theory, and an ultra-materialist in practice . . . what shall I do?' What he in fact does in *The Water-Babies* is give most space to scientific induction, leaving the 'superstition' to fend for itself.

This goes also for another area in which, as MacDonald did with the same idea, Kingsley might have produced a mystic sense of divine immanence. This is his application of the idea of moral (d)evolution, by which, through God's providential working, the body of a creature is brought to express the condition of its soul. We first find it dramatised in *Alton Locke* (1850), where Locke has a fever vision in which he finds himself relegated to a low form of life and forced to work out his evil through long ages of evolution:

> He who falls from the golden ladder must climb through ages to its top. He who tears himself in pieces by his lusts, ages only can make him one again. The madrepore shall become a shell, and the shell a fish, and the fish a bird, and the bird a beast; and then he shall become a man again, and see the glory of the latter days.[16]

As Kingsley formulated this idea for himself, in often-heated debate with Thomas Huxley, it became more a way of answering

Darwin than of revealing God. For Darwin's theory of evolution removed all sense of a plan from nature, reducing natural history to a process of the survival of the fittest; but by arguing, however incapable either of proof or disproof it was, that creation had evolved to higher and higher forms because the spiritual condition of life had generally advanced, Kingsley could keep nature meaningful and avoid having to accept life's forms as merely random.[17] Clearly, in order to maintain his argument he had to believe in the perfectibility of creation on earth – and in fact his outlook was imbued with a strong utopianism that the Great Exhibition and the scientific progress of his age could only reinforce: 'if ... those forefathers of ours could rise from their graves this day, they would be inclined to see in our hospitals, in our railroads, in the achievements of our physical science, confirmation of that old superstition of theirs, proofs of the kingdom of God, realisations of the gifts which Christ received for men, vaster than any of which they had ever dreamed'.[18]

At any rate, Kingsley twice states that this idea of moral (d)evolution is at the centre of *The Water-Babies*: the 'doctrine of this wonderful fairy tale ... is, that your soul makes your body, just as a snail makes his shell' (p. 86); and, when Tom has grown prickles as a result of stealing Mrs Bedonebyasyoudid's sweets, he reminds us that 'you must know and believe that people's souls make their bodies just as a snail makes its shell' (p. 217). Other illustrations of the idea are the transfiguration of the female hoodie crow, the transformations undergone by coarse sailors (who have become molly-mock birds) and the mutation of the Doasyoulikes (who have devolved to apes). In Tom's case such changes are not so immediately obvious, since he retains his form as a water-baby from first to last; but it is possible to argue that his changing surroundings can be seen as a larger body, and that the move from the narrow stream to the broad river and the open sea figures a growth and expansion of his soul. This may perhaps be problematic in view of the fact that it is equally possible to argue that Tom does not develop morally at all, that the body which teases the beasts in the stream is still found tormenting the sea-creatures when he has arrived at Mrs Bedonebyasyoudid; or that Tom is found committing one of the most heinous of the sins of a child, according to Kingsley, when he has reached the sea.[19]

But, whatever the moral facts, for us the main point must be the extent to which this idea of moral (d)evolution shows itself to be fused with a Christian vision. In fact, wonderful and 'supernatural' though the idea is, it is presented as an autonomous process within nature, rather than as one sustained and operated by God and the spiritual conditions of reality. If we compare Kingsley's presentation of the idea with that of MacDonald in his fantasy, we find that the latter has set us in a medium so evidently that of the spirit under the aegis of the divine that we are in no 'doubt' about its source and context. It is the numinous fire of purgatorial roses in the old lady's room that enables Curdie in *The Princess and Curdie* to be able to tell through a handshake what shape the inner soul is growing into. It is the state of their souls that determines the form of North Wind perceived by different people in *At the Back of the North Wind*. But Kingsley has put the numinous source underneath rather than on top of nature. He has even to some extent downplayed the 'spiritual' character of the soul. We tend to be directed to Tom's and others' *actions* as the causes of bodily change: the soul, or evil as metaphysical categories, are not really considered. The physical analogy of shell-making snail to soul-making body is rather a 'giveaway' here.

But this is by no means all there is to be said on the Christian content of *The Water-Babies*. If there is not a ready sense of God's immanence in nature, or of His working through the spiritual process of soul-making body, there is still the process described in the whole of Tom's journey in the story, a process which is clearly *meant* to be Christian. Tom, when we are first introduced to him, is described as a boy who 'had never been taught to say his prayers. He had never heard of God, or of Christ, except in words which you have never heard' (pp. 1–2). In this heathen state his blackness as a chimney-sweep is symbolic: he is outcast. But, as in Blake's Song of Innocence 'The Chimney Sweeper' (to which Kingsley seems part-indebted), the black bodies of exile will come off at 'death' (which figures entrance to a new spiritual life): Blake's Tom the sweep dreams at night 'That thousands of sweepers, Dick, Joe, Ned, & Jack, / Were all of them lock'd up in coffins of black', and an angel with a bright key comes by and releases them. 'Then down a green plain leaping, laughing, they run, / And wash in a river, and shine in the Sun.' And that is what will happen when Kingsley's Tom enters the water and leaves his black 'husk and shell' behind (p. 76; reminiscent of Blake's 'The Little Black Boy' too). In Tom, then, Kingsley figures the heathen who are so through no fault of their own, the truths of the Gospel having been kept from them.

For Kingsley, Tom's case is even worse, for he has been brought up in a supposedly Christian society. For that, the system and also his coarse master Grimes are to blame: 'Grimes', we note, is by name better suited to chimneys than Tom is, and it is chimneys and volcanoes that he is to sweep out in purgatory. A poor Irishwoman meets Tom and Grimes when one day they are going from the town to Harthover House in the country to sweep the chimneys, and she is more concerned to walk with Tom than with his master. Arriving at a spring, Tom is astonished to see Grimes wash himself; and, though Grimes tells him he did it to be cool rather than to be clean, his attraction to water at this point is still left strange. Grimes refuses to let Tom dip his head in the water also; and the Irishwoman rebukes him, saying she knows of a hidden evil deed of his, at which he grows blustering and frightened. She asks him if he is not ashamed of himself, and, when he says no, agrees, saying, 'If you ever had been ashamed of yourself, you would have gone over into Vendale long ago' (p. 13). This is to prove highly significant in relation to Tom later. Before mysteriously disappearing she says, 'Those that wish to be clean, clean they will be; and those that wish to be foul, foul they will be. Remember.' Clearly, however solidly she may be presented, she is intended to represent the working of grace in nature on the unregenerate soul.

When they arrive at Harthover, the house is described as a mass of different styles grown together, which 'looked as if somebody had built a whole street of houses of every imaginable shape, and then stirred them together with a spoon':

> *For the attics were Anglo-Saxon.*
> *The third floor Norman.*
> *The second Cinque-cento.*
> *The first-floor Elizabethan.*
> *The right wing Pure Doric.*
> *The centre Early English, with a huge portico*
> *   copied from the Parthenon.*[19]

And so on, mentioning a '*back staircase from the Tajmahal at Agra*' (there is later to be much emphasis on the backstairs from the Other-end-of-Nowhere). What we have here is the first sign of destructuring in the narrative: first, the description of the house is a digression; and, secondly, the house is a mass of 'digressions' from itself, held together only by the reconciling hand of time. To those who complained that the house has no unity, Sir John Harthover replied that he liked it for that, because it 'looked like a real live house, that had a history, and had grown and grown as the world grew' (p. 20). Here a piece of seemingly dead architecture is given life, as later the creatures in the stream are given personalities; and this animation we may suppose does not express mere pathetic fallacy, but rather the moral (d)evolutionary idea by which nature is throughout spiritually alive. In this light we may see the whole process by which Tom meets and talks with the water-creatures – who are all given quite human personalities – as more than a mere convenience; rather, it is a way of showing how, seen close as Tom sees it, nature is not only more infinitely various, but also more strangely alive, than we suppose.

But the destructured description of the house here may also suggest some prelude to destructuring in Tom. This house, stirred together as by a spoon, is halfway, in this transformation of hard stone and constrictive chimneys, to the fluidity of water, which we may say symbolises the spirit. Tom himself starts with a hard brick in his hand, ready to throw at people; now his desire for water is growing. What is more, the house as described is an impossibility. The attics could not be Anglo-Saxon if the third floor were Norman. If this house has 'grown and grown as the world grew', the world grows backwards. But then, in a sense, going backwards is later to be the way of advancing, as Tom must go backwards to be an eft, a form of foetus, and must journey backwards to the Other-end-of-Nowhere, and as the scientific giant Epimethus he finds there must run in reverse.

Within Harthover House Tom is to have his first sight of Christ, and of himself; and within the labyrinth of its chimneys, which might figure the unconscious mind, he loses himself and eventually emerges in the bedroom of little Ellie. The room is all in white, in contrast to his own black. He sees a picture of a man laying his hand on children's heads, and another of a man nailed to a cross, which makes him sad and awed. And then he sees – beautiful, golden, white and all clean – little Ellie sleeping in her bed. Of course, as we read, Ellie is 'just a little Yorkshire girl'; but let the context and Tom's later relation with her work on us, and we shall see that in a sense she figures the soul as it may be. He thinks her 'an angel out of heaven', and wonders if she has got to look like that by washing: which is true at a level which he does not yet know. And then suddenly he catches sight of a figure standing close to him, 'a little ugly, black, ragged figure, with bleared eyes and grinning white teeth'. When he realises it is himself reflected in a mirror, he is so distressed 'with shame and anger' that he tries to go back up the chimney again, but upsets the fender and fire-irons with a crash as he does so. This wakens Ellie, who screams, thus bringing in her nurse to collar Tom – at which she fails, and he escapes through the window (pp. 26–7). Tom's shame at himself will now lead him, as the Irishwoman said, to Vendale, a deep cut in the earth which may be said to figure a descent into the self and the unconscious current of the world to be presented in the watery medium that will be his home. His shame, while ultimately beneficial, is not wholly 'deserved', since his blackness has been given to him by the world rather than by himself and deeds of his own choosing. Kingsley wrote elsewhere of urban children,

> Their souls are like their bodies, hidden by the rags, foul with the dirt, of what we miscall civilization. But take them to the pure stream; strip off the ugly shapeless rags; wash the young limbs again, and you shall find them, body and soul, fresh and lithe, graceful and capable.[20]

But all this shame in Tom, and his wonder at the little girl, is now taking place unknown to him under the aegis of Christ, who comforted children and died that they might be saved. After Tom leaves the house, pursued as it were by all the world, thinking him a thief, his way is both guided and followed unseen by the Irishwoman, whose feet 'twinkled past each other so fast that you could not see which was foremost' (p. 36). Already in one sense he has changed. His previous life was circumscribed and ordered. He was controlled by Grimes, and sent into chimneys. Now he is in the open, away from town, away from buildings, away from the chimneys within buildings, running first through the garden and grounds with their many obstacles, then free across the open moor. Now he must choose for himself. If he may be likened to a little black gorilla as he flees, there is no 'big father gorilla' around to help him against his pursuers: he does not remember having a father and expects 'to have to take care of himself'; when he is stuck in some thickets he says to himself, 'I must get out of this ... or I shall stay here till somebody comes to help me – which is just what I don't want' (pp. 31–3). So it is that he chooses to go the way his pursuers will not expect after crossing the wall. Before, his future life had been inevitable to him, a mere cyclic repeat of that of Grimes, in which he would drink and dice and keep dogs and beat his apprentices in turn (pp. 2–3). Now it is as uncertain as his direction, and he must choose it. That will be the main difference in his life when he has become a water-baby: he will have been given free moral choice and, with it, the responsibility of making such choices.

What happens when Tom enters the stream? He has become fevered from his long climb down into Vendale: physically, one could say, he is suffering from sunstroke. He hears church bells ringing, and thinks it is Sunday; but they are audible to him alone. He feels he would like to go to church, for he has never seen the inside of one before. But first he feels he must be clean, and the refrain of the Irishwoman on cleanliness sounds in his head. He goes to the stream nearby to wash, and the church bells ring still louder in his mind. He falls into the water; and in two minutes he has swum out leaving his old shell behind, transformed to a little water-baby. That he is a baby of course implies a fresh start. It is fair to say that in our sense he has 'died': certainly that is what Sir John and the others make of it when they find the rest of his body. But in Kingsley's view 'Tom was quite alive; and cleaner, and merrier, than he ever had been' (p. 76), because he has changed to another form. He is in a purgatorial 'intermediate state' within this world, where he will be given another chance. In one way it is fair to see the whole of Tom's life in the water as his terrestrial purgatory.[21]

But it is also true that the water is a symbol of baptism, particularly in its association with church bells and Tom's first desire to enter a church. Tom's 'godmother', here also a symbol of continuing grace as she enters the water after him, is the Irishwoman, who sees him into the stream and then turns into the Queen of the Fairies and floats away. Though baptised, though permanently immersed in the water which symbolises acceptance of him through God's grace, he is still ignorant of the fact; and because, as the Queen tells the fairies, 'He is but a savage now, and like the beasts which perish' (p. 58), they must not reveal themselves to him. Yet they continuously will represent the 'infinite network of special providences' which make up 'the whole history of the universe'.[22]

We do have, then, in *The Water-Babies* something of a spiritual presence, in the pictures of Christ, in the Irishwoman and the fairies, in the beauty of Ellie, in the sound of church bells, and above all in the now-pervasive medium of water – the kind of fictional mystical experience that we do not more directly derive from Kingsley's 'natural theology' or his idea of moral (d)evolution. The water of course is a wonderful symbol, not only of baptism itself, but of that intercommunication of all life under grace which forms Christ's body, the Church. The church bells that Tom heard, and for which he wished to clean himself, actually came from the water, for 'the farther he went in, the more the church-bells rang in his head' (p. 56).

However, it must also be borne in mind that many of the specifically supernatural elements here – the Irishwoman meeting Tom and Grimes at the fountain, following Tom over the moor and entering the water as the Queen of the Fairies – were added to the serialised first version of *The Water-Babies* as it appeared in 1862–3 in *Macmillan's Magazine*. It has been argued that Kingsley did this in order to reconcile the Victorian context of Yorkshire with the more magical life of the stream.[23] In fact, however, we find similar additions right down the stream until Tom meets with water-babies in the sea. We are told that the water-babies long to teach him not to play naughty tricks on the creatures in the stream, and to play with him, but cannot because of the Queen of the Fairies' inter-diction: in the serial Kingsley simply leaves us with the warning, which is also in the book, of 'a certain old lady who is coming' (p. 91).[24] Similarly the serial has no mention of the water-babies who help drive off the otter to protect Tom, or who appear for an instant to him when he is about to set off downstream; nor of the fairies watching over Tom on his journey, making sure that sailors in river towns do not see him and that he does not fall foul of sewers and mill-races. Further, the serialised version is without the epigraphs of often supernatural import which Kingsley added to the chapters of the book. For instance, in the book the second chapter begins with a quotation from Spenser's *The Faerie Queene*, II.viii:

> 'And is there care in heaven? and is there love
> In heavenly spirits to these creatures base
> That may compassion of their evils move?
> There is: – else much more wretched were the case
> Of men than beasts: But oh! the exceeding grace
> Of Highest God that loves His creatures so,
> And all His works with mercy doth embrace,

That blessed Angels He sends to and fro,
To serve to wicked man, to serve His wicked foe!'

Similar effects are achieved in other chapters with quotations from Wordsworth and Coleridge: these help to give the story a matrix of supernatural meaning it might not otherwise have shown. In short, Kingsley has *imposed* some of the supernatural significance on his story after the fact; and all his additions are for this purpose.

Here we see evidence that Kingsley was not sure that his readers would see the mystical or baptismal significance of Tom's spiritual journey as he first presented it. Originally it was exactly fitted to his notion of 'a living, immanent, ever-working God'[25] who is indistinguishable from His own works and their operation. Thus, in the serial version, while Tom's journey is intended to be a Christian one, and his immersion baptism, this significance is carried within a perfectly 'natural' appearance, whereby a little sweep takes fright on first seeing himself in a mirror and flees over the moor and down the crag, until exhaustion and delirium drive him to the stream. Kingsley's procedure here was to be like that with his 'natural theology': one was to proceed with nature until eventually, by a process of analysis, one 'found absolute divine miracle at the bottom of all', or water-babies at the bottom of the sea. So, a process of apparently moral development in Tom would have been crowned as 'sacred' development after his action of helping the lobster triggered his meeting with the fairies. But by introducing the water-babies earlier in the look, and by inserting a fairy, however well disguised, into the Yorkshire content, Kingsley has gone near to presenting the very kind of supernatural action he found impossible to sustain as a scientific Christian – that of 'an interfering God – a master-magician', as he called it.[26] The fact that he was prepared to do this testifies to the tension in Kingsley between the materialist and the mystic. Most people are happy with the final version of *The Water-Babies*, so that is not perhaps a live issue. But it does bear important witness to the fact that the 'supernatural' level of reading the water, or the influence of the picture of Christ, is conditioned by other and overtly magical or sacred elements added to the narrative after its first appearance. In this sense Kingsley literally converted *The Water-Babies* to Christianity. The conversion may look natural, may not feel awkward, but it has been accomplished for all that.

Tom's history after the point we have reached may be more

briefly dealt with. At first he is with what the lady salmon sees as 'low company' (p. 24) in the stream – flies, grubs and minnows. We have already seen some of the ways in which his company changes as he journeys: he meets creatures that have more families or links with one another, and which explain themselves more to him – in short, there is more interrelating. But he also progresses to meeting higher forms. It is the otter family which appears and bids him go down to the sea. There he meets much larger aquatic creatures: the salmon, the sun-fish, the lobster. At the same time he has developed from living under water to looking about him on its surface. It is thus that he meets a seal, porpoises, basking sharks, a giant eel and the lobster. For the sea and the tide represent a new medium which transforms his relation to the water: 'He felt as strong, and light, and fresh, as if his veins had run champagne; and gave, he did not know why, three skips out of the water, a yard high, and head over heels, just as the salmon do when they first touch the noble rich salt water, which, as some wise men tell us, is the mother of all living things' (pp. 135–6). Now he spends more time out of the water, going on the sands or the rocks by the shore. And, when he has set off from St Brandan's Isle to the world's end, he travels across the surface of the ocean. At the same time, his companions have changed from creatures that live in the sea to birds that live above it: he starts with the wingless Gairfowl, but then is with the petrels ('Mother Carey's chickens') and the mollys. In a sense his soul could be said to have developed wings. Certainly the stages by which he has got here imply this.

But it is not just that he has developed: he has also *been* developed by the medium of grace in which he is now set. It is a rainstorm and a momentary vision of water-babies, as well as the urging of the otter, that sends him forth from the stream down the river. It is a bruising he gets from the trout and the relationship he develops with the dragon-fly that helps him to learn such a lesson 'that he did not torment creatures for a long time after' (p. 98). All the time he is under the watchful providence of the fairies. And all the time, as the Queen of the Fairies said he must, he is learning 'from the beasts which perish' (p. 58). His movement from stream to river to sea expresses a choice of wider and deeper life – his spirit becomes enlarged. He literally learns to see for greater distances as the story proceeds: at first only a few inches to the next water-beast, but by the end from horizon to horizon. When he has reached the sea he is capable of an act of selfless generosity: he risks his life to save the lobster. When he has done this, the water-babies reveal themselves to him; or rather, as they put it, he becomes capable at last of distinguishing them. Now he has reached a point where he is no longer the isolated soul in spiritual quarantine. But his conduct with the larger body of water-babies brings responsibility too. He must go on acting for others all the time, not just the once that he helped the lobster. The water-babies spend their time working on behalf of other creatures in the sea, and so must Tom.

But he is still selfish, and therefore must still learn. Indeed his worst evil is still to come, as though driven into a last corner. He not only starts tormenting water-creatures again, but one day steals Mrs Bedonebyasyoudid's sweets – that is, steals from all (as he thinks) to gratify himself alone. Yet it is part of the gracious environment in which he is set that the punishment devised for him should be such as to make him better. The prickles his body grows as a result, and his isolation, eventually lead him to confess all to Mrs Bedonebyasyoudid, who at once forgives him and brings Ellie to him to teach him how to get rid of the prickles. All this expresses Kingsley's view of the universe as a benignly determinist medium, in which all evil will be set right: 'Evil, as such, has no existence; but men can and do resist God's will, and break the law, which is appointed for them, and so punish themselves by getting into disharmony with their own constitution and that of the universe; just as a wheel in a piece of machinery punishes itself when it gets out of gear';[27] and in *Madam How and Lady Why* (1869), we are told that Lady Why, the spiritual organiser of nature, 'will take care that you always come across a worse man than you are trying to be, – a more apish man . . . or a more swinish man . . . or a more wolfish man . . . and so she will disappoint and disgust you, my child, with that greedy, selfish, vain animal life, till you turn round and see your mistake, and try to live the true human life, which also is divine'.[28]

Ellie's instruction of Tom might be said to represent his confirmation into the Church, when one becomes aware of the grace received under baptism, and voluntarily offers oneself again. And, when the teaching is done, Ellie and Tom can recognise one another again for what they are: for the first time Tom remembers his previous life. This recovered consciousness of course represents a further growth in spiritual perception beyond that whereby Tom became able to perceive the water-babies for the first time. Now, we must feel, he has recognised not only the things of the spirit, but also the place to which they belong. For Ellie, unlike the water-babies, is a visitor from heaven, the 'home' to which she goes on Sundays, and to which Tom longs to go too. But before that is possible he must go to the Other-end-of-Nowhere, which represents by its distance the sheerness of the effort required; and now help not someone he likes, such as the lobster, but someone he does not like or wish to help, his old master Grimes. In this way he is made finally to go against his own nature, so extremely that he goes out of it into a new nature altogether. And this is partly symbolised in the way he goes backwards to the Other-end-of-Nowhere.

Thus we may say that there is a very marked Christian pattern behind the narrative of *The Water-Babies*, and present in its symbolism. It is a pattern derived partly from Bunyan's *The Pilgrim's Progress* (a favourite book of Kingsley's), particularly in the idea of a pilgrim running away from a city across a plain, and in the idea of a channel or path of development; but it is also very much Kingsley's own. It is also sheerly different from MacDonald's fantasy, where no such obvious pattern was to be discovered but all was finally lost in mystery and the numinous. MacDonald turned away from allegory; Kingsley by contrast seems to embrace it, with the stark labels he gives his great fairies, and the clearly decipherable scheme of Christian development beneath his narrative. And yet in Kingsley this clarity emerges from a narrative of apparently the most amazing confusion and variety, full of disgressions, objects and creatures. Kingsley's object is to create sense out of seeming chaos, but not by force; to let nature be itself and yet reveal patterns; to be at once empirical and artless in approach, and thus reveal divine truth. It is the reverse with MacDonald: he takes the familiar world we take for granted, and defamiliarises it; he turns all that we know to obscurity and mystery. Thus Anodos at the beginning of *Phantastes* 'wakes' one morning to find the ordinary lineaments of his bedroom – the basin, the bed-hangings, the carpet – turning to parts of the landscape of Fairy Land before his eyes. Kingsley's approach to nature is much more 'Victorian' and 'scientific': for him the world accepted as it is, untreated, will link up to speak the things of God. Where MacDonald's fantasy moves towards the 'disconnected', as Novalis called it, Kingsley's moves from apparent chaos to connectedness.

This sense of 'connectedness-in-multiplicity' in Kingsley is furthered in the way his universe is portrayed as a network of interrelationships founded ultimately on divine charity. For Kingsley the Christian universe is one in which Christ works through nature for the ultimate good of all his creatures. *The Water-Babies* describes the breadth of a love that will work to save even those who never heard of Him, and that will then harness that soul to help begin the salvation even of an oppressor (Grimes). What Kingsley thus gives us is a world oriented towards heaven, all life tipping into eternity. In MacDonald's fantasy, apart from *Lilith*, the concern is more with the salvation of the individual, as in many previous Christian works; but Kingsley's purview is all being. Tom may be the centre, may often be alone; but throughout *The Water-Babies* we are made to feel that he is part of the larger common-wealth of life around him. Anodos in *Phantastes* was the focus of interest, the peculiarity, Fairy Land expressing his nature; but the marine world in Kingsley's book is an objective one, and Tom is just one among many water-babies to attend the classes of the fairies Bedonebyasyoudid and Doasyouwouldbedoneby. The sense of relationship among a whole variety of creatures is very marked. The trout are known to the salmon, who themselves have met water-babies: not only physically, but biologically, the land is connected to the sea. The sheer variety of the creatures Tom meets and whose characters he learns begins to make the world a huge fabric of interconnecting being and personality. Without the help, for instance, of the petrels, the mollys and the dog, Tom would never have reached the Other-end-of-Nowhere. Symbolically the last Gairfowl, who refuses relationship, dies.

And then there is the personality of the author, which finds its quirky way into every nook and cranny of the book, as pervasive as the watery medium itself, as immanent almost as the personal God who made this peculiar nature. 'A water-baby? You never heard of a water-baby. Perhaps not. That is the very reason why this story was written. There are a great many things in the world which you never heard of' (p. 67). 'Here I come to the very saddest part of all my story. I know some people will only laugh at it, and call it much ado about nothing. But I know one man who would not; and he was an officer with a pair of gray moustaches as long as your arm' (p. 211). Kingsley never draws any analogy between the author of a fairy tale and God the maker of the world, but the parallel is there, and all the more suggestive for the fact that Kingsley did not believe in art, felt it his business to mirror the character of reality without selection or distortion: the world of *The Water-Babies* is meant to be a mirror of our own. The picture as said is one of a great interdependent community, with man as but one, if the highest, member. Even 'things' are brought to life of a sort, from the shirt-pin Sir John Harthover's groom loses over Lewthwaite Crag to the 'mountain-loaves and island-cakes' made in the oven of the sea-mother (pp. 65, 284).

Kingsley's style contributes to all this, by being endlessly digressive, constantly picking up all sorts of bits and pieces and bringing them together. Huge excursions – on the architecture of Harthover House, the reality of fairies or water-babies, the many punishments of Professor Ptthmllnsprts, the history of the Mayor of Plymouth and the lobster, and the Other-end-of-Nowhere – pepper the book. And at smaller levels Kingsley will not keep his eye only 'on the object', as when at Tom's escape from Harthover House he turns to describe in detail all the various people who set out in pursuit, and what they were doing before, until by the end he has got to the point of turning the whole thing into a joke: 'Only my Lady did not give chase; for when she had put her head out of the window, her night-wig fell into the garden, and she had to ring up her lady's-maid, and send her down for it privately, which quite put her out of the running, so that she came in nowhere, and is consequently not placed' (pp. 29–30). And so it is throughout, in constant sidetracks, shifts of tone, importations of all sorts of matters into the one under review. This habit of drawing all sorts of things together in one place is almost 'conceited', and certainly derives from Kingsley's reading of Rabelais, from who he said he had 'learnt immensely';[29] but its tone and application, in being imitative of the commonwealth of nature in which all things share and have a part (even the apparently 'outside', symbolised in the black heathen Tom[30]), are peculiarly Kingsley. His justification of this 'yeasty' style is on these lines:

> The idea of self-evolution in a story, beautiful as it is, is just one of those logical systems which is too narrow for the transcendental variety of life and fact. . . .
>
> In the greatest Christian pictures you see figures thrown in ἐυπαρέργου which are not required by the subject, *e.g.* the Pope and St Theresa in the Madonna di San Sisto. Their use, conscious or unconscious, is to connect the subject with the rest of the universe, even with the present time, and show that it does not stand alone, that it is not a world of itself (to which alone self-evolution would be completely applicable), but is connected with the rest of the world. . . .

Now in the modern novel you ought to have all this, if it is to be a picture of actual life.[31]

And that of course is part of the ethic of *The Water-Babies*. Kingsley's stylistic method is at once imitative of nature, and moral or spiritual in portraying all things as bound together. He will not give us only Tom's development, because that would cut him off from life. Thus the unity of his book becomes as ramshackle, but still 'natural', as that of Harthover House,[32] or even as a caddis-fly's home (pp. 88–9) or a lobster (p. 145), composed of a mass of random bits and pieces. And, we may remark, Kingsley has brought together a good many bits of himself in *The Water-Babies* as in no other of his books: the Christian, the socialist, the marine biologist, the fisherman, the geologist, the nationalist, the sanitary reformer, the mystic, the educationalist, the evolutionist, the poet. By this means he would hope to show not only the co-operativeness of the universe, its being a great network of charity and exchange (as Charles Williams would put it), but also that it has a unity far greater, and composed out of far more diverse materials, than any that we could make. This idea of universal charity, and of the universe as a unique concord-in-discord, might refer us beyond it to a divine explanation and source. And certainly, as something like a correlative to 'a living, immanent, ever-working God', as Kingsley called Him, the style of *The Water-Babies* is remarkably dynamic and ever-moving. Even the mystic moment with the great fairies at the end is one of movement, for they continually seem to change form before Tom and Ellie (pp. 325–6). And throughout there is a sense of energy and vitality that seems to come from a kind of joy that has to do with more than nature itself:

> The sea breeze came in freshly with the tide and blew the fog away; and the little waves danced for joy around the buoy, and the old buoy danced with them. The shadows of the clouds ran races over the bright blue bay, and yet never caught each other up; and the breakers plunged merrily upon the wide white sands, and jumped up over the rocks, to see what the green fields inside were like, and tumbled down and broke themselves all to pieces, and never minded it a bit, but mended themselves and jumped up again. And the terns hovered over Tom like huge white dragon-flies with black heads, and the gulls laughed like girls at play, and the sea-pies, with their red bills and legs, flew to and fro from shore to shore, and whistled sweet and wild.
>
> (pp. 137–8)

This is a style that seems as vigorous and ever-changing as the water, both physical and mystical, in which the story is set.

As we have seen, for Kingsley the true Christian fantasy of the world, the most fantastical of fantasies, is to be found not in the inventions of man but in nature, even in the most 'ordinary' things of nature:

> 'We are fearfully and wonderfully made,' said old David; and so we are; and so is everything around us, down to the very deal table [on which Kingsley is writing]. Yes; much more fearfully and wonderfully made, already, is the table, as it stands now, nothing but a piece of dead deal wood, than if, as foxes say, and geese believe, spirits could make it dance, or talk to you by rapping on it.   (p. 76)

His fantasy refuses 'other' worlds or images and symbols taken from past literatures: its context is the turning world as it is now. *The Water-Babies* is a highly contemporary fantasy, connected in every way to the world in which Kingsley lived, and to issues of his day – among them the American Civil War, Robert Lowe's Revised Education Code of 1862, positivism, the fountains in Trafalgar Square, the setting up of Broadmoor Criminal Lunatic Asylum on Easthampstead Plain in 1863, American 'greenbacks', Napoleon III's annexation of Nice, the Acclimatisation Society, the *Hippocampus minor* controversy between Richard Owen and T. H. Huxley, the rejection of Monckton-Milnes's bill (March 1862) to permit marriage with a deceased husband's brother, or a deceased wife's sister.[33] There are scarcely any such references in MacDonald's fantasy, but then he is not concerned with this world so much as with the next, or with the outer world so much as with the inner. But for Kingsley such connection of 'the subject with the rest of the universe' is essential.

At the same time, while *The Water-Babies* has obvious literary antecedents in Rabelais, Bunyan, Blake and Wordsworth, we do not need to be aware of these writers or their works to understand it. At one point in his revisions Kingsley is, as a matter of fact, to be found removing biblical references from his story;[34] and certainly he has not made it difficult to understand the symbolism of his story from the account he has given us. MacDonald's fantasy is rooted in the past – its very landscapes are of another age, and its symbolism often comes from far back, even from primordial stages of human development in the case of its 'archetypal' imagery. But Kingsley does not look back like this. Indeed, there is that in him that does not believe that the past is active in the present – which considering that he became a professor of history at Cambridge, is astonishing. But, given his belief in life as a continual progressive movement forward, an ever-dynamic evolution to better things, the past was bound not to be important. Certainly each stage of *The Water-Babies* tends to 'forget' the last. The effect is that, as observed earlier, MacDonald's fantasy has depth, but Kingsley's has *spread*. Kingsley's radiates outwards horizontally, to take in everything in sight, whereas MacDonald's takes a few things and broods on them till further significances emerge from within them. It is natural therefore, that the Christian aspect should be much less present in *The Water-Babies* than it is in MacDonald's fantasy. For Kingsley was describing the world largely as it was, and hoping that it would show itself to be more than it appeared. He was using an empirical aesthetic to portray a divine reality, and a scientific method to try to show the great artificer. In the end it is his boldness that stands out.

15

Twentieth-Century Christian Fantasy

Of straightforwardly Christian fantasists in this century there are probably only three main ones – Charles Williams, T. F. Powys and C. S. Lewis – and of these Powys rather minimises the fantastic, and to some extent the Christian, element, so that he may explore the spiritual complexities of life in their light. Otherwise we are dealing with fantasies which may be Christian, such as Tolkien's *The Lord of the Rings* or Richard Adams' *Shardik* (1974), with religious fantasy which avoids being Christian, such as Mikhail Bulgakov's *The Master and Margarita* (1928–40), or with science fiction which transfers numinous awe from God to the alien or the remote. We shall consider all these, because they are very much part of the story of what has happened to Christian fantasy; but our main concern will be with the work of Charles Williams and C. S. Lewis.

With the gradual disappearance of an ostensibly 'Christian' society after the First World War, Christian fantasy had a still more lonely position than it occupied in the Victorian period. The exception to this was the period from the beginning of the Second World War to some way into the 1950s, during which there was a quickening of faith under the pressure of extreme experience; and most of Lewis's fiction was written at this time. Both his and Williams's fantasy shows preference for older societal and even cosmic structures. Williams aligns his views with those of Dante; his work is full of Christianised symbols from the Middle Ages and the Renaissance – the Platonic 'Ideas' behind life, the Tarot, the Cosmic Dance, the stone of the first Matter, the Holy Grail; his universe is inter-correspondent and hierarchical. Lewis, who saw himself as belonging to an 'Old Western' culture which died out around 1830, re-creates a medieval and Christian concentric universe in his 'space trilogy', and a monarchic and pastoral society in his *Chronicles of Narnia*. It must be said, though, that Charles Williams does set his fantasies in very contemporary and often urban situations in a way that Lewis does not. And again, before we assign this adherence to an older order to the embattled situation of the modern Christian fantasist, we should note that Williams never explicitly registered such a feeling. Nevertheless there is a real-enough desire registered in the fantasy of Williams and Lewis for a coherent, ordered and stable universe – a desire echoed in the pastoral and feudal societies which form the base in Tolkien, Ursula Le Guin's 'Earthsea' trilogy, Mervyn Peake's 'Titus books, T. H. White's *The Once and Future King*, Robert Silverberg's 'Valentine' books, John Crowley's *Little, Big*, and many other works.

In this, modern contrasts markedly with Victorian fantasy. For i could be said that Victorian fantasies seek to subvert settled ways of thinking about the world, as MacDonald shows the transforming power of the imagination, or Kingsley how much more miraculous nature is than we suppose; such fantasies are in a sense revolutionary working against set social modes. This is surely one of the primary underlying reasons for their being written in dream-like or fragmentary narratives. By contrast Williams, Lewis and Tolkien give us *structured* universes in their fantasy, whether the 'diagram of glory' that Williams continually celebrates, or the highly wrought cosmic plan in Lewis, in which 'all is pattern', even down to the extremely complex 'literary' unity of his *Perelandra*, or the very detailed consistency of the world of Middle-earth in *The Lord of the Rings*. Modern fantasies are thus often much more reactionary, their worlds the fictional re-establishment of values, as much social and pastoral as Christian and spiritual, that have gone from or are under threat in the environment in which they are written. This may explain why metamorphosis, which is so recurrent an idea in Victorian fantasy, where forms are in continual flux according to an implicit ethic of change, is not often to be found in twentieth-century fantasy – apart from its more recent postmodern variety in Borges, Pynchon or García Márquez.

Twentieth-century fantasy is also distinctive in its creation of self-consistent 'other' worlds. In Victorian fantasy we often find the 'fictional microcosm' invaded, whether by narrative interpolations or authorial interruption. MacDonald's *Phantastes* is broken up by alternative stories and episodes in which the central character Anodos partakes; and Kingsley in *The Water-Babies* continually addresses the reader: 'Am I in earnest? Oh dear no! Don't you know that this is a fairy tale, and all fun and pretence; and that you are not to believe one word of it, even if it is true?'[1] But in writers such as Lewis, Eddison, Tolkien, Peake or Le Guin the object is the creation of as solid and inviolate a world as possible, which our minds may enter for the duration of the story.

The important point to emphasise here is the 'otherness' of such worlds in much twentieth-century fantasy. Lewis wanted to make wholly different worlds from our own, and realised this in his Mars, Venus and Narnia. Tolkien, who wrote an essay in praise of 'sub-created' worlds, built up his Middle-earth, a realm which has little direct relation to our own world. T. H. White's Gramarye allows him to enjoy a re-creation of the 'Age of Individuals'. Peake's Gormenghast is a realm which Peake almost seems to inhabit as much as this world: he wrote, 'For it is one's ambition to create one's *own* world in a style germane to its substance, and to people it with its native forms and denizens that never were before.... '2 Victorian fantasy rarely creates a fantastic world for its own sake. Carroll's Wonderland and Looking-Glass World are not places to look at: strictly they are not even places, but really a series of positions and encounters to be moved through. Each of the creatures and people met is highly memorable and fantastic, but we are much less aware of a fantastic world, existing on its own. The Fairy Land in MacDonald's *Phantastes* is also a series of encounters set in a medium which changes in parallel with the development of the protagonist. In a sense where previously, in MacDonald, God was the artist, now the artist is God: he creates universes in the image of the Making of his Creator. At this level, where before the relation of the fantasy to divine truth was one of inspiration, here it is one of imitation, and the bond is less immediate; just as the created world itself is in less immediate spiritual relation to our own.

There are other differences between Victorian and modern fantasy which have influence on the Christian form. One is the much more 'epic' or social mode of modern fantasy. Previously the hero was usually solitary, and events related to him or her alone – thus Tom, Anodos, Alice, each of whom is cut off from 'normal' life and set in a strange world with which his or her individual psyche reacts. In modern fantasy the protagonist is often part of a group – the groups of children in E. Nesbit's stories or C. S. Lewis's Narnia books, the four princes in E. R. Eddison's *The Worm Ouroboros* (1922), the company of the Ring in Tolkien's epic, the Round Table in T. H. White's *The Once and Future King*. Even when the hero is single, he is often interacting with other people – Ransom with the Un-man and the Lady on Perelandra, Lester Furnivall with Simon the Clerk, Betty Wallingford, Evelyn Mercer and her husband in Charles Williams' *All Hallows' Eve*. Often on the actions of these central figures the fate of a whole world depends. If Ransom fails on Perelandra, the Lady and with her the planet may fall, and a huge act of redemption may be necessary. On the actions of Tolkien's Frodo and the Company depends the survival of Middle-earth Unless Anthony Durrant can find some way of controlling the wild Principles released into the world by the magician Berringer, in Williams' *The Place of the Lion*, all life may be destroyed.

In parallel to this we find that, where the moral vice most frequently attacked in nineteenth-century fantasy is individual greed, the desire to feed the self, in twentieth-century fantasy it is power-lust, the megalomaniac desire to subdue others or whole worlds to one's will which has been a recurrent feature in the politics of this period Thus, where in Kingsley's *The Water-Babies* Tom is self-punished for stealing Mrs Bedonebyasyoudid's sweets, and in *Phantastes* Anodos's evil shadow makes him appropriate and pervert the wonders of Fairy Land, in more modern fantasy we find Williams' Giles Tumulty who wants to control this world, and his Simon the Clerk, who wants to control the next world also. So too we find Lewis's Un man trying to bring Perelandra beneath its power, Tolkien's Sauron determined to secure the One Ring and with it final mastery of Middle-earth, or Peake's Steerpike, feeling his way towards power over all Gormenghast. This epic and social aspect tends to make modern Christian fantasy a total vision of a Christ-based world rather than the more provincial form of an individual experience and yet at the same time this social vision makes it more fantastic more wished-for, more remote from realisation.

Frequently we find that twentieth-century fantasy is more ecological than moral, concerned with the preservation of a world at least as much as the transformation of an individual. Charles Williams could hardly be said to have been interested in ecology and the 'countryside' as we generally mean it now, but his fantasy certainly shows an impulse towards the protection of the world from threat or subversion by magic, which is conceived rather like the politically destabilising influence of an anarchist. C. S. Lewis, much more responsive to the pastoral impulse, portrays the maintenance of rural rather than urban paradises. In Victorian fantasy the moral emphasis demands not that the individual should stay still, but that the spirit should change. Further, it could be said that there is sometimes almost as much emphasis on protection of the land as of its people in modern fantasy, as in Tolkien or Ursula Le Guin.

A further aspect of twentieth-century fantasy is its sense of frailty Where change and subversion are the norm, where all is 'at risk', as in Victorian fantasy, that is not an issue. Where there is continual struggle to preserve and protect, where there is the recurrent sense that one individual – a Simon the Clerk, an Un-man, a White Witch, a Sauron, a Steerpike, a Mordred or a Cob – can ruin a whole world, the feeling of frailty becomes marked. Thus it is that Christian and other fantasy of the twentieth century is full of a sense of crisis. This is appropriate no doubt to an age in which the assassination of one man could set the whole 'civilised' world at war, or in which the press of a finger may terminate that world for ever. At any rate modern fantasy has much more sense of an antagonist. Whereas in Victorian Christian fantasy the enemy is the self, and lies within, in one's own alterable greeds and coldnesses of heart, in Williams and Lewis it is outside the control of the self in an 'other', and is more difficult to check.[3]

Lastly, we may observe that from Kingsley to C. S. Lewis there is an increase in the number and variety of Christian fantasies produced by each writer. With Kingsley we have only *The Water-Babies*: what Kingsley gives us is the world as it 'is', and he therefore needs to say it only once. The same is true of most of the writers of Christian fantasy prior to Kingsley. With MacDonald we enter the more fluid world of the imagination, which throws out images at seeming random; and thus we find several different fictions, from the quasi-medieval world of *The Princess and the Goblin* to the region of the seven dimensions in *Lilith*. Again in Charles Williams, though not here because of a source in the imagination, we find a series of Christian 'fictions' embodied in six novels set in contemporary England but all with different modes of the supernatural, and also in two Arthurian poems and a number of plays. There is, however, a certain similarity of idiom among these multiple fantasies: faërie in one form or other runs through all MacDonald's work, and Williams' novels all have a roughly similar context and orientation. The same cannot so readily be said of the many fictions of different worlds created by C. S. Lewis, from his Perelandra to Narnia to Glome: indeed sometimes it would be hard to tell that the same writer was behind them all. Thus in twentieth-century fantasy there is a spread, a fragmentation, call it what we will, of the divine presence in fiction.

It would be rash to draw too much from this. Clearly Christian fantasy is not radically different from other modern works of literature in this respect, save only in that its greater dependence on the imagination makes its fictions necessarily more scattered in character: we live in a period which has put a far higher premium on fiction and free invention than ever before, and this is simply being reflected here. But, if the causes are not unique, the consequence may be. For multiple fictionality means in a sense multiple textuality we are no longer dealing with a quasi-biblical 'set text', a single mod in which the Word manifests itself, but rather with a series of differen versions, all of which are variously inaccurate renderings of the truth This does bring us to a position where the 'Christianity' of Christian fantasy trembles on the verge of mutation. Some of those mutation – not at all necessarily representing a decline or even a loss – w shall consider after looking at Charles Williams and C. S. Lewis.

Nevertheless, as earlier observed, all these Christian fantasies whether of the nineteenth or the twentieth centuries, retain one thing in common: the emphasis on God as creator and their orientation towards praise of His creation. Each work is designed ultimately to manifest the 'pattern of the glory', as Williams has it: human conduc is important, and the Christian life and spiritual development o the protagonists are significant, but in contrast to Bunyan, say, it i the richness of divine creation variously revealed through their action and travels that is of ultimate consequence. This goes together with their sense that good is stronger and finally more real than evil there is not one 'wicked' character in Kingsley, MacDonald, William or Lewis but finds his or her evil subverted or subsumed in som larger divine pattern; or, as MacDonald's Anodos puts it at the end of *Phantastes*, 'What we call evil, is the only and best shape, which for the person and his condition at the time, could be assumed by the best good.' At the heart of all these modern fantasies is contemplation contemplation of holy reality. And of Charles Williams in particular our next author, it is fair to say that his novels may be conceived a virtual ceremonies of praise.

16

Charles Williams

Of all the writers of Christian fantasy we have considered, Charles Williams is perhaps the most apparently serene; and this at a time when serenity has seemed least possible for the Christian. Williams belonged to the Church from the start, and never 'doubted' in the sense in which that term is generally understood. What he did was embrace doubt as an essential part of the living dialectic of his faith: agnosticism, even unbelief, was to him part of the balance that made up life. In this sense nothing that happened during his life – not the First World War, not the establishment of an atheist communist state in Russia, not the racist nationalism of Germany – could be excluded from his faith in the operations of God: this is shown in the closing pages of his 'history of the Holy Spirit in the Church', *The Descent of the Dove* (1939).[1] Williams experienced pain and loss in his life, but the whole disposition of his spirit was open to accept them. For him there is no beleaguered character to his faith, no condition of its being embattled in a hostile modern age: for him it embraces everything, or, in MacDonald's words, 'There is no word to represent that which is not God, no word for the *where* without God in it; for it is not, could not be.'[2] In this sense Williams is not a dualist; and in this he seeks to align himself with the theology of Kierkegaard, whose 'life of scepticism was rooted in God'.[3] So secure does he sit within his faith that his 'apologetics', or rather his theological writings, do not assume an audience of any other than spiritual initiates: he does not address a world 'outside' – perhaps because for him there is no 'outside', since all is within what he called the divine 'Co-inherence'. And, if we think of his life, particularly his long career in the small society of Oxford University Press, that is remarkably secure and insulated too.

This assurance in Williams, together with a certain lack of engagement with the common difficulties and questionings of modern man, lends a hieratic and esoteric character to both the ideas and the style of his work: he is not nearly so well known as C. S. Lewis. But what is important for our purposes here is the sense that as a Christian fantasist he thus seems one whose faith we can least locate and explain in relation to his own times. It seems as though in this direction at least it will not make much final sense to call him a 'twentieth-century writer of Christian fantasy'. He himself would have smiled at the notion that one's Christianity is for any time: for him the acts of Christ are continuous, not historical, and time and space only modes of thought.[4]

For all that, it is possible to argue that certain of the highly idiosyncratic ideas in his theology do implicitly register a response to 'modern reality' which he would otherwise disclaim.[5] Of those we might single out his insistence on the universe in God being highly patterned, even diagrammatic: in his view, 'God always geometrizes', and 'heaven is always exact'.[6] The entirety of his poem *Taliessin through Logres* (1938) is in a sense a picture of the web of this glory. 'The word glory, to English ears, usually means no more than a kind of mazy bright blur. But the maze should be, though it generally is not, exact, and the brightness should be that of a geometrical pattern.' Or, 'The prophets are sent out from the visible mathematics of the glory to proclaim the moral mathematics of the glory.'[7] All this emphasis on order and precision, which overgoes even Dante, may express an unconscious response to the formlessness, the absence of structure and direction in the modern world, where knowledge has become relative, where God himself has been seen as an imprecise metaphor, where total war, collectivisation and the degradation of human as much as divine values have led to loss of meaning. Through a theology which transfigures the world to a place whose least item plays a crucial part in a hugely complex pattern, Williams at once does justice to the multifariousness of the world and shows it as highly ordered and charged with divine significance. As said, it would be wrong to say that he intends to do this; but that is what may readily be taken to happen.

The same might be said of his idea that a divine act is never past, but always 'co-inherent' (to use his favoured word) within creation. The fall is constantly recurrent, the crucifixion is perpetually present, the Last Things are about us with the First. Far from this being a world without God, or one that has drifted away from Him, it is one from which He cannot go, with which He is everlastingly married and infused. Such a theological position denies historicism, making Christ ever-present; counters demythologising, making myths continually active. At one sweep Williams puts aside the simple notion of Christ as being 2000 years gone, if ever He was, and puts

Him with us now and ever.[8] What neater way of recharging the
world with the supernatural? And it is worth emphasising that,
though Williams aligns himself with Kierkegaard, his theology has
little of the harshness and pain of the Dane's, little of the stress that
he lays on the absurdity of the world and the sheer alienness of
God and His commands (Abraham's experience in *Fear and Trembling*).
For Williams the cosmic news is good, and its mysteries benign.
How much that is a product of an assurance untried, how much of
a need for an optimistic faith, cannot be judged. But in effect it
gives us a theology and a faith that remake the world to sustain the
belief that all things will be well.

The remarkable thing about Williams is how *much* of a sense of
the supernatural he has as active within this world. So much is this
the case that in his life and work both he seems to have been
engaged on a kind of continuous mystical experience. Kingsley and
MacDonald also had a sense of divine immanence, but for Kingsley
this immanence was elusive, and for MacDonald it was more in the
imagination than in the 'real' world, and imperceptible to all but
the child-like mind. Prior to Romanticism (and Wordsworth, to
whom Williams owed much), the emphasis on mysticism of the
'affirmative way', or *via positiva*, is much rarer. Christian fantasy is
more concerned with behaviour, with how to win or lose heaven,
than with the experience itself of the divine. And the world is often
felt to be an unhallowed and sinful place. It may seem strange,
therefore, that just at the time when the sense of the numinous and
of the existence of the divine was beginning largely to fade from
man's experience, we should have in Williams so full a realisation
and re-creation of it within this world – though in one sense that
may be precisely the reason.

At the theological level this sense of the supernatural comes from
the centrality of Christ and the incarnation to Williams' thought
and feeling. Because Christ has come into the world and made it a
part of His nature, it must necessarily be inescapably supernatural.
Each least apparently secular thing in the world thus participates
directly in His nature, and, because His nature is Charity, all things
are joined together by links of charity into that body of continual
exchange which Williams called 'the Co-inherence'. Here then we
have a Christian fantasy which is so by being finally *about* Christ.
Other such fantasies might consider Christian behaviour, or the
way to heaven, or the quest for God in this world, or how to see

spiritual things, but these look straight to Christ Himself. And that is partly why Williams aligns himself with Dante. For Dante too had a strong incarnational sense, founded on the transfiguration of his vision of Beatrice: in the *Vita Nuova* as in the *Purgatorio* he describes how his love for her as a mortal realised itself as much more a longing for the Christ of whom she was an image: romantic love became hallowed as love for the divine. So Williams describes the process in his reading of Dante, *The Figure of Beatrice* (1943). And in Dante's highly ordered and symmetrical cosmos, which is yet fluid with continual movement, he found an image that matched his own sense of a universe of correspondences and patterns which are interlinked in Christ. It is fair in some sense to say that much of Williams' work is a reinterpretation of Dante's vision.

Williams' prose fantasies are *Shadows of Ecstasy* (1929, 1933); *War in Heaven* (1930), *Many Dimensions* (1931), *The Place of the Lion* (1931), *The Greater Trumps* (1932), *Descent into Hell* (1937) and *All Hallows' Eve* (1945). He also wrote a Christianised story of Arthur in two poems, *Taliessin through Logres* (1938) and *The Region of the Summer Stars* (1944). All the novels are set in 'this' world, though the world is subject to penetration by 'supernatural' events. In each, the supernatural is gradually introduced and its significance increased, steadily eroding the characters' assumptions about the world with ever-deeper revelations. Most of the stories involve an attempt by evil people to gain supernatural power, whether through control over some magical object such as the Holy Grail or a wonder-working stone made of the 'First Matter of Creation', or else directly through control over other souls: it then becomes the business of characters aligned towards goodness to put themselves at the disposal of the divine and order-restoring forces of the universe. In this way the evil become as it were a stimulus for the revelation of the holy nature of reality.[9] The total effect of these works is invariably to show us how quite other their worlds are than the secular things they seem to be. We start *War in Heaven* with an office murder that turns out to link with the discovery of the Holy Grail; in *The Place of the Lion* an escaped lioness seen by two walkers is later subsumed in the leonine form of one of the sacred Principles of creation; in *All Hallows' Eve* we begin with a girl looking over a bridge in wartime London and only gradually realise that she is dead.

The world so revealed is still very much the every-day, even more so than in Kingsley, who tended to reject its more ugly side. Thus in

All Hallows' Eve the central character, a dead woman called Lester, reflects on the debris she sees floating in the Thames:

> The evacuations of the City had their place in the City; how else could the City be the City? Corruption (so to call it) was tolerable, even adequate and proper, even glorious. These things also were facts. They could not be forgotten or lost in fantasy; all that had been, was; all that was, was. A sodden mass of cardboard and paper drifted by, but the soddenness was itself a joy, for this was what happened, and all that happened, in this great material world, was good. The very heaviness of the heavy sky was a wonder, and the unutilitarian expectation of rain a delight.[10]

At the human level of the 'every-day', we find a railway porter in the same novel, a traffic policeman in *The Greater Trumps* and a secretary in *Many Dimensions* all variously transfigured. From the point of view of Williams' theology, all things live in Christ's nature; from the point of view of modern Christian fantasy, we might see this as an attempt to leave nothing out.

Williams' interest in 'Christianising ordinariness' is seen in his treatment of the supernatural, the extraordinary, in his fiction. Magic and miracle may come into this world and their misuse disturb it, whether in the shape of a magic Tarot pack which controls the elements, or the animate forms of the great Principles of life; but all of them are present not for their own sake, but to show how they have been made incarnate in this world: indeed their naked presence, while testifying vividly to the divine power from which they emanate, is dangerous, and must be removed.

Thus in *The Place of the Lion* the errors of a magician have loosed into the world the Platonic Principles of life – the Lion of strength and wrath, the Serpent of subtlety, the Lamb of meekness and charity, the Eagle of balance and insight, the Phoenix of rebirth, the Horse of speed, the Butterfly of beauty and so on – and one of the functions of these beings within the novel is to show both that these forces are real and that life is normally a mixture and balance of them, so that it partakes in the eternal while being a part of time. In the context of his knowledge of the Lion, the world presents itself to the protagonist Anthony Durrant in

> an apparition of strength. How firmly the houses were set within the ground! with what decision each row of bricks lay level upon

the row beneath! Spires and towers and chimneys thrust into the sky, and slender as they were, it was an energetic slenderness. The trees were drawing up strength and displaying it, and the sunlight communicated strength. The noises that came to him from the streets resolved themselves into a litany of energy. Matter was directed by and inspired with this first and necessary virtue, and through the vast spaces of the sky potential energy expanded in an azure wonder.[11]

Very often in Williams' novels we find statements as fervently direct, even abstract-seeming, as this. Yet it is part of his vision that the world is the Word made flesh, that (and particularly in this novel) the abstract and the concrete, a thought and an experience, are not to be divided, for all are under the reconciliations of Christ's incarnation. What, for Williams, is happening in the passage quoted is not more Anthony Durrant having an intellectual vision than an intellectual vision having Anthony Durrant. As he listens, the sounds seem to change and become more various, suggesting not just one principle but a balance of many in life, though from time to time a particular one may come forward:

But the sounds that came to him, though they reached him as a choric hymn, sounding almost like the subdued and harmonious thunder of the lion's roar, were yet many. A subtlety of music held them together, and the strength whose epiphany was before him was also subtilized into its complex existence. Neither virtue could exist without the other: the slender spires were a token of that unison. What intelligence, what cunning, what practice, had gone to build them!

Having now added the Serpent, he goes on to add the Butterfly, the Horse, the Eagle, the Phoenix and the Lamb until he has attained a total vision not only of the balance of all those forces in himself but of their presence among the stars and the whole fabric of the universe.[12] What has happened is that the 'bare' supernatural of the Principles has acted as a catalyst to reveal the supernatural present in far more subtle and mixed form in life itself.

And this happens in most of the novels that portray an incursion of the supernatural: it is gradually seen only as one concretion of many forces that move already within life. In *Many Dimensions* the Stone enshrines healing, justice and self-transcendence; and eventually it finds its path back to its place through the body of the self-giving Chloe Burnett, secretary to the Lord Chief Justice: 'all began to flow out, out from the Stone, out into the hands that held it, out along the arms and into the body and shape of which they were a part'.[13] What is revealed is not a singleness – though there is singleness in the Holy Grail in *War in Heaven*, which is considered much more as an object than in relation to the fabric of life – but an organic complexity. And indeed organic complexity is for Williams the thing. For him two images in particular – that of the human body and that of the city, both forms of complex interaction within a unity – are spiritually meaningful. For him glory is no solitary thing: 'The pattern of the glory is a pattern of acts.'[14] That is why, in a sense, he writes novels, which are patterns of acts. It is the living co-operation of the societies of being that for him manifests the everlasting.

To this we will return; for the moment our point is that, as he learns his own vision, Williams comes less and less in his novels to look beyond the world, or even at the wonder of the supernatural things themselves. It is as though he no longer needs the 'artificial respiration' provided for the world by this means and learns how to show it irradiated from within. In *War in Heaven* we are still looking at the Holy Grail, and are allowed to wonder at the power it contains, power which is here detached from the world, and indeed which scarcely manifests itself in the way that the Stone or the Principles do: here it is the task of the mortals to preserve it inviolate, rather than to share in its nature; here too is the only novel in which the object has a supernatural guardian, in the (rather absurd) form of Prester John in 'a light grey suit and soft hat'. At the end Prester John becomes in a church the priest king, and then a figure of Christ Himself, surrounded by half-apprehended angels; the emphasis is on the approach of another world, not the salvation of this one, as the Archdeacon of Fardles comes to his long-desired death:

> Faster and faster all things moved through that narrow channel he had before seen and now himself seemed to be entering and beyond it they issued into similar but different existence – themselves still, yet infused and made one in an undreamed perfection. The sunlight – the very sun itself – was moving on through the upright form before the altar, and darkness and light together were pouring through it, and with them all things that were.[15]

In the novels following this one it is already different. In *War in Heaven* the world was not threatened by misuse of the supernatural;

in the novels of 1931–2 – *Many Dimensions, The Place of the Lion* and *The Greater Trumps* – that has become the situation. Giles Tumulty wants to use the Stone in *Many Dimensions* to gain autocratic power; the released Principles in *The Place of the Lion* begin to pursue a widening spiral about their point of origin which will eventually destroy the world; the misuse of the mystic Tarot pack in *The Greater Trumps* lets loose a storm on the world that threatens to ruin it. In every case what is emphasised at the end is the restoration of the world's true nature and balance through the removal or control of the supernatural, rather than interest in the supernatural or that which lies beyond the world for themselves. In a sense we could say that Williams' novels grow progressively less 'other', or 'fantastic', in the transcendental sense. Now his vision is more incarnational: now the supernatural in its naked form is seen as dangerous more than desirable, best realised within the lineaments of flesh and blood. At the end of *The Place of the Lion*, 'The guard that protected earth was set again; the interposition of the Mercy veiled the destroying energies from the weakness of men', and, once they have regained their 'normal' selves, Anthony is returned to Damaris. By the time we reach the novels *Descent into Hell* and *All Hallows' Eve* there are no supernatural objects from some far source at all. Indeed, we might say that the whole sequence of Charles Williams' novels shows a gradual implanting of the supernatural within the world. All his theological works, one might note, emphasise the divine coming down into creation – *He Came down from Heaven* (1938), *The Descent of the Dove* (1939) and *The Forgiveness of Sins* (1942). So in Williams' Christian fantasy the accent is very much on this world. But it is a world which through the incarnated Christ is able to be much more truly itself than it could 'normally' be. That is the point of Anthony Durrant's vision of the strength and subtlety manifested in the world: it is not that they are functions of the Principles, rather that the Principles reveal what in far more complex forms is in them. As seen, Williams calls the whole fabric of this world 'the Co-inherence': for him the world is an organic body or unity imbued with Christ.

This sense of the supernatural multifariousness of the world is, as previously said, accompanied by an equally strong sense of pattern and order within it. In his cycle of poems *Taliessin through Logres* (1938), Williams images the countries of the world as part of the human body, with the head at Britain, the breasts in Gaul, the hands in Rome, the buttocks in Caucasia. The passage quoted above from *All Hallows'*

Eve about the glory of rubbish on the Thames finds it glorious not as rubbish alone but as rubbish that is part of the city's evacuations, part of the order that governs the civic body. Similarly Williams could portray the patience of the railway porter in the same novel as transfiguring him and his office: 'Golden-thighed Endurance, sun-shrouded Justice, were in him, and his face was the deep confluence of the City'; or, in what might seem perhaps to us an excess of fervency, describe the traffic policeman in *The Greater Trumps* as sharing identity with all the controllers and rulers of the world, or a doctor in *The Place of the Lion* as taking on the lineaments of Aesculapius, the great original of all doctors.[16] Wild and multiple though the universe may appear, it is informed by an elaborate patterning that accounts for every least thing and action, all being founded in Christ.

This is why also the 'smallest' acts can be as important as the greatest. The newly dead Lester Furnivall in *All Hallows' Eve* remembers how her husband Richard would bring her water at night when she was thirsty, and to her the deed is a part of universal charity: 'a kind of vista of innumerable someones doing such things for innumerable someones stretched before her . . . . [It] was a deed of such excelling merit on his part that all the choirs of heaven and birds of earth could never properly sing its praise.'[17] Within the web of charity all things can take on a significance which transcends the merely local. In *The Place of the Lion*, which is much concerned with the idea of naming things, we find that names themselves assume larger meaning within the narrative. The house of the magician Berringer, who through his meddling brings the dangerous Principles of being into the world, is called The Joinings; the names of the misguided characters who align themselves with the Lion and the Serpent are Foster and Miss Wilmot. The central character, who succeeds in balancing the principles, is called Anthony Durrant; he edits a local journal called *The Two Camps*. The bookseller Richardson, who, while devoted to God, refuses the Principles and eventually goes to his own destruction, lives at Bypath Villas. The sensible doctor is called Rockbotham. It is true that other main figures, such as Damaris Tighe and Quentin Sabot, do not have such immediately resonant names, but it is not pattern's part to be wholly open to us. These 'significant' names are not just allegorical: they are names that were predestined parts of the pattern from the first. (C. S. Lewis was to use a similar idea with his Ransom in *Perelandra*, who is brought by Maleldil to realise that 'It is not for nothing that you are named Ransom.'[18]) So too, in *The Greater Trumps*, Sybil Conningsby turns out to be 'a sybil indeed'.[19]

Williams' theology, founded on the idea of the participation of all life in the being of Christ, allowed him the belief that any being could exchange its nature with any other; or that, to put it in terms of an'answer' to the modern condition, nothing is finally isolated. In *The Place of the Lion* Anthony Durrant is transfigured at the end to Adam, so that he may enter Eden once more to name the beasts, and in naming them make the world safe once more from the dangerous incursions of the untamed Principles. In *Many Dimensions* the living force of Justice itself breathes through Lord Arglay. In *Descent into Hell* Battle Hill near Hastings becomes the form of Christ's body; in *All Hallows' Eve* Lester feels herself crucified as she intercedes to save Betty Wallingford from the evil Clerk Simon, and later Betty herself re-enacts Christ's miracles of healing. Equally it is possible for a character to take on or participate in the nature of Satan, if he chooses that road long enough. In *War in Heaven* the magician Gregory Persimmons comes to a position where 'He was hungry – but not for food; he was thirsty – but not for drink; he was filled with passion – but not for flesh. He expanded in the rush of an ancient desire; he longed to be married to the whole universe for a bride'; and for a moment he gains 'ecstasy of perfect mastery, marriage in hell, he who was Satan married to that beside which was Satan'.[20]

'The pattern of the glory is a pattern of acts.' Not only are Williams' novels filled with characters or incidental events which can take other and 'larger' being; they are also *sequences* of pattern and rule: thus story and 'history' are made significant (as Williams made a pattern out of his history of the Church in *The Descent of the Dove*, 1939). The operations of the supernatural in particular are highly formalised. In *The Place of the Lion* the Principles enter in stages through Berringer's house: first the Lion, then the Serpent, then the Butterfly, and so on. The Lion begins slowly to pace out an ever-widening circle about the house; and later the Serpent follows the same course. Others remain static, such as the hovering Butterfly or the Phoenix in its burning nest of the house, or later the Lamb standing quietly in the midst of a field while madness goes on about it (embodying the still centre of peace). Others still, such as the Unicorn of speed, flash outwards; or fly above the world, as the Eagle does. But the total effect is of a graded process by which the world is gradually sucked back into the Principles from which it derived its life. Over humans, who are made of all the Principles, no single one of them has immediate power, unless they choose to give themselves to it. But the gradual incursion of the Principles soon involves the removal of all creatures like them: birds and butterflies disappear; the horses of the world follow the Unicorn. And bit by bit strength (the Lion) and intelligence (the Serpent) are removed from the works of man. Eventually man himself may be deprived of power and reason: unless he is a perfect balance of all the Principles he will be drawn into one or other of their orbits depending on his tendency. It is only under the divine mercy that man is saved from this, when in reliving Adam's primal naming of the beasts in Eden Anthony Durrant is able to free the world once more of their wild archetypes.

Similar 'patterns of glory' can be found in *The Greater Trumps*, where the informing idea is of the Cosmic Dance, which the actions follow; or in *Many Dimensions*, where acts of law and mercy interweave with one another about the nature of the Stone. In *Descent into Hell* the very nature of acts themselves is dramatised in the form of the masque all the characters are helping to present. As a masque, in which the characters will act out symbolic versions of their natures, it marries 'unreality' (artistic illusion) with reality. It is also a symbol of co-operative charity. As 'art', the play begs the question of its own status, and by implication that of the novel itself. Its symbolic truth is more than accident or merely human arrangement: it is there because it is part of the pattern of the acts which make up the realisation of this particular divine family of man. The whole novel, as with all of Williams' works, is such that the human characters increasingly appear as actors in some great and eternal drama. Williams believed that from the standpoint of God, in whom all time is eternally present, 'It is finished; we ... do but play out the necessary ceremony.'[21]

In *All Hallows' Eve* the pattern of the acts is subsumed in the workings of the 'co-inherent' City. That city is immediately London, in which the action takes place, and in a ghostly form of which the two dead girls, Lester Furnivall and Evelyn Mercer, walk. But it is also the City, the image of potential charity among men, domiciled within the suffering body of Christ. To give oneself to its workings, to be one with it, is one thing; the other is to seek to pervert it, to bend it to one's will, to attempt mastery where one should submit. On the one side is, as she gradually comes to it, Lester, who disposes herself to the City's nature by diverting to herself the malignity intended for the girl Betty Wallingford, and by trying to the last to save Evelyn Mercer from hell. On the other is the magician Simon the Clerk, who has defied the laws of being by manufacturing an immortality for himself. He has done this also by breaking down the barriers between the world of the living and the dead, by transgressing time to steal facts from the future, by abusing the human body to beget a spiritual slave child, and by perverting his own identity into simulacra of himself which he has sent about the world to do his bidding. All those acts return on Simon by the exact and exacting operation of the laws of the City. The Jew who has sought to make himself a god meets in a roseate cloud and a rain of crucified blood with the God who made Himself a Jew: 'that Jew [Christ] had gone up into the law and according to the law. Now the law was filling the breach in the law.'[22] And this same law, which brings together in hellish collision the separated selves of Simon, at the same time finally divides the dead Lester from her husband Richard. By the law she has in that purgatorial afterworld been able to choose her path, and, having chosen it by virtue of her acts of compassion on behalf of Betty and Evelyn, she must tread it. No facile happy ending here: the note is one of eternal division and glad resignation together (p. 226); the emphasis is on the sharp and precise divisions of the law which is both law and mercy. That same law can even offer some hope of redemption for Lady Wallingford, whose last conscious act, despite her years of hatred for her, was to try to save her daughter from Simon: 'since in that gift she had desired the good of another and not her own, since she had indeed willed to give her self, the City secluded her passion, and took her gift to its own divine self' (p. 238). Within the Christ-ordered web of charity that is the City, all acts become meaningful, and all subject to the co-inherent patterning and law that is the City's nature.[23]

This precision and patterning in Williams' novels can operate in the smallest areas of style also, as one might expect of works founded on the image of a co-inherent body in which every last part exchanges its nature with the greatest. Here for example is the historian Lawrence Wentworth in *Descent into Hell* choosing his reaction to the news that his rival Aston Moffatt has been given a knighthood:

> There was presented to him at once and clearly an opportunity for joy – casual, accidental joy, but joy. If he could not manage joy, at least he might have managed the intention of joy, or (if that also were too much) an effort towards the intention of joy. The infinity of grace could have been contented and invoked by a mere mental refusal of anything but such an effort. He knew his

duty – he was no fool – he knew that the fantastic recognition would please and amuse the innocent soul of Sir Aston, not so much for himself as in some unselfish way for the honour of history. Such honours meant nothing, but they were part of the absurd dance of the world, and to be enjoyed as such. Wentworth knew he could share that pleasure. He could enjoy; at least he could refuse not to enjoy. He could refuse and reject damnation.

With a perfectly clear, if instantaneous, knowledge of what he did, he rejected joy instead. He instantaneously preferred anger, and at once it came; he invoked envy, and it obliged him.[24]

Throughout there is the sense of the way he is going to choose: he had an opportunity; if he had not done this he could at least have done that, or even that, and still Christ would have accepted the tiny motion of goodness. He knew that the honour was no increase of vanity to Sir Aston, knew precisely the comic status of such honours. And yet. It is all in the past, finished. The undertow of the tenses, the bleak, atomised syntax, the portrayal of goodness proffered from outside, not coming from within, sucks all beneath the surface. It is a very telling demolition of Wentworth. It leaves him no motive at all for his refusal save mere habit. It needed the least gesture, and he himself knew the hollowness of such honours. His refusal then is for no reason, for nothing. And 'nothing' is precisely the character of evil, mere 'motiveless malignity', the endless void into which he is eventually to descend.

The precision of the analysis here could be said to express Williams' sense that 'heaven is always exact'. Each paragraph is balanced by its opening statement: in the first he has 'at once and clearly' the chance for joy; in the second he has 'perfectly clear, if instantaneous, knowledge of what he did'. Every word operates to define. If not joy, then the intention; if not intention, then intention to intend. The direction is towards infinite regress, so long as there is *something* at the bottom of it. The infinity that is Christ would accept the infinitesimal movement of the will. The phrase 'contented and invoked' is again fine: no mere passive satisfaction, but also an immediate answering operation of grace. And the obscurity of the negative phrase, 'a mere mental refusal of anything but such an effort', exactly catches how such a positive motion of the will could be almost buried in hedging refusals. Then again the careful discriminations concerning Sir Aston's response – 'please and amuse the innocent soul', and not for himself but history. And then at the end, halting the movement of thought, emerging stark from the complexities of possible immediate behaviour, the implications of his decision: 'He could refuse and reject damnation.' It is typical no doubt of Wentworth's own precision as a historian that his refusal of joy instead should still be couched in exact and apparently controlled terms; yet the precision now lies altogether beyond him, for he is leaving it, his knowledge of what he is doing 'clear, if instantaneous'. His choice of anger and envy is precisely not choice, but a yielding of the self. The ordered language here now records an absence; it depicts its own abolition in the formlessness that is hell. This sort of exactitude, this sort of reflectiveness too, is found throughout Williams' writing. He sets every action, thought or decision within a larger spiritual context, or at least extends and schematises its implications. In this way nothing, not even hell, is left merely itself: it is always seen as part of a larger system and order of interaction.

One other form of patterning and precision-making in the novels arises from the use of recurrent images, which are more than images. In *All Hallows' Eve*, for instance, there is frequent imagery of water. Lester and Evelyn are killed near the Thames. Thereafter for a time they wander in dry places of the City. The picture that Jonathan Drayton the artist has done of Clerk Simon portrays him as a harsh figure standing on a rock preaching to beetle-like disciples who seem to recede inwards towards a fissure that will engulf them. (One is reminded of the 'rock and no water' sequence in Eliot's *The Waste Land*.) But Lester, who previously did her no charity, goes in to Betty. First she asks Betty's remembrance of all she did to her, and her forgiveness, and is given it. At this Betty describes her earliest memory, of being in a lake or a very broad river and being surrounded by fish and borne up by a giant one, till she came to a shore where a woman was standing saying, 'There, dearie, no-one can undo that; bless God for it' (p. 122). In actual fact this is an image of her secret baptism by her old nurse (p. 185). But it is also a continuous action of Christ the fish, in the water of grace, by which she has been able to remember and forgive Lester, and in which she will be able just to bear what the Clerk intends for her. After this she says, almost casually, 'We might go and look at the Thames some time, you and I and Jonathan' (p. 123). The whole chapter (6) is called 'The Wise Water'. When, 'in exchange', Lester gives herself to help Betty and is in the midst of her suffering, she herself has a transfigured vision of water, in the form of her husband Richard bringing her the glass of water at night, through which and her own unselfish act she sees now how easy it is to be free of 'the receding death-light of earth' (p. 147). Lester's charity to Evelyn expresses itself once in a vague idea of giving her 'a drink, a cup of tea or a sherry or a glass of water – something of that material and liquid joy' (p. 164). The Clerk knows nothing of the lake from which Betty sprang: the water in the City is there, but (as in MacDonald's *Lilith*) mysterious and hidden (p. 170).

And so it goes on. Lester returns to the river; sees the rubbish on it and glorifies it; realises too that the river portends a more final division coming between her and this life: 'The under-river sang as it flowed; all the streets of London were full of that sweet inflexible note – the single note she had heard in Betty's room, the bed on which she had safely lain. This was it – bed and note and river, the small cold piercing pain of immortal separation' (p. 198). The water, active in itself, is in a dance of opposition, uniting and separating, binding more strongly in separation. Last, the water becomes rain, the spiritual rain that washes away the sins of the world in Simon, that glues Lady Wallingford to her own cross; and finally it turns into the rain of crucified blood that both redeems and finds the irredeemable. Water thus makes a pattern of a very deep order in the book, and typically of Williams it is a pattern in which the water continually changes its nature, while still remaining itself; nor is it any *mere* symbol or imposed motif, but is portrayed as an active spiritual agency in its own right. And in others of Williams' novels, though perhaps not quite so elaborated as it is here, we have other such recurrent 'images': the Stone, whose solidity expresses the Law and whose organic integration with the body of Chloe Burnett displays the Mercy, in *Many Dimensions*; the motif of naming in *The Place of the Lion* and *All Hallows' Eve*; the 'play' and drama imagery that pervades *Descent into Hell*.

The images in the later novels seem to come from a deeper spiritual level than those in the earlier ones. Here they are not objects or principles, but the very lineaments of the world itself. Here it is not a case of the supernatural, whether in the form of Grails, stones, cards or primal forces, being brought *into* the world, for here the world is, properly seen, supernatural in its very ordinariness. As seen, these later novels are much more directly Christian and incarnational than the earlier ones, where some supernatural object interposed itself between God and man, even if it bespoke the things of heaven. Here, in the imagery of wood or water, of City or human body, the God who was born and died for men seems much closer, more immediate in His actions. Perhaps another way of putting it is that the imagery is less arbitrary and occult, and now much more sacramental and *hallowed*, while still being shaped in Williams' peculiar idiom. Certainly, for him, three 'givens' in life were peculiarly channels for divine action: the image of the beloved, the human body, and the City;[25] all three of these images are fundamental in *Descent into Hell* and *All Hallows' Eve*. In the beloved, as for Dante, is caught a desire for Christ which is made manifest in the pure desire for another human. In the co-operative life both of the body and of the City Williams found the lineaments of the Co-inherence, the interconnection and sharing of all things, which partakes in the nature of heaven. Therefore these last novels radiate a much more mystical sense of immediate and immanent divine action; and this comes over all the more strongly because they deal with situations that permit 'belief' more readily than Holy Grails or magic stones of the First Matter of Creation. We are faced in *Descent into Hell* with the 'ultimate implications' of ordinary-seeming actions, and in *All Hallows' Eve* with a post-death experience which is so much a continuation of life, and so undramatically presented as matter-of-fact, that we half-allow the possibility of such a thing actually happening. (And, one should add, Williams is very skilful in showing the gradual transitions by which Lester realises that she is dead, and eventually grows further into her death.)

But still these sacramental images are only images. Williams used to say of them, 'This also is Thou; neither is this Thou.'[26] Christ is in them; and He is not. God is more than any image; and His nature is such that His presence and His absence may be together in one place, through the co-inherent dance of which He is the centre. Williams' treatment of the images here is slightly more 'incarnational' than that of Lewis. Lewis saw certain images – and they were much more romantic, 'other' and non-sacramental than those of Williams – as suggestive, through the emotions they awoke, of a desire for something more than they. Thus the images were always in a sense mere 'push-buttons' for the deity, and might vary from person to person. Further, what Lewis tended to desire (if we exclude perhaps his last novel, *Till We Have Faces*) was a place, a landscape – the lost Paradise, heaven. What Williams desired was a person. His whole world is conceived of as the body of a man. It is the incarnation and the Cross that move him, not so much the far country from which the God–man came.

And that is why, if we like, Williams never takes us very 'far' imaginatively is his novels. Certainly, of course, he has no interest in space travel. Nobody has to travel anywhere. What happens happens generally in one place. Either the supernatural enters the world somewhere, and must be got rid of there; or, where evil chooses to try to disturb the Co-inherence, it must be answered. All the novels are set in England, and usually in very localised parts of it. In *All Hallows' Eve* the Clerk sends his evil second selves abroad to other nations, but we do not follow them there. In that same novel there is a vision of the co-inherent City of London as containing in itself all other forms of itself – Stone Age, medieval, Elizabethan, Victorian – that have been since the beginning, and also as containing all other cities that are in the world.[27] But the vision is microcosmic: we are being asked to apprehend the city's 'connections', its relatedness, not to travel outwards. Even in the poetry, *Taliessin through Logres* and *The Region of the Summer Stars*, though we move from time to time about the organic and co-inherent body of the world, from the skull of Thule to the breasts of Gaul or the buttocks of the Caucasus, and also to the 'antipodean' world that inverts ours, P'o-L'u, none the less the focus is all on Logres in Britain, and on Camelot: there is never the sense that any place is more wondrous than another by virtue of distance, but rather that all exchange natures with one another within what Williams saw as the diagrammatised web of the glory. To repeat, the emphasis is human. And, rather as in T. S. Eliot's Christian plays, the 'exploration' involves not a journeying outwards of the self, but a journeying into the self, to deeper and deeper awareness of one's true spiritual nature. In this sense Williams is closer to MacDonald than to Kingsley or Lewis (except the Lewis of *That Hideous Strength* and *Till We Have Faces*).

But he is unlike MacDonald – and Eliot – too in that the knowledge of what one is is found in relationship. Lester in *All Hallows' Eve* has never more truly understood her relationship with her husband than when she is dead; and she only goes further into herself when she gives herself to help Betty Wallingford. It is part of Damaris Tighe's self-discovery in *The Place of the Lion* to allow Anthony Durrant to help her; and Anthony's own knowledge of himself and of the world is quickened by his wish to help his friend Quentin Sabot. Relationship is often supposed by the very fact of having interconnected groups of supernatural objects or happenings. The whole of Williams' vision here is founded on the relationship between God and man in the incarnation: 'brothers and sisters in Christ' is to be the aim.

By virtue of this larger relation the 'good' do not need to act, though they must choose: if they choose to put themselves at another's disposal, Another will help accomplish the intended good. It is the evil who seek to change things, who initiate acts: they let the Principles of creation into life, try to get hold of a magic stone or a Grail or gain control over the world of the dead to amass power to themselves. Their opposites wait, watch, and then give themselves. Anthony gives himself to the Eagle of balance; Nancy Coningsby lets the Greater Trumps work for themselves within her hands; Chloe Burnett gives herself to the Stone; Margaret Anstruther makes herself open to the damaged spirit of the suicide from Battle Hill; her daughter Pauline bears the burden of physical pain suffered by her ancestor. Often these acts are accomplished literally while lying down, or at least sitting. Their inactivity heightens our sense of the wonder of what is being done through them. 'The pattern of the glory is a pattern of acts'; but those acts are of a different order from what we know of as act.

That is why the form of the novels has a closer affinity to masque (a genre in which Williams was writing between 1927 and 1929[28]) than to plain story: the object is one of progressive revelation, of showing as far as may be done the ultimate implications of a situation. (Here Williams' analytic, intellectual mode of style is uniquely appropriate too.[29]) The Principles in *The Place of the Lion* seem at first merely a rather large Lion or Serpent, say; then they take on supernatural power; then a book on the angelic hierarchies is found to explain something of what they may ultimately be, and how they all interrelate; then Anthony Durrant learns much more about them by his identification with the Eagle of balance and insight. Finally, the Principles are understood yet further when, in order to stop the threat to the order of the world they represent, Anthony must, through the web of the Co-inherence, become Adam as he was in Paradise, and name the raw energies of life so that they will manifest themselves only in the mild form of beasts. By the end of the novel the universe has been set before us as an incredibly rich, complex and, to the uninitiated, dangerous web of charity. At the same time characters have as it were realised the full implications of their own natures. Damaris Tighe, for instance, who, locked in intellectual and personal pride, saw no relation between her study of Platonic Ideas and real life, finds a vision of herself turned inside-out when she encounters in a menacing pterodactyl her perversion of the Eagle of balance.

Williams' novels are a peculiar mixture of the realistic and the everyday with the starkly 'other'. For some readers the mixture may be more than they can take. An ordinary meal at table, in this context, can turn into a Communion; giving one's seat up in the bus can partake in the vicariousness of Christ; studying one's toe in the bath can lead to a sense of Christ's body – 'How sweet of Love to have a toe like that!';[30] a young man of the 1930s can put on skins and turn into Adam. Some will find it difficult to make such connections: here Williams' vision of the Co-inherence seems much more real than his ability to render it convincing. This is not always so: indeed there are many successes. But Williams' novels will perhaps always remain a minority taste precisely because they attempt such a junction between the apparently banal and the everlasting. For Williams such a junction was what Christ came down to effect; but the belief is not always enough by itself.

Williams' vision is a highly individual one, more so even than those of Kingsley or MacDonald, for our minds are relatively free to enter their worlds and find their spiritual bearings. But Williams' novels come to us with a whole ready-made system of ideas which we have to understand to enter the work. In *The Place of the Lion* there is always the sense that a system is there, and that the gap between the beginning and the end of the novel measures the spiritual and intellectual distance to be covered by Anthony Durrant in compre- hending it. And this is the case in all the novels: there is a curiously liturgical or sacerdotal quality to their vision, as though part of a service,[31] all the more curious when we feel that the source of the vision is most immediately Williams himself. The ideas of co-inherence and substitution, of the geometry of the glory, the images of the City or of the body, are quite specific to Williams' theology, even while they have their source in the nature of Christ. The fantastic world we have to enter in Williams' fiction is doubly fantastic: first a world made strange, and then a body of alien Christian belief.

There is small attempt to make this vision easy for us. Indeed, the harder, the more complex, the more intellectually demanding it is, the more it matches Williams' notion of the glory of God as an incredibly complicated web of exchange. Thus, we are to think; we are to think very hard; and we are to accept the peculiar thoughts we are asked to think. Williams' work is much more *a priori*, much more enclosed, than that of any other writer we have considered. This makes the growing comprehension of his meaning peculiarly rewarding, but it severely limits his appeal. If Williams' theology stresses a God who came down from heaven, we do not have a Williams who comes down to the reader: he always talks from some further coign of vantage, and we are never without the pressure of his larger view.

Most esoteric of all his works, perhaps, are the Arthurian poems *Taliessin through Logres* (1938) and *The Region of the Summer Stars* (1944). The overall scheme is unfinished, but Williams was not concerned with narrative sequence so much as with a series of reflections on aspects of the Arthuriad: that is partly why there is little adherence to chronology in the separate poems. Among the themes explored is the relation of poetry to culture and order, and the extent to which its sympathies, structures and exchanges may be said to mirror the pattern of divine glory: this is why Williams has the spiritually educated poet Taliessin and his perceptions often at the centre. Another is, once more, the idea of the Co-inherence, given form through the focus of the Empire at Byzantium, re-created in the Round Table, and literally 'embodied' in imperial Europe, considered as a human anatomy. The idea of the transfigurations and degradations possible within romantic love runs through the poem, from the relation of Bors and Elayne, through that of Lancelot and Guinevere, to that of Lamorack and Morgause.

Within the lineaments of the Arthuriad, Williams could also explore the Christian pattern of established order and creation, innocence, fall, redemption and ascension, in the establishment of the balance that was the Round Table, the Dolorous Blow that began its destruction, the birth of Galahad out of Lancelot's sinfulness, and the passing of Galahad and the ending of the civilisation in Logres. In Williams' view, of course, such a pattern is not merely a figure of the Christian story, but re-enacts it, through the exchange that is the Co-inherence, at the centre of which is 'a god dominant, miraculous and yet recurrent'.[32] It may be that this is also why Williams does not tell a story here, a sequence of one thing before another: if the last is so mingled with the first, that suggests the bridging of time; if the pattern emerges from a seeming *melange* of separate impressions, that shows all the more the strength of its presence. But in a sense the past is not recurring: Galahad not only 'relives' Christ in his forgiveness of Lancelot and by implication the sinfulness in Arthur's court, but he is also one mode of the Parousia, the *Second* Coming of Christ, described in 1 Corinthians 15.23ff.[33] This promised advent, like all others, is not yet fulfilled, and the vision of co-inherent life on earth is withdrawn: it is at once a lost apocalypse and a stronger assurance of the one to come.

All these ideas, images and movements surge within a poem that sometimes labours under their weight, sometimes flashes with real poetic apprehension – a poem made still more inaccessible to us than the novels, dealing as it does not only with 'mythological' material in a non-narrative mode, but glancing so intensively at its packed ideas that they often shiver and multiply before us:

> On the forms of ancient saints, my heroes, your thumbs,
> as on a winch the power of man is wound
> to the last inch; there ground is prepared
> for the eared and seeded harvest of propinquant goodwill,
> drained the reeded marches, cleared the branched jungles
> where the unthumbed shapes of apes swung and hung.
>
> ('Bors to Elayne: On the King's Coins')

For Williams, part of the dialectic of the glory was always between flesh and the bone beneath, between the image and the idea: whether the intellectual lineaments of his poetry overwhelm their embodiment must, however, be the question. He wrote, in *Taliessin through Logres*, 'When sensation slips from intellect, expect the tyrant': and elsewhere, 'eternity always insists on being analysed'.[34]

One further point concerning Williams' use of fantasy must be the degree of reality he felt to inhere in his own invented worlds. The worlds of *All Hallows' Eve*, *Descent into Hell* and the poems, for example, seem closer to divine reality than those of *Many Dimensions* and *The Greater Trumps*, with their more fictive supernatural agents. For all, though, it would in greater or lesser degree be a case of 'This also is Thou; neither is this Thou.' Williams was, as said, fond of masque, which impacts directly on the real world; in *Descent into Hell* and *All Hallows' Eve* art is seen to shape reality, which is itself patterned like art. Virgil and Taliessin in *Taliessin through Logres* alike build civilisations through pen or harp. Williams wants to show that the real world does not exist to and for itself, that it is permeable. That is why he has it 'invaded' or 'shot through' with the supernatural in his work. Nothing is cut off: all is part of the Co-inherence, and subject to exchange of nature. For him, therefore, 'myth' and 'fact' are interchangeable: 'In a sense, of course, history is itself a myth; to the imaginative, engaged in considering these things, all is equally myth.'[35]

For all that, it has to be said that Williams' Christian fantasy is more immediately fictive than that of Kingsley or MacDonald. In *The Water-Babies*, the empiricist Kingsley gives us as near as possible an imitation of nature as it is, and then tries to show how God may be deciphered in it. He suggests that the world of his story is to be seen as 'nature' rather than 'art', and he gives a model of what we can do for ourselves by the same means in the scarce-different world outside. (The individual actions of his characters are, however, more fictive, as is the account of Tom's baptism and confirmation: this is Tom's personal history, and, though we may experience some form of it, we will not do so in this mode.) As for MacDonald's fantasy, and the worlds it presents, it is always intended as an expression of the unconscious imagination: that is, its peculiarities come directly from the God-inspired faculty that is within man, and in that sense it is again directly connected to our world and a mirror of one aspect of it.

Williams, however, presents us with a world remade to express his vision: this is the world as it variously might be, a world less given than invented. Some images – of the body, the City, the beloved, or of pattern and rule – seem to have an almost sacramental character for Williams, but the imagined worlds are seen, like most other created things, as contingent in their reality. There is no direct pressure in Williams' work to have us believe in any one of them, only to wonder at the complexities of divine design and love, portrayed through an imagery which is no more adequate than any other to express them – even while it does demonstrate Williams' general belief in the permeability of the world to Christ. In this sense Williams' Christian vision has less immediate and specific relation to us than Kingsley's or MacDonald's. The process – if we may call it this – is taken further in the work of C. S. Lewis; for there God and Christianity are portrayed through the even greater fictionality of invented worlds remote from our time or space. Lewis, however, we shall also find much more concerned to help us travel there.

17

C. S. Lewis

Lewis owed much in his fantasy to both George MacDonald and Charles Williams (which gives some idea of how much of a small modern group these writers make). His debt to MacDonald was not just literary: his first reading of *Phantastes* in 1916 came at a crucial stage in his spiritual development, and he felt that the experience 'baptised' his imagination and pushed him out of agnosticism and over the Christian frontier.[1] So influenced did he feel by MacDonald's work and the character within it that he had a fictional George MacDonald take part in his *The Great Divorce*, meeting the narrator in a borderland of Heaven and discussing the nature of providence and damnation; and in the same year, 1946, he edited a selection of MacDonald's work – *George MacDonald: An Anthology*. As for Williams, Lewis wrote to him after reading his *The Place of the Lion* in 1936, and, when Williams moved to Oxford with Oxford University Press during the war, he and Lewis became quite close friends, and he joined the select group of Oxford Christians known as the 'Inklings', which included Tolkien. Lewis wrote a detailed explication of Williams' Arthurian poems, *Arthurian Torso* (1948); and his *That Hideous Strength* is in idiom and setting very much indebted to Charles Williams' novels. To MacDonald's work Lewis owes much of his idea of *Sehnsucht*, his feeling that certain images in the world peculiarly subsume the divine, though they must never be mistaken for it. This is one of the leitmotifs of his fiction. With MacDonald also he shares a sense of some 'great good coming', the feeling that this world is not our true home, but some other place which we have either long since lost or never yet found. To Williams he feels drawn partly for his strong feeling for Christian medievalism, and his re-creation of universes of energetic and hierarchic love in his fiction. Williams also appealed for his clarity, his sense of order and pattern behind the world; and, like MacDonald, for his sacramentalist approach to images.

Yet we should not exaggerate the influence of these two. Lewis looked for sources as he looked for friends: he is essentially gregarious in his vision. One is struck also by the many sheer differences between him and these writers. Unlike Williams', for instance, his fantasy takes place off-world. *The Pilgrim's Regress: An Allegorical Apology for Christianity, Reason and Romanticism* (1933) is set in a landscape of the soul; *Out of the Silent Planet* (1938) and *Perelandra* (1943) take the reader on trips to mythical versions of Mars and Venus; *The Great Divorce: A Dream* (1946) starts in Hell and takes us by bus to a region near Heaven; the *Chronicles of Narnia* (1950–6) are set in a little universe reached through a magic wardrobe and by other means; *Till We Have Faces: A Myth Retold* (1956) occurs in a country named Glome to the north of Greece in classical times. Lewis said that he resorted to such realms because the world had been so fully explored that there was no place left for wonder:

> Those who wish to visit strange regions in search of such beauty, awe, or terror as the actual world does not supply have increasingly been driven to other planets or other stars. It is the result of increasing geographical knowledge. The less known the real world is, the more plausibly your marvels can be related near at hand. As the area of knowledge spreads, you need to go further afield: like a man moving his house further and further out into the country as the new building estates catch him up. Thus in Grimm's *Märchen*, stories told by peasants in wooded country, you need only walk an hour's journey into the next forest to find a home for your witch or ogre .... Homer, writing for a maritime people has to take Odysseus several days' journey by sea before he meets Circe, Calypso, the Cyclops, or the Sirens .... By the eighteenth century we have to move well out into the country. Paltock and Swift take us to remote seas, Voltaire to America. Rider Haggard had to go to unexplored Africa or Tibet; Bulwer Lytton, to the depths of the Earth. It might have been predicted that stories of this kind would, sooner or later, have to leave Tellus altogether.[2]

What is notable here is that Lewis associates wonder with distance: for him it is something removed from our everyday experience. This is precisely opposite to Charles Williams, who sought to show that the everyday and the commonplace, the 'known', were themselves wonderful. For Lewis it is precisely the *super*natural that is interesting, where it was not for Williams. Further, Williams 'collapses' distance in his idea of Christ's acts as ever present within 'the Co-inherence': all times and all places may be seen to interweave with one another. For Lewis, 'He is not here, but is risen':[3] Christ's acts, while they have accomplished our redemption, are historical and past. Williams, it might be said, lives in Christ, while Lewis lives towards Him. Lewis's very mention of 'wonder' and its desirability suggest the need to thirst towards something: he is essentially goal-seeking. This may account for the fact that narrative matters rather more to him than it does to Williams. In Williams' stories something has often temporarily gone wrong and has to be put right so that the world can remain much as it is. Foolish or evil men admit supernatural forces into the world and these have to be checked or tamed by people acting within the Co-inherence. But Lewis's stories are more in the nature of quests towards an end. There is more certainty in Williams' work that the evil will be circumscribed: indeed, its energetic opposition to good is seen almost as part of the heavenly scheme; thus in a sense it is always 'going nowhere'. But there is much more suspense in Lewis's narratives. We do not know what Ransom will find on Mars, nor how the temptation of the Lady on Perelandra will end, nor how the gods in *Till We Have Faces* will answer Orual. The central characters have an aim that sends them on a journey, whether it is to save a primally innocent Lady from a tempter, or to find a lost prince, or the island of one's desires.

But the larger aim behind most of the stories is the realisation of 'otherness'. Lewis could write of David Lindsay and his *A Voyage to Arcturus* (1921), 'He is the first writer to discover what "other planets" are really good for in fiction. No merely physical strangeness or merely spatial distance will realize that idea of otherness which is what we are always trying to grasp in a story about voyaging through space: you must go into another dimension.'[4] Thus not only has he moved beyond Earth to the planets, but they are the planets mythically conceived, not those as science knows them:

> I took a hero once to Mars in a space-ship, but when I knew better I had angels convey him to Venus. Nor need the strange worlds, when we get there, be at all strictly tied to scientific probabilities. It is their wonder, or beauty, or suggestiveness that matter. When I myself put canals on Mars I believe I already knew that better telescopes had already dissipated that old optical delusion. The point was that they were part of the Martian myth as it already existed in the common mind.[5]

Lewis's desire for 'wonder-in-distance' may in part account for the fact that he has created so many sheerly different fantastic worlds,

each quite 'other' in relation to the last – the allegorical world of
The Pilgrim's Regress, Mars, Perelandra, the environs of Heaven, Narnia,
Glome. Williams' fantastic world is always this one; and the fantastic
worlds in George MacDonald are not so sheerly different from one
another as those in Lewis – for instance, the Fairy Land that Anodos
wanders in in *Phantastes* is not unlike the 'region of the seven
dimensions' which Vane of *Lilith* enters, nor even the fairy-tale context
of castles, mines, magic old ladies, wild beasts and evil cities in the
'Curdie' books. It is fair to say that 'otherness' and fantasy-making
are in one sense, for Lewis, synonymous.

This sense of otherness, and the spiritual desire or *Sehnsucht* it
awakens, is one of the central threads of Lewis's experience as a
Christian. It was the experience of that otherness in the form of
'holiness' in reading MacDonald's *Phantastes* that transformed him.
All through his life he found that an image or event could
unexpectedly become luminous with promise and fill him with the
sense of an 'unnameable something, desire for which pierces us like
a rapier at the smell of a bonfire, the sound of wild ducks flying
overhead, the title of *The Well at the World's End*, the opening lines
of *Kubla Khan*, the morning cobwebs in late summer, or the noise of
falling waves'.[6] This desire, though awakened by these things, is
not to be identified with them, or it will leave them: 'For they are
not the thing itself; they are only the scent of a flower we have not
found, the echo of a tune we have not heard, news from a country
we have never yet visited.'[7] And that far-off country is heaven, the
longing for which is implanted in us by God. Lewis went so far as
to claim that the course of his spiritual experience as described in
his *Surprised by Joy* followed a kind of lived proof of God's
existence, in as much as by refining away the 'dross' of false
apprehensions of images he came to find their true source in
heaven.[8] And to this he could readily add a condensed 'logical'
argument to clinch the matter:

> We remain conscious of a desire which no natural happiness will
> satisfy. But is there any reason to suppose that reality offers any
> satisfaction to it? 'Nor does the being hungry prove that we have
> bread.' But I think it may be urged that this misses the point. A
> man's physical hunger does not prove that that man will get any
> bread; he may die of starvation on a raft in the Atlantic. But
> surely a man's hunger does prove that he comes of a race which
> repairs its body by eating and inhabits a world where eatable

substances exist. In the same way, though I do not believe (I wish I did) that my desire for Paradise proves that I shall enjoy it, I think it a pretty good indication that such a thing exists and that some men will. A man may love a woman and not win her; but it would be very odd if the phenomenon called 'falling in love' occurred in a sexless world.[9]

(Just such a phenomenon of falling in love in a sexless world – though Lewis would say it is not 'falling in love' in his sense – is portrayed by George MacDonald in *Phantastes*, in the story of the strange planet which Anodos finds in the fairy palace.) This longing in Lewis for the 'wholly other' (in Rudolf Otto's phrase[10]), this feeling that the world has only broken imagery of it, this wish to get among new created worlds beyond our own – all these come, of course, from a desire for heaven, as Lewis says; but they also could be said to come from an escapist impulse which is peculiar to our times and to certain 'reactionary' responses to it. Lewis praised Tolkien's defence of the escapist impulse of fantasy in terms of the right of a prisoner of war to escape his barbed-wire surroundings.[11] Tolkien had small love for the modern industrialised world; and, on the evidence of *That Hideous Strength* alone, neither did Lewis.[12] While Lewis might, like Tolkien, find beauty in natural scenes, he also felt radically unhappy with a world to which he felt he did not truly belong, a world which, looked back on from Mars in *Out of the Silent Planet*, is seen as cut off from the 'celestial commonwealth' and subject to the Black Archon, and so constituted that the messages of God are 'gleams of celestial strength and beauty falling on a jungle of filth and imbecility'.[13]

MacDonald shares a sense of alienation from this world. But his is less conditioned by a reaction to its modern aspect: he simply knows it mystically, as a poor shadow of a greater world beyond it – 'Oh dear, what a mere inn of a place the world is! and thank God! we must widen and widen our thoughts and hearts. A great good is coming to us all – too big for this world to hold.'[14] That good can be intuited now, if we live, like God, in our own unconscious minds. MacDonald does not believe in the divine distance: He is most poignantly present, and man has only to cast off this worldly garment in death to be with Him – 'Home is ever so far away in the palm of your hand, and how to get there it is of no use to tell you', Mr Raven says to Vane in *Lilith*;[15] 'distance' is of spirit only. In his belief that we should live mystically, MacDonald is much more akin to Williams than to Lewis. He and Lewis may both be 'Platonists', but they differ in the nature of their world-renouncing. And in the same way, though MacDonald shares with Lewis the concept of Romantic yearning, or *Sehnsucht*, in Lewis the yearning is for something wholly other and beyond, while in MacDonald it is for one's true self – 'man is dead if he know not the Power which is his cause, his deepest selfing self; the Presence which is not himself, and is nearer to him than himself; which is infinitely more himself, more his very being, than he is himself'.[16]

Because Lewis so looks beyond the world, and beyond or outside the 'given' in our experience, whether it be the mind as in MacDonald, or this world itself as it is variously in Kingsley and Williams, his fantasy is necessarily even more fictional. The imagined realms of *Phantastes* and *Lilith* may be 'untrue' by themselves, but they are also pictures of the unconscious mind which we are all encouraged to enter. The actual created worlds of Charles Williams' *The Place of the Lion* or *All Hallow's Eve* may be invented, but they are also images of the world as Williams believed it supernaturally to be, and as he would have us perceive it too. But Lewis's Mars, with its vertical spires of rock, its bizarre vegetation and its various alien races, is in no sense an image of our world, nor is it meant to be taken as at all 'real'. Rather, it is *desirable*, as a desirable image of a world entirely invented by one man may be. Of course, it may have final reality, along the lines of Tolkien's 'All tales may come true; and yet, at the last, redeemed, they may be as like and as unlike the forms that we give them as Man, finally redeemed, will be like and unlike the fallen that we know.'[17] Lewis had his own way of putting this belief: he argued that 'what was myth in one world might always be fact in some other';[18] thus within his own work he has the myth of the Cyclops become reality on Mars, and realises the Garden of the Hesperides on Perelandra, and Medusa on the Moon.[19] But none of this alters the fact that the worlds in which these things are made to become 'real' are still imaginary.

How then is the sense of this 'otherness' realised in Lewis's fantasy? The procedure is broadly akin to that which we find in other writers of nineteenth-and twentieth-century Christian fantasy: we start with an ordinary-seeming world and then find it transformed to something of far greater depth than could ever have been guessed. MacDonald begins with the world and then draws us deeper and deeper into the mind until we realise something of its divine roots; Kingsley takes us into nature to the point where the principles behind it appear, and then further, to sense what it is that sustains the principles. Williams starts with an ordinary person on a London bridge; then gradually reveals this person to be newly dead; then builds up a picture of the 'supernatural' City she now inhabits; then shows how through her acts she may reveal that City to be a network of divine action founded in Christ. In a similar manner Lewis in *Out of the Silent Planet* starts us with a man out on a walking-tour; has him happen across two men who are about to travel to Mars in a spaceship they have constructed; then has him captured and taken to Mars as a sacrifice for the supposedly hostile inhabitants. Thereafter he has him encounter the strangeness of Mars and then of its rational inhabitants; and last has him meet an angelic intelligence or Oyarsa who governs the planet, and who conveys something of the divine nature of the universe in which Mars is set, from awareness of which the inhabitants of Earth are excluded. Thus seen, the process is a form of analysis, and exemplifies the kind of tapering which allows the reader the more readily to move from one mode of understanding reality to another.

But in Lewis's case the process is also somewhat different. For one thing, Lewis tends to focus much more than the others on the unseating of previous assumptions. For him the displacement of one level of reading reality by another is the key, for in that sudden enlargement of consciousness, that sense of 'fallings from us, vanishings',[20] he found one form of the experience of otherness. Lewis saw that as the effect of mythic narrative on the reader also:

It goes beyond the expression of things we have already felt. It arouses in us sensations we have never had before, never anticipated having, as though we had broken out of our normal mode of consciousness and 'possessed joys not promised to our birth'. It gets under our skin, hits us at a level deeper than our thoughts or even our passions, troubles oldest certainties till all questions are re-opened, and in general shocks us more fully awake than we are for most of our lives.[21]

For Lewis the experience of shifting from one level of understanding to another is important in itself, because it gives that sudden shock of alienation that opens our spirits. The more we are dislocated from old modes of seeing, the more we will be able to align ourselves towards God. Thus, while Lewis's books do operate as analyses towards deeper levels of reality, the experience of the process itself is important. For Lewis the Christian theologian, our limited consciousness is a direct product of the fall; to have that consciousness continually broken down is to escape from self and come nearer to God. For Lewis the Christian apologist, however, we are also blinkered by modern secularism. Ransom's experience in *Out of the Silent Planet* is one of a continual opening to a wider reality. His terrors of Mars give way to scientific curiosity and wonder, and as they do so he is able to meet and communicate with the different species of the planet and eventually with its guiding spiritual intelligence as the other men who took him there cannot: because they remain stuck in their old selves they do not understand the Malacandrian races, do not come to love the planet and cannot see the Oyarsa.[22]

This process of undercutting assumptions takes many different forms. In *The Pilgrim's Regress* it is a journey of *Sehnsucht* or spiritual yearning itself. The central character, John, has been brought up to fear the grim-seeming Landlord of his country (a Calvinist view of God). One day he has an experience which completely changes all his previous views of the world: he is out in the road near his home when he hears a very sweet musical note, and a voice bidding him, 'Come.' Then he sees that in the stone wall by the road there is a window, which he has never seen before; and through the window he sees a woodland full of primroses which he seems to remember from early childhood; yet it seems still further back,

> very long ago – so long that even in the moment of remembering the memory seemed still out of reach. While he strained to grasp it, there came to him from beyond the wood a sweetness and a pang so piercing that instantly he forgot his father's house, and his mother, and the fear of the Landlord, and the burden of the rules. All the furniture of his mind was taken away .... It seemed to him that a mist which hung at the far end of the wood had parted for a moment, and through the rift he had seen a calm sea, and in the sea an island, where the smooth turf sloped down unbroken to the bays, and out of the thickets peeped the pale, small-breasted Oreads, wise like gods, unconscious of themselves like beasts, and tall enchanters, bearded to their feet, sat in green chairs among the forests. But even while he pictured these things he knew, with one part of his mind, that they were not like the things he had seen – nay, that what had befallen him was not seeing at all. But he was too young to heed the distinction: and

too empty, now that the unbounded sweetness passed away, not to seize greedily whatever it had left behind.[23]

'All the furniture of his mind was taken away': that is what is progressively to happen; but only for a moment here. What follows is that John makes the discovery of this supposed island his object in life. Because of his limited perception, and his greedy desire to possess things, he for long confuses the island with others of his desires, whether for sex, power or the intellectually daring. He then passes through a period of disillusion from which the use of his reason releases him. And so through progressively more 'sophisticated' and profound misapplications of his longing, until under the influence of Mother Kirk, who enables him to cross a grand canyon (his and man's fallen sinfulness), he begins to apprehend something of the true source of his longings. He is told that they are sent by the Landlord, and that the picture forms they take vary from time to time and from man to man. Then he is shown the island of his desires itself, and realises that he no longer needs it. At the same time he is brought to realise that the shape of the island is the shape of the Landlord's mountain which he left so long ago, and that in travelling apparently away from the Landlord he has been travelling towards him. His whole world-view is reversed, just as he now must return all the now-changed way he has come to reach his divine goal.

A not dissimilar mode of 'otherness' occurs in Lewis's *Till We Have Faces*, where the main character, Orual, is brought to realise that her long complaint against the gods for 'stealing' her friend Psyche from her, and for refusing fully to reveal themselves, is its own answer; further that, all the time that Psyche is supposed to have been carrying out the tasks set by the god, the burden of those tasks has in fact been carried by Orual herself. Truth reveals itself at deeper and deeper levels: she comes to see that 'nothing is yet in its true form'.

In these fantasies it is largely the self and its promptings that are found to be ultimately 'other'. In many of his works Lewis is concerned to portray a journey through a deepening sense of otherness in the 'outer' world. He does this not so much through the technique of reversal we have just witnessed as through a linear or sequential displacement, from the 'natural' to the supernatural and divine. We have already seen something of this process in *Out of the Silent Planet*, in Ransom's journey from Earth to Mars and its innocent inhabitants and thence to its angelic intelligence and the larger divine reality it represents. In *The Lion the Witch and the Wardrobe* (1950), the children move from the 'real' twentieth-century world through the magic wardrobe to the realm of Narnia, where are witches, dwarves, fauns and talking beavers; then Narnia's winter is changed to spring with the arrival from outside of the great lion Aslan, who is much more than lion; then beyond that Aslan opposes to the magic of the evil White Witch a far deeper magic from beyond the beginning of time, through which, by his offering his life as sacrifice in place of another's, he may after his death come to life once more. This last is a divine level of truth which, having been reached, ends with Aslan going again from Narnia for a time, leaving the children to govern for some years before they in turn find their way back to their original world. Only in *The Last Battle* (1956) does the divine truth that was inside Narnia become the truth that opens it to final realities, as Aslan opens the door out of the dying world of Narnia to the new and ever-better Narnias beyond. This journey through 'otherness' is also seen in the progressively more magical, until sacred, places visited by the ship in *The Voyage of the Dawn Treader* (1953). In *Perelandra* Ransom's first vision of the planet is in terms of random lines and then shapes; then a 'solid', as he becomes aware that he is swimming in a huge ocean; then, as he encounters, in sequence, a floating island, plants and trees, animals, a primally innocent woman and Maleldil in her, he ascends the ladder of being. With each step his previous assumptions about the character of reality are displaced.

'As though we had broken out of our normal mode of consciousness': 'out of' is the Key phrase here. The process is often one of literally going out of one's previous narrow purview – *Out of the Silent Planet*, out from the confines of Hell in *The Great Divorce* to the precincts of Heaven, out from home into the wider spiritual world in *The Pilgrim's Regress*, out from the fearfulness of the veiled self in *Till We Have Faces*. In *That Hideous Strength* Lewis portrays hell through a reverse image of this: the book is set on Earth, subject to the devil's power, and Mark Studdock, who has in part unwittingly allied himself to agencies ultimately in league with hell, discovers this fact through a progressive narrowing of his purview, until he finds it in a little room; further, what he finds is nothing, only the infinitely banal and vacuous. In *The Great Divorce* hell turns out to be a tiny crack in the grassy floor of the heavenly region visited, and 'a damned soul is nearly nothing: it is shrunk, shut up in itself'.[24] People who live in safe groups, or confined to buildings, tend to be people who are spiritually lost or in danger in Lewis's fiction: for him exposure, opening-out, imaged in the naked body and receptive soul of the Lady on Perelandra, are the ways away from self and towards the 'other'.[25] It is interesting here again to contrast Williams with Lewis; for, whereas in Lewis's work we usually move outwards, in Williams' things come into focus in one place, person or object. For both, though, the object is the same: to make things other than they seem to the modern agnostic mind (whether of characters within the books or of the reader).

But the most highly wrought presentation of otherness is undoubtedly *Perelandra* (1943). The protagonist, Ransom, who went to Mars by spaceship in *Out of the Silent Planet* is here sent to 'Venus' in a white coffin-shaped casket through angelic agency. On arriving, he finds the planet to be largely oceanic, with islands of floating vegetation, though there is some solid, or 'fixed', land too. Though the ocean and its waves are gigantic and the floating islands are novel, nothing is *wholly* unlike our world. On Mars, by contrast, the world is at once wholly alien, entirely conditioned by a theme of perpendicularity which makes every least hummock of earth or wavelet on a lake into a spout of earth or water; and each rational species is quite different from the others, the long, furred, seal-like *hrossa* from the tall, spindly, humanoid *sorns*, and both from the frog-like *pfifltriggi*.

And yet, for all that it has likenesses to our world, Perelandra is quite other at a spiritual level. The ocean, for one thing, is part animate, the expression of the character of Venus herself. We see this most when Ransom meets a human figure floating on one of the islands. This figure turns out to be not the man he supposed, but a green lady. Nor is she just a green lady. As he talks to her, and she tells him of her love for her husband and her love for 'Maleldil', who made her, we realise that she is unfallen, and that the whole planet with her is in a sense primally innocent. Nor is this lady to be seen as 'a new Eve': her innocence is *sui generis*. Lewis once said that 'where the god and the *idolon* [here Maleldil and his image in the Lady] were most nearly one there was least danger of confounding them'.[26] Thus Ransom's early assumptions about her are undercut, and the planet is always more truly strange for seeming to have features like ours. As he speaks to her, the gulf between them opens even as they speak: Ransom comes to realise that he is not dealing only with an alien psyche, but with one that is wholly apart from his.

There was no category in the terrestrial mind which would fit her. Opposites met in her and were fused in a fashion for which we have no images. One way of putting it would be to say that neither our sacred nor our profane art could make her portrait. Beautiful, naked, shameless, young – she was obviously a goddess: but then the face, the face so calm that it escaped insipidity by the very concentration of its mildness, the face that was like the sudden coldness and stillness of a church when we enter it from a hot street – that made her a Madonna. The alert, inner silence which looked out from those eyes overawed him; yet at any moment she might laugh like a child, or run like Artemis or dance like a Mænad. (pp. 71–2)

The Lady's innocence is a unique blend of ignorance and far superior knowledge: the attitude towards her flickers between an impulse towards condescension and one towards worship. She does not know what time is, or what to possess a thing means; when Ransom asks her to take him to her home, the 'place where people live together and have their possessions and bring up their children', she replies by spreading out her hands, 'to indicate all that was in sight. "This is my home," she said.' Paradise here is no single place as on Earth, but the whole planet. On *Perelandra* any one view is transformed by another, just as the huge ocean is endlessly moving and as the floating islands no sooner look like one sort of landscape than by virtue of the shaping action of the sea beneath them they change to one quite different. Indeed the 'enemy' on Perelandra is in a sense fixity: Maledil has forbidden the Lady and her Lord to sleep on the fixed Land, and it is the objective of the evil Un-man to persuade her to do so. At the end of the novel the Lady describes to Ransom how she has been brought to see precisely what would be evil in doing this:

How could I wish to live there except because it was Fixed? And why should I desire the Fixed except to make sure – to be able on one day to command where I should be the next and what should happen to me? It was to reject the wave – to draw my hands out of Maleldil's, to say to Him, 'Not thus, but thus' – to put in our own power what times should roll towards us.... (p. 239)

It is part of such awareness that, even while this is true here, fixity of land or even of purpose is not on other worlds an evil, as on Earth or

Malacandra: as the angelic song has it at the end of *Perelandra*, in this idiom, 'Never did He make two things the same' (p. 246).

Ransom is continually being thrown out of his previous assumptions. The Lady knows nothing of pain, evil or death, and has no concept of self, of ownership or of home. She welcomes everything to the planet, even an emissary of the devil, because it is in the character of her innocence to accept every 'wave', every experience, viewing it as sent by Maledil. When the Un-man 'tempts' her to sleep on the Fixed Land, this is not to her a temptation, but a matter for rational discussion. The Un-man itself is no hideous or melodramatic devil, but the devil in the body of a middle-aged Cambridge scientist.

As for the temptation itself, it is a whole series of spiritual displacements for Ransom. For instance, at one point the Un-man says that if Eve had not fallen men would never have experienced the colossal gift of Christ's redemption of them; out of the fall comes not evil but a better good. Ransom is temporarily floored by this (pp. 137–8). He begins to think, as the Un-man presses home its attack by 'third-degree' methods of ceaseless propaganda, that the Lady must fall, and that, while the devil is all too present, God is not (p. 159). But then a 'Voice' – typically it is not identified with Maleldil – speaks in his mind by night, telling him that 'God' is present: for he, Ransom, is His representative. Moreover, 'It is not for nothing that you are named Ransom': Ransom sees that his name, which to him has been contingent, is part of a great pattern in which he has been the projected key through all time (168–9). On Earth it is reasonable for us to distinguish between the accidental and the essential. 'But step outside that frame and the distinction drops down into the void, fluttering useless wings. He had been forced out of the frame, caught up into the larger pattern.' Beyond this an even more terrifying piece of knowledge is given to Ransom: '"My name also is Ransom", said the Voice' (168). He realises that, if he does not save the Lady, Maleldil will have to redeem the planet in 'some act of even more appalling love, some glory of yet deeper humility' (p. 169) than he accomplished as Christ on Earth.

And yet what is being asked of him seems so *unreasonable*. For the Voice is suggesting to him that he defeat the Un-man not through argument but by fighting it, physically. Ransom thinks this as absurd as if the elephant should have trodden on the serpent in Eden. But he is brought to realise that comparisons with other contexts are irrelevant, for 'This chapter, this page, this very sentence, in the cosmic story was utterly and eternally itself; no other passage that had occurred or ever would occur could be substituted for it' (p. 166). Furthermore, the story suggests that the categories of 'mental' and 'physical' are irrelevant: that in a sense Ransom has been fighting the Un-man with his body while he has been arguing with it hitherto, and that when he attacks it physically he will also in a sense be continuing the debate. We begin to see too that Ransom's objections to fighting the Un-man are founded not simply on rational grounds: he is terrified of it. Yet here too he is shifted to a new level of awareness and courage as he begins to see that a physical fight between him and the Un-man will be a fairly even match, involving 'one middle-aged, sedentary body against another' (p. 166).[27]

And that is how the whole book works, shifting us out of assumptions to deeper knowledge, and revealing even that deeper knowledge to be of only provisional reality. The rest of the story is partly an account of Ransom's development towards an understanding of the paradoxical nature of truth, celebrated in a vision spoken and given to him by the Oyéresu or planetary guardians of Mars and Venus at the end, in which he learns how in Maleldil all things are at once supremely important and superfluous, central and peripheral, how time is both serial and eternally co-present, how God is in the meanest grain as in the greatest angel. Mere mortal Ransom may still remain at the end of this book; but he has also been translated beyond all knowing, and the bleeding heel with which he is sent back to Earth is no more the mark of his approaching end than it is the signature of Maleldil that will bring him back to Perelandra and the blessed isle of Aphallin.

By means of dislocation, upset expectation, tapering towards the supernatural, and paradox, Lewis makes us experience something of the abyss of thought that is God. In a moment we shall look at the means by which he not only makes us feel it, but makes us desire to feel more of it. For the present let us just consider what is happening in Lewis's work. All this stress on 'otherness' and on realising God's existence is peculiarly appropriate for one who like Lewis was all his life either hounded or haunted by the divine presence. As an atheist Lewis felt that God searched him out; as a Christian he all too often felt he had to prove Him. The 'further' he was from God, in this sense, the more real He was: perhaps that partly explains why Lewis keeps rewriting Him off the world into fairy lands or other planets; after all, we have seen him associating wonder with distance. But the effect of this stress on his works is quite distinctive. It makes them a unique blend of exciting narrative and contemplation, of things happening and things being looked at. For all Lewis's love of stories, their sequence was in the end a means, though an essential one, towards catching an elusive 'quality':

> In real life, as in a story, something must happen. That is just the trouble. We grasp at a state and find only a succession of events in which the state is never quite embodied. The grand idea of finding Atlantis which stirs us in the first chapter of the adventure story is apt to be frittered away in mere excitement when the journey has once been begun . . . . All that happens may be delightful: but can any such series quite embody the sheer state of being which was what we wanted? . . .
>
> In life and art both, as it seems to me, we are always trying to catch in our net of successive moments something that is not successive. Whether in real life there is any doctor who can teach us how to do it, so that at last either the meshes will become fine enough to hold the bird, or we be so changed that we can throw our nets away and follow the bird to its own country, is not a question for this essay ['On Stories']. But I think it is sometimes done – or very, very nearly done – in stories. I believe the effort to be well worth making.[28]

Actually the elusive bird is for Lewis to be found also in images. It is not with narratives, but with pictures, that his fantasies begin:

> All my seven Narnian books, and my three science fiction books, began with seeing pictures in my head. At first they were not a story, just pictures.[29]

> Everything began with images; a faun carrying an umbrella, a queen on a sledge, a magnificent lion.[30]

> The starting point of the second novel, *Perelandra*, was my mental picture of the floating islands. The whole of the rest of my labours in a sense consisted of building up a world in which floating islands could exist.[31]

It was a sense of holiness – of a quality – that Lewis felt came through the story of George MacDonald's *Phantastes*.

The need to demonstrate the *existence* of God is, as said before, one peculiar to the modern period, in which it is deemed less and less certain. The need for fantasy to be oriented towards being rather than becoming, towards the contemplation of a Reality at least as much as action within it, is one that is also peculiar to post-Romantic Christian fantasy. Lewis does not differ from others in kind so much as in degree. The paradox is that his contemplativeness, the dominance of emotion in his work, comes out of narratives which are far more 'narrative', and far more concerned with objectives and suspense, than those of MacDonald, Kingsley or Williams.

At the centre of Lewis's fantastic worlds is desire, and the desirable. In a sense many of his fantasies are designed around creative worlds which are images conveying *Sehnsucht*. The great ocean of Venus, with floating islands of feathery vegetation on it, is full of a pleasure at once physical and far more:

> The water gleamed, the sky burned with gold, but all was rich and dim, and his eyes fed upon it undazzled and unaching. The very names of green and gold, which he [Ransom] used perforce in describing the scene, are too harsh for the tenderness, the muted iridescence, of that warm, maternal, delicately gorgeous world. It was mild to look upon as evening, warm like summer noon, gentle and winning like early dawn.   (p. 39)

Ransom feels drawn to a floating island by night by a desire that reaches beyond all time:

> The cord of longing which drew him to the invisible isle seemed to him at that moment to have been fastened long, long before his coming to Perelandra, long before the earliest times that memory could recover in his childhood, before his birth, before the birth of man himself, before the origins of time. It was sharp, sweet, wild, and holy, all in one.   (p. 116)

Images of desire, if of less immediate spiritual intensity, are also to be seen in Mars and Narnia. Ransom at the beginning of *Perelandra* regrets that he is not returning to Malacandra: 'I'd give anything I possess . . . just to look down one of those gorges again and see the blue, blue water winding in and out among the woods' (p. 22). And Narnia, with its forests and plains, its castles and towns, its talking beasts and Telmarine men, its surrounding sea and its permeability to the great lion Aslan, that too is an image of the desirable, however subject to mortality it may be: here as with Mars we feel the wonder of a created world in so far as it expresses the craftsmanship or sacrifice of God; nothing is 'for itself', for everything is an image of its not-absent Maker. And sometimes we may come close to an image of the land of that Maker, in the sacred places where Aslan is found, whether as lion or as lamb, at the furthest edges of the Narnian universe, in *The Voyage of the 'Dawn Treader'* and *The Silver Chair*: in the former the ship travels by progressively stranger realms until the children row through a sea of lilies and beyond a huge static wave to a grassy place beyond where a lamb is sitting by a fire offering them fish to eat (the reference is scriptural here, to John 21.9–13). With these images, the experience of a fantastic world by Lewis is one of awakened desire and loss.

Lewis is not simply concerned with the portrayal of otherness or the desirable for their own sakes. He is determined that his readers should experience them too. The strange thing with him is that, for all that his fantastic worlds are far more invented or fictional than those of MacDonald, Kingsley or Williams, he has persuaded more people to entertain the idea of their existence. He is much more of a Christian apologist than the others: they tend to write from within their beliefs, demonstrating or 'showing' truths, as Kingsley has it, or else leaving the truth to propagate itself by chance, like the wind on an Aeolian harp, as MacDonald puts it. But in a sense every one of Lewis's books which portrays growing contact with the supernatural or a journey towards it relives his own conversion. He seeks to draw us into his worlds, to make us travel imaginatively and maybe a little way spiritually with his characters. He is always supremely aware of the unconvinced reader, and of the need to appeal to his audience, by awakening desire through his images, or appealing to reason, or even 'masculine' good sense. His protagonists are nearly always sceptics who ask the sort of questions we might in such fantastic situations. MacDonald's characters hardly ever consider the wonder of what is happening to them, or express much surprise at being tipped into Fairy Land; and the protagonists of Charles Williams' novels are less bemused than concerned to find patterns in their experience. As for Kingsley's Tom, he most often takes what happens unthinkingly. But Lewis seems much more directly sensitive to the modern drift away from Christianity. Perhaps this is because he himself, unlike Williams, was for much of his early life an atheist or an agnostic. Lewis wrote quite a few books of apologetics: for instance, *The Problem of Pain* (1940), *Beyond Personality* (1944), *Miracles* (1947), *Mere Christianity* (1952), *Letters to Malcolm* (1964). Charles Williams, by constrast, wrote works of theology. In his *Surprised by Joy* Lewis describes the route by which he came to be a Christian, a process described in fictional and less personal form in *The Pilgrim's Regress*. During the war he gave many radio broadcasts grappling with the problems of ordinary people trying to retain their faith in wartime. In *The Screwtape Letters: Letters from a Senior to a Junior Devil* (1942) he presents an imagined account of how the devil is at work in our most ordinary and banal spiritual lapses.

Here is an example of Lewis's apologetic technique in his fiction, from *That Hideous Strength*: it is Mark Studdock's eventual response to the hellish 'Objective Room' in which he is placed by Professor Frost of the National Institute of Co-ordinated Experiments.

> After an hour or so this long, high coffin of a room began to produce on Mark an effect which his instructor had probably not anticipated. There was no return of the attack which he had suffered last night in the cell. Whether because he had already survived that attack, or because the imminence of death had drawn the tooth of his lifelong desire for the esoteric, or because he had (in a fashion) called very urgently for help, the built and painted perversity of this room had the effect of making him aware, as he had never been aware before, of this room's opposite. As the desert first teaches men to love water, or as absence first reveals affection, there rose up against this background of the sour and the crooked some kind of vision of the sweet and the straight. Something else – something he vaguely called the 'Normal' – apparently existed. He had never thought about if before. But there it was – solid, massive, with a shape of its own, almost like something you could touch, or eat, or fall in love with.[32]

The narrative addresses us. It offers us a range of possible reasons for Mark's reaction, all of which are true, but the last (the response to his call for help) more significantly true than the others; and leaves us to prioritise them for ourselves. But in doing this it also imitates Mark's present state of spirit, poised halfway between a secular and a more religious understanding of the universe. Thus, it is exact. So too is the 'probably not anticipated' of the first sentence: in one way of course

Curry had not anticipated this; in another it is precisely right not to know what goes on in the heads of the evil. All the time the style is being both casual and reasonable – 'After an hour or so', 'drawn the tooth'; then the three possible explanations for the absence of attack. We are invited in. The suspension of the long third sentence, delaying its centre till the very last word, also does this; while at the same time illustrating syntactically the preponderance of negative events which eventually beget this first flicker of the positive. And, if anything further were wanting, it is provided by the use of everyday comparisons with the strange events going on here – the desert teaching a man to love water, or absence arousing affection. Finally the substance of this 'Normal', in contrast to the vagueness with which Mark names it, and with which we ourselves often apprehend it, is conveyed in almost material terms of weight, shape and size, like a huge piece of furniture. Thus at every stage Lewis addresses the 'ordinary reader', and is at pains to make the 'supernatural' as solid and immediate and everyday as he can – which is exactly his understanding of Christ's nature also. By contrast, the passage we looked at from Williams (pp. 226–8, above) was directed at objective analysis rather than explanation to a reader.

We will find these methods – the use of appeals to reason, analogies taken from common human experience, precision, carefully (but unconsciously) weighted invitations – in all Lewis's fantasy. Particular forms of it are seen in *Out of the Silent Planet* and *Perelandra*. In the former, Ransom is presented as quite scientific in his approach to Mars. As a philologist he is fascinated by the different languages used by the three rational races on the planet, but his curiosity is seen in all areas, as he inspects the vegetation, discusses the different forms of social behaviour, or considers the various adaptations of creatures to their environments. Even at the end, returned to Earth, he is still adding details of his investigations which he regrets could not be got into the body of the story.

> For instance, because I always take a thermometer with me on a holiday ... I know that the normal temperature of a *hross* is 103°. I know – though I can't remember learning it – that they live about 80 Martian years, or 160 earth years; that they marry at about 20 (= 40); that their droppings, like those of the horse, are not offensive to themselves, or to me, and are used for agriculture; that they don't shed tears, or blink; that they do get ... 'elevated' but not drunk on a gaudy night .... [33]

This of course gives the story much more solidity and conviction – a feature added to by the very way the story on its own is shown by this postscript to be inadequate: the 'fictional microcosm' is worn away a little.

This approach we again find in *Perelandra*, especially in the way that anything that cannot be seen clearly at once has its vagueness later removed – as when, seen closer to, the Fixed Land, which previously from afar seemed 'a single smooth column of ghastly green standing up' (p. 41), becomes 'a cluster of columns . . . rather like exaggerated dolomites' (p. 81). Likewise Ransom sees, through the moss of the Fixed Land, creatures that at first he takes for insects but discovers 'on closer inspection, to be tiny mammals' (p. 218). But the persuasiveness of *Perelandra* also comes from the thoroughness with which Lewis has thought through the character of the Lady's innocence, and integrated it with the planet. She lives on floating islands that shape themselves to every varying wave of the ocean; and this is made more than analogous to her innocence, by which she accepts whatever experience Maleldil sends her. At the same time, just as her islands mould themselves to the surface of the ocean, so she identifies herself entirely with her experience. She thought she was Maleldil's creature; but Ransom teaches her that she chooses every act she makes, however unconsciously. Because she did not have self-consciousness, she could not have a larger perspective, and therefore had no sense of time, or of 'home' or of owning things. Ransom gives her this self-consciousness, but it is a double-edged gift, for the Un-man can seek to turn self-awareness into self-dramatisation and egotism. It is all very 'neat', and rings so intellectually true at every point, that we are drawn in to give it more ready 'belief'. And, as the pattern further unfolds and we are told that what seemed at first an arbitrary prohibition – against sleeping on the Fixed Land – in fact makes sense at the symbolic level of preferring what one can hold on to for oneself to what Maleldil sends in the form of the waves, then we feel that this is not so much a world made by Lewis as a harmonious structure which further reveals the nature of Maleldil.

Another apologetic technique used by Lewis is the disguising of his Christian themes so that they may be more readily assimilated. In the fantasy of MacDonald, Kingsley and Williams, too, the Christian content is not directly named, because their object is to portray the nature of reality first, and how that reality falls naturally into divine patterns. Lewis, as we have seen, is not portraying any form of 'our reality': his worlds are made ones, and this arguably makes him more 'manipulative'and apologetic in tendency. In *The Lion, the Witch and the Wardrobe*, the slaying and resurrection of Aslan the lion obviously parallel the Passion story in the Gospels, while the breaking of the stone table recalls the abrogation of the Old Law. We should remember, however, that the one story is not *simply* a version of the other: Lewis believed that what was myth in one world could be fact in some other, and that every event in the cosmic story was utterly and eternally itself, not to be compared with any other. Nevertheless his object is clearly apologetic: even if he is not retelling the Gospel story alone, he is trying to inculcate the rhythm of divine reality in any world.

> I thought I saw how [fairy tales]...could steal past a certain inhibition which had paralysed much of my own religion in childhood. Why did one find it so hard to feel as one was told one ought to feel about God or about the sufferings of Christ? I thought the chief reason was that one was told one ought to. An obligation to feel can freeze feelings. And reverence itself did harm. The whole subject was associated with lowered voices; almost as if it were something medical. But supposing that by casting all these things into an imaginary world, stripping them of their stained-glass and Sunday school associations, one could make them for the first time appear in their real potency? Could one not thus steal past those watchful dragons? I thought one could.[34]

That this 'worked' so far as the disguise was concerned is attested to by many readers who did not consciously recognise the Christian and biblical 'source' of what they were reading. No such ignorance would for long have been possible with Charles Williams.

Part of the reason for the success of this method is that Lewis's 'figurative' disposition is not towards what we may still wish to call the metaphor, by which different contexts are fused, but towards the simile, by which they are compared. His vision is not 'incarnational' in the way that that of Williams is. For him we can be *like* Christ; we cannot participate in Him. So he puts God in another world, myth divided from fact, and surprises us with Him there. He has us leave Earth or our own dimension for another, and tells us that reality on other planets or in fairy land, far from being as different as we expect, repeats the spiritual patterns of our own.

He gives us a sense of otherness in all his fiction, and yet makes the other ultimately very recognisable. With Lewis we have a double vision: one of a fantastic world quite alien to our own, and another of that world reflecting and re-enacting some of the deepest truths of our spiritual history. This is precisely parallel to Lewis's dual insistence on the singularity of his fantastic worlds, where nothing is a copy or model of anything else, and, at the same time, on their likeness to events in our economy, articulated in his constant use of simile in his work. His paradoxical unification of this duality is seen in his comment on the likeness of the Lord of Perelandra to Christ: 'Where likeness was greatest, mistake was least possible' (p. 236). That is the other mode of the experience that we have: for us, what seemed to be singular and alien comes to have links and likenesses to our world, while remaining itself; here, where unlikeness seems greatest, kinship is most suggested. And it is this curious method of going away to come closer that makes Lewis's apologetic intent peculiarly effective.

Unlike MacDonald, Kingsley or Williams, Lewis deals with the interplay of two worlds: Earth on the one hand, and Mars, Venus, Narnia or the borderlands of Heaven on the other. The protagonists in the other three writers are simply absorbed into, or literally immersed in, a transfigured world (the exception here would be, to some extent, Macdonald's *At the Back of the North Wind*): Tom is in the water; Anodos lives his way through Fairy Land; the characters in a Charles Williams novel accept the revealed supernatural character of reality without great surprise. But we always know with Ransom or Mars or Venus that he is an outsider, a man from another and fallen world. Further, except in *That Hideous Strength*, he always remains like us, an ordinary man in the midst of extraordinary scenes. And, if Lewis can present us with worlds far above us and ours in spiritual purity, he can also explore that which is spiritually beneath us, in his devils or in hell. But the special poignancy of his work lies in putting us so close to his visions of innocence with his earthly protagonists, so near to a sense of God's direct workmanship, that we can almost feel it and touch it, and yet at the same time know the pain of the sheer gulf that divides us from it, know too that it is 'only' an image made by an earthly and 'fallen' writer:

> And all the time the little jewel-coloured land went soaring up into the yellow firmament and hung there a moment and tilted its woods and went racing down into the warm lustrous depths

between the waves: and the Lady lay sleeping with one arm bent beneath her head and her lips a little parted. Sleeping, assuredly – for her eyes were shut and her breathing regular – yet not looking quite like those who sleep in our world, for her face was full of expression and intelligence, and the limbs looked as if they were ready at any moment to leap up, and altogether she gave the impression that sleep was not a thing that happened to her but an action which she performed.   (p. 141)

Lewis's predilection for simile becomes a precise measure of how much and at the same time how little like ours the other world is. It is all right when it comes to comparing the shifting trees of a floating island to the masts of yachts swaying at anchor; but in itself a floating island defies analogy as much as attempts to stay upright on it, and the 'provincial' attempts of the mind to see it in terrestrial terms are continually subverted:

Sometimes his own land and a neighbouring land would be on opposite slopes of a trough, with only a narrow strait of water between them; and then, for the moment, you were cheated with the semblance of a terrestrial landscape. It looked exactly as though you were in a well-wooded valley with a river at the bottom of it. But while you watched, that seeming river did the impossible. It thrust itself up so that the land on either side sloped downwards from it; and then up farther still and shouldered half the landscape out of sight beyond its ridge; and became a huge greeny-gold hog's back of water hanging in the sky and threatening to engulf your own land, which now was concave and reeled backwards to the next roller, and rushing upwards, became convex again.   (p. 56)

By switching to the second person Lewis puts us as close as he can. In part the ocean and the floating lands on it express the vitality and variety of Maleldil, which are always supremely *there*, as in the massive and solid waves, and yet as uncapturable as their shapes. Here again otherness undermines our notions of reality, our quantifications of it; and does so literally with Ransom, by continually throwing him on his face. The prohibition on Perelandra relates as we have seen, to staying on the Fixed Land, symbol of the imposition of the self on the divine flux of phenomena. Yet the desire to make analogies and connections between one world and another is not seen as inherently wrong: it is so only where it does not simultaneously recognise its own inadequacy. *Perelandra* ends with an elaborate hymn on the dialectical and paradoxical nature of reality, the Great Dance, sung by the angelic intelligences. So too Lewis brings us extraordinarily close to his images of spiritual desire, only to have them shrink from us as we approach, and say, as it were, 'It is not I. I am only a reminder. Look! Look! What do I remind you of?'[35] By that means he continually displaces our appetite for the 'other' towards a hunger for the Wholly Other.

A sense of division seems to underlie much of Lewis's work. The Earth, 'a jungle of filth and imbecility', is cut off from the Celestial Commonwealth and under the power of the Black Archon. Each fantastic world Lewis creates is divided from ours and from every other; and what is myth in one world may be fact only in some other. Any image which awakens in us all our desire and longing must be forsaken for the Reality that, while it speaks through it, comes from far beyond it. The opposition of God and devil, heaven and hell, runs through Lewis's work. His strongest Christian sense is of our fallen condition, cut off from the primal innocence and closeness to God which was once ours. In Narnia he shows us innocence continually lost and recovered; in Perelandra a fallen mortal is brought into poignant closeness to an unfallen lady from whose state he is for ever separate.[36] As we have seen, too, Lewis, unlike Charles Williams, has difficulty with some of the 'incarnational' aspects of Christianity: he registers only a willed acceptance of the idea behind the sacraments,[37] and the accounts he gives of Christ stress not His coming into the world but His leaving it through His death and resurrection (Aslan; Mark Studdock's experience in *That Hideous Strength*).

Lewis is himself always profoundly self-conscious, watching himself or surrogates of himself having experiences or emotions and commenting on them, always organising them into a pattern: his autobiography *Surprised by Joy* is a remarkable treatment of himself as a specimen of a certain pattern of Christian conversion. He feels also cut off from his own times, a cultural dinosaur, an 'Old Western Man' of an age long gone: here too he speaks of himself as 'a specimen'.[38] He feels divided against even himself, his strongly imaginative and emotional side at war with his ever-guiding rational faculty: he wrote, 'Who [can] make imagination's dim exploring touch / Ever report the same as intellectual sight?'[39] In himself he continually dramatises the debate between those within and those outside the faith: his apologetics have always been popular because he never ceases to share the position of the unbeliever as much as that of the believer. This mixture of scepticism and belief may give strength to his faith, but it is unusual among modern writers in admitting the draught from outside.

There is a sense in all this division, in this painful separation of man from God, earth from heaven, image from reality, of a departure, as though for Lewis God has now removed to a distance – even if that distance is also for him a guarantee of His reality. And, for all Lewis's peculiarities, this seems to be echoed in later writers. The Christian fantasies that follow his work are in the main derivative, self-conscious and founded on wish-fulfilment rather than true belief; and nearly all of them are set on other worlds and planets. There are, however, works which come near to Christian fantasy but which shape Christian imagery to the purposes of other religious views – Sufic, Gnostic, Judaic: some of those we shall consider in the next chapter. The appetite for novelty that drives, the sense of flux that conditions and the feeling of complexity that characterises the later part of the twentieth century works against the stabilities, tradition and ultimately profound simplicities of Christian fantasy: either it is written within a protected fence, or it becomes other than traditionally Christian or it is not written at all.

18

Other Writers

There is a surprisingly wide range of modern fantasies and science-fiction works on religious topics involving the 'supernatural', even if there are few plainly Christian fantasies of any stature, apart from those of Williams and Lewis. We shall be looking here at writers who are in varying degrees obliquely Christian, at some who while Christian are too 'fantastic' or removed from reality, and at a range of science-fiction mutations of Christian vision. All of them, however singular in outlook, in some sense depend on Christianity.

An instance of a fantasy which is obliquely Christian is J. R. R. Tolkien's *The Lord of the Rings*. Tolkien was a Christian, and in his short story 'Leaf by Niggle' (1938–9) he did produce a little Christian fable, but the affinities of his larger work are much more immediately with the outlook found in his beloved *Beowulf*, with its sense of doomed heroism;[1] further, Tolkien maintained of the work that, 'As for any inner meaning or "message", it has in the intention of the author none. It is neither allegorical nor topical.'[2] Nevertheless, although The *Lord of the Rings* is not consciously directed to Christian purpose, it may indirectly work to this end. Frodo, who must bear the terrible burden of the Ring to save all Middle-earth, is like Christ carrying the Cross and the burden of man's sin that all may be redeemed. To that we may add that the Fellowship of the Ring is analogous to Christ's disciples.[3] But there is no further to go here, for these disciples bear witness to no new faith, and Frodo's act preserves rather than transforms the world, even if Sauron is almost finally defeated. There is, however, another pattern of the Christian story suggested within the narrative: namely, Christ's temptation in the wilderness. Frodo travels for forty days, hungry and thirsty during his time in Mordor, from the peace of Lothlórien to Mount Doom. He wanders in waste places, constantly tempted by the power in the world that the Ring offers. When at the last Gollum, the spiritually diseased hobbit, is put down, it is like the putting-down of Satan. Nevertheless here too there are differences. Frodo is not alone in Mordor; nor does his will hold out at the end, when only 'providence' saves him from falling. Whether these reticences and discrepancies in the narrative permit the Christian significance to come over, or even to come over more strongly than it otherwise might, precisely because it is implied rather than stated, one cannot say.[4] Certainly Tolkien has more 'on hand' in his story than Christian purpose – the invention of a world, the education of a hero, the creation of languages (his declared primary interest in *The Lord of the Rings*). On the evidence of the readership of his fantasy it has seemed to move in an ecological rather than a Christian direction, to speak more to the environment outside people than that within them.

Tolkien, of course is not the only 'Christian fantasist' to write obliquely: Coleridge (from whom he drew many of his ideas on the imagination and on creation) does it in 'The Rime of the Ancient Mariner' (1798). The mariner who shoots the albatross, figure of Christ, commits a primal sin, for which all his fellows die, while he continues in a state of living death. After long punishment under the law of nature he has violated, and in a region of aridity symbolising that of his soul, grace is granted him by angelic spirits, and his ship is eventually guided home; though not to rest for him. In Charles Maturin's *Melmoth the Wanderer* (1820), the beautiful Immalee is tempted in her garden island by a satanic wanderer (C. S. Lewis owed much to this novel for his story of the temptation of the unfallen Lady by the Un-man in his *Perelandra*). And later we shall be looking at some writers who are far more indirectly Christian than this.

For the moment let us look at the different obliqueness of Mikhail Bulgakov's celebrated *The Master and Margarita* (1928–40), which describes the arrival of a group of devils in the Moscow of the 1920s, and the chaos they cause to 'respectable' people. This story is surrounded by an account of the last days on earth of one Yeshua Ha-Notsri, comprising his interviews with Pontius Pilate and his subsequent execution. The Christ Bulgakov gives us is in no way definitely 'supernatural' as his devils are, with their amazing powers and transformations: this Christ reveals human emotion in His talk with Pilate, and seems almost a wispy nonentity; no supernatural events accompany either His expiry or the subsequent disposal of His body. Of course, we are invited to attempt connections between these two different areas of the story, the one serious and ominous, the other both comic and menacing. The devils are not *obviously* evil: they expose corruption and punish it. They hold centre stage. 'Following' Blake, Bulgakov shows us the world from their perspective.

Similarly, he gives us a Christ seen from Pontius Pilate's perspective. There is another and divine authority who begs Woland (Satan) to give the 'Master' and his Margarita a place of eternal rest, but His ambassador is the ragged and fanatical Matthew the Levite, whom Woland regards with contempt.

A central theme of the book is the deceptiveness of appearance. With some sinister, and one obvious, difference, the devils come disguised as a sort of Muscovite Marx Brothers – the difference being Behemoth, the man-sized black cat, first seen trying to board a tram. They put on an entertainment of conjuring at the Moscow Variety, in which among other tricks they remove and restore the head of a man, tell the intimate secrets of a random member of the audience, and rain apparently genuine banknotes on the assembled company; they also offer all the women in the audience a variety of the most modish clothes, which subsequently disappear from them in the street. They live in rooms which usually appear empty, or which can be transformed to enormous dimensions for a ball. They spend their whole time shifting between jest and earnest, between predicting a death for the chairman of the literary club MASSOLIT, which we then gorily witness, and having a harmless shooting-match with the pursuing police, with Behemoth firing pistols while swinging on a chandelier. Numbers of people are sent to the Moscow Clinic for variously avowing the existence of supernatural happenings.

There is much play on names in the text, suggesting that all identifying labels are suspect. The devil assumes the Goethean name of Woland, which no one can quite remember; and when the devils have all gone, their 'true' names become confused. 'Jesus' is changed to 'Yeshua Ha-Notsri'. The 'Master' of the story, who has been writing a story of Pontius Pilate, has no known name at all; indeed he says it no longer exists.[5] By this means it is suggested that we cannot be certain of the identity of anything, least of all of the devils. The devils could be seen as disguised angels, so long as one realised that this identity too was shifting. 'Yeshua' is, and is not, the Jesus who we know.[6]

A subtle process of alienation, of defamiliarisation, is going on. At the beginning of the story two Moscow literati are accosted by a man in the park, who tells them that he was with Pilate in his interview with 'Jesus', and then proceeds to tell them part of the story of what happened then. The story is taken up again much later, in the manuscript of the Master, who has 'independently' been writing a story about Pilate, to the point of Christ's execution and Judas's subsequent secret murder by Pilate. This story substantially alters the account in the Gospels. It has Yeshua as a fairly inoffensive man who seems to have blundered into falling foul of the law, and whose death is recorded only in disgusting physical detail: there is no mention of dying for the sins of man, or of rising again; and indeed the body is recovered after the crucifixion and buried with those of the thieves. Yeshua himself predicts that His followers will misrepresent Him and His teachings in what will become the Gospels, 'These good people . . . are unlearned and have confused everything I said. I am beginning to fear that this confusion will last for a very long time' (p. 28). By 'this confusion' is meant the Christian faith as we know it.

What then is the truth?[7] The subject is continued through the topic of writing. The Master's story about Pilate is the one that Woland begins. Is it the only true one, then? Or is it simply another way of rewriting the past? Not quite the latter, for when the Master truly finishes the story he does so by saying that Pilate is free. For two millennia Pilate has remained static in a kind of limbo, tortured by the thought of his moral failure – which may be why he almost alone in the story has a biblical and fixed name – and he has been reading the Master's story about him. Indeed the story has as it were incorporated him, so that its bleak initial end becomes the one that he has suffered so long. For this story, although written in the time of the twentieth century, has entered eternity and is 'already' known to those who inhabit that eternity; the vision is a Gnostic one, whereby the doings of the spirit are everlastingly interactive.[8] Thus a 'story' becomes a 'fact', makes things happen in another world, just as the story of Christ made things happen in this one.

And what then of the book we are reading, *The Master and Margarita?* Bulgakov continually breaks down categories. If we say that his account of Yeshua desupernaturalises the Bible, his picture of the devils in Moscow resupernaturalises an atheist materialist state. If the book begins with Woland opposing the atheistic assertion of the editor Berlioz that 'all the stories about . . . [Christ] were mere invention, pure myth' based on earlier pagan myths (pp. 13, 14), Woland's assertion that 'Jesus did exist, you know' (p. 23) is still ambiguous as to the mode of 'exist'; for, after he himself has attested that he was with Pilate, and Berlioz has questioned the non-Gospel character of his account, he says, 'surely . . . you of all people must realise that absolutely nothing written in the gospels actually happened' (p. 49). And yet, beyond and before that he has asked, 'if there is no God, then who, one wonders, rules the life of man and keeps the world in order?' (p. 18); and as Berlioz goes, to his 'accidental' death under a tram, Woland tells him that he is about to demonstrate the seventh proof of God's existence (p. 52) – a proof he says he has already mentioned, when in fact he got no further than an undisclosed sixth (p. 17). Bulgakov does not desupernaturalise the Gospels: he tells us that the reality behind them may be far more and far less wondrous than we suppose, and that at any rate it is quite other.

For Bulgakov – as for Blake – truth seems to lie in ceaseless movement between different positions, symbolised in the mobility, deceptiveness and ground-removing wit of his devils. God exists and does not; Jesus is real and 'ordinary'; the devils are moral and renegade; fiction may become actual, but actuality may be perverted to fiction (the biblical 'Jesus' story). Certainly the function of such movement is to shake mankind loose from settled assumptions. It is because she can make that sort of imaginative leap, in acting as hostess to the obscene damned at Woland's ball, that Margarita has his favour and he brings the Master out of the clinic for her. As for most of the other Muscovites, the complacency of several of them is permanently shattered, but society as a whole is able to convince itself that nothing extraordinary really happened. We know differently, and therefore lastingly know the frailty of the crust on which man's assumptions are founded. By such means Bulgakov could depict the transience of an apparently monolithic state – as readily as that of a similarly monolithic Gospel text.

But movement, however united to spiritual uplift, is not everything: there seems to be much more to this novel. It feels as though in stirring up the whole issue of Christ's existence, in suddenly making His reality at once more vulgar and more alien than we could have imagined, it succeeds in reincarnating Him in a sense. The Gospels are suddenly reconverted to something 'rich and strange', as are our own lives. Who, after all, is this mysterious Master, seemingly a mere mortal beside Woland, and yet capable of rediscovering history and changing life in eternity? Why have the devils come to Moscow at this time? May this not be another Christ story in modern times? Or a Gnostic Second and more successful Coming? At Woland's ball Margarita re-enacts the Last Judgement, when the dead are reclothed in their bodies[9] – yet from her there is no judgement, only grace and compassion for the wretched. If anyone, she is the Christ figure (Margarita = Pearl = Christ, the pearl of great price), and the Master the Creator both of book and world. Yet these identifications must be partial, no sooner glimpsed than left.[10] The total effect of Bulgakov's novel is one of enormous zest and wonder, a spiritual shaking-loose of the foundations, and the sense somewhere of a god turning as though about to look at us. It is at once a peculiarly 'postmodern' book in its insistence on the 'textuality' of reality, and at the same time somehow imbued with a pulse as old as the Cross and as old as the lonely Roman governor living out the centuries with a head aching with guilt.

A word is called for here concerning other modern Russian writers of 'Christian' fiction, particularly the Symbolists of the turn of the century, of whom Bulgakov has sometimes been seen as a late representative.[11] It has recently been argued that there is a marked measure of Christian supernatural presence in such works as Dostoevsky's *The Idiot* (1866), Andrey Bely's *Petersburg* (1910–11) or Boris Pasternak' *Dr Zhivago* (1958): all these books have been seen to follow an apocalyptic pattern based on the Bible, demonstrating that their events stem ultimately from the ever-present acts and Word of God within their narratives, even while such events seem most immediately the product of human wills.[12] Vladimir Solovyov's (traditional) 'Story of Antichrist' in his *Three Conversations* (1900) is cited as a stimulus for Bely's *Petersburg*.[13] It is true that in *Petersburg* Christ does make an occasional appearance (as enigmatically as at the end of Alexander Blok's poem *The Twelve*, 1918), as does the figure of a giant bronze horseman who inspires the enervated revolutionary Dudkin to murder his political master Lippanchenko;[14] true too that the vision of Petersburg is of a world of fragments, emptied of spiritual content – provocative perhaps, through its very drained inertia, of the political volcano that will be its apocalypse within time. Yet the evidence for a Christian reading of the novel must be tentative, as too the argument that the apocalypse predicated here is one not of final circularity and inertia, but of spiral progress and ascent beyond the end. While the claim that '*Petersburg* was not simply a window to the West, as it had been for its founder, but a window to the beyond. Each epiphany in the novel is a small-scale template of the cosmic revelation at hand',[15] is an exciting and potentially enriching one, it must remain one open to debate, subject to the enigmatic quality of the novel. And the same is true of the assertion that throughout the less Christian *Dr Zhivago* '[God's] History lies concealed within history, time that is meaningful and emplotted "from beyond" exists within time that is meaningless and tragic.'[16]

There is one other work of literary complexity that comes near to Christian fantasy, and that is T. F. Powys's *Mr Weston's Good Wine* (1927). The book describes the coming to the village of Folly Down, one November, of a travelling wine-salesman, Mr Weston, and his assistant, a young man called Michael. Mr Weston's wine, although presented as an alcoholic beverage, is a much more moral and spiritual drink. Mr Weston is God, and Michael is His angel, although we only gradually realise this; further, He is not the scriptural and 'aloof' God, but one sorrowfully and lovingly involved in His creation. Much of the story seems at first more an analysis of the spiritual state of the village than an account of Mr Weston and his doings. There is the twisted Mrs Vosper ('viper'?) who rejoices in bringing girls to be raped by the sons of squire Mumby beneath an oak-tree; there is young Tamar Grobe, who is in love with her vision of an angel; there is her father the vicar, who has lost his faith in God after his wife was killed in an accident; there is Thomas Bunce the landlord, who blames God for every ill that has come to Folly Down; and there is Mr Grunter the church clerk, who has attempted suicide because he believes he is nothing.

The 'supernatural' acts in the book, though real enough, are often unknown to others, or unobtrusive. A curious boy looks in the back of Mr Weston's van and gets a terrible fright, though it is only much later that we can guess what he saw. On the hill before Folly Down, Mr Weston advertises himself in lights on the night sky by connecting the car battery to 'a curious network of wires, sustained in the air by two stout rods'.[17] In the middle of the story, time and the clocks are suddenly seen to have stopped, but life goes on much as before; and eventually time starts again. Tamar, after marriage to her angel, Michael, is taken to heaven when Grunter's curse of the evil oak-tree is followed by a lightning-stroke which destroys it and kills her. Mr Grobe, who longs for death, is given Mr Weston's darkest wine to enable him to find it. A well of water is turned briefly to wine so that young Luke Bird can meet the stipulation of the father of the girl he loves in order to gain her. Squire Mumby's sons are pursued in the night by the heavy tramp and roar of some great beast; and Mrs Vosper's heart is invisibly torn to pieces by its claws, until she lies dead of an apparent seizure. At the end, returned to the hill outside Folly Down, Mr Weston has Michael set fire to the van by dropping a match in the petrol tank, and they both vanish in the smoke.

But Mr Weston's presence is more pervasive than the slightness of these intrusions might suggest. For one thing, he as it were enfolds the story, which begins and ends with him and Michael, like creation itself, and in which the space given at the beginning of the novel to converse between Mr Weston and Michael is exactly the same as that given to their 'supernatural' activities at the end. Being very arbitrary, we could say that, as it appears, the first quarter of the book is given to God, the next half to man, and the last quarter to God's interaction with man – something like a Hegelian process of thesis, antithesis and synthesis, realised in the imagery of the salesman of wine on the one hand, the potentially resistant customers on the other, and the culmination in relatively successful transactions. Such schemes are blurred by the fact that for these country people there is not such a sharp division between 'nature' and 'supernature' as there is for more 'sophisticated' minds. When time stops and Grunter tells the people in the inn, 'eternity have begun' (p. 139), they are all just as ready to live in this new dimension without demur.[18] This is a world in which Luke Bird can preach to and convert the beasts of the field, a girl falls in love with the idea of marrying an angel, a long-running debate can exist as to whether it is God who is deflowering girls beneath the oak-tree, and the existence of an angel can be believed as readily as that of a policeman (pp. 231–2). And that for the novel is the truth about the world: it is a place surrounded by the everlasting, and uniquely penetrable by it, as in this story. The story may be non-canonical, but it is certainly incarnational, in its sense of a God who comes down to earth out of love for His creation, and puts on, like Christ, the lineaments and mores of that world that He may do it good.

The story is certainly in part allegory, in so far as Folly Down may be taken as a microcosm of mankind. God has come down to His creation to test its spiritual character through the offer of His wine. He has used other methods of approach before, 'signs and wonders, war and earthquake, fire and tempest, plague and famine, and all because we wish to draw their attention to our good wine' (p. 60): the reference to the Old Testament God is clear enough. Allowing for the fact that the people of Folly Down are odd and quite unlike city-dwellers, and for the absence of representation of man's sinfulness – the dominant sin here is betrayal of love – we may still take them as a picture of the world. For the book sees love as that on which all else depends. Her love for the angel is to be Tamar's joy; his love for creation is Luke Bird's gift, and his requited passion for Jenny Bunce the gift of God; Grobe's love for his dead wife has lost him his faith in God and his pleasure in life, but can give him back joy in the life to come; Grunter's failure of love for himself is expressed in his attempted suicide and his wish to 'matter' by being thought of as the local seducer. Others have been blighted by love – Ada Kiddle, seduced and later self-killed, her sisters Phoebe and Ann reduced to wretched and abused spirits in Mrs Vosper's house. The centre of the evil is in Mrs Vosper, who 'has the greatest dislike – an inherent dislike – of her own sex, until they grow old enough to be as a vindictive as she. Her jealousy has charged her heart with a bitter cruelty, and she goes the way of her kind in having her revenge' (p. 53). At her encouragement, the torpid souls of the Mumby sons have reduced love to rape. For that they are terrified into amendment of life by Mr Weston's release from his van of a supposed lion, the devil, previously (and scripturally) bound for a thousand years (p. 302), but now set loose for a season.[19] Mrs Vosper, however, is killed by the beast and taken to hell (p. 299). (Charles Williams' *The Place of the Lion* probably owes a great deal to this novel.)

The whole story is a kind of Second Coming, as with Bulgakov's *The Master and Margarita*, but there is nothing apocalyptic here except our revived sense of the contingency of the world which Mr Weston has made and could unmake in an instant. This is no Last Judgement, but the insertion of a spiritual litmus paper into humanity. As already noted, the nearest analogy is with Christ's acts. Mr Weston comes down not only to review humanity in Folly Down, but to help it. His wine, which expresses itself as joy, spiritual awareness or death, is always love. The narrative portrays at first a series of isolated individuals in their separate homes and episodes: Mr Weston first brings them all together in his mind in his discussion with Michael, then links them by going round visiting them all, and finally saves them from their loneliness – bringing Tamar together with her angel, Luke Bird with Jenny Bunce, Mr Grobe with his dead wife, Mr Grunter with the world he has found meaningless, and even Martin and John Mumby with the bedraggled spirits of Phoebe and Ann Kiddle.

The theme of marriage, of coming together, is central to the book, and occurs in every detail, right down to the remarks of Mrs Meek and Mrs Grunter about their husbands; in one form or another, it is virtually the sole topic of the novel. And this makes the book doubly incarnational in character, for marriage of the sexes is an image of the marriage of heaven and earth. And this larger marriage, the bond between heaven and earth, is portrayed in the relation between Mr Weston and the world he created. Beholding that world at its best, 'even the Creator of the universe can wish to forget Himself for a season and be born again, in the exquisite loveliness of one lonely daisy' (pp. 57–8). The very way in which Mr Weston and Michael in their car are so much the travelling salesman and his assistant, attests to this. The divine fits into the 'ordinary' world just as that world sits in the hand of God. To God in a sense the world is as much miracle as He to it. When Michael writes Mr Weston's name in light in the sky with the apparatus connected to the car battery, the result is at once a supernatural and an electronic event: the miracle is literally earthed. And Mr Weston is so simultaneously the ingratiating hawker of his wares and the God concerned for humanity that no wedge can be thrust between them.[20]

As with others of Powys's novels, particularly *Unclay* (1931), *Mr Weston's Good Wine* has a strongly physical emphasis. Set in the country as it is, we are continually aware of the earth, of trees and of animals. Even the names of the people suggest the animal – Mumby, Grunter, Kiddle, Vosper, Bird, Bunce, Grobe. Love is conceived of as a strongly sexual experience: that is something that the more intellectual Grobe found hard always to comprehend in his wife. When girls – Ada, Phoebe, Ann, Tamar, Jenny – are in love, their first thoughts are of lying with their lovers in 'the oak-tree bed'. Life is conditioned to the rhythm of the seasons and to day and night. It is not surprising that Powys, who sat in Hardy's seat at school in Dorchester, should have become a friend of that novelist's. But the difference between *Mr Weston's Good Wine* and *Unclay* is also marked: *Unclay* takes us to the hideous fact of death and rubs our faces in it, till we feel we could never rise again from the miry clods, but *Mr Weston* somehow conveys that the closer we get to the physical world the more we find that it is more than physical. Sitting talking to the animals, Luke Bird brings out their souls and converts them; laying bare the decomposed body of Ada Kiddle in her grave for the Mumbys to behold is to give them 'My good wine, gentlemen', as Mr Weston tells them (p. 292). The 'sacredness' of the physical is at the heart of the book: it is partly because she debases it to the *merely* physical, making human love nothing more than the servicing of cows by bulls, that Mrs Vosper is evil.

Indeed it is Mr Weston's sadness that he is not fully part of this world. His enjoyment of its variety throughout the story is manifest. But his is only a visit, and his departure elegiac; his melancholy reminder to Michael that 'All things tend to their end' seems almost a way of protecting himself from sorrow, especially in the ironic counterpoint that immediately follows: 'Mr Weston sighed. He turned towards Folly Down. The dawn was near. A lantern, a moving star, lit a carter's way from his cottage to Mr Mumby's stable; a wakeful cock crew; the pleasant scent of wood smoke was in the air, and the clatter of a well-bucket was heard' (p. 315). As for Michael, who so 'loved' Tamar, he no sooner marries and delights her than she dies. And Mr Weston, who gave it to man, has not, he says, experienced death; though he may have done so through Christ (pp. 65–6). It is a gulf between him and his creation, and one that gives him pain, both because it is hard for his creatures and because he is cut off from it. He tells Grunter of the eighth day of creation, when he gave death to the people he had made, because they seemed sad; but then they blamed him (p. 301). He says, 'Grunter ... I long to die. I long to drink my own dark wine'; and, 'not a death happens in all the world but I wish it were mine own, and I would have every dying one to know that I long to die with him' (pp. 300, 301). When that time comes, the 'firm' – that is, all heaven and earth – will end (p. 228). As a creator, Mr Weston had created more than he thought to – the strange beauty of a real world:

> He possessed in a very large degree a poet's fancy, that will at any moment create out of the imagination a new world.
> Mr Weston had once written a prose poem that he had divided into many books, and was naturally surprised when he discovered that the very persons and places that he had but seen in fancy had a real existence in fact.   (p. 28)

Having thus created, and created in his spiritual idiom, Mr Weston feels a responsibility to keep what he has made as close to its original idea as possible. Hence his visit. And yet, as creator of this wonderful thing out of his heart, Mr Weston must feel the desire to lose his separateness, to become fully a part of it, and thus to die and become nothing. He and Grunter, who are often together, are much alike: Grunter wanted before to commit suicide because he felt himself nothing; Mr Weston will in the end commit suicide and all will become nothing.

Beyond this we may reflect, as we did with *The Master and Margarita*, on the relation between God as author of creation and the writer as author of his book. (This issue is not infrequent in modern Christian fantasy, where the interest is in God the creator and the relation of man's creation to His.) The world is made by God the author, an author who has a writer's nervous pride in his creation, and who has the same attitude to His more immediately literary creation, the Bible (p. 259). Even His wine may on occasion be literary, as when He temporarily substitutes it for Mr Grobe's Bible: on the Bible's return Grobe wonders, 'But where was the wine? Had he been all the evening drinking out of that great book? Had that book been Mr Weston's Good Wine?' (p. 305). Mr Weston's creations have flaws, and he has an author's sense that 'it's always so, when one has finished a book, and it is printed, a new idea comes that would have made it all so much more interesting' (p. 262); for him, such ideas were woman, death, and a strange 'long snaky root', which he added to his original creation (pp. 151–2, 255, 301). His first two acts before he enters Folly Down are to open his 'tradesman's' book, and to write his name in the sky.

Analogies are implied between Mr Weston as author, and Powys as author of the book in which he so features. In his own book Mr Weston says, 'I have noted and taken into account all the vagaries of human nature from its first beginning' (p. 49): the vagaries that he finds in Folly Down are those also found in Powys's book. The relation between 'fiction' and 'fact' is thus continually present. Since God's created 'facts' are also parts of a 'fiction', one cannot say that they are more real than stories. Having described the switch in the story from time to eternity Powys asks, 'And yet this story remains a true one, and why should it not be true? (p. 200). he goes on to say that our scientists tell us that such 'miraculous' jugglings with time can happen throughout the universe. On the other hand, Mr Weston says it is mistaken to believe the words of another, in particular those in the Bible, because they are the productions of an artist with an eye for effect: 'The best books have to end unhappily; that is their only chance of success' (p. 273). Sometimes Powys can speak like 'God': 'And now that this November day has slipped into its grave, Thomas Bunce sets a match to his parlour fire. And we – we will have no garish sunshine in our story, but only a long evening to prepare us for the everlasting night' (p. 121); 'if we – and a writer has, as Mr Weston himself knows, a privilege in this matter – may be permitted for a moment to look into this wine merchant's heart …' (p. 151). The country people, we hear, read nature as a book, and rightly (p. 67). Heaven is far more interested in the working-out of a 'fiction' which contains reality, than in 'a mere battle between wandering tribes' (p. 200). All is simultaneously fiction and reality: the old contrast between fiction and truth which we saw in pre-1800 Christian fantasy is here denied even more than in most modern fantasies. Just as God partakes in the reality of the world by being Mr Weston, so the world too partakes in His reality; and the invented world of the novel is part of His invention.

Of other near-Christian fantasies there is none which is either complex enough or else Christian enough to call for detailed consideration here. One may start by mentioning Richard Adams' *Shardik* (1974), a story which has certain affinities with that of Christ. A giant bear god (Shardik), whose return has long been anticipated, appears to a tribe whose leader (Kelderek), instead of simply worshipping the bear, harnesses it to his aims of secular conquest. Though Kelderek thus gains temporary mastery of a kingdom, Shardik escapes, bringing the downfall of Kelderek, who is cast into exile. As the bear escapes the cage into which he thrust it, so the cage of reason and success with which Kelderek surrounded himself is taken away, and he is exposed to steadily more of the brutish and irrational in human nature until he learns humility and the true godhood of Shardik. Shardik has a supernatural aura about him even while – perhaps most while – he behaves as a beast. The victory of Kelderek over the army of the Beklan kingdom occurs when Shardik's cage careers out of control downhill at the enemy and he climbs enraged from its ruin to attack all those about him; and Shardik's later 'rescue' of Kelderek and a group of slave children at the cost of his life comes about when the slave-master Genshed provokes his rage by firing a burning arrow into his eye. Such Christian analogies as there are, however, cannot be drawn tightly. At the end Kelderek sets up a new society in the wilderness, run by destitute children and founded on worship of Shardik: it is tempting to see this as the young Christian faith under the New Law, as the previous worship of Shardik as a tribal totem organised by aged priestesses could be seen as life under the Old; but the point should be no more than hinted. A similar reserve should be maintained when we perceive that Adams' earlier novel *Watership Down* (1972) could be read as the story in the Pentateuch of the journey out of Egypt by the Israelites to the eventual Promised Land.[21]

Another problematic case is the science-fantasy sequence *The Book of the New Sun* (1980–7) by the American writer Gene Wolfe. It is clear that darkened Urth's search for a new sun to replace its burnt-out one may be seen in terms of a 'How long, O Lord?' and a desire for the Second Coming; yet the sequence, more typically of science fiction than of fantasy, prefers metaphysical complexities to spiritual truths, and is indeed highly recondite on the nature of truth.[22] It is full of Christian patterns – as we might expect from an author who is himself a Christian – such as the idea that the least thing may be the greatest and the greatest become the least, or that through the incarnation time partakes in eternity; and some quaint ideas too, such as that Christ was, like the protagonist Severian, a torturer;[23] but there is no clear overall Christian world view and evidence less of a desire to change people's spirits than of a wish to displace philosophic assumptions. It may be that some inherent Christian reading may be elicited from this series – as any book can, if faintly congenial to it, be made to depict such a pattern – but it does not make a convincing claim to be the sole and intended meaning.[24]

There are a considerable number of Christian fantasies that have been written in America, mainly over the last two decades. Many of them are heavily influenced by Lewis and Tolkien; and many are addressed to children. The general aim is to put over some form of Christian vision by using fantasy as a vehicle.[25] One will often find that the Christian element is not organic but is grafted onto these stories – the exact converse of what goes on in Adams' *Shardik*, where it is so latent as to be in doubt. Stephen Donaldson, in his 'Thomas Covenant' novels (1977–83) has a Christian framework in the books, with 'Covenant' (the name is deliberate) representing Christ and the New Law, while Lord Foul, the devil cast out by the Creator, has so corrupted the magical 'Land' that it lives at best under Law and at worst by blood-sacrifice. There is a crucifixion and resurrection motif also. All this is very well; but the story is mainly a fantasy in which the Christian element is not essential to the characters, who talk and act simply as heroes and heroines of romance; and Covenant, who shows little love for the people of a Land he believes only in so far as it may be an extension of himself, is hard to feel vitally as a Christ figure.

In Richard Ford's *Quest for the Faradawn* (1982) we have what is basically a 'rescue of animals' story with a Christian layer on top. (The book owes much to Tolkien and to *Watership Down*.) Man was created by an evil elf-lord as a punishment for animals; but a few men are good, and the story begins with an abandoned man-child being brought up by woodland animals. Together with a little Tolkinian company, he must eventually set off in quest of the Faradawn, the essence of the three elvish kingdoms, and thereby open to animals the secret paths by which they may go underground to save themselves from the holocaust by which man is about to destroy himself. This rather misanthropic tale is given a semi-Christian dimension via a single conversation with the elvish Lord Wychnor *en route* (ch. 12): this draws on the conversation between the Fellowship of the Ring and Elrond at Rivendell in *The Lord of the Rings*, but, whereas in Tolkien the presence of the larger dimension described by Elrond has been felt from the first, in Ford it is a mythological addendum. Ashgaroth, the Creator of Good (God), fought and overthrew Dreagg, Lord of Evil, in the Efflinch Wars and confined him to the Halls of Dragorn. But Dreagg fought back, and drained life and innocence from the world, till Ashgaroth created the elves to oppose him. Then Dreagg seduced one of the elves; and this eventually led to the evil in man's creation. However, Ashgaroth promised a saviour, who turns out to be the child left in the forest. No further Christian significance arises in the narrative itself: certainly the hero is not shown behaving like Christ. The Christian framework does no more than supply a sort of penumbra about the story, a mythological power-tap by which it may make itself more significant than it really is.

Many of these books are fully 'fantasies' in that they afford too-ready consolations without much sense of the reality of pain and evil save as bogeys for heroes to drive away. C. S. Lewis, by contrast, knows that the White Witch is beautiful and that she never really goes. Thus in Stephen Lawhead's *In the Hall of the Dragon King* (1982) the hero Quentin, who has previously served the old gods, is told that in order to receive the 'Blessing' of the one true God, 'All that is required is a true heart and a desire to receive it.'[26] The evangelical tendency of this author partly accounts for this: only believe, and you will be saved. In Muriel Leeson's *The Path of the Promise Keeper* (1984) the children have only to keep to the strict instructions of the Promise-Keeper and hold to the path (the story owes much to Bunyan) to win through to the treasure of the Golden Cave. In John White's *The Tower of Geburah* (1978), *The Iron Sceptre* (1981) and *The Sword Bearer* (1986) the children are helped by Gaal (Christ) in their various trials, and learn again that to succeed they must follow Gaal's instructions and keep to the path so that the evil Goblin Prince may be killed and the land of Anthropos (Man) freed from the 'Mystery of Abomination'. We may suppose that the fact that these books are addressed to children explains some of their gentle character, but, as the authors themselves sometimes admit, no book written only for children can be of any worth.

Other books are a little more sophisticated. Madeleine L'Engle in

A Wrinkle in Time (1962), *A Wind in the Door* (1973) and *A Swiftly Tilting Planet* (1978) has a very good sense of character which in the first novel at least makes a success of the interaction of the human and the supernatural. Each of the stories portrays children battling against an ultimate evil, called 'It' or 'Echthroi', which threatens variously their father, the world and the universe. In each case they are helped by a form of angel: in the first book by three shape-changing old women called Mrs Whatsit, Mrs Who and Mrs Which; in the second by a many-winged and -eyed cherubim called Proginoskes; and in the third by a unicorn named Gaudior. The good are clearly linked to the purposes of God, and the evil to those of the devil, who invests the world: but there is no theology or doctrine, only an ethic of love. Through a Christ-like act of self-sacrifice, for example, Proginoskes annihilates himself to save all life from being destroyed by the Echthroi. The plots are rather strained and absurdly melodramatic, but a vision of joy does come through. What these stories suggest is that, if we can only open our eyes wide enough, we will see the wonderful spiritual reality all about us, as well as its terrors. The parents of the children are scientists, and science, finding out about the universe, is seen as a way of finding out about God. The very choice of apparently insignificant children as protagonists in a setting which may range across the whole universe, or into the micro-universe within the cell, or into the depths of time, is an image of our seeming littleness and isolation made coherent within a larger pattern. That is particularly shown in *A Wind in the Door*, where damage by the forces of evil to the almost-invisible farandolae, which are essential to life, is destroying creation; and where the children enter the dying body of their brother to fight with the Echthroi and save his farandolae and him. Everything is seen as significant: the object of these books is to give back spiritual meaning to the lives of their readers.

How well they succeed it is hard to say. The child protagonists are privileged and intelligent bourgeois, and the attempt to widen the social range by including the more proletarian Calvin O'Keefe only involves him in throwing in his hand with the middle classes and marrying the daughter. This is a problem with many such books. Further, the rather abrupt transitions of the books, whereby we no sooner meet a strange old woman than she shifts us to 'Uriel, the third planet of the Star Malak in the spiral nebula Messier 101',[27] makes them rather hard to take: C. S. Lewis, L'Engle's primary source, is much more gradual in his introductions of the extraordinary and the supernatural. More than this, one feels that if these stories were taken away there would be not much left to believe in. It is possible for readers to feel that Narnia or Perelandra have a reality beyond the books in which they are portrayed – certainly Lewis himself felt so with Perelandra[28] – but the worlds of Echthroi and farandolae, or of 'It' on the planet Camazotz, seem to have no existence beyond the covers of their books. The ultimate reason for this, as with much modern Christian fantasy, is the evangelical pressure, the desire to put over a Christian vision, which reduces the fantastic worlds to mere tools. It is interesting to note how little time there is for contemplation in these books: we are always being hurried from one place or event to another, as part of a growing pattern of spiritual significance.

Many of these Christian fantasies have quite negative feelings about the earth, which is seen as in some way blighted. The desire to escape is very strong and expresses itself in the very creation of alternative worlds which offer more excitement or more joy than our own. That is why they look most to the example of C. S. Lewis, who not only had, but deliberately expounded, this outlook. Lewis's Christian concept of *Sehnsucht*, or spiritual yearning, in particular keys in to the mixture of 'American dream' and desire for another world. One can see these strands in Robert Siegel's *Alpha Centauri* (1980), where a modern girl goes back to a time when there were still centaurs in the world. These centaurs themselves are an image of desire, representing in themselves the union of the rational and the animal. But that desire is shrinking. Once, the centaurs lived in joy under the wise governance of the First Ones, in a world that was a garden. But then one of First Ones, Kalendos, dreamt not of the pleasures that he had, but of the Thing That Is Not (phrase derived from Swift, meaning 'lie'), until he went to find it; and when he had it he went mad and evil, and cursed nature, which then 'fell', and he went to the east. Later his descendants, eventually called Rock-Movers, returned and began to drive the now dwindling First Ones and centaurs westwards into Britain. These Rock-Movers practise blood-sacrifice and are aligned to the ways of the Warper, or Satan, while the First Ones follow the Shaper, whose son will be the Healer. Before the fall of Kalendos, it had been possible for all the Shaper's creatures to travel freely and instantaneously to any of his worlds in the universe: the centaurs, whose home world is Alpha Centauri, became confined to earth when the gate between worlds in a 'Singing Stone' was closed. It is the task of the girl protagonist Becky to open this stone for the centaurs so that they may return to their paradisal home, 'where oceans break on translucent cliffs ten thousand feet high, and winged horses nest in the lords of trees, and purple grasses run forever under a violet moon'.[29]

The whole story is full of the sense of the loss of Paradise and the consequent blighting and shrinkage of the centaur world. While the more evil Rock-Movers are overthrown at the end of the narrative, we know that the world in our time is still more corroded and near its end: Becky is told, 'In your time, or later, when the earth has been chained and desecrated, when man is finally sick of himself and the machines he has enslaved himself to, there will be a time of great troubles' (pp. 199–200). Loss also runs through the book, as the centaurs are steadily driven from their place in the world to their last hope in escape from it. One of the ruling images of the book is the contrast between the absolute freedom of will they once had, and the increasing restriction on them in the story, till they are no longer able to exist in the world and have only one exit from it. The story is full of episodes involving captivity; and of contrasts between the relatively free forest life of the centaurs and the static citified life of the men of stones, the Rock-Movers. The narrative is governed also by the shrinkage of time. Before Kalendos, whose name relates to time's movement, all was eternal spring in the world; and timelessness is the element of the First Ones (p. 74). But time steadily narrows in the story: by the end there are only five days for Becky to return from the First Ones to bring the centaurs to the Singing Stone, a task whose final achievement 'only in the nick of time' is more than a mere piece of narrative suspense. Becky returns to her own dark century – appropriately through the 'Eye of the Fog' with the promise that the centaurs will return to earth in the last days, and that she, as the long-awaited saviour of the centaurs, is a person of particular divine favour. Thus the book contains the kind of apocalyptic that is congenial to the American psyche, together with a sense of an everlasting American dream beyond the Second Coming: 'In that time the earth will be remade as it was meant to be, and the glory of it shall be a hundredfold for all the centuries of its suffering' (p. 200; cf. p. 236).

The story is quite complex and subtly organised, but, for all that, its characters and settings are not very full-bodied. One of the reasons is that the author has not been able to give a strong idea of the 'differentness' of a centaur: usually we find ourselves thinking of them more as men than as men–horses, and those who make friends with Becky speak and behave often as American children might.

The influence of Lewis and Tolkien (Becky as Ransom, the centaurs as 'Ents' looked after by Eldar in a threatened Middle-earth) is so felt that perhaps it inhibits creativity; and this is true of a large proportion of these American Christian fantasies. If their light approach is to be explained by the fact that they are written for children, we should ask why so many of them *are* written for children in the first place. Their drift, whatever conflicts they dramatise, is towards the escapist, towards 'good' feelings and the sense that God is on *our* side and that there will be a glorious life beyond this one. Where other Christian fantasies might take more account of the mixture of good and evil in every man, these fantasies show their protagonists as pure, and evil as a force from outside: their view of life and the world thus becomes simplistic. They reject the world as it is, not out of asceticism as with Bunyan or the *Queste*, but out of what in the end is evasion, the refusal to accept its complexity and fallenness and seek to amend them from within. Their other worlds, centaurs and cherubim, are 'ways out': they write fantasy because their answers involve turning away from the real world. These are hard sayings, but the perspective of all the works considered in this book calls for them.

Another way of putting this is that one feels with these writers that they like the idea of being Christians, but they do not seem fully to know what it is like. Other writers speak from within a long spiritual experience of Christianity: Kingsley as a pastor constantly fighting to preserve his faith, MacDonald with his Christian hope in relative exile from society, Williams living within the 'Co-inherence', Lewis developing in depth of knowledge of God until the end of his life. With them we feel the presence of a spirit that has made a journey behind every book that they write. With the writers we have just considered we feel rather their adherence first to a system of ideas rather than to experience. Their books are governed either by literary patterns derived from 'model' writers, or by clear schemes taken from the Bible. Repeatedly one finds various forms of narrative relating to Satan's expulsion from heaven, the creation of the world, the seduction of man, the redemption in Christ, and the apocalypse and the creation of a new heaven and earth. These *schemata* feel rather *voulus*, read as though they are a substitute for full and long conviction. This is in no way to deny that they may encourage readers at least to think about Christianity, but the quality of the faith they might partly stimulate seems thin and complacent. It is sad to have to say of this mini-renaissance in the writing of Christian fantasy that it marks not a new start but something of a terminal decline.

Beyond these one can simply list a range of works which, while they could be called 'Christian fantasy', are only partially so. *A Romance of Two Worlds* (1886), one of several such works by Marie Corelli, is as much true-love romance as it is revelation, and in recompense for earthly insecurities promises a Christian heaven of electrical energy for well-bred spiritual initiates. In G. K. Chesterton's *The Man Who Was Thursday* (1908) a police hunt for a group of anarchists trembles on the verge of envisaging apocalypse. Georges Bernanos's *Sous le Soleil du Satan* (1926) is an attempt by a Catholic writer to 'hollow out' the realism so dominant in the novel by showing it to be open to another, Christian supernatural, reading. In Paul Gallico's *Father Malachi's Miracle* (1931) a priest's request for a miracle in an unbelieving world is answered by the transportation of an Edinburgh dance hall to the Bass Rock in the Firth of Forth; yet no one proves one whit the more ready to believe in God or even the miracle itself. Finally, in Kingsley Amis's *The Green Man* (1969) a rather uneasy God intervenes to ensure the defeat of a ghost and a devil who have been plaguing a hotel and its epicurean owner. In all these works, either fantasy or Christianity is not fully present.

We come now to a work that demands mention even though it is not Christian in its supernatural emphasis – David Lindsay's *A Voyage to Arcturus* (1920). It is to this book that C. S. Lewis in turn was indebted, though here not slavishly, for many of the images of his fantasy. Lindsay's book is the reverse of those we have just been considering in that it is full of a violent succession of extraordinarily vivid images. Indeed, originality is in one sense almost of the essence in Lindsay's world. The hero Maskull has agreed to come to Tormance from Earth because 'I was tired of vulgarity'; on Earth, 'Originality is a lost habit' (a typical witty paradox).[30] His whole experience on Tormance is of one shock after another, until at the end, when he climbs to seek the god Muspel, what he finds is nothing.

Yet on the planet his every experience of startling difference is accompanied by a sense of sameness: all who die have on them the same sickening grin of the Crystalman–devil who has the world in his sway. And all the incredible landscapes and creatures of the planet are alike the products of Crystalman's 'Shaping'. The very faculty that is revered as God or Shaper in Siegel's *Alpha Centauri*, the creative principle, is here seen as somehow corrupt and corrupting. Maskull's journey across Tormance is one that involves a growth in perception and resistance to the seductive images of Shaping and his world.[31] Unlike in the fantasies we have just reviewed, the world is rejected not to find an easier or more consoling one, but to penetrate to a harsher reality; to get beyond all life's blandishments to the bleak truth. We have the paradox here that the 'other' world is the true one, while this world is 'false and deceitful, to the very core', so that 'reality and falseness are two words for the same thing' (p. 145). What Maskull finds is that the true god Muspel (the name is from Norse mythology) is 'wholly surrounded by Crystalman's world . . . and consisted of himself and the stone tower on which he was sitting' (p. 247). This work is Gnostic and Manichaean in its view of the world, and certainly on its view of creation has no place for an incarnated god; rather its journey is a *via negativa* towards a deity who turns out to be no transcendent being but one caught in desperate conflict (it is typical of this book to end with a god who refuses to be a point of rest[32]).

But for our purposes Lindsay is significant because he says 'no' to the imagination and creativity themselves, the very features that are most salient in modern Christian fantasy and its picture of God as maker of worlds. Lindsay's book in part constitutes an attack on Romanticism and all forms of emotional attitude: he wishes to get beyond feelings and imaginative attachments to the true objectivity that is Muspel. The urge is remotely 'Christian' only in so far as the world is seen as given over to the devil, who is master of lies, so that to reach God one must leave the world entirely.[33] Otherwise it is an instance of the highly individual and idiosyncratic course that modern religious fantasy has often taken.

Our last area of concern must be with science fiction, Christian and religious. Perhaps the two best-known works of Christian science fiction, written at almost the same time, are James Blish's *A Case of Conscience* (1958; written 1953–8) and Walter M. Miller Jr's *A Canticle for Leibowitz* (1960; written 1955–7). Both are written from the standpoint of the Roman Catholic Church as an institution, though Blish puts more emphasis on the theological difficulties of an individual priest; it is at least interesting that the church which most stands for institutionalised values should be the one that most frequently appears in the value-challenging genre of science fiction.

Blish's novel describes a commission sent by Earth to investigate the nature of an inhabited planet Lithia, to decide both on its commercial potential and its status as a created object in God's universe. Lithia is a paradise in which the rational inhabitants live without original sin in total harmony and contentment. Since this harmony is achieved without any belief in God, since this is an Eden without a divine maker, Father Ramon Ruiz-Sanchez, the priest–commissioner, is forced to conclude that Lithia is a construct of the devil. He decides that the Lithian paradise was made by the devil to evacuate the Bible of meaning, to convey to man that he could be supremely happy without any need for a deity. Here Blish touches of course on a belief which, despite his book, has become very much a part of modern consciousness. Lithia then becomes another of the devil's lies, and must be destroyed. In order to report this, however, Father Ruiz-Sanchez is forced himself into a 'devilish' heresy: namely, the supposition that the devil can create. The Pope, however, argues that the planet is not a creation but a hallucination, and one that can be banished by exorcism. That exorcism, when carried out, 'coincides' with a dangerous experiment in nuclear fission on Lithia (actually it was so arranged by the Pope), so that when the planet blows up the Church benefits from a manifestation of divine judgement which rides on the back of what may well have been the consequence of a nuclear chain reaction.

Thus no overt supernatural act occurs during the entire book, and it is up to faith to decide whether divine power is at work. For Blish's interest in the novel is not to put forward a Christian world view – though he is certainly more sympathetic to the Father than to the other characters, not least in telling the story from his point of view. He is fascinated by intellectual dilemma, and the mind's interaction with and interpretation of phenomena. His interest is, in short, scientific: what is the precise nature of this thing? Father Ruiz-Sanchez is himself a scientist in his biological investigations of Lithia; but what the book describes at the theological level also is a process of assembling data, formulating a hypothesis, testing it, and finally acting on it. The point about Lithia is that it looks so convincing and is filled with such rational and sensible inhabitants that the rigour required in determining its essence and holding to that determination is considerable. Whether in fact the Father is right cannot fully be known: the Church and the Pope are satisfied, but the Father at the end is 'alone with his God and his grief'. Thus the presence of any form of supernatural agency is left in doubt. Such doubts and ambiguities are of the essence of Blish's intellectual understanding of reality.[34]

Blish, we should remark here, wrote two more novels in which the supernatural 'definitely' appears, *Black Easter* (1968) and *The Day after Judgment* (1971). Both of these could be said in part to reflect

his apocalyptic view, following that of Oswald Spengler, of the
terminal decline of the West. In *Black Easter* a group of black magicians
call up some devils for their own limited purposes, but in fact they
release the whole population of hell on the earth, which is then
devastated; nor is there any divine power to oppose them, because
'God is dead' [35] In *The Day after Judgment*, Satan is forced to occupy
God's vacant throne and rule us, which causes his own collapse and
return to hell. Neither of these books supposes the real existence of
the devil or hell – no new religious world view is put forward. Part
of the purpose is to express the stupidity of man from the perspective
of a supernatural being well acquainted with stupidity: that is, to
provide a vantage point giving unique insight. Another urge is, as
with *A Case of Conscience*, that of the scientific experimentalist: here,
'Suppose one did this, what would happen?' If Satan were allowed
to win and then had to rule the universe as God, what would be the
result? Then there is the fascination with a theological proof of a
particularly arcane character: the fact that the very victory of the
devil entails his defeat suggests the great power of good and the
possibility that God still exists somewhere, detached from events.
Last and most simple, there is the Faustian and black-magic urge to
extend experience and push knowledge to the limit: such an urge is
common to science fiction, though rarely seen in this mode. It is
paradoxical that *A Case of Conscience*, which contains no *identifiable*
Christian supernatural occurrence, should be nearer to a serious
consideration of Christianity's place in the modern world than those
later books with their direct presentation of hell; but it may serve to
instance something of how the 'angle' of science fiction on Christianity
has changed over this period.

Miller's *Canticle for Leibowitz* does not even offer any supernatural
event in its narrative. We deal with the Church about 700 years after
a nuclear holocaust, preserving what frail relics of past civilisation
remain; then we move 500 years further to see the rise of a new
scientific civilisation; then 500 years more, to the eve of another and
final thermonuclear war, with the Church preparing a rocket so that
God's created image may escape the earth – again taking knowledge
with him. But, even as the book records what appears the secular
folly of man, and history as blind cycle, it invites us to consider all
these events as expressions of the divine will. The historical cycle
portrayed, which repeats, within the same temporal compass, the
patterns of our own, moves from dark ages to renaissance to the
separation of the state from the Church and finally to the accelerated

secularism that produces holocaust. Seen from a Christian perspective, the pattern is at the same time one of a move from fall to redemption in Christ:[36] this is imaged at the end as the rocket bearing humanity's last home ascends to the heavens like a phoenix from amid the ashes of the earth. Similarly, while man is the architect of his own ruin, that ruin may be seen also as caused by God: the first holocaust is known as the 'Flame Deluge' by the monks, meaning that like the Flood it was sent to purge and cleanse mankind. Nor again does this prevent the onset of war at the end of the story from being seen as the workings of Satan (who after all was God's 'factor' in the sufferings of Job): 'The visage of Lucifer mushroomed into hideousness above the cloudbank, rising slowly like some titan climbing to its feet after ages of imprisonment in the Earth.'[37]

The condition of mortality is duality. Every fall of man brings about both a resurrection and a new fall: a resurrection of spiritual life in the ensuing 'dark ages'; a resurrection of learning thereafter. But the two are disjoined: the monks of the dark ages do not understand the meaning of the knowledge they protect for future generations, and these future generations spurn the spiritual understanding of the monks. The Flame Deluge is both a purgation and a punishment. Science used to bring light is a wonder; but it is also a curse. The two-headed mutants that thread the three sections of the book seem to symbolise man himself: one has two female heads, the one suggesting the fallen woman Eve, the other the woman of redemption, Mary. An air of scepticism and irony characterises the Christianity of the story: there are no easy victories or consolations here, only the wondrous recurrence of divine patterns, through the apparent 'mere' agency of human choice, for us to admire and be terrified by. This book is without doubt not only a powerfully 'realistic' Christian vision of history; it is one of the most deeply felt and convincing science-fiction works ever written. Not least potent is the way that, almost by accident, each of the three sections ends with the death of its protagonist, and with predators: in the first two sections, buzzards, who devour the body; in the last, a creature of the relatively un-poisoned medium of the sea, a shark, who does not so devour – 'He was very hungry that season.'

Among recent followers of Miller's book perhaps the most distinguished is Russell Hoban's *Riddley Walker* (1980), which, like *Canticle*, shows a conflation of science with religion, and describes a process whereby the ignorant mythologising of past events gives way to a scientific knowledge that could re-create the holocaust: the difference here is that in the teeth of pessimism the hero stays on earth to try to stop it happening. There is a Christ-likeness in Riddley's behaviour, but that is really only a way of glossing it: despite an air of indeterminacy between natural and supernatural planes of being that seems to run through the novel, there is no direct Christian vision here.

Since the 1950s science fiction has rather moved away from the presentation of any form of Christian world view. This has rarely been owing to any hostility, more to do with science fiction's innate expansiveness, which will not brook confinement within any one metaphysic. Indeed science fiction is often in its element displacing our assumptions – whether moral ones, as in John Wyndham's *The Day of the Triffids* (1951), or ontological ones, as in Aldous Huxley's *Brave New World* (1934), or even narrative assumptions, as in Frederik Pohl's 'The Tunnel under the World' (1954): as the hero of Wyndham's book puts it, 'life has to be dynamic and not static'.[38]

One side of this is a greater concern with constantly learning and finding out about the universe than with teaching. Here knowledge does not exist in a bible or any authority, but in the process of discovery. Thus, while there are science-fiction books with a hortatory or even moral aim – for instance, those warning against nuclear weapons – the large majority are 'scientific' in the sense of 'finding out' only; and to that extent virtually the whole area of human spiritual conduct drops out of consideration and with it what amounts to a central part of the Christian life. In contrast to Christian fantasy, science fiction rarely has much of a moral sense, or makes distinctions between good and evil: it does not generally accept the fixity of position that would make such distinctions possible. Nor, on the other hand, as a genre which puts man and his struggle to survive at its centre, can science fiction often give a place to the idea of man as rescued or saved by some larger being than himself – particularly not by a being who was at the same time as weak as ourselves. There are partial exceptions to this point, to which we shall come – but the idea of a Christ like us whom we murdered is uncommon enough. As for the 'terminal' mythology of Christianity, the First and Last Things, the story of creation, fall, Messiah and judgement, these appear quite frequently in science fiction, but commandeered for secular purposes. In particular the genre has seized on the concept of the Last Things with which to portray catastrophe or nuclear holocaust – indeed it has been argued that the very existence of science fiction testifies to a millenarian death wish in Western civilisation,[39] although it would be fair to say that the genre has shown itself as much concerned with the origins of the world as with its end.

The strange fact is that, for all this absence of true Christian vision from science fiction, it is one of the most religious of literary genres, in the sense that it is for ever constructing, in a world that has largely abandoned one 'mythology', a whole series of others with which to give 'meaning' to man's position in a vast and impersonal universe.[40] The difference, apart from inherently, between these and the previous Christian vision is that few science-fiction writers believe or have lived their mythologies, which are most of them only invented, fictive, literary. Of course, there is the frequent suggestion that in a universe of boundless possibility, an invented world need be no less real than the one we see; but what is at issue here is neither possibility nor even credibility, but the degree of conviction behind any such invented world: to give a simple answer, George MacDonald 'believes' in his Fairy Land or C. S. Lewis in his 'impossible' Malacandra in ways that Frank Herbert does not with his *Dune*. That said, the concern in science fiction is very often with the ultimate: our ultimate source, our ultimate end. It is there from the first in H. G. Wells's *The Time Machine* (1895), which explores human development into the far future and the eventual terminus of the sun's death, or in Mary Shelley's *Frankenstein* (1818), or, later, in Arthur C. Clarke's *Childhood's End* (1953) and *2001: A Space Odyssey* (1968). It is present too in many of the stories in which men travel to other planets or stars, or meet the alien, symbol of the unknown in self and life.[41] Each such story implicitly makes a fictive pattern out of the purposelessness of life. Each can in some way find an answer to the question 'why?' In so literary an age as ours, the answers they pose may often be sufficient to satisfy. There are many prepared to be taken in by the proposition of Arthur C. Clarke that intelligence was conferred on man by visiting aliens in the prehistoric past: for the blind dynamic of Darwinian nature is substituted a purposive rational act, making us at once part of a larger cosmic scheme and part of a scientific experiment. 'Someone else is looking after us': that is one of the strong impulses science fiction draws on to enhance its credibility, from Spielberg's films *Close Encounters of the Third Kind* (1977) to *E. T.* (1982).

As an instance of the combination of 'religious' impulse and 'Christian' imagery to a purpose other than Christian we can consider Clarke's *Childhood's End*. Man, on the verge of nuclear self-destruction, is visited by a fleet of alien starships, the inhabitants of which remove man's destructive potential and establish a golden age on Earth. These aliens, when they eventually reveal themselves, turn out to have the aspect of devils, giant forms with wings and horns. Karellen, the leader of these 'Overlords', as they are called, explains that man's image of the devil, associated with the end of the world, was in fact based on a faint prevision of these aliens, who have come to preside over what may well be the dissolution of the world. Thus the 'devil' imagery comes not from a past event but from a future event which has leaked into the past. So much then for the traditional imagery of the devil. These Overlords follow the unfathomable purposes of an Overmind, which is a hundred times further beyond them intellectually than they are beyond man: God here is, as in much science fiction, a colossal scientist. The Overmind perceived that humanity was about to beget a super-race of children who would be of enormous intelligence and power, and sent the Overlords to oversee the safe emergence of this race. The story then describes how the children become increasingly remote from their parents, until they have to live separately; how the previous generation of the human race dies out or, warned of the approaching end of Earth, commits suicide; and how finally the children leave the Earth in a funnel of fire, having so gathered its nature into themselves that on their departure its being is so thin that it collapses and blows apart.

In this story the idea of spiritual progress beyond death that we saw in Dante has been translated into intellectual advance. The notion of each individual as an immortal soul is here shifted to a notion of the immortal soul of the race. It is frequently the case in science fiction that human life is seen in terms of the race and from an Olympian standpoint. In the Christian fantasy we have considered, however vast its compass, the focus is on an individual: the vision we have in the *Commedia* may be 'objective', but it is at the same time the very particular one of Dante; and always the sense is there that the decision of a single soul is as crucial as that of a million, for matters of mere size and number do not matter in Christianity as they do in science fiction. For Christianity, too, humanity at the end of time is no more morally advanced than humanity at the beginning, after Eden: all are alike fallen. The concept of evolution and of expansion outwards is a post-Renaissance one to which science fiction is particularly receptive. The change in mental power portrayed in *Childhood's End* occurs not through gradual evolution but through an abrupt switch in the manner of a metamorphosis, as when a pupa turns into a butterfly.

Typically of much science fiction, the story sees death as the enemy, and continued physical and mental survival as an important good. There are not very many 'terminal visions' in science fiction which end with no further hope for a future.[42] Here, though 'old' humanity dies, it continues – indeed, transcends itself – in its wonderful children. Karellen tells obsolete *homo sapiens*, 'For what you have brought into the world may be utterly alien, it may share none of your desires or hopes, it may look upon your greatest achievements as childish toys – yet it is something wonderful, and you will have created it. When our race is forgotten, part of yours will still exist.'[43] This urge to cheat death is not that of Christianity, where death is seen both as a horror and as the way to God: science fiction does not find a 'philosophic' place for it to the degree that Christianity does.

In its insistence on 'childhood's end', too, the book is in marked contrast to Christianity. The Gospels suggest that, unless we become as children we shall never enter heaven, and that Christ had a particular love for children. The implication often is that the road to spiritual betterment lies in going backward, in unlearning the ways of the world. The Christian has to exercise will, but he perhaps comes nearest to God and divine assistance in self-abnegation and humility. Christ's life was largely one of humility and sufferance; and his Passion was an image of willed passivity, a trust in the Father – in a sense an image of perfect sonship. But in Clarke's book childhood is done with: mankind is to grow to adulthood, and to develop in power over phenomena. In the paradoxical, mind-shifting way typical of science fiction, childhood's end is found in the children, and it is the adults who are, comparatively, infantile. It is remarkable, when one thinks of it, how often the children in science fiction have nothing very child-like about them, from the hostile little party members of *Nineteen Eighty-Four* or the telepathic youths of John Wyndham's *The Chrysalids* (1955) to the precocious seers of Herbert's Dune novels or the worldly innocents of Samuel R. Delany's novels. Even William Golding's *Lord of the Flies* (1954), in portraying how children would 'really' behave if cut off from adult help on a desert island, still aligns their behaviour to that of primitive adult societies.

Clarke's book is also distinct from Christianity in its stress on distance. The children steadily grow apart from the adults: they look like children (though their faces gradually take on a group similarity), but they are utterly alien and emotionally indifferent to their parents. Their intelligence is of a character sheerly different, and increasingly dangerous, to all but themselves. Their 'home' is not here on Earth, but travelling the universe. What they will do is quite unknown, since what they are is equally beyond comprehension. In a sense they have become like gods, accomplishing huge 'miracles'. They start the Moon turning on its axis and slow the Earth. God in Christianity is also unknowable, but He is also nearer to us than any other person: He is the truest of our selves. The fascination with distance in *Childhood's End* as in much science fiction is part of a lust for the infinite as a substitute for God. Which of us does not, in his or her post-Romantic soul, thrill to the picture the Overlords record of the way one of the children's minds quests outwards to the centre of the galaxy and beyond?

> It might have been Earth. A white sun hung in a blue sky flecked with clouds, which were racing before a storm. A hill sloped gently down to an ocean torn into spray by the ravening wind. Yet nothing moved: the scene was frozen as if glimpsed in a flash of lightning. And far, far away on the horizon was something that was not of Earth – a line of misty columns, tapering slightly as they soared out of the sea and lost themselves among the clouds. They were spaced with perfect precision along the rim of the planet – too huge to be artificial, yet too regular to be natural.
>
> ('Sideneus 4 and the Pillars of the Dawn,' said Rashaverak, and there was awe in his voice. 'He has reached the centre of the Universe.'
>
> 'And he has barely begun his journey,' answered Karellen.)
>
> (p. 148)

Clarke is always at pains to show how utterly reality is beyond us, how small our understanding is even as it reaches out (see for example p. 178).[44] This is in part a religious experience of our utter nothingness before the infinite God; but, when we also realise that Clarke has in a sense made infinity into God, the feeling may become the rather more secular one of a gigantic intellectual inferiority complex. And this reverence for the infinite, rather than for infinity contracted to a span in Christ, is typical of science fiction, from Stapledon's *Star Maker* (1937) to Greg Bear's *Eon* (1985) and *Eternity* (1988).

There are a few science fiction stories which put forward what looks like a Christian supernaturalist vision, and it is instructive to consider what happens with them. In the first place it is interesting that most of them are in the form of short stories.[45] The aim is not to provide a vision, or to spend any length of time on the Christian world view, but simply to make a brief and often witty point, and move on. We can take two examples here, Ray Bradbury's 'The Man' (1949) and Gardner Dozois' 'Disciples' (1981). In Bradbury's story 'the first rocket expedition to Planet Forty-three in Star System Three'[46] lands on a planet apparently inhabited by human beings. No one welcomes them: angry, the captain sends his lieutenant, Martin, to the nearest town. Martin returns dazed, to say that the people there had more important things on their minds than rockets that day, for they were visited by a man who was clearly Christ. The captain disbelieves this and maintains that it was another rocket's captain, Burton, playing a practical joke. When it turns out that no other expedition had come to the planet before them, he is forced to believe that the Messiah has appeared here, and he tries by violence to make the mayor of the town tell him where he is. It is he who asks the question, 'But you must know where he went?': he assumes that the Messiah has now gone. He cannot derive information from the mayor, who says to him, 'There's no way . . . to tell you anything' (p. 51). Because of that the captain, now obsessed by the quest for the Messiah, leaves the planet with a reduced crew, in search of him. Meanwhile the mayor tells Martin that from planet to planet the captain will always be just too late,

> And finally he will miss out by only a few seconds. And when he has visited three hundred worlds and is seventy or eighty years old he will miss out by only a fraction of a second, and then a smaller fraction of a second. And he will go on and on, thinking to find that very thing which he left behind here, on this planet, in this city –. (pp. 52–3)

Martin and the mayor then go to meet the Messiah in the city.

The main concern of this story is not with the Messiah, who never appears, but with the behaviour of humanity confronted by him. The captain is in a sense like science fiction itself, with his obsession with movement: 'Why do we do it, Martin? This space travel, I mean. Always on the go. Always searching. Our insides always tight, never any rest' (p. 43). He can never accept what is there: it is not the Messiah, it is Burton playing a joke; and, if it is the Messiah, he must be somewhere else. The captain does not really *want* to find him; he wants to be continually moving in search of him. If he ever finds him, 'Why, I'll ask him for a little – peace and quiet' (p. 52). He blames the need for continual search on Darwin and the loss of faith: there has been no peace and quiet since with the theory of natural selection 'everything went by the board, everything we used to believe in', and man was forced to look for his soul on other planets (p. 43). But even when he could have found his soul the captain refuses it. In this Bradbury seems to satirise the need of modern man always to have some goal before him: the journey of the rocket to other places becomes a measure of his distance from his true self.

The story is powerful in the way that it encapsulates the blind and isolating nature of this modern need for continual purpose: it is not that the truth or 'God' has left man, but that he has left the truth, deluding himself with phantoms so that he may preserve a false picture of the world. For we understand the story best when we see the captain not running in search of the Messiah, but running away from him: he is, as the mayor says, quite unable to accept a reality that challenges his. His rocket that protects him from space is an image of the ego that shuts him from truth.

He cannot see the Messiah in the city because he will not. The story is about man's alienation from himself. The hope is in those representatives of modern man who stay on the planet; the captain, who would like to destroy it because it does not send him a welcoming party, is the lineal descendant of a Pizarro or a Cortes. By irony his very rocket, in lifting from the planet 'on a pillar of fire', provides the Old Testament sign of God's presence to the Israelites journeying to the Promised Land (Exodus 13.21–2). The story, then, is not so much about the rediscovery of Christ among the stars as about man's inability to find peace within himself.

Gardner Dozois' 'Disciples' portrays a 'thin, weaselly-looking man' called Nicky the Horse, who earns his limited keep in a crowded city by handing out leaflets for the 'Lordhouse', warning of the Last Days and the Coming of Jesus. He has to keep clear of other religious groups with their own messages to peddle, such as the 'Hairy Krishnaites' and the Moonies. As he is thinking of lunch at the nearby hot-dog stall, the stall's owner Saul Edelmann comes by to tell him that he has given away the stall and everything he owns because the Messiah is coming. This Messiah is one Murray Kupferberg, a plumber from Pittsburgh. Nicky laughs in disbelief, saying that Jesus is the only Messiah, and eventually takes angry leave of Saul, who is expecting this Messiah to come and gather his people to him that day. Nicky's rage is largely at having missed Saul's benefaction; as later in the afternoon, when a little parade of people goes by and a woman throws away an ermine stole which lands on a xylophone-player standing near him. Later still, all enthusiasm for his occupation as messenger of doom gone, Nicky suddenly hears an enormous trumpet-like noise of music, and looks up:

> As he watched, a crack appeared in the dull gray sky. The sky split open, and behind the sky was nothingness, a wedge of darkness so terrible and absolute that it hurt the eyes to look at it. The crack widened; the wedge of darkness grew. Light began to pour through the crack in the sky, blinding white light more intense and frightening than the darkness had been. Squinting against that terrible radiance, his eyes watering, Nicky saw tiny figures rising into the air far away, thousands upon thousands of human figures floating up into the sky, falling *up* while the iron music shook the firmament around them, people falling up and into and through the crack in the sky, merging into that wondrous and awful river of light, fading, disappearing, until the last one was gone.
>
> The crack in the sky closed. The music grumbled and rumbled away into silence.
>
> Everything was still.
>
> Snowflakes began to squeeze like slow tears from the slate gray sky.
>
> Nicky stayed there for hours, staring upward until his neck was aching and the last of the light was gone, but after that nothing else happened at all.[47]

This event is almost an extension of Nicky's bad luck. Just as he has missed out on life, on the gifts of this and the previous day, so too he has 'bet' on the wrong heaven and has to see, yet again, someone else having a far better time than he. Of course, so far as religion is concerned, the point is that any of them could be right, and the 'absurd' existence of Murray Kupferberg the plumber from Pittsburgh seems to confirm this – until we recall that the carpenter's son Jesus from Nazareth would have seemed an equally preposterous Messiah in his own time.

Christianity and its agents seem to fail one another in this story. Nicky says that Jesus is his Messiah and rejects that of Saul Edelmann, but he knows nothing of the real nature of Christ and has not read the Bible: nothing very generous drives him, only the animal wish for food and comfort. The title of the story, 'Disciples', is a mockery. If anything, the story portrays how 'Jesus' is now a mere name debased in the streets, and perverted by those who hear it (a group who jeer at 'Jesus loves you' as a homosexual's wish; a woman who assaults Nicky for mentioning the name of Jesus). A harsh irony of the story is that it is not the Messiah of the poor who comes, but the Messiah of the frequently well-to-do: Nicky is the 'heavy-laden', but he remains without rest. The apocalypse that comes is harsh and violent in sound and sight: this suggests that it partakes in the coarse nature of the world on which it intrudes.

Yet it cannot be denied that the story conveys an air of terrible longing for escape from a hideous world. Nicky himself was not more unpleasant than his degraded surroundings; and his desire for food and sleep, his sole objective in putting himself in these mean streets, is a version of the desire for ultimate escape, even when it is seen in terms of 'hot stew ... the bottle of strong raw wine, his mattress in the rustling, fart-smelling communal darkness, oblivion'. Nevertheless, the vision of the souls ascending to heaven is brief, opening and shutting like a box, and we are left with the bleak world of disillusion as opposed to illusion.

If Nicky is at all representative, he is a picture of man always in the wrong place or time, always hoping and being frustrated. The story shows how degraded and misunderstood the Christian message has now become; but its emphasis, like Bradbury's 'The Man', is on that which makes man live outside the moment, whether driven by neurotic compulsions or by loathing of a world of which he feels no part. For that is the point about Nicky: streetwise though he is, he is alone and not really a part of his surroundings: his very message of the imminence of the Last Things distances him from them, both in its peculiarity and its content. The emphasis, then, is social and human, not Christian; and certainly not Christian so far as any compassion for Nicky goes. The story reads as a rather ruthless stripping-down of all things to coarse and unlovely and unjust basics. As with most such science-fiction short stories, there is no pervasive emphasis on a Christian vision, only the use of a mystical moment to drive home a contrast. The use of such moments is also guided by the speculative impulse of the genre, which is for ever asking 'What if ...?' or 'Suppose the extraordinary really happened?': the urge is the exciting exploration of the possible fantastic, rather than any approach to the more probably Real. Perhaps the further extraordinary contrast lies in the publication of this story in the lubricious and expensively fleshed *Penthouse*.

There are many science-fiction works which utilise the stored-up power of Christian imagery for their own purposes, or else invert it into other religious modes. Philip José Farmer's *To Your Scattered Bodies Go* (1971), the first book of his 'Riverworld' series of novels, begins with all humanity from the earliest times being apparently resurrected along the banks of a vast and seemingly endless river on a strange world. For much of the book there are conjectures about whether this is the Christian life after death and they are in some kind of purgatory; and there are visits by mysterious persons who suggest angels. But increasingly it becomes clear that all the people are the products of a computer that has stored blueprints of all humanity, and that they are on a giant planet near the galactic core, run by alien social engineers conducting an experiment with them (for what purpose is never entirely clear). Thus the 'frisson' of the Christian supernatural is exploited to give the story at its outset an enormous thrust of mysterious excitement – until the whole thing shrivels down, as it frequently does in science fiction, from the numinously sacred to the alien secular.[48]

A contrast to this is the 'Canopus in Argos' series of novels by Doris Lessing, particularly the first, *Shikasta* (1979). This tells of the colonisation and seeding of Earth with benign spiritual impulses by an 'enlightened' race on Canopus, and the transformation of monkeys to intelligent and innocent humans living in a terrestrial paradise. This utopia is poisoned by the evil force from the planet Shammat, and gradually descends into the wretched history that we know, terminating in thermonuclear war. But obviously Canopus takes the role of God the Creator (even while it is a single and fallible stellar empire), and Shammat that of the devil, while the success of Shammat parallels the destruction of Eden. Similarly, the race of giants recalls that in Genesis, and the frequent visits to Earth of emissaries from Canopus are like visits of angels or infusions of divine grace. (However, possibly owing to Lessing's Sufism,[49] the story contains no Christ figure – unless one counts the suffering Johor, agent of Canopus on Earth.)

Essentially what this story does from the outset is go in reverse direction to Farmer's: it suggests that the Christian or supernaturalist view of our spiritual history is a misinterpretation of what are much more 'scientific' events; mythology is rewritten as an experiment in cultural anthropology (if there is still a mystical dimension). The further difference between Lessing and Farmer, which in large part explains why she is seen as the more 'serious' writer, is that she partly means what she says – she has, form the evidence of this and the later novels, enough of the mystic or would-be mystic in her, and certainly enough social concern, for the imagery of other worlds that she creates to be partly founded on believed truth. That makes her quite an exceptional figure in science fiction. It does not necessarily make her a good writer of it: indeed her very earnestness may at times reduce the value of her books as literature, and their suasive power. But it does make her a writer of genuine vision; and that would put her alongside C. S. Lewis or others here, were it not for the simple fact that her vision is not Christian – that indeed she has so recast some of the central narratives of the Bible as to suggest the obliteration of Christianity. Most of all she has taken away that side of Christianity which depends on the notion of man's ultimate dependence on Christ and His redemption: she is more concerned that people learn their own responsibility and try to develop into love and true community, if helped by agents from Canopus. It is a utopian rather than an apocalyptic vision, one concerned more with bettering the world than with learning to do without it in death and eventual resurrection.

Nearer to a Christian vision, and more 'open-ended' and eclectic in approach, is Philip K. Dick in his late novels *Valis* (1981) and *The Divine Invasion* (1981). Dick's vision is a mainly Gnostic one, and it is interesting to note that this type of religious outlook is evident in several other leading writers in the field – not least Lindsay, Bulgakov and Lessing, and even, to some extent, Powys. Gnosticism is a religion which is arguably well suited to speculative fiction, for like science fiction it rates increased intellectual awareness very highly; it is a dynamic and expansive religion rather than one enclosed within First and Last Things; it similarly seeks to escape from a world perceived as restricting; and it emphasises man's ability to save himself, rather than any sin-bound dependence on divine grace and mediation.[50] Dick, however, would see his Gnosticism as not so much a rejection of Christianity, more a possible continuation of it in a new form.

Valis and *The Divine Invasion* are fine achievements, particularly in the way Dick is able to combine cosmic topics with the mundane or even the absurd without forfeiting the character of either. They are hard to summarise. *Valis* is about one Horselover Fat, a dark side of 'Philip Dick' the character in the book, who is brought to madness and despair by the deaths of close friends, but sustained by communications from a source which, he is able to satisfy himself, is God. Eventually he makes contract with an incarnation of God – the little daughter, Sophia, of the rock stars Eric and Linda Lampton, in northern California; but she is accidentally killed, and Fat, who had disappeared on her discovery, returns to continue his search for the Saviour. The novel gives full scope to the possibility that Fat is deluded about God for at least part of the time, particularly in relation to a strange pink light that conveys his first revelation; and the 'supernatural', if we may speak of it this way, is not very overtly present, being often absorbed in apparently natural events. This is in part the point; for the book is largely concerned with searching reality to find its divine nature and source. It confronts life in all its obstinate corruption, pain and sheer banality, to find that which transcends them; but it suggests that such a confrontation is the only route to the divine. The search, of its nature, is never complete *sub specie aeternitatis* – which is why the revealed Messiah must once more be withdrawn.

More immediately apposite to our concerns is the more evidently 'supernatural' *The Divine Invasion*. It has been well said of the two novels that, where in *Valis* man seeks out God, in *The Divine Invasion* God seeks out man.[51] It might be added that, where *Valis* was based on actual experience, *The Divine Invasion* is an invented story founded on belief.[52] So far as the theology goes, the book is based on the notion that God (Yahweh) was expelled from Earth with the destruction of the Jews at Masada in AD 70. At the time of the novel, 200 years beyond that of *Valis*, God has decided to return to Earth as a child, and seeds Himself in an earthwoman living on a planet far from Earth. He then enables her to return to Earth, which is now given over to evil and entirely hostile to the things of God. The birth is achieved, but at the cost of loss of memory in the young Emmanuel through an accident. Eventually he links up with Zina, who is half of Yahweh's nature left on Earth, and with her help and through the agency of the developing charity of the human protagonist Herb Asher he is able to overthrow the released force of Belial and begin the final war with the forces of nihilism. If *Valis* was a dark novel, this is an optimistic one. Dick originally entitled it *Valis Regained*[53] (Valis = Vast Active Living Intelligence System = God); he wrote the novel in twelve days in a mood of joy.[54] Dick called it 'a study of Judaism', which he researched extensively before writing.[55] But, while he claimed in an interview that 'Christianity is renounced and denounced in the book. God is specifically Yahweh, as in the Old Testament', he could still say, in the same interview, 'I snuck in some Christianity. I finally got back to Christianity. It's inserted insidiously into the book. It's a Christian thing, which you would never identify as Christian.'[56]

What is certain is that, if the book is to be considered as Christian, Dick has rewritten Christianity, integrating it with religious and metaphysical beliefs it would normally exclude. God is not a trinity, but a duality, which through the action of the book becomes a unity in duality. The one side, vested in Emmanuel the child of Yahweh, is in some sense the judging God of the Old Testament, the transcendent world-condemning God, while the other, seen in the 'nature' figure Zina who has remained on Earth, is the Shekhina, the loving, more immanent, even incarnate God of the New Testament. Emmanuel thinks, of Zina, 'These two portions of the Godhead ... have been detached from each other for millennia. But now we have come together again, the male half of the Godhead and the female half'; and 'You the kind side, he thought; the compassionate side. And I the terrible side that arouses fear and trembling. Together we form a unity. Separated, we are not whole; we are not, individually, enough.'[57] This duality and synthesis could not be predicated of the nature of the Christian God, who is seen as present wholly in each mode of the Trinity, as each in Him.

Again, the main conflict of the book is not with evil, which comes only at the end, but with one's other self, and one's ignorance: Emmanuel must find out for himself what he is and who Zina is – that is one essential character of Gnosticism, although usually applied only to mortal understanding. Gnostic also is the idea that the universe is a continually maintained thought in the mid of God (hence VALIS), in which all times and places are eternally present, and awareness of which puts one directly in touch with the divine. Thus the physicality of 'the world as it is' is denied: within the novel the central action occurs in an alternative Earth constructed by Zina's mind; and Emmanuel is born not so much as baby, in which role we never see him, more as a prodigious mind which must discover itself through a 'disinhibiting stimulus'. This is all the more remarkable when we consider how much the novel, with its prophet Elias and its new Joseph and Mary in the human protagonists Herb Asher and Rybys Rommey, seems to re-create the incarnational story as we have it in the Bible. But in the novel Christ's mission is seen as a failure, and this Second Coming in the space age is the true one. Platonic, Spinozan, Judaic, Zoroastrian, Gnostic and Christian elements interweave: it is as though Dick is creating a new composite theology.

And yet at the centre of the book is love both divine and human, and that may, as with Powys's *Mr Weston's Good Wine*, be its most Christian aspect: the love the binds Herb and Rybys, Herb and the singer Linda, Emmanuel and Zina. Yahweh may have come down to Earth to defeat Belial, but His coming is not just a victory, but a marriage with His lost half: here God is not all-powerful, but is as emotionally retarded by His division as He is intellectually retarded in the accident that follows His return. God is thus humanised in another sense than the incarnational one: He has weaknesses, biases, which have to be corrected. Just as Herb Asher must learn to consequences of cutting himself off from humankind, so must Yahweh, who mocks him, learn the spiritual price of His own exile: they follow a parallel journey after the accident, whereby they gradually remember their true natures and pasts, and this additionally unites God and man. But it has to be said that this is by the most peculiar and unorthodox means.

How then does this novel stand in relation to Christianity? Certainly there is no suggestion by Dick that his theology is wholly 'right': it is too provisional for that, too much the local and eccentric construct of one individual, even while it is recognisably Gnostic. Gnosticism itself does, however, have a certain proximity to Christianity, as a mode of which one branch of it flourished during the first two centuries after Christ's death, until it was suppressed by the Church Fathers. Just as it existed as one version of the truth before 'orthodoxy' extinguished it, Dick and many others like him might say, so it may return when orthodoxy is itself crumbling (and syncretistic religions once more flourishing) and provide an alternative 'Christian' faith to Christianity itself. For the Christian, of course, there are no alternatives to belief in Christ as the redeemer who saved us from our fallen sinfulness, and who will return in final judgement in the Last Days. Nevertheless, it might be argued that in a universe now seen to be of infinite possibility and indeterminate character, and in a postmodern world of multiple planes of reality, a God who is seen as having chosen only one means by which to manifest Himself, or allowed only one interpretation of any one manifestation, is hard to accept. Especially does this seem to be felt by the science-fiction writer, for whom there is not one universe but an unlimited series available to creation by man's imagination; and more still by Philip Dick, for whom our so solid Earth is in reality a mental construct which can flicker into another form in a moment.

It is such 'breaking-out' of the imagination that Dick's theological novels represent. Rather than seeking to subvert Christianity, they may be seen as working to give it flexibility beyond rigid parameters of belief and institution, to make it able to expand beyond hallowed but confining modes; their Gnosticism is in a sense the religious correlative of the modern belief in enlarging mental awareness. Whether we regard this as one way in which Christianity may sustain itself through change, or as heresy, or simply as the loss of truly Christian vision, is for us to determine. If the former, then Christian fantasy continues, but by changing out of recognition; if the latter, then we must admit its increasingly tenuous position in modern literature.

For beyond this one can only list some of the themes explored by religious works of science fiction, as we are no longer dealing with works that have much direct bearing on Christianity as we know it. Robert Heinlein in *Stranger in a Strange Land* (1961) describes a world in which everyone who 'groks' is God; and shifts between polytheistic and monotheistic theologies. Roger Zelazny in ' A Rose for Ecclesiastes' (1967) portrays the attempt of an agnostic called Gallinger to persuade the Martians out of a fatalistic self-abandonment to the ways of their god: he fails, but in so doing confirms them further in their faith, and inadvertently fulfils the role of their of long-prophesied messiah. The 'Dune' novels of Frank Herbert contain a religion of power based on psychic forces, in which those who can tap their collective unconscious most profoundly may become almost gods. P. J. Farmer's *Night of Light* (1966) presents a battle of good and evil gods every seven years on a planet called Dante's Joy, these gods being projections of the collective spiritual psyche of the population over the period, and the success of one or the other expressing a judgement on them. Harlan Ellison's 'The Deathbird' (1973) makes the serpent the protector of Earth against a maniacal deity, and the re-creator of Adam in the person of one Nathan Stack, who realises the folly of worshipping this god. In Michael Moorcock's *Behold the Man* (1969), the Christ who died on the cross is portrayed as a bungling and weedy time-traveller from the present day who gets caught up in events beyond his control. Robert Sheckley's *Dimension of Miracles* (1968) attacks fundamentalist notions of God, denying the adequacy of any of our images of Him. In these and other novels Christianity is still present as an implicit comparator, but it is melting into a multinational sea of faith where no belief system remains.

If we look back at our account of modern Christian fantasy, it will be seen that the issue in such fantasy has been how to relate the old 'supernatural' to a world of much greater change and complexity than has hitherto existed. As previously observed, in Dante, in Spenser, in Milton, Bunyan or Swedenborg, the world is felt to be inadequate before God, a place whose pleasures and variety are as nothing to those of heaven. Post-Romantic Christian fantasy, while not admitting it, seems to register something of the opposite sense. The world seems much less directly dependent on God, and the wonders of the world, or the mysteries of the mind, have to be considered first: God's power and glory are seen more immanently, as manifested within phenomena. Even this mode of uniting God with our world is one that is possible mainly in the nineteenth century; in the twentieth, in more 'fictional' fantasy, 'God' tends more often to exist off-world, in outer space, whether in Lindsay's *A Voyage to Arcturus* or Lewis's space trilogy or Dicks's 'Valis' novels; or to come to the world from outside as an anomalous visitor, as in Powys. Increasingly the Christian supernatural becomes located in wholly fantastic worlds; or else is made still more remote-seeming by being subsumed within other religious visions. From a possibly 'continuous presence', the Christian supernatural in literature slips to an occasional one – and thence to a presence no longer really believed in at all.

Yet there are those who have answers to this, those who now argue that to look for the continuance of the 'supernatural' in the Christian faith is to be out of touch with the times. For them the search for the 'wholly other' is a form of escape from our condition. For them too the Bible is neither a narrative to be believed nor even a myth to be explained, but a work of literature which has all the open-endedness, multidimensionality and indeterminacy which characterises what is known as postmodern fiction – a work the experience of which is capable of opening deeper levels of ourselves than we could ever have imagined, through our experience of its continued challenge to our every assumption.[58] For such critics the experience itself of such texts is crucial, and not to be characterised by such fixed terms and goals as God, Christ, Heaven, Hell. And a similar move away from historicism, objectivism and orthodoxy, whether of Church or Bible, distinguishes much modern 'anthropotheology', in Rudolf Bultmann, Karl Rahner and Paul Tillich.[59]

In a sense the whole history of Christian fantasy that we have traced has been a gradual process of 'deconstruction', to the point where it can perhaps find itself only in a deconstructed form. Looked at one way, the journey appears one towards loss. Yet from another point of view, from the aspect of Christianity as a growing and developing faith rather than what may be considered a static set of assertions and narratives to which credence must everlastingly be given, it may be that this is only the beginning, a point where a genuine and unforced merging of the old categories of nature and supernature, God and man and world, may take place, just as it so sweetly and painfully happened, and still happens, beyond all our comprehension, two millennia ago as now, in Christ and on the Cross.

Notes

The following abbreviations are used in references to journals.

E in C	*Essays in Criticism*
ELH	*English Literary History*
ELR	*English Literary Renaissance*
ES	*English Studies*
JEGP	*Journal of English and Germanic Philology*
MLN	*Modern Language Notes*
MLQ	*Modern Language Quarterly*
MP	*Modern Philology*
N & Q	*Notes and Queries*
PQ	*Philological Quarterly*
SEL	*Studies in English Literature 1500–1900*
SP	*Studies in Philology*
TSLL	*Texas Studies in Literature and Language*
UTQ	*University of Toronto Quarterly*

CHAPTER 1   INTRODUCTION

1. Quoted in George P. Landow, *Victorian Types, Victorian Shadows: Biblical Typology in Victorian Literature, Art and Thought* (London: Routledge and Kegan Paul, 1980) p. 55.
2. The initial stimulus for this was David Friedrich Strauss, *Das Leben Jesu* (1835). See Hans W. Frei, *The Eclipse of Biblical Narrative: A Study in Eighteenth and Nineteenth Century Hermeneutics* (New Haven, Conn., and London: Yale University Press, 1974) chs 12, 14; Robert Alter and Frank Kermode (eds), *The Literary Guide to the Bible* (London: Collins, 1987). One of the most seminal works of theology this century has been Rudolf Bultmann's demythologising essay 'New Testament and Theology' (1941).
3. On the last see Northrop Frye, *The Great Code: The Bible and Literature* (London: Routledge, and Kegan Paul, 1982); Alter and Kermode, *The Literary Guide to the Bible*; and David Jasper, *The New Testament and the Literary Imagination* (London: Macmillan, 1987).
4. J. R. R. Tolkien, *Tree and Leaf* (London: Allen and Unwin, 1964) p. 62.
5. Francis Bacon, *The Advancement of Learning* (1605), in J. E. Spingarn (ed.), *Critical Essays of the Seventeenth Century*, 3 vols (London: Oxford University Press, 1908), I, 7.
6. Sir William Davenant, 'Preface to *Gondibert*' (1650), ibid., II, 5.
7. Abraham Cowley, 'Preface to *Poems*' (1656), ibid., II, 89–90.

8. Sir Philip Sidney, *An Apologie for Poetrie* (1583), in G. Gregory Smith (ed.), *Elizabethan Critical Essays*, 2 vols (London: Oxford University Press, 1904) I, 157.

9. Tolkien, *Tree and Leaf*, p. 63. See also Helen Elsom in Alter and Kermode, *The Literary Guide to the Bible*, pp. 568–9, on the Gospels as examples of a contemporary romance genre, and read as such. It is, incidentally, a mistaken notion of fantasy's capacity to identify it with mere 'fancy', as opposed to truth-bearing 'imagination', as does Jasper (*The New Testament and the Literary Imagination*, ch. 7, pp. 83–96, esp. pp. 84–6).

10. I have defined fantasy's more general use of the supernatural in similar terms in C. N. Manlove, *Modern Fantasy: Five Studies* (Cambridge: Cambridge University Press, 1975) ch. 1; supplemented in C. N. Manlove, 'On the Nature of Fantasy', in Roger C. Schlobin (ed.), *The Aesthetics of Fantasy Literature and Art* (Notre Dame, Ind.: University of Notre Dame Press, 1982) pp. 29–30. By 'unambiguous' here, in relation to the supernatural, I am referring to the definition of 'the fantastic' (not *fantasy*) by Tzvetan Todorov in his *The Fantastic: A Structural Approach to a Literary Genre* (1970), tr. Richard Howard (Cleveland: Case Western Reserve University Press, 1973): 'The fantastic ... lasts only as long as a certain hesitation: a hesitation common to reader and character, who must decide whether or not what they perceive derives from "reality" as it exists in the common opinion' (p. 41). This is the sort of disguised 'fantastic' to be found in some of the novelists described in Malcolm Scott's *The Struggle for the Soul of the French Novel: French Catholic and Realist Novelists, 1850–1970* (London: Macmillan, 1989).

11. On such visions and reports see Howard Rollins Patch, *The Other World: According to Descriptions in Medieval Literature* (Cambridge, Mass.: Harvard University Press, 1950) chs 4, 5; and Carol Zaleski, *Otherworld Journeys: Accounts of Near-Death Experience in Medieval and Modern Times* (New York: Oxford University Press, 1987) chs 2–5.

12. Tolkien, *Tree and Leaf*, p. 49. See also p. 50.

13. St Thomas Aquinas, *Summa Theologica*, I. i. 9 ad 1.

14. Lewis has another reason: that the Bible has all sorts of 'Sunday school' associations that put us off. To get past those 'watchful dragons' he put scriptural truths in a 'faërian' context. See his 'Sometimes Fairy Stories May Say Best What's to Be Said' (1956), repr. in his *Of Other Worlds: Essays and Stories*, ed. Walter Hooper (London: Geoffrey Bles, 1966) pp. 36–7.

15. Charles Williams, *'He Came down from Heaven' and 'The Forgiveness of Sins'* (London: Faber and Faber, 1950) pp. 25, 102–3.

16. C. S. Lewis, *The Pilgrim's Regress: An Allegorical Apology for Christianity, Reason and Romanticism*, 3rd edn (London: Geoffrey Bles, 1965) p. 171.

17. Wendy Holden, 'Non-Vital Statistics in Minds of Americans', *Daily Telegraph*, 12 Aug 1989, p. 3: '1% of Americans do not believe in God'. Cf. also *Observer*, 31 Mar 1991, p. 18: '232 million of the 266 million inhabitants [of the United States] profess to be Christians.'

CHAPTER 2   THE FRENCH *QUESTE DEL SAINT GRAAL*

1.   Jacques Le Goff, 'The Marvelous in the Medieval Imagination' (1985), in *The Medieval Imagination,* tr. Arthur Goldhammer (Chicago and London: University of Chicago Press, 1988) pp. 28–9.
2.   For accounts and translations see Watson Kirkconnell, *The Celestial Cycle: The Theme of 'Paradise Lost' in World Literature with Translations of the Major Analogues* (Toronto: University of Toronto Press, 1952) pp. 3–43.
3.   See Howard Rollins Patch, *The Other World: According to Descriptions in Medieval Literature* (Cambridge, Mass.: Harvard University Press, 1950).
4.   A striking exception is *Beowulf* (c. 700–50), with its dragons and monsters, but this poem issued not from the Church but from recently converted Anglo-Saxon and heathen culture; and its outlook is only partly Christian, referring only to the Old Testament and omitting all mention of Christ.
5.   Le Goff, *The Medieval Imagination,* p. 29. See also the whole essay ('The Marvelous in the Medieval Imagination'), pp. 27–44.
6.   Ibid., pp. 32, 29. But the Church was still 'allergic to the marvelous', and the marvellous itself resisted incorporation (pp. 42, 36).
7.   See Roger Sherman Loomis, 'The Origin of the Grail Legends', in Loomis (ed.), *Arthurian Literature in the Middle Ages: A Collaborative History* (Oxford: Clarendon Press, 1959) pp. 274–95. There are recent translations of Chrétien and *Perlesvaus* by Nigel Bryant, published as *Perceval: The Story of the Grail* (Cambridge: D. S. Brewer, 1982) and *Perlesvaus: The High Book of the Grail* (Cambridge: D. S. Brewer, 1978), respectively; and of Wolfram's *Parzival* by A. T. Hatto (Harmondsworth, Middx: Penguin, 1980).
8.   And than any of its successors: see for instance Eugène Vinaver, *Malory* (Oxford: Clarendon Press, 1929) pp. 70–84. Pauline Matarasso, in the Introduction to her translation *The Quest of the Holy Grail* (Harmondsworth, Middx: Penguin, 1969) p. 28, remarks, 'Whereas to the author of the *Quest* the tale was merely a vehicle for expressing spiritual truths in an idiom which would make them live in the minds of a sophisticated but secular public, for Malory the tale was paramount, the doctrines, in so far as he understood them, of very secondary importance. Furthermore the *Quest* with its overt condemnation of the pride and pomp of chivalry conflicted with Malory's conception of the knightly ideal.'
9.   Matarasso, Introduction to *The Quest,* p. 9. Cf. Mary Hines-Berry, 'A Tale "Breffly Drawyne Oute of Freynshe"', in Toshiyuki Takamiya and Derek Brewer (eds), *Aspects of Malory,* Arthurian Studies, I (Cambridge: D. S. Brewer; Totowa, NJ: Rowman and Littlefield, 1981): 'From the first, the reader is invited to see through the story . . . . The action is constantly elaborated in such a way that we see the real meaning lies not in things or in actions, but in their deeper significance' (p. 94); 'The literal story of the Grail quest is only a vehicle for a very precise exposition of a mystical understanding of the Eucharist' (p. 102).

10. Translated extracts from the *Queste* are by Matarasso; parenthetical page references relate to this edition. (See above, note 8.)

11. See Frederick W. Locke, *'The Quest for the Holy Grail': A Literary Study of a Thirteenth Century French Romance* (Stanford, Calif.: Stanford University Press, 1960); and Pauline Matarasso, *The Redemption of Chivalry: A Study of the 'Queste del Saint Graal'* (Geneva: Librairie Droz, 1979).

12. See also Hines-Berry, in Takamiya and Brewer, *Aspects of Malory*, pp. 94–5.

13. On the facility with which the medieval mind could let enchanted mingle with terrestrial geography, unseen with seen, see Carolly Erickson, *The Medieval Vision: Essays in History and Perception* (New York: Oxford University Press, 1976) pp. 3–13, 27–8; Le Goff, *The Medieval Imagination*, p. 33.

14. Matarasso, *The Quest*, p. 293 n. 44, remarks that the concept of the *aventure* in the *Queste* relates not to mere random doings and experiences, but is 'above all God working and manifesting Himself in the physical world'.

CHAPTER 3   DANTE: THE *COMMEDIA*

1. Cf. A. D. Nuttall, *Overheard by God: Fiction and Prayer in Herbert, Milton, Dante and St John* (London: Methuen, 1980) pp. 139–43.

2. Umberto Cosmo, *A Handbook to Dante Studies*, tr. David Moore (Oxford: Basil Blackwell, 1950) p. 152, writes, 'Certainly the journey is a fiction, but a fiction which from the poet's point of view it is both desirable and necessary that his readers should accept as the truth.' Erich Auerbach, in 'Dante's Addresses to the Reader', *Romance Philology*, 7 (1954), repr. in Robert J. Clements (ed.), *American Critical Essays on 'The Divine Comedy'* (New York: New York University Press, 1967), comments, 'the contemporary reader already knew that all this: mission, journey, and actual revelation in Purgatory and Heaven, was poetical fiction. But a fiction so fused with reality that one easily forgets where its realm begins' (p. 46); and again, 'The appeal to divine authority was the natural and normal way to express strong political convictions in medieval civilisation' (p. 49).

3. There is some possible mountain precedent, but nothing of the placing in a southern ocean, nor the notion of spiral ascent via cornices: see Jacques Le Goff, *The Birth of Purgatory*, tr. Arthur Goldhammer (London: Scolar Press, 1981) pp. 116–17, 126–7, 334–55.

4. Patrick Boyde, *Dante Philomythes and Philosopher: Man in the Cosmos* (Cambridge: Cambridge University Press, 1981) pp. 109–11.

5. For an overview of sources see William Anderson, *Dante the Maker* (London: Hutchinson, 1983) pp. 274–80, 329–30, 418–23. For 'Vision of the Other World' sources see Howard Rollins Patch, *The Other World: According to Descriptions in Medieval Literature* (Cambridge, Mass.: Harvard University Press, 1950); and Carol Zaleski, *Otherworld Journeys: Accounts of Near-Death Experience in Medieval and Modern*

Times (New York: Oxford University Press, 1987). For possible Islamic sources see Miguel Asin, *Islam and the Divine Comedy*, tr. H. Sunderland (London: John Murray, 1926); but cf. Theodore Silverstein, 'Dante and the Legend of the *Mi'raj*: The Problem of Islamic Influence on the Christian Literature of the Otherworld', *Journal of Near Eastern Studies*, 11 (1952) 89–110, 187–97.

6. See for example Patch, *The Other World*; Zaleski, *Otherworld Journeys*; and Eileen Gardner (ed.), *Visions of Heaven and Hell before Dante* (New York: Italica Press, 1989). Irma Brandeis, *The Ladder of Vision: A Study of Images in Dante's Comedy* (London: Chatto and Windus, 1960) p. 18, remarks that the subject till Dante 'had been given only the simplest and crudest of pious representations in the Christian west'. Cosmo, *Handbook*, p. 145, goes so far as to claim, 'The *Comedy* is assuredly a creation of such powerful originality that no resemblance to it is to be found in any previous work.'

7. Gerard Watson, 'Imagination and Religion in Classical Thought' and Thomas Finan, 'Dante and the Religious Imagination', in James P. Mackey (ed.), *Religious Imagination* (Edinburgh: Edinburgh University Press, 1987) pp. 48–53, 65–85. Of Dante, Watson says, 'With Dante the imagination gains a higher place than it had yet been accorded in poetry or philosophy.... Imagination had become the pathway to the divine life' (p. 53).

8. Dante, *Vita Nuova*, II: 'certo di lei si potea dire quella parola del poeta Omero: *Ella non parea figliuola d'uomo mortale, ma di deo*' ('in all certainty one could ascribe to her those words of Homer: "She seemed the daughter not of a mortal man but of God"').

9. Anderson, *Dante the Maker*, pp. 304–5.

10. Ibid., pp. 175–6, 239. In his treatise on the vernacular, *De Vulgari Eloquentia*, Dante's central theme is 'nobilior est vulgaris' ('the vernacular is more noble [than Latin]').

11. Ernst Robert Curtius, *European Literature and the Latin Middle Ages*, tr. W.R. Trask, Bollingen Series, XXXVI (New York: Pantheon, 1953) pp. 48–61. On the limited interest in literature *qua* literature in the medieval period see J. W. H. Atkins, *English Literary Criticism: The Medieval Phase* (Cambridge: Cambridge University Press, 1943) ch. 1, pp. 1–35.

12. Apart perhaps from the educational and scientific cosmic voyage in Bernardus Silvestris's *Cosmographia* ('Microcosmos', chs 3–9; followed in *Anticlaudianus*, IV–V). Both Bernardus and Alanus in his *De Planctu Naturae* invent new 'myths'–the one of creation, the other of creation gone wrong – but these myths are less narratives than sequential encyclopaedias of being, or being depraved. On Bernardus's novelty see Brian Stock, *Myth and Science in the Twelfth Century: A Study of Bernard Sylvester* (Princeton, NJ: Princeton University Press, 1972) esp. p. 274: it is clear from Stock's account that Bernardus's creation of myth would be such as to tie it more and not less to a conceptual and allegorical function, in the face of the attacks being made on myth in the mid twelfth century by the 'new science' and rationalism (pp. 59–60). On Dante's contrastive originality in 'baptising' pagan

imagery see Anderson, *Dante the Maker*, pp. 322–3: 'there is no earlier example amongst Christian mystics for his [Dante's] daring juxtaposition of divine theme and pagan images'. On his debt to Virgil for his 'strong story-line' and his 'grandiose and glowing images' see also pp. 421–2.

13.   In common with his contemporaries Dante approached the *Aeneid* as a work to be understood morally and allegorically, and to be retranslated into Christian terms. On this, see for example Teodolinda Barolini, *Dante's Poets: Textuality and Truth in the 'Comedy'* (Princeton, NJ: Princeton University Press, 1984) pp. 201–70, esp. pp. 214–18; Robin Kirkpatrick, *Dante: 'The Divine Comedy'* (Cambridge: Cambridge University Press, 1987) pp. 7–10. But in the *Commedia* Dante's attitude to the *Aeneid* is markedly different from that of his nearest predecessor in this field, Bernardus Silvestris, who, while praising the poem for its narrative, sees that narrative only as subserving a Christian allegory of the pilgrimage of a human soul through the world, from an infantine confinement to the body, via a lapse into concupiscence (Dido) and a descent into knowledge of the soul (Hades), to an approach to divine vision – in short, as a psychomachia. In Bernardus's view, 'Virgil is a philosopher. His procedure is to describe allegorically and by means of an integument what the human spirit does and endures while temporarily placed in the human body . . . . The integument is a type of exposition which wraps the apprehension of truth in a fictional narrative, and thus it is also called an *involucrum*, a cover' – Bernardus Silvestris, *Commentary on the First Six Books of Virgil's 'Aeneid'*, tr. Earl G. Schreiber and Thomas E. Maresca (Lincoln, Nebr., and London: University of Nebraska Press, 1979) Preface, p. 5. Thus, though Bernardus observes 'the double point of view of philosophy and poetic fiction' required to read the *Aeneid* (p. 3), it is the former that is important in his *Commentary*. As Schreiber and Maresca point out in their introduction, Bernardus reads the *Aeneid* as an 'allegory of poets' rather than an 'allegory of theologians': 'Narrative, the story, is the *fictum*, the made-up; the meanings of words are the real' (p. xviii). Dante, by contrast, values the story not only as a means to an educative end but also on its own terms. 'In Dante's vision, Aeneas' intellectual quest . . . owes a great deal to the neoplatonists' interpretations. But Dante departs from Bernardus' exegesis at the very outset in a fundamental way. Vergil appears primarily as a poet . . . . The emphasis on Vergil as a poet serves for Dante as a way of focussing precisely on the tension – partly bypassed by Bernardus – between literature and philosophy and as a way of questioning the notion that poetic language can directly lead to an extrapolation of philosophical "truth"' – Giuseppe Mazzotta, *Dante, Poet of the Desert: History and Allegory in the 'Divine Comedy'* (Princeton, NJ: Princeton University Press, 1979) pp. 156–7.

14.   Translated extracts from the *Commedia* are from Dante Alighieri, *The Divine Comedy*, tr. Charles S. Singleton, 3 vols, Bollingen Series, LXXX (Princeton, NJ: Princeton University Press, 1970, 1973, 1975). Line

references relate to this edition. *Inferno, Purgatorio* and *Paradiso* abbreviated in references as *Inf., Purg., Par.*

15. On Dante's scientific picture of the workings of the universe in the *Commedia* see Boyde, *Dante Philomythes.*

16. Charles S. Singleton, 'Dante's Allegory' (1954), in Clements, *American Critical Essays*, pp. 91–103; Anderson, *Dante the Maker*, pp. 333–5. Francis Fergusson, *Dante* (London: Weidenfeld and Nicolson, 1966) p. 95, argues that 'Dante, following the allegorical mode of Scripture as he understood it, built the three allegorical "meanings", or ways of understanding action, into the successive stages of the journey to make it one of progressive enlightenment – literal in Hell, moral and then allegorical in Purgatory, and then anagogical in Heaven.'

17. On the last see Kenelm Foster, *The Two Dantes, and Other Studies* (London: Darton, Longman and Todd, 1977) pp. 7–10.

18. Dorothy L. Sayers (tr. and ed.), *Dante, 'The Divine Comedy'*, I: *Hell* (Harmondsworth, Middx: Penguin, 1949) p. 205.

19. J. R. R. Tolkien, *Tree and Leaf* (London: Allen and Unwin, 1964) p. 48.

20. Mervyn Peake, *Gormenghast* (London: Eyre and Spottiswoode, 1950) p. 454.

21. Cf. Philip McNair, 'The Poetry of the "Comedy"', in U. Limentani (ed.), *The Mind of Dante* (Cambridge: Cambridge University Press, 1965) p. 29: 'Dante's travels are not intended to be fantastic, like Baron Münchhausen's: they are intended to be credible. Hence the *Comedy* is not pure fiction in which anything might happen: it is controlled by a reality independent of itself. Dante is describing the universe which is.'

22. Anderson, *Dante the Maker*, pp. 284–6, 384, on numerology in the *Commedia*; Cosmo, *Handbook*, p. 165, declares that 'the very structure of the work is modelled on the order of the universe'.

23. This is parallel to the Augustinian three levels of vision 'by which, progressively, man may apprehend divine truth: corporeal vision, spiritual vision, which mediates between the first and third kinds, and intellectual vision, which is the highest' (Anderson, *Dante the Maker*, p. 299).

24. The visionary journeys to the worlds beyond death that precede the *Commedia* are brief and mainly involve visits to Hell, Purgatory or a usually earthly Paradise. See Patch, *The Other World*; and Zaleski, *Otherworld Journeys.*

25. See also Ernest Hatch Wilkins, 'Reminiscence and Anticipation in the *Divine Comedy*', in Clements, *American Critical Essays*, pp. 52–63.

26. For a fine modern understanding of this human–divine relationship see Charles Williams, *The Figure of Beatrice: A Study in Dante* (London: Faber and Faber, 1943).

27. On Beatrice as Christ figure see also Charles S. Singleton, 'The Pattern at the Centre', *Dante Studies I, 'Commedia': Elements of Structure* (Cambridge, Mass: Harvard University Press, 1954) pp. 45–60.

28. Linear in that the second line of each tercet rhymes with the first and third of the next; circular in that the bounding lines of each tercet rhyme. See also John Freccero, 'The Significance of Terza Rima'

(1983), repr. in *Dante: The Poetics of Conversion* (Cambridge, Mass: Harvard University Press, 1986) pp. 258–71.

CHAPTER 4   THE MIDDLE ENGLISH *PEARL*

1. On the backgrounds of the poem as 'Vision of the Other World' and 'Consolatio', respectively, see Thomas C. Niemann, '*Pearl* and the Christian Other World', *Genre*, 7 (1974) 213–32; and John Conley, '*Pearl* and a Lost Tradition', *JEGP*, 54 (1955) 332–47, repr. in Conley (ed.), *The Middle English 'Pearl': Critical Essays* (Notre Dame, Ind.: University of Notre Dame Press, 1970) pp. 50–72. See also Howard Rollins Patch, *The Other World: According to Descriptions in Medieval Literature* (Cambridge, Mass.: Harvard University Press, 1950) chs 4, 5.

2. References are to *Pearl*, ed. E. V. Gordon (Oxford: Clarendon Press, 1953).

3. See Ian Bishop, '*Pearl' in its Setting: A Critical Study of the Structure and Meaning of the Middle English Poem* (Oxford: Basil Blackwell, 1968) pp. 51–61. Bishop, pp. 62–72, also finds present an 'allegory of the poets'.

4. On the pearl as symbol see also A. C. Spearing, 'Symbolic and Dramatic Development in *Pearl*', *MP*, 60 (1962) 1–12, repr. in Conley, *Pearl*, pp. 122–48; Patricia M. Kean, '*The Pearl': An Interpretation* (London: Routledge and Kegan Paul, 1967) pp. 138–61; Bishop, '*Pearl' in its Setting*, pp. 92–8.

5. It is even potentially heretical in the sense that the child was not even a *late* labourer: she never worked at all. On possible medieval precedent for this, see D. W. Robertson Jr, 'The "Heresy" of *The Pearl*', *MLN*, 65 (1950) 152–5, repr. in Conley, pp. 291–6; Bishop, pp. 122–5.

6. See also Wendell Stacy Johnson, 'The Imagery and Diction of *The Pearl*: Toward an Interpretation', *ELH*, 20 (1953), repr. in Conley, *Pearl*, pp. 46–9; and Charles Moorman, 'The Role of the Narrator in *Pearl*', *MP*, 53 (1955), repr. in Conley, *Pearl*, pp. 118, 120.

7. See for example Nikki Stiller, 'The Transformation of the Physical in the Middle English *Pearl*', *ES*, 63 (1982) 402–9.

8. There have been earlier suggestions that the dream expresses the psychology of the dreamer, but they tend to relate only to the 'dream-like' structure and transitions of the poem: there is little idea of the content of the vision as symbolic expression of the moral nature of the dreamer. See Constance B. Hieatt, *The Realism of Dream Visions: The Poetic Exploitation of the Dream-Experience in Chaucer and his Contemporaries* (The Hague: Mouton, 1967) pp. 61–6; and A. C. Spearing, *Medieval Dream-Poetry* (Cambridge: Cambridge University Press, 1976) pp. 111–29. A recent partial exception on medieval dream-visions generally is J.A. Burrow, *Essays on Medieval Literature* (Oxford: Clarendon Press, 1984) pp. 206–12: Burrow remarks tentatively, for instance, of the second vision from the first part of *Piers Plowman* (V–VII) that the 'quite unexpected twists in the allegorical fiction suggest imaginatively, it seems to me, the continuous corkscrewing movement of the spirit, adopting and then rejecting successive

images, definitions and external observances as it works towards inwardness and truth .... The story and the meaning seem to interpenetrate, in a way that Neo-Romantic criticism is especially well fitted to describe' (p. 212).

9. There have been occasional remarks on the maiden's coldness: for instance by Spearing, in Conley, *Pearl*, pp. 135, 138; by Kean, in *The Pearl*, pp. 198–9; and by Larry M. Sklute, in 'Expectation and Fulfillment in *Pearl*', *PQ*, 52 (1973) 675. Kean, however, sees it as a function of the fact that she is 'Reason', and Sklute as an expression of her distance as a heavenly being from our merely human modes of feeling. No suggestion is made that her aspect expresses the dreamer's way of seeing things. An exception here is Theodore Bogdanos, *Pearl: Image of the Ineffable: A Study in Medieval Poetic Symbolism* (University Park, Pa: Pennsylvania State University Press, 1983) p. 87, which speaks of 'the poets' intentional accentuation of divine heartlessness . . . to elicit a powerful response in the reader as human sufferer. The poet wishes to heighten the dramatic tension between man in his frailty and the absolute, inscrutable decrees he must measure up to.' My own interpretation of *Pearl* has, it should be said, certain affinities with Bogdanos's fine account of the poem, particularly his treatment of the maiden's parable and the picture of heaven; but Bogdanos is much more concerned to see the 'unaccommodating' aspects of the vision from the point of view of God's ineffability rather than the dreamer's particular frailty.

10. On this possibility, and on the similarities between *Pearl* and the *Commedia*, see Kean, *The Pearl*, pp. 120–31, 138; and Niemann, in *Genre*, 7, pp. 223–5.

11. One should, however, also bear in mind Kean's observation that 'Vision literature, on the whole . . . favours the enclosure' (*The Pearl*, p. 96).

12. On the poem as a subversive, self-consuming artifact which continually tests the reader by undermining his espousal of the rational see Howard V. Hendrix, 'Reasonable Failure: "Pearl" Considered as a Self-Consuming Artifact of "Gostly Porpose"', *Neuphilologische Mitteilungen*, 86 (1985) 458–66.

13. The *Iter ad Paradisum* is a medieval topos: see Patch, *The Other World* ch. 5, and Kean, *The Pearl*, pp. 89–113, citing likely sources in Mandeville, the Alexander Romances and the *Roman de la Rose*, as well as Dante. Nevertheless, as Patch, *The Other World*, p. 190, says, it is also highly original.

14. On the significance of the stones see Milton R. Stern, 'An Approach to *The Pearl*', *JEGP*, 54 (1955), repr. in Conley, *Pearl*, p. 84. Stern notes latent significance in the three precious stones specified in the stream-bed (p. 81).

15. Previous commentators have seen it as a three-stage ascent reflective of the gradations of the narrator's spiritual development: thus Louis Blenkner, OSB, 'The Theological Structure of *Pearl*', *Traditio*, 24 (1968) 43–75 [repr. in Conley, *Pearl*, pp. 220–71], and 'The Pattern of Traditional Images in *Pearl*', *SP*, 68 (1971) 26–49; John Finlayson, '*Pearl*: Landscape and Vision', *SP*, 71 (1974) 314–43; Stiller, in *ES*, 63.

CHAPTER 5   SPENSER: *THE FAERIE QUEENE*

1. C. S. Lewis traces the cause to the recovery in the twelfth century of the texts of the 'philosopher of divisions', Aristotle: 'Heaven began, under this dispensation, to seem further off.' But for him the full consequence is not evident until the seventeenth century and Descartes. See C. S. Lewis, *The Allegory of Love: A Study in Medieval Tradition* (New York: Oxford University Press, 1958) p. 88.

2. *The Terrors of the Night, or, A Discourse of Apparitions* (1594), in *The Works of Thomas Nashe*, 5 vols, ed. R. B. McKerrow, rev. F. P. Wilson (Oxford: Basil Blackwell, 1958) I, 349, citing St John Chrysostom.

3. 'A Letter of the Authors expounding his whole intention in the course of this worke', annexed to the first three books of *The Faerie Queene* in 1590, addressed to Sir Walter Raleigh, and dated 23 Jan 1589.

4. Ibid.

5. *The Quest of the Holy Grail*, tr. Pauline Matarasso (Harmondsworth, Middx: Penguin, 1969) p. 158.

6. Contrast Frederick W. Locke, *'The Quest for the Holy Grail': A Literary Study of a Thirteenth Century French Romance* (Stanford, Calif.: Stanford University Press, 1960) p. 67: 'The *Queste* is not a "darke conceit"'. Spenser, in his dedicatory letter to Sir Walter Raleigh, felt a need to supply a key to his poem. The author of the *Queste*, on the other hand, presented his work with an assurance that he would be understood in spite of the incontestable darkness that envelops his book at certain points. His was a confidence based on the knowledge that his readers possessed a body of symbols that were public in nature.'

7. This is not to exclude her roles as a cult epithet for Queen Elizabeth, and as figuring the One True Church of England in opposition to Roman Catholicism: for recent accounts of which, see, respectively, Michael O'Connell, *Mirror and Veil: The Historical Dimension in Spenser's 'Faerie Queene'* (Chapel Hill: University of North Carolina Press, 1977) pp. 44–51, 60–5, and Anthea Hume, *Edmund Spenser: Protestant Poet* (Cambridge: Cambridge University Press, 1984) pp. 85–9.

8. The evidence of R. M. Cummings (ed.), *Spenser: The Critical Heritage* (London: Routledge and Kegan Paul, 1971) pp. 6–10, is that it did not.

9. References are to the Longmans Annotated English Texts edition of *The Faerie Queene*, ed. A.C. Hamilton (London and New York, 1977).

10. Paul Alpers, 'Narrative and Rhetoric in *The Faerie Queene*', *SEL*, 2 (1962) 28.

11. As by Hamilton, who glosses the cup of gold as that of the Holy Sacrament, the serpent as a healing symbol of Aesculapius and as a figure of Christ (John 3.14), and the book as the New Testament sealed by the blood of Christ's death (*The Faerie Queene*, Longmans Annotated edn, p. 132).

12. See also A. C Hamilton, *'The Structure of Allegory in 'The Faerie Queene'* (Oxford: Clarendon Press, 1961) pp. 1–43, on the importance of the literal, or narrative, level in the poem; and on Spenser's debt to Dante.

13. On which see also Rosemary Freeman, *'The Faerie Queene': A Companion for Readers* (London: Chatto and Windus, 1970) ch. 4, pp. 87–127.

14. The source is ultimately Revelation 12.15 and 16.13, where the dragon vomits a flood to stop the passage of the beautiful woman; but it seems almost certain that Spenser drew directly on the account of the books vomited by Philology in Martianus Capella's *De Nuptiis Philologiae et Mercurii* (AD 410–29), §§ 135–9.

15. On the flexibility of interpretation required cf. Thomas H. Cain, *Praise in 'The Faerie Queene'* (Lincoln, Nebr., and London: University of Nebraska Press, 1978) ch. 3, pp. 58–83, esp. pp. 71–3.

16. James Nohrnberg, *The Analogy of 'The Faerie Queene'* (Princeton, NJ: Princeton University Press, 1976) pp. 103–5, 119–30, puts a similar view much more fully.

17. Isabel G. MacCaffrey, *Spenser's Allegory: The Anatomy of Imagination* (Princeton, NJ: Princeton University Press, 1976) pp. 67–71, also sees Fairy Land in these terms.

18. For an interpretation of the development of Redcrosse in terms of a gradual movement from a corruptible 'fantasy of faith' to true vision see Sean Kane, 'Spenser and the Frame of Faith', *UTQ*, 50 (1981) 253–68.

19. See also O'Connell, *Mirror and Veil*, pp. 41–2.

20. For an interesting argument for the literalising of metaphor in literature see Samuel R. Levin, *Metaphoric Worlds: Conceptions of a Romantic Nature* (New Haven, Conn.: Yale University Press, 1988).

21. For Lewis's views on myth and fact see below, ch. 17 n. 18.

22. Sir Philip Sidney, *An Apologie for Poetrie* (1583), in G. Gregory Smith (ed.), *Elizabethan Critical Essays*, 2 vols (London: Oxford University Press, 1904) I, 156. The view of the poet as maker of a new and self-consistent world imitating God's is also advanced by Tasso, in *Discorsi del Poema Eroico* (1594): see Torquato Tasso, *Discourses on the Heroic Poem*, tr. Mariella Cavalchini and Irene Samuel (Oxford: Clarendon Press, 1973) pp. 77–8.

CHAPTER 6   MARLOWE: *DR FAUSTUS*

1. Paul H. Kocher, *Christopher Marlowe: A Study of his Thought, Learning and Character* (Chapel Hill: University of North Carolina Press, 1946) pp. 79–86, gives a thorough critique of this view.

2. References to *Tamburlaine* and *Dr Faustus* are to the texts in *Christopher Marlowe: The Complete Works*, ed. Fredson Bowers, 2nd edn, 2 vols (Cambridge: Cambridge University Press, 1981).

3. W. W. Greg, 'The Damnation of Faustus' (1946), repr. in Clifford Leech (ed.), *Marlowe: A Collection of Critical Essays* (Englewood Cliffs, NJ: Prentice-Hall, 1964) pp. 103–6, sees Faustus as committing 'the sin of demoniality, that is, bodily intercourse with demons' (p. 106). Judith Weil, *Christopher Marlowe: Merlin's Prophet* (Cambridge: Cambridge University Press, 1977) pp. 73–5, points out the blasphemies and corruptions of the speech in its perversions of biblical and other

Christian language; and at p. 195 n. 39 argues the weakness of one case made against that of Greg – by T. W. Craik, in 'The Damnation of Faustus Reconsidered', *Renaissance Drama*, 2 (1969) 192–6.

4.   J. C. Maxwell, 'The Plays of Christopher Marlowe', in Boris Ford (ed.), *The Pelican Guide to English Literature, 2: The Age of Shakespeare* (Harmondsworth, Middx: Penguin, 1963) p. 173. On Faustus's materialism see also Leo Kirschbaum, 'Religious Values in *Dr Faustus*' (1962), repr. in Willard Farnham (ed.), *Twentieth Century Interpretations of 'Dr Faustus': A Collection of Critical Essays* (Englewood Cliffs, NJ: Prentice-Hall, 1969) pp. 77-87; Michael Mangan, *Christopher Marlowe, 'Dr Faustus': A Critical Study*, Penguin Masterstudies (Harmondsworth, Middx: Penguin, 1987) pp. 45–6.

5.   Cf. *The New Catholic Encyclopaedia*, 17 vols (New York: McGraw-Hill, 1967) IV, 1007: 'separation from God is the theological idea of hell'.

6.   For other aspects of confinement in *Faustus* see Frank Manley, 'The Nature of *Faustus*', *MP*, 66 (1968–9) 220–1; Marjorie Garber, '"Infinite Riches in a Little Room": Closure and Enclosure in Marlowe', in Alvin Kernan (ed.), *Two Renaissance Mythmakers, Christopher Marlowe and Ben Jonson: Selected Papers from the English Institute, 1975–6*, n.s., 1 (Baltimore: Johns Hopkins University Press, 1977) pp. 5, 17–21.

7.   Roland M. Frye, 'Marlowe's *Doctor Faustus*: The Repudiation of Humanity' (1956), in Farnham, *Twentieth Century Interpretations*, pp. 56–7.

8.   See also A. L. French, 'The Philosophy of *Dr Faustus*', *E in C*, 20 (1970) 137.

9.   See also James Smith, 'Marlowe's *Dr Faustus*', *Scrutiny*, 8 (1939) 39–40, 49.

10.   See for example C. D. Baker, 'Certain Religious Elements in the English Doctrine of the Inspired Poet during the Renaissance', *ELH*, 6 (1939) 300–23.

11.   French, however, is prepared to accuse Marlowe of such blatant self-contradiction (*E in C*, 20, pp. 126–30).

12.   On which see Mangan, *Dr Faustus*, pp. 31–2.

13.   J.B. Steane, *Marlowe: A Critical Study* (Cambridge: Cambridge University Press, 1965) p. 165, finds this sense of shrinkage one of the dominant impressions conveyed by the play.

14.   See also French, in *E in C*, 20, p. 128; and Roy T. Eriksen, *'The forme of Faustus fortunes': A Study of 'The Tragedie of Doctor Faustus' (1616)* (Oslo: Sorlum; and Atlantic Highlands, NJ: Humanities Press, 1987) p. 36.

15.   Eriksen, *'The forme of Faustus fortunes'*, p. 37, also makes this point.

16.   See also Mangan, *Dr Faustus*, p. 34.

17.   By C. S. Lewis, in his *A Preface to 'Paradise Lost'* (London: Oxford University Press, 1942) p. 95.

18.   Weil, *Marlowe: Merlin's Prophet*, p. 62, cites James H. Sims, *Dramatic Uses of Allusion in Marlowe and Shakespeare* (Gainesville: University of Florida Press, 1966) p. 25, referring Faustus's reaction to the '*Homo fuge*' ('If unto God, hee'le throw me downe to hell') to Psalm 139. 7–10 on the omnipresence of God, in hell as in heaven. Weil remarks,

'For the joyful psalmist, God is everywhere. In order to express his hope of escape, Faustus has chosen words which point to an inevitable reunion with God.' This further extends the idea of all in *Faustus* happening within the divine presence.

19. See also Steane, *Marlowe: A Critical Study*, p. 135.
20. On such inversions see also, for example, Smith, in *Scrutiny*, 8, pp. 36–7; Helen Gardner, 'The Damnation of Faustus' (1946), in Farnham, *Twentieth Century Interpretations*, p. 39; J. P. Brockbank, *Marlowe: 'Dr Faustus'* (London: Edward Arnold, 1962) pp. 56–9; Leonard H. Frey, 'Antithetical Balance in the Opening and Close of *Doctor Faustus'*, *MLQ*, 24 (1963) 350–3.
21. C. L. Barber, '"The form of Faustus' fortunes good or bad"', *Tulane Drama Review*, 8 (1963–4) 106–12.
22. Michael Hattaway, *Elizabethan Popular Theatre: Plays in Performance* (London: Routledge and Kegan Paul, 1982) pp. 175–6, remarks, 'Mephostophilis' answers disappoint Faustus . . . . The devil's knowledge is drab . . . . All he [Faustus] draws from Mephostophilis is a denial of the crystalline sphere introduced to explain the phenomenon of planetary trepidation. Marlowe may have been indebted to Augustinus Ricius for this modification of orthodox Ptolemaic cosmography, but the dramatic point is that this sphere is invisible and that Faustus is unable to entertain any knowledge that is not empirical.'
23. Cf. Mangan, *Dr Faustus*, p. 86: '[Mephostophilis] rarely lied to Faustus. Indeed we have seen him being astonishingly honest with Faustus . . . hardly ever lying or deceiving.' This of course does not suggest that the devils could not lie, only that it is amazing that they did not.
24. Henry M. Pachter, *Paracelsus: Magic into Science* (New York: Henry Schuman, 1951) pp. 12–16.
25. Ernst Cassirer, Paul Oskar Kristeller and John Herman Randall, Jr (eds.), *The Renaissance Philosophy of Man* (Chicago: University of Chicago Press, 1948) p. 225 (tr. Elizabeth Livermore Forbes). A similar view, of the poet as creator, is advanced by Sidney in *An Apologie for Poetrie* (quoted above, pp. 71–2).

CHAPTER 7   THE METAPHYSICAL POETS

1. Jacopo Mazzoni, 'On the Defence of the *Comedy* [of Dante]' (1587), in *Literary Criticism: Plato to Dryden*, ed. and tr. Allan H. Gilbert (Detroit: Wayne State University Press, 1962) pp. 387, 366.
2. A. C. Hamilton, *The Structure of Allegory in 'The Faerie Queene'* (Oxford: Clarendon Press, 1961), pp. 124–7.
3. As in Castelvetro, Sidney and Tasso: see *Literary Criticism*, pp. 305–7, 324, 412–14, 435, 439, 470–1.
4. Louis Martz, *The Poetry of Meditation: A Study in English Religious Literature of the Seventeenth Century*, rev. edn (New Haven, Conn.: Yale University Press, 1962) pp. 50–2, and Barbara Kiefer Lewalski, *Protestant Poetics and the Seventeenth-Century Religious Lyric* (Princeton, NJ: Princeton University Press, 1979) pp. 268–9, argue for Ignatian

meditative structure in the sonnet; William H. Halewood, *The Poetry of Grace: Reformation Themes and Structures in English Seventeenth-Century Poetry* (New Haven, Conn.: Yale University Press, 1970) pp. 80–5, suggests a post-Reformation Augustinian one.

5.   See on this C. N. Manlove, *Literature and Reality, 1600–1800* (London: Macmillan, 1978) pp. 8–10. It has been maintained that this insistence on divine grace is a product of Calvinism and the belief that man is totally depraved, but the accent of these poems is so much on the personal, so suggestive of an irresponsible or truant will rather than of a helpless one, and so often critical of God's inactivity, that this attempt to square the Holy Sonnets with orthodox Calvinism seems rather strained: see for example Lewalski, *Protestant Poetics, passim*, esp. pp. 18–23, 264–75. Acknowledgement of the difficulties, and an attempt still to see them as part of a Calvinist theology behind the sonnets, may be found in John Stachniewski, 'John Donne: The Despair of the "Holy Sonnets"', *ELH*, 48 (1981) 677–705 (esp. p. 690 on 'Batter my heart').

6.   It is frequently argued that the Holy Sonnets should be seen as a sequence of spiritual development or conversion, so that each one till the 'end' produces only a varyingly partial vision: in this sense it would be wrong to take the vision of one sonnet at face value and criticise it in these terms. See for instance Carol Marks Sicherman, 'Donne's Discoveries', *SEL*, 11 (1971) 84–8; Lewalski, *Protestant Poetics*, pp. 264–75; Stephenie Yearwood, 'Donne's *Holy Sonnets*: The Theology of Conversion', *TSLL*, 24 (1982) 208–21. But this assumption of sequence in the sonnets is based in part on conjecture, originating in Helen Gardner's edition of *The Divine Poems* (1952), regarding Donne's intentions and is not strikingly supported by the sonnets as we read them. See also Stachniewski, in *ELH*, 48, pp. 677–84.

7.   Nevertheless such readings, based on the three images of the poem and the supposed threes (actually twos and fours) of the verbs, are frequently made: see the references in William Kerrigan, 'The Fearful Accommodations of John Donne', *ELR*, 4 (1974) 353 n. 52; and R. D. Bedford, 'Donne's Holy Sonnet "Batter my heart"', *N and Q*, 227 (1982) 16.

8.   A similar point is made by Sharon C. Seelig, in *The Shadow of Eternity: Belief and Structure in Herbert, Vaughan and Traherne* (Lexington, Ky: University Press of Kentucky, 1981) p. 45: 'Herbert's chief aim ... is the bending of his will to God's whereas Vaughan desires more ardently to see God than to obey him.'

CHAPTER 8   MILTON: *PARADISE LOST*

1.   For a full account see Barbara Kiefer Lewalski, *Milton's Brief Epic: The Genre, Meaning, and Art of 'Paradise Regained'* (Providence, RI: Brown University Press, 1966) chs 3–4, pp. 37–101. There is a useful series of lists of biblical epics in Watson Kirkconnell, *Awake the Courteous Echo: The Themes and Prosody of 'Comus', 'Lycidas' and 'Paradise Regained', with*

Translations of the Major Analogues (Toronto: University of Toronto Press, 1973) pp. 315–22.

2. Lewalski, *Milton's Brief Epic*, ch. 4.

3. See Mario A. Di Cesare, *Vida's 'Christiad' and Vergilian Epic* (New York: Columbia University Press, 1964); and Sister Mary Edgar Meyer, OSF, *The Sources of Hojeda's 'La Christiada'*, University of Michigan Publications, Language and Literature, XXVI (Ann Arbor: University of Michigan Press, 1953).

4. The bulk of the 'sources' and analogues of *Paradise Lost* tend to focus only on one or sometimes two aspects of the cosmic drama – the war in heaven, the creation of the world, the fall of man, and man's subsequent history. There are more expansive (largely non-English) exceptions – 'Caedmonian' *Genesis* (*c.* 700–850), Old German *Genesis* (*c.* 1070), Eysteinn Asgrunsson's *Lilja* (*c.* 1360), the Middle English *Clannesse* (*c.* 1375), Rupertus Tuitiensio's *Opus Originale de Victoria Verbi Dei* (1487), Jacob Ruff's *Adam and Heva* (1550), Gasparo Murtola's *Della creatione del mondo* (1608), Andrew Ramsay's *Poemata Sacra* (1633); but, apart from the first, few of these are very inspired and none is a clear source for Milton. See Watson Kirkconnell, *The Celestial Cycle: The Theme of 'Paradise Lost' in World Literature with Translations of the Major Analogues* (Toronto: University of Toronto Press, 1952) pp. 510–12, 517–18, 527, 531, 541, 559–60, 588–90. Of the more likely sources for *Paradise Lost*, Avitus's *Poematum de Mosaicae Historiae Gestis* (AD 507) focuses on the creation of man, his fall and its consequences; Du Bartas's *La Sepmaine* (1578) describes the creation; Erasmo di Valvasone's *L'Angeleida* (1590) portrays the war in heaven; Hugo Grotius's drama *Adamus Exsul* (1601) treats the fall itself (with some report, by an angelic visitant to Adam, of the creation of the world); and Joost van den Vondel's drama *Lucifer* (1654) concentrates on the war in heaven and, in a brief report, the fall of man. None of these has much of Milton's plastic energy, or the sense in his work of the whole cosmos extending behind each location – Vondel, perhaps the nearest to Milton, adheres to the 'unities' by having all the immediate action occur in one place in heaven and with a limited number of actors. (Translations of these works, in full or in part, appear in Kirkconnell, *The Celestial Cycle*, pp. 19–43, 47–58, 80–7, 96–220, 361–421.)

5. On this see for example Roland M. Frye *Milton's Imagery and the Visual Arts: Iconographic Tradition in the Epic Poems* (Princeton, NJ: Princeton University Press, 1978); Murray Roston, *Milton and the Baroque* (London: Macmillan 1980).

6. There are obvious analogues (Frye's book points out numbers of the artistic ones) for the nature of celestial experience within heaven, for the pastoral *locus amoenus* of Eden and for the place of darkness and of mingled fire and ice that is hell, but the spatial and geographical character and interrelation of these places as described in Milton are relatively new. There is perhaps some precedent for his continental hell in the Irish *Fis Adamnáin* of the eighth century, as is pointed out in C. S. Boswell, *An Irish Precursor of Dante: A Study on the Vision of*

*Heaven and Hell Ascribed to the Eighth-century Irish Saint Adamnán,
with Translation of the Irish Text*, Grimm Library, no. 18 (London:
David Nutt, 1908) pp. 39, 43, 173, 203.

7. For an attempted diagram of Milton's cosmos see Walter Clyde
    Curry, 'Some Travels of Milton's Satan', *PQ*, 29 (1950) 234 – though
    the circular form of the diagram does need the corrective observation
    that the universe is circumscribed only by a boundless and infinite
    deity (pp. 234–5). Curry remarks, 'Satan's wanderings cover amazing
    stretches of hyperbolical infinitudes – infinitudes which may be said
    to represent the expanded universe of Milton's mind' (p. 235).

8. Marjorie Nicolson, 'Milton's Hell and the Phlegraean Fields', *UTQ*, 7
    (1937–8) 500–13, argues that Milton probably visited the famous
    volcanic Phlegraean Fields while in Italy, from parallels between
    features of the Fields and passages in *Paradise Lost*. See also Frye,
    Milton's Imagery, p. 132.

9. Milton published *A Brief History of Muscovia* in the 1640s: see *The
    Works of John Milton*, ed. F. A. Patterson, 18 vols (New York: Columbia
    University Press, 1931–8) X, 327–82; pp. 331–2 and 342–4 are most
    suggestive in relation to the quotation here, and Milton cites his
    sources in such writers as Purchas, Hakluyt, Willoughby and
    Chancellor. See also Robert R. Cawley, 'Milton and Russia', *Milton
    and the Literature of Travel* (Princeton, NJ: Princeton University Press,
    1951) ch. 3, pp. 42–64.

10. See for example Howard Rollins Patch, *The Other World: According to
    Descriptions in Medieval Literature* (Cambridge, Mass.: Harvard
    University Press, 1950); and Kirkconnell, *The Celestial Cycle*. Isabel G.
    MacCaffrey, *'Paradise Lost' as 'Myth'* (Cambridge, Mass: Harvard
    University Press, 1959), calls the voyage 'Milton's greatest "original"
    creation' (p. 193; see also p. 194).

11. In the interplanetary journeys in most writers prior to Milton, from
    Lucian to Kepler or De Bergerac, apart possibly from the voyage in
    Bernardus Silvestris's *Cosmographia*, there is scant attention to the
    experience of the journey itself and its distances; see also Marjorie
    Hope Nicolson, *Voyages to the Moon* (New York: Macmillan, 1960)
    chs 1–2. In her 'The Discovery of Space', in O. B. Hardison, Jr (ed.),
    *Medieval and Renaissance Studies: Proceedings of the Southeastern Institute
    of Medieval and Renaissance Studies, Summer, 1965* (Chapel Hill, NC:
    University of North Carolina Press, 1966) p. 57, Nicolson writes,
    'Nowhere in poetry do we find more majestic conceptions of the
    vastness of space than in the work of this blind poet, in those scenes
    of cosmic perspective in which we, like Satan on the one hand, God
    on the other, look up and down to discover a universe majestic in its
    vastness.' On Milton's spatial imagery see also MacCaffrey, *'Paradise
    Lost' as 'Myth'*.

12. In the Introduction to book II of *The Reason of Church Government*
    (1641), Milton speaks in vatic terms of poetic inspiration, looking
    forward to the eventual writing of a work (to become *Paradise Lost*)
    which will be helped into being through 'devout prayer to that
    eternall Spirit who can enrich with all utterance and knowledge, and

sends out his Seraphim with the hallow'd fire of his Altar to touch and purify the lips of whom he pleases' (*Works*, III.i, 241). Kirkconnell, *The Celestial Cycle*, p. 496, points out, however, that claims of divine inspiration are common to almost all accounts of the fall.

13. MacCaffrey seems on the verge of this: 'Satan's pilgrimage through the dark towards Paradise re-traces the necessity that life imposes on us all' ('*Paradise Lost' as Myth*', p. 191).

14. The idea of the snake as penetrating Eve occurs in Gnosticism: see Jacques Lacarrière, *The Gnostics* (London: Peter Owen, 1977) pp. 81–2. There is also precedent for the idea of Satan as seducer in rabbinical sources, with which Milton was acquainted: see *The Jewish Encyclopaedia*, ed. Isidore Singer, 12 vols (New York: Funk and Wagnalls, 1901–6) s.v. 'Eve', 'Lilith'; and J.M. Evans, '*Paradise Lost' and the Genesis Tradition* (Oxford: Clarendon Press, 1968) pp. 33, 46–8, 55. The notion is also implied in 2 Corinthians 11. 2–3. The sources and analogues in Kirkconnell, *The Celestial Cycle*, occasionally touch on the idea of physical seduction (pp. 68, 111, 284, 366–7, 489, 528); it can be found also in Phineas Fletcher's *The Purple Island* (1633) XII. 29. In Act I of Vondel's *Lucifer*, the account of Eve by Apollyon is lascivious and awakens like feelings in his companions.

15. The famous physician William Harvey, discoverer of the circulatory principle of the blood, asserted in his *Exercitationes de Generatione Animalium* (1651) that all animals, including man, are produced from an egg, but nevertheless could still believe in spontaneous generation, and hold that the seminal fluid influenced the egg by an incorporeal shaping process involving no transmission of material – Harvey, *Disputations Touching the Generation of Animals*, tr. Gweneth Whitteridge (Oxford: Blackwell Scientific Publications, 1981) pp. 22, 112–13, 175, 203, and 214–39 (chs 47–50). In Harvey's view the power by which the semen seemed to shape the egg without adding anything material to it was ultimately attributable only to the plastic creative agency of God: in effect Harvey makes God the father of every creature in an intimate way, since He is active in the conception (pp. 234–9). It was not till 1677, ten years after the publication of *Paradise Lost*, that male spermatozoa were first seen – by Leeuwenhoek, using a microscope.

16. 'A Study in the Process of Individuation' (1950), 'Concerning Mandala Symbolism' (1950) and 'Mandalas' (1955), in *The Collected Works of C. G. Jung*, tr. R. F. C. Hull, 20 vols (London: Routledge and Kegan Paul, 1953–79) IX.i: *The Archetypes and the Collective Unconscious*, 2nd edn, pp. 290–390.

17. See the two sets of plates in Jung, (ibid.) between pp. 292 and 293, 356 and 357, esp. plates 3–5, 9, 10, 13 and 22 in the first set, and 10, 14–24 and 51 in the second; and the commentaries at pp. 305–23, 362–3, 366, 368–71, esp. pp. 311–2 on Mercurius as the world-egg-encircling snake.

18. Jung, *Works*, IX. i and XIV: *Mysterium Coniunctionis: An Inquiry into the Separation and Synthesis of Psychic Opposites*, pp. 187–8, on the alchemists' propagation of the ideal of quaternity (trinity + the 'serpent'), and pp. 340–3 on the origin and double aspect of the snake as death and

life together, and as Christ and Antichrist. Evidence for the duality of Satan also comes from even an apparently negative source: in Willard McCarthy, 'The Catabatic Structure of Satan's Quest', *UTQ*, 56 (1986) 283–307, it is suggested that Satan's descent to hell and reascent to earth are a form of the classical *katabasis*, the descent of the hero to an underworld and subsequent return; McCarthy's point is that Milton has done this in an ironically inverted form which continually exposes Satan, but this is to allow Milton's purpose entirely to subvert the primal force of the image itself, in terms of which Blake's account of what happened is in one sense 'right': 'It indeed appear'd to Reason as if Desire was cast out; but the Devil's account is, that the Messiah fell, and formed a heaven of what he stole from the Abyss' *(The Marriage of Heaven and Hell)*. McCarthy, incidentally, remarks the sexual analogies in Satan's entry into Paradise (p. 300). Margaret Stocker, *Paradise Lost* (London: Macmillan, 1988) pp. 40–1, citing discussions by MacCaffrey *('Paradise Lost' as 'Myth')* and R. J. Zwi Werblowsky ('Antagonist of Heaven's Almighty King', 1952) observes, 'Certainly MacCaffrey's elevation of Satan as a human archetype raises more strongly the very question it is designed to answer: whether an attractive Satan undermines the poem's theology. If as Werblowsky ... suggests, Satan shares the mythic value of Prometheus, Milton is certainly playing with fire. Prometheus the fire-bringer was also light-bearer (cf. "Lucifer", Satan's angelic name), whose revolt against the prohibitions of Zeus may have transgressed divine law but was absolutely necessary to man's survival' (p. 40).

19. They are explored further in C. N. Manlove, *Literature and Reality, 1600–1800* (London: Macmillan, 1978) pp. 50–6.

CHAPTER 9 BUNYAN: *THE PILGRIM'S PROGRESS*

1. References are to *The Pilgrim's Progress*, ed. J. B. Wharey, rev. R. Sharrock (Oxford: Clarendon Press, 1960).

2. It has been suggested that Bunyan had written *The Pilgrim's Progress* by 1666 (near the time when he is assumed to have written the analogous work *The Heavenly Footman*) and that he then held it back from publication through uncertainty concerning its worth and possible reception: see Christopher Hill, *A Turbulent, Seditious, and Factious People: John Bunyan and his Church, 1628–1688* (Oxford: Clarendon Press, 1988) pp. 197–8. This only adds to our sense of the danger Bunyan felt in using such an earthly method to put over unearthly truths. On the evidence of the book's reception by his fellow believers, Bunyan was right to be nervous of his use of fiction: see Roger Sharrock, *John Bunyan* (London: Macmillan, 1968) p. 139.

3. Various stages on the journey – the City of Destruction, Evangelist, the Slough of Despond, Worldly Wiseman, the Wicket-gate, Hill Difficulty, Interpreter's House, Apollyon, Vanity Fair, Doubting

Castle, the Delectable Mountains – can be paralleled in *Grace Abounding*. See Sharrock, *Bunyan*, pp. 72–87.

4. This episode with Charity, along with Christian's initial return to his house to plead with his wife and family to come with him, were added by Bunyan to the second edition to soften Christian's apparent restlessness and the offence by implication to Bunyan's own wife.

5. There have been those who suggest that Bunyan suspended his elective and predestinarian theology here: Nick Davis, 'The Problem of Misfortune in *The Pilgrim's Progress*', in Vincent Newey (ed.), *'The Pilgrim's Progress': Critical and Historical Views* (Liverpool: Liverpool University Press, 1980) p. 198, says, 'The doctrine of election, which has such a central place in Bunyan's theological writings, is virtually elided from *The Pilgrim's Progress*. This has to do with Bunyan's deliberate adoption of a human rather than a divine perspective in his presentation of Christian's struggle: election *qua* property of the divine will cannot be a part of human experience.' See also Gordon Campbell, 'The Theology of *The Pilgrim's Progress*', ibid., pp. 256–7. It has been argued also that the sense of free will and of election are both present in the allegory: see for example Hill, *A Turbulent, Seditious, and Factious People*, pp. 209–10; and Gordon Campbell, 'Fishing in Other Men's Waters: Bunyan and the Theologians', in N. H. Keeble (ed.), *John Bunyan, Conventicle and Parnassus: Tercentenary Essays* (Oxford: Clarendon Press, 1989) pp. 149–51.

6. There have recently been various attempts to deny our understanding of 'progress' as 'moving forward' or 'advance' (*OED*, sb. 1, 4). Stanley E. Fish, 'Progress in *The Pilgrim's Progress*', in *Self-Consuming Artifacts: The Experience of Seventeenth-Century Literature* (Berkeley and Los Angeles: University of California Press, 1972) pp. 224-64, suggests that Bunyan continually subverts his narrative so that our illusion of forward motion is exposed. This 'non-progressive' approach goes together with an acceptance of Bunyan's 'elective' theology as dominant in *The Pilgrim's Progress*: Gordon S. Wakefield, '"To be a Pilgrim": Bunyan and the Christian Life', in Keeble, *Bunyan*, p. 131, says, 'It has been questioned whether there is any real pilgrim's *progress* . . . . Is it not a matter of imputed righteousness to the end . . .?', and concludes that this is the case (pp. 131–3). Others question the seventeenth-century meaning of the word 'progress': for example, Philip Edwards, 'The Journey in *The Pilgrim's Progress*', in Newey, *The Pilgrim's Progress*, p. 111; and Hill, *A Turbulent, Seditious, and Factious People*, pp. 221–2. (The debate has also occupied other grounds than these.) For various replies see Vincent Newey, 'Bunyan and the Confines of the Mind', in Newey, *The Pilgrim's Progress*, pp. 21–48; David Mills, 'The Dreams of Bunyan and Langland', ibid., p. 165; Nick Shrimpton, 'Bunyan's Military Metaphor', ibid., pp. 205–24 (which attempts a synthesis of 'progressive' and 'anti-progressive' views). Here it may simply be maintained (1) that the examples of subversion of Bunyan's narrative cited by Fish are relatively infrequent; (2) that 'progress' had its 'progressive' meaning well-

established by Bunyan's day, and that it is unlikely that he would have chosen the word at all if one of its meanings so flew against an anti-progressive intention. No one has asked why Bunyan did not call his work, say, *The Pilgrim's Journey*, if that was what he meant; Bunyan had no especial penchant for alliterative titles. (Actually the word 'Walking' would have been still more appropriate, as it was used by several Puritan manuals of spiritual conduct at the time: see James Turner, 'Bunyan's Sense of Place', in Newey, *The Pilgrim's Progress*, p. 106.)

7. This makes it incorrect to claim that Christian's journey is entirely the expression of his particular spiritual condition: see Fish, *Self-Consuming Artifacts*, pp. 230–1.

8. For a fuller account see C. N. Manlove, 'The Image of the Journey in *Pilgrim's Progress*: Narrative versus Allegory', *Journal of Narrative Technique*, 10, no. 1 (Winter 1980) 16–19, 30–1. The references to Simon Patrick's *The Parable of the Pilgrim* are to the 3rd edn (1667), pp. 323, 386.

9. U. Milo Kaufmann, 'The Pilgrim's Progress' and Traditions in Puritan Meditation (New Haven, Conn.: Yale University Press, 1966) esp. pp. 134–6, locates *The Pilgrim's Progress* in a Puritan tradition oriented towards *mythos* rather than *logos* in the dissemination of faith, and in particular relates it to an affective tradition based on heavenly promise.

10 Both of these are cited in Kaufmann, 'The Pilgrim's Progress' and Traditions, pp. 180–1.

11. It really matters little that the landscape is occasionally absurd, as in the 'wide field full of dark Mountains' in which either Formalist or Hypocrisy comes to grief (p. 42): the narrative drives us to visualise, however improbably. For an alternative view see Turner, in Newey, *The Pilgrim's Progress*, p. 104ff.: 'The only real space traversed by pilgrims is the verbal' (p. 107).

12. This theologically orthodox view is taken by Fish. Contrast John R. Knott, Jr, 'Bunyan's Gospel Day: A Reading of *The Pilgrim's Progress*', *ELR*, 3 (1973) 443–61; Newey, 'Bunyan and the Confines of the Mind', *The Pilgrim's Progress*; and David Seed, 'Dialogue and Debate in *The Pilgrim's Progress*', ibid., pp. 74, 80.

13. Turner, in Newey, *The Pilgrim's Progress*, p. 108, says that Hill Difficulty 'represents the problems of reconciling contradictions in the Bible'. There is small evidence of this; and, were it the intended meaning, the actual presentation of the Hill is hardly such as to put us strongly in mind of it.

14. Parts of this reading are indebted to Dorothy Van Ghent, 'On *The Pilgrim's Progress*', in *The English Novel: Form and Function* (New York: Harper and Row, 1961) pp. 23–5, though with different interpretation.

15. See also Campbell, in Newey, *The Pilgrim's Progress*, pp. 258–61. Of the roll, for example, Campbell says, 'The narrative function of the roll has superseded its allegorical function. It is Bunyan's invention, and takes on a life of its own.'

16. Henri A. Talon (ed.), *God's Knotty Log: Selected Writings of John*

Bunyan (Chicago and New York: Meridian 1961) p. 301 nn. 42, 48. See also Wharey (ed.), *The Pilgrim's Progress*, p. 321; and Hill, *A Turbulent, Seditious, and Factious People*, p. 217, agreeing.

17. Roger Sharrock, 'Life and Story in *The Pilgrim's Progress*', in Newey, *The Pilgrim's Progress*, pp. 63–6.

18. Similarly, while it has been suggested by Fish (*Self-Consuming Artifacts*, pp. 228–9) that the 'way' is Christ Himself – from John 14.6: 'I am the way, the truth, and the life: no man cometh unto the Father, but by me' – there is no scope for such a mystical level in the allegory. Nor, as Fish admits, is this biblical text ever cited; and indeed we have much closer equation between the Wicket-gate and Christ from the marginal citation of Matthew 7.13–14 (p. 22). Newey, 'Bunyan and the Confines of the Mind', *The Pilgrim's Progress*, p. 27, says that the obvious metaphoric possibilities of the way are not exploited because, 'While the shape, components and preferred values of his [Bunyan's] vision are naturally determined by his religion and its doctrines, these latter do not constitute either its vital principle or the boundaries of its meaning'. This principle Newey sees as an 'engagement with the individual and his interior life'. Contrast, however, Brian Nellist, '*The Pilgrim's Progress* and Allegory', ibid., pp. 150–1, arguing that the singular absence of Christ from *The Pilgrim's Progress* (in contrast to *Grace Abounding*) is to be explained by the fact that He here features as the 'way': 'The Road functions not as a proposition but as the location of all the experiences Christian passes through. Its effects upon his personality are educative rather than instructional and Christian's relation to it, his regret at leaving it, his joy on finding it again, his total, unanalytical acceptance of it, is like a loving relation with a person.' The analogy that ends this is really no more than analogy: Christian's relation with the path is to do with his relative security, not with any loving exchange between him and his medium.

CHAPTER 10   SWEDENBORG: *HEAVEN AND HELL*

1. Colleen McDannell and Bernhard Lang, 'Swedenborg and the Emergence of a Modern Heaven', *Heaven: A History* (New Haven, Conn., and London: Yale University Press, 1988) pp. 181–227.

2. For this and much other information on Swedenborg see Cyriel Odhner Sigstedt, *The Swedenborg Epic: The Life and Works of Emmanuel Swedenborg* (New York: Bookman Associates, 1952).

3. Ibid., pp. 59–63, 74–9, 107–17, 133–40, 149–59, 166–73, 174–81.

4. Ibid., pp. 178–9.

5. The text used here is the Everyman's Library edition of *Heaven and Hell*, intro. J. Howard Spalding (London: J. M. Dent, 1909).

6. For other examples of biblical 'translation' see nos 81, 119, 129, 287, 434, 471. The same process is at work in Swedenborg's *Arcana Coelestia, or the Heavenly Secrets which are in the Sacred Scripture or the*

Word of the Lord, disclosed . . . (1749–56), and *The Apocalypse Revealed* (1766).

7. McDannell and Lang, *Heaven: A History*, pp. 181–227.
8. Spalding, Introduction to *Heaven and Hell*, p. xi.
9. Sigstedt, *The Swedenborg Epic*, pp. 202–3, is sure that Swedenborg had read *Paradise Lost*.
10. This idea is directly parallel to the mechanical principles governing the universe as portrayed in Swedenborg's *Principia* in vol. I of his *Philosophical and Mineralogical Works* (1734). See Sigstedt, *The Swedenborg Epic*, pp. 111–15, 490.
11. For an account of Swedenborg's influence on utopian and millenarian thought in later eighteenth-century England see Clarke Garnett, 'Swedenborg and Mystical Enlightenment in England', *Journal of the History of Ideas*, 45 (1984) 67 ff.
12. Geoffrey Rowell, *Hell and the Victorians: A Study of Nineteenth-Century Controversies concerning Eternal Punishment and the Future Life* (Oxford: Clarendon Press, 1974).

CHAPTER 11   BLAKE: 'THE LITTLE BLACK BOY' AND *THE MARRIAGE OF HEAVEN AND HELL*

1. Kathleen Raine, *Blake and Tradition*, 2 vols (London: Routledge and Kegan Paul, 1969) I, 10–14, believes 'The Little Black Boy' to be 'Blake's most completely – and most successfully – Swedenborgian poem' (p. 10). While it is hard to accept Raine's statement that 'The black boy and the white boy are evidently related to Swedenborg's good and evil angels, each in his ambient sphere', it is almost certain that Blake took over Swedenborg's imagery of the deity as a supernatural sun distributing the light of divine truth and the heat of divine love to the heavens (*Heaven and Hell*, nos 116–40): 'But though neither the sun of this world is seen in heaven, nor anything derived from that sun, yet there is a sun there and light and heat . . . . The Lord appears in heaven as the Sun because He is Divine Love from which all spiritual things and by means of the sun of this world all natural things exist' (no. 117). But, while using Swedenborgian imagery, the mother has confounded its meaning, for she equates God with our natural and physical sun, thus making physical and divine light and heat one and the same thing. This is to be one main source of the confusions of the poem.
2. G. R. Sabri-Tabrizi, *The 'Heaven' and 'Hell' of William Blake* (London: Lawrence and Wishart, 1973) ch. 3, pp. 71–134, finds references to *Heaven and Hell* throughout *The Marriage*. A useful overview is Morton D. Paley's '"A new heaven is begun": William Blake and Swedenborgianism', *Blake: An Illustrated Quarterly*, 13, no. 2 (Fall 1979) 64–90, esp. pp. 74–5.
3. Jacob H. Adler, 'Symbol and Meaning in "The Little Black Boy"', *MLN*, 72 (1957) 415, points out the further contradiction that 'souls, free from the "clouds" of the body, cannot obscure the light'.

4. Cf. also Zachary Leader, *Reading Blake's 'Songs'* (London: Routledge and Kegan Paul, 1981) pp. 110–11, describing the mother's placatory 'illusion': 'Though comforted by what his mother says, the little black boy's anxieties are never quieted .... The mother's explanations, with their implied superiority of black over white – cannot wipe away the fears of his own inferiority that we have discovered in the words the child speaks in stanza 1.'

5. For a fuller account, and a consequent reconsideration of Innocence and Experience as fixed categories, see C. N. Manlove, 'Engineered Innocence: Blake's "The Little Black Boy" and "The Fly"', *E in C*, 27 (1977) 112–21.

6. That the poem is dialectical has also been observed by Harold Bloom, *The Visionary Company: A Reading of English Romantic Poetry*, rev. edn (Ithaca, NY: Cornell University Press, 1971) pp. 39–41. Bloom anticipates one or two of the points made here: his concern, however, is more with the poem as exposure of the Christian dualism between body and soul, and the mother's 'Urizenic confusions'. 'The mother's metaphors are badly chosen; blackness is not a cloud or a shady grove if heat is love, as blackness absorbs love. Having learned so odd a lesson from his mother, the little black boy seizes both ends of the paradox, unknowingly defying his instruction' (p. 40); 'The poem's final irony is the dark child promising to shield his English friend from God's love until the less favored can bear with joy the blackening beam of divine energy and affection' (p. 41). See also Bloom's *Blake's Apocalypse: A Study in Poetic Argument* (London: Gollancz, 1963) pp. 48–51.

7. Harold Bloom, 'Dialectic in *The Marriage of Heaven and Hell*' (1958), repr. in M. H. Abrams (ed.), *English Romantic Poets: Modern Essays in Criticism* (New York: Oxford University Press, 1960) p. 77. Bloom's article has considerably influenced the view of *The Marriage* advanced here.

8. Bloom, 'Dialectic', in Abrams, *English Romantic Poets*, p. 78; Martin K. Nurmi, *William Blake* (London: Hutchinson, 1975) p. 77.

9. Nurmi, *Blake*, p. 76, points out that *The Marriage* as a whole is 'arranged structurally into an opening Argument and then into six alternating expository sections each followed by a "memorable fancy"': this provides an interesting large-scale parallel to the structure here.

10. See also Bloom, 'Dialectic', in Abrams, *English Romantic Poets*; Nurmi, *Blake*, pp. 74–6; and Dan Miller, 'Contrary Revelation: *The Marriage of Heaven and Hell*', *Studies in Romanticism*, 24 (1985) 491–509. Miller remarks that '*The Marriage* disallows both dualism and monism, yet permits no middle ground' (p. 500); that 'Reading Blake's expositions and narratives of contrariety involves a regress; it means understanding that reason and energy are opposites, then that they are mutually dependent, then that they nevertheless conflict, yet cannot be separated, yet are and ever should be separated' (p. 505); and that 'there is no presentation of contrariety in *The Marriage* that is not complicated by dramatic context, figural discourse, and rhetorical motives' (ibid.).

11. Contrast the millenarian reading of Bloom ('Dialectic', in Abrams,

English Romantic Poets, p. 79) associating the unrest and promise of the French Revolution with the Last Things, and following Northrop Fyre in his *Fearful Symmetry* (1947) in seeing 'the central idea of the *Marriage* as being the analogy of this unrest to the Biblical time of troubles that precedes the end of the world'.

CHAPTER 12   MODERN CHRISTIAN FANTASY

1. God may have retired from literature, as J. Hillis Miller describes it in his *The Disappearance of God* (Cambridge, Mass.: Harvard University Press, 1963), but He stayed very much in the hearts of millions of ordinary churchgoers: see Owen Chadwick, *A History of the Victorian Church*, 2 vols, II: *1860–1901*, rev. edn (London: A & C. Black, 1972) esp. chs 4–5.

2. See also Hans W. Frei, *The Eclipse of Biblical Narrative: A Study in Eighteenth and Nineteenth Century Hermeneutics* (New Haven, Conn., and London: Yale University Press, 1974), which particularly emphasises the sources in late-eighteenth- and early-nineteenth-century German theology and philosophy.

3. Though of course there are earlier isolated instances of this, as in Cyrano de Bergerac's *L'Autre Monde* (1657).

4. Bernard McGinn, 'Revelation', in Robert Alter and Frank Kermode (eds), *The Literary Guide to the Bible* (London: Collins, 1987) II, 539.

5. Frei, *The Eclipse of Biblical Narrative*, pp. 233–46; James P. Mackey, *Jesus: The Man and the Myth* (London: SCM Press, 1979) pp. 30–7.

6. Gillian Beer, *Darwin's Plots: Evolutionary Narrative in Darwin, George Eliot and Nineteenth-Century Fiction* (London: Routledge and Kegan Paul, 1983) pp. 14–17.

7. Charles Kingsley, *Alton Locke, Tailor and Poet*, in *The Works of Charles Kingsley*, 28 vols (London: Macmillan, 1879–83) III, 411. Cf. George MacDonald, *The Miracles of our Lord* (1871), ed. Rolland Hein (Wheaton, Ill.: Harold Shaw, 1980) p. 13, describing miracles as 'a possible fulfillment of [nature's] . . . deepest laws'.

8. On the 'immanentist' emphasis of nineteenth-century and to some extent twentieth-century theology and Christian belief see J. S. Lawton, *Miracles and Revelation* (London: Lutterworth Press, 1958) esp. p. 142; and Chadwick, *A History of the Victorian Church*, II, 31. T. B. Tennyson, 'The Sacramental Imagination', in U. C. Knoepflmacher and G. B. Tennyson (eds), *Nature and the Victorian Imagination* (Berkeley, Calif.: University of California Press, 1977) pp. 370–90, writes, 'The pervasive appeal of [Keble's] *The Christian Year* disposed many Victorian minds to view Nature as Keble and the Tractarians viewed it, as God's book which he who runs might read as a means, for the rightly disposed Christian soul, of experiencing through the visible world that contact with the invisible one that is normally effected through the sacraments' (p. 379).

9. Colleen McDannell and Bernhard Lang, *Heaven: A History* (New Haven, Conn., and London: Yale University Press, 1988) p. 275.

10. Walter Taverner, 'The Historical Antecedents of Rudolf Otto's Concept of the Numinous' (unpublished PhD thesis submitted to Edinburgh University Divinity Faculty, 1949).

11. See for example Carlyle's *Sartor Resartus* (1836) and Tennyson's *In Memoriam* (1850).

12. Evinced most signally in Arnold: see Stephen Prickett, *Romanticism and Religion: The Tradition of Wordsworth and Coleridge in the Victorian Church* (Cambridge: Cambridge University Press, 1976) pp. 213–17.

13. See Nathan Scott, Jr, *Craters of the Spirit: Studies in the Modern Novel* (London: Sheed and Ward, 1969). See also Ian Gregor and Walter Stein (eds), *The Prose for God: Religious and Anti-Religious Aspects of Imaginative Literature* (London: Sheed and Ward, 1973); Patrick Grant, *Six Modern Authors and Problems of Belief* (London: Macmillan, 1979). Recently there have been attempts by post-modernist 'literary' theologians to identify literary and ultimately 'Christian' experience: see for example David Jasper, *The Study of Literature and Religion* (London: Macmillan, 1989); and Robert Detweiler, *Breaking the Fall: Religious Readings of Contemporary Fiction* (London: Macmillan, 1989).

14. Letter to F. D. Maurice, summer 1862, repr. in *Charles Kingsley: His Letters and Memories of his Life*, ed. Frances E. Kingsley, 2 vols (London: Kegan Paul, 1978) II, 137.

15. Charles Williams, *'He Came down from Heaven' and 'The Forgiveness of Sins'* (London: Faber and Faber, 1950) p. 97.

16. C. S. Lewis, 'On Stories', *Of Other Worlds: Essays and Stories* (London: Geoffrey Bles, 1966) p. 20.

17. On such stories in the nineteenth century see Margaret Maison, *Search Your Soul, Eustace: A Survey of the Religious Novel in the Victorian Age* (London: Sheed and Ward, 1961); and Robert Lee Wolff, *Gains and Losses: Novels of Faith and Doubt in Victorian England* (London: John Murray, 1977).

18. This is what happens, if indirectly, with some of the writers of German Romantic fairy tale in the period 1790–1820. On the whole subject, Burton Feldman and Robert D. Richardson, *The Rise of Modern Mythology, 1680–1860* (Bloomington: Indiana University Press, 1972), is invaluable; see esp. pp. 303–4: 'Romantic myth may in part be described as a revival in secular or idealist form of an older Christian hope.' See also M. H. Abrams, *Natural Supernaturalism: Tradition and Revolution in Romantic Literature* (New York: W.W. Norton, 1971) esp. ch. 1, section 6.

19. Lewis, 'Sometimes Fairy Stories May Say Best What's to Be Said', *Of Other Worlds*, p. 36.

20. George MacDonald, 'The Imagination: Its Functions and its Culture', *A Dish of Orts, Chiefly Papers on the Imagination, and on Shakspere* (London: Sampson Low, 1893) p. 28.

21. Charles Williams, *The Greater Trumps* (London: Faber and Faber, 1964) pp. 94–5.

22. Lewis, *Out of the Silent Planet* (London: Pan, 1963) pp. 170–1.

23. D. H. Lawrence, *A Propos of 'Lady Chatterley's Lover'* (London: Mandrake Press, 1930) p. 55.

24. J. R. R. Tolkien, *Tree and Leaf* (London: Allen and Unwin, 1964) pp. 51–8.
25. The term is Robert Reilly's: see his *Romantic Religion: A Study of Barfield, Lewis, Williams, and Tolkien* (Athens, Ga: University of Georgia Press, 1971).
26. MacDonald, 'The Fantastic Imagination', *A Dish of Orts*, p. 321.

CHAPTER 13   GEORGE MACDONALD'S FAIRY TALES

1. George MacDonald, *The Princess and Curdie*, 2nd edn (London: Chatto and Windus, 1888) p. 46.
2. MacDonald, 'The Imagination', *A Dish of Orts, Chiefly Papers on the Imagination, and on Shakspere* (London: Sampson Low, 1893) p. 25.
3. William Blake, *The Ghost of Abel*, i. 3; *Jerusalem*, 77.
4. MacDonald, 'The Imagination', *A Dish of Orts*, p. 4.
5. Ibid., p. 25.
6. C. N. Manlove, 'The Unconscious in MacDonald's Fairy-tales', in *Modern Fantasy: Five Studies* (Cambridge: Cambridge University Press, 1975) pp. 71–5.
7. For the source, see Novalis, *Schriften*, ed. Paul Kluckhohn and Richard Samuel, 3 vols (Stuttgart: Kohlhammer, 1960–68) iii, 281, no. 237: 'Unser Leben *ist* kein Traum – aber es soll und wird vielleicht einer werden.'
8. Novalis, *Schriften*, iii, 454, no. 986: 'Ein Mährchen ist wie ein Traumbild ohne Zusammenhang. Ein Ensemble wunderbarer Dinge und Begebenheiten, z. B. eine musikalische Phantasie, die harmonischen Folgen einer Aeolsharfe, die Natur selbst.'
9. MacDonald, 'The Fantastic Imagination', *A Dish of Orts*, pp. 316–22.
10 The most obvious analogue for this is the 'myth of the cave' in Plato's *Republic*, 7.7.
11. As in *The Pilgrim's Progress* (at Doubting Castle), of which MacDonald was particularly fond.
12. MacDonald, 'The Imagination', *A Dish of Orts*, p. 18.
13. MacDonald, 'The Fantastic Imagination', ibid., p. 317.
14. Ibid., p. 318.
15. Ibid., p. 319.
16. Ibid., pp. 320–1.
17. MacDonald, *At the Back of the North Wind*, 2nd edn (London: Blackie and Sons, 1886) p. 77.
18. Ibid., p. 143.
19. I am indebted for these insights to Lesley Smith (née Willis) in an unpublished book on MacDonald's longer fairy tales for children: 'George MacDonald's Fantasy for Children: "Light Out of Darkness" in *At The Back of the North Wind, The Princess and the Goblin* and *The Princess and Curdie*', chs 1–3.
20. MacDonald, *At the Back of the North Wind*, p. 363.
21. Ibid., pp. 320–1.
22. G. K. Chesterton, Preface to Greville MacDonald, *George MacDonald*

and his Wife (London: George Allen and Unwin, 1924) pp. 10–11; C. S. Lewis (ed.), *George MacDonald: An Anthology* (London: Geoffrey Bles, 1946) pp. 19–20.

23. Tony Tanner, 'Mountains and Depths – an Approach to Nineteenth-Century Dualism', *Review of English Literature*, 3, no. 4 (Oct 1962) 52–4.

24. Robert Lee Wolff, *The Golden Key: A Study of the Fiction of George MacDonald* (New Haven, Conn.: Yale University Press, 1961) p. 166.

25. For a critique of these more specific interpretations see Manlove, *Modern Fantasy*, pp. 84–7.

26. On the symbolism here, and its sacramental character in MacDonald's work, see ibid., pp. 87–90, 95–8.

27. MacDonald, *The Princess and Curdie*, pp. 66–7.

28. George MacDonald, *'Phantastes' and 'Lilith'* (London: Victor Gollancz, 1962) p. 83.

29. Ibid., p. 89; cf. pp. 81–2, 194.

30. Ibid., p. 227.

31. Ernst Robert Curtius, *European Literature and the Latin Middle Ages*, tr. W. R. Trask, Bollingen Series, XXXVI (New York: Pantheon, 1953) pp. 159–62.

32. C. S. Lewis, *The Pilgrim's Regress: An Allegorical Apology for Christianity, Reason and Romanticism*, 3rd edn (London: Geoffrey Bles, 1943) p. 10.

33. MacDonald, *'Phantastes' and 'Lilith'*, p. 18.

34. MacDonald, 'The Fantastic Imagination', *A Dish of Orts*, p. 322.

35. MacDonald, *'Phantastes' and 'Lilith'*, pp. 195–6; cf. p. 253.

36. MacDonald, *At the Back of the North Wind*, pp. 212–13.

37. MacDonald, *'Phantastes' and 'Lilith'*, p. 179.

38. MacDonald, *At the Back of the North Wind*, p. 364.

39. MacDonald and his family toured the country presenting *The Pilgrim's Progress, Part 2*, with MacDonald playing the part of Christian, from 1877 to 1889. See William Raeper, *George MacDonald* (Tring, Herts: Lion, 1987) pp. 338–58.

40. On this see C. N. Manlove, 'Circularity in Fantasy: George MacDonald', in *The Impulse of Fantasy Literature* (London: Macmillan, 1983) pp. 74–92.

41. MacDonald 'The Fantastic Imagination', *A Dish of Orts*, p. 320.

42. MacDonald, 'Essays on Some of the Forms of Literature', *A Dish of Orts*, p. 234.

CHAPTER 14   CHARLES KINGSLEY: *THE WATER-BABIES*

1. Charles Kingsley, *Yeast: A Problem*, in *The Works of Charles Kingsley*, 28 vols (London: Macmillan, 1879–83) II, 312.

2. David Newsome, *Two Classes of Men: Platonism and English Romantic Thought* (London: John Murray, 1974) esp. pp. 1–7.

3. R. A. Forsyth, *The Lost Pattern: Essays on the Emergent City Sensibility in Victorian England* (Nedlands: University of Western Australia

Press, 1976) pp. 54–5. Cf. Tony Tanner, 'Mountains and Depths – an Approach to Nineteenth-Century Dualism', *Review of English Literature*, 3, no. 4 (Oct 1962) 60: 'The Cartesian dichotomy of mind and matter [is] . . . part of the landscape of the nineteenth-century mind.'

4. Kingsley, letter of 8 Feb 1857, in *Charles Kingsley: His Letters and Memories of his Life*, ed. Frances E. Kingsley, 2 vols (London: Kegan Paul, 1878) II, 18–19.

5. For a more extended comparison see C. N. Manlove, 'MacDonald and Kingsley: A Victorian Contrast', in William Raeper (ed.), *The Gold Thread: Essays on George MacDonald* (Edinburgh: Edinburgh University Press, 1990) pp. 140–62.

6. George MacDonald, *Unspoken Sermons: Third Series* (London: Longmans, Green, 1889) p. 62.

7. Charles Kingsley, *The Water-Babies: A Fairy Tale for a Land-Baby*, 4th edn (London: Macmillan, 1889) pp. 326–7. Page references are to this edition.

8. Kingsley, *Madam How and Lady Why, or, First Lessons in Earth Lore for Children, Works*, XIII, 145, 125.

9. *Kingsley, Letters and Memories*, II, 67; cf. I, 413.

10. Kingsley, *Westminster Sermons, Works*, XXVIII, xxviii, xxvii; cf. p. 195.

11. Kingsley, *Letters and Memories*, II, 18.

12. Kingsley, *Westminster Sermons*, p. xxii.

13. Kingsley, *Alton Locke, Tailor and Poet, Works*, III, 412. On Kingsley's difficulties here see C. N. Manlove, *Modern Fantasy: Five Studies* (Cambridge: Cambridge University Press, 1975) pp. 32–8, 266–7.

14. Kingsley, *Glaucus, or, The Wonders of the Shore, Works*, V, 131–3.

15. Kingsley, *The Good News of God: Sermons, Works*, XXIV, 229. See also Kingsley, *The Gospel of the Pentateuch, A Set of Parish Sermons; and David, Five Sermons, Works*, XXV, xv ('In the power of man to find out God I will never believe'); *Westminster Sermons*, pp. xix–xxi, 187; Kingsley, *Discipline, and Other Sermons, Works*, XXVII, 83.

16. Kingsley, *Alton Locke*, p. 376.

17. On the relations between Darwin's and Kingsley's transformationist theories see Gillian Beer, 'Darwinian Myths', in *Darwin's Plots: Evolutionary Narrative in Darwin, George Eliot and Nineteenth-Century Fiction* (London: Routledge and Kegan Paul, 1983) pp. 122–39. On Kingsley's relations with Thomas Huxley (the model for Professor Ptthmllnsprts) see Charles S. Blinderman, 'Huxley and Kingsley', *Victorian Newsletter*, 20 (Autumn 1961) 25–8. This idea of purposive evolution did not remain peculiar to Kingsley: it later gained considerable popularity through Henry Drummond's *Natural Law in the Spiritual World* (1884).

18. Kingsley, *Sermons on National Subjects, Works*, XXIII, 109–10. See also *Yeast*, pp. 293–6; *Westminster Sermons*, pp. 277–9; *Scientific Lectures and Essays, Works*, XIX, 308.

19. On this whole subject of Tom's evolution see Manlove, *Modern Fantasy*, pp. 38–53.

20. Kingsley, *Letters and Memories*, II, 325.

21. Kingsley wrote in 1872 to the Committee for the Defence of the Athanasian Creed, suggesting the revival of 'a somewhat neglected Catholic doctrine – that of the intermediate state, or states' (*Letters and Memories*, II, 395–7). See also *Letters and Memories*, I, 318–19, 392–6, 469–71, and II, 41–2, 106, 207; *The Good News of God*, pp. 57–66; *The Water of Life, and Other Sermons*, Works, XXVI, 71–6; *Alton Locke*, pp. 353-5. Kingsley felt the hope 'that this, our present life, instead of being an ultimate one, which is to decide our fate for ever, is merely some sort of chrysalis state, in which man's faculties are so narrow and cramped, his chances (I speak of the millions, not the units,) of knowing the good so few, that he may have chances hereafter, perhaps continually fresh ones to all eternity' (*Letters and Memories*, I, 483).

22. Kingsley, *Glaucus*, p. 100. See also for example *The Gospel of the Pentateuch*, p. 231; *The Water of Life*, pp. 176–88; *Discipline*, pp. 24–5; *Westminster Sermons*, pp. 214–16; *Letters and Memories*, II, 175, 338.

23. Arthur Johnston, 'The Water-Babies: Kingsley's Debt to Darwin', *English*, 12 (1959) 219.

24. *Macmillan's Magazine*, VI (Oct 1862) 435.

25. Kingsley, *Letters and Memories*, II, 171.

26. Ibid.

27. Ibid., II, 28. On the insubstantiality of evil see also ibid., I, 317; and, on the inexorability of God's laws of nature, Kingsley, *Village Sermons, and Town and Country Sermons*, Works, XXI, 52–8; *Town Geology* (London: Strahan, 1872) pp. xviii–xix; *Westminster Sermons*, p. 125; *Sermons on National Subjects*, pp. 483–4.

28. Kingsley, *Madam How and Lady Why*, p. 263. On natural punishment see also ibid., pp. 298–9; *Literary and General Essays*, Works, XX, 44–6.

29. Kingsley, *Letters and Memories*, I, 210; see also p. 211. Kingsley would read some at least of Rabelais every year: see Elspeth Huxley (compiler), *The Kingsleys: A Biographical Anthology* (London: Allen and Unwin, 1973) p. 117.

30. Kingsley might not have felt so had Tom not been white underneath: the racist position of *Westminster Sermons*, pp. xvi–xviii, or of *Sermons on National Subjects*, pp. 265–8, 415–16, is clear enough, even seeing 'savage' peoples as images of the lower-than-brutish state to which man can be reduced by original sin. Nevertheless Kingsley can also insist on Christ's acts as redeeming all men: see *Sermons on National Subjects*, p. 71.

31. Kingsley, *Letters and Memories*, II, 39.

32. Manlove, *Modern Fantasy*, pp. 26, 36; Stephen Prickett, *Victorian Fantasy* (Brighton: Harvester, 1979) pp. 156–9.

33. Johnston, in *English*, 12, p. 216. See also Valentine Cunningham, 'Soiled Fairy: The Water-Babies in its Time', *E in C*, 35 (1985) 121–48.

34. Possibly to prevent fright to his child readers, he omitted from the serial account mention of the inclusion among the water-babies of children thrown by Darius to the lions and of boys eaten by bears for mocking Elisha. See Larry Uffelman and Patrick Scott, 'Kingsley's Serial

Novels II: *The Water-Babies'*, *Victorian Periodicals Review*, XIX, no. 4 (Winter 1986) 125.

CHAPTER 15   TWENTIETH-CENTURY CHRISTIAN FANTASY

1. Charles Kingsley, *The Water-Babies: A Fairy Tale for a Land-Baby*, 4th edn (London: Macmillan, 1889) p. 76.
2. Mervyn Peake, Introduction to *Drawings by Mervyn Peake* (London: Grey Walls Press, 1949) p. 11.
3. Colin Manlove, 'Victorian and Modern Fantasy: Some Contrasts', in Donald Morse, Marshall Tymn and Csilla Bertha (eds.), *The Celebration of the Fantastic: Selected Papers from the Tenth Anniversary Conference on the Fantastic in the Arts* (Westport, Conn.: Greenwood Press, 1991).

CHAPTER 16   CHARLES WILLIAMS

1. See also Charles Williams, *'He Came down from Heaven' and 'The Forgiveness of Sins'* (London: Faber and Faber, 1950) pp. 98–9, outlining how everything appalling within the universe exists because God chose to allow it to be: 'There is no split second of the unutterable horror and misery of the world that he did not foresee ... when he created; no torment of children, no obstinacy of social wickedness, no starvation of the innocent, no prolonged and deliberate cruelty, which he did not know.'
2. George MacDonald, *Unspoken Sermons: Third Series* (London: Longmans, Green, 1889) p. 252.
3. Charles Williams, *The Descent of the Dove: A Short History of the Holy Spirit in the Church* (London: Longmans, 1939) p. 213.
4. In a 'mythological scrap-book' of 1912–16, Williams made this note: 'Knowledge that Time and Space are only modes of thought. "is not this the beginning of all magic?" (E. Nesbit. – *Amulet*.)' Cited in Charles Williams, *'The Image of the City' and Other Essays*, sel. and intro. Anne Ridler (London: Oxford University Press, 1958) p. 171.
5. For an excellent survey of Williams' theological ideas see Mary M. Shideler, *The Theology of Romantic Love: A Study in the Writings of Charles Williams* (New York: Harper and Bros, 1962).
6. Williams, *He Came down from Heaven*, p. 34; *Collected Plays* (London: Oxford University Press, 1963) p. 298.
7. Williams, *He Came down from Heaven*, pp. 33, 35. Cf. *Thomas Cranmer of Canterbury* (1936), in *Collected Plays*, p. 31: 'none there to escape / into the unformed shadow of mystery mere, / but find a strong order, a diagram clear, / a ladder runged and tongued'.
8. These views can be found in *He Came down from Heaven*, *The Descent of the Dove*, and the theological essays in *The Image of the City*.
9. See C. N. Manlove, 'Fantasy as Praise: Charles Williams', in *The Impulse of Fantasy Literature* (London: Macmillan, 1983), pp. 15–30.

10. Charles Williams, *All Hallows' Eve* (London: Faber and Faber, 1945) p. 197.
11. Charles Williams, *The Place of the Lion* (London: Faber and Faber, 1965) p. 183.
12. Ibid., pp. 183–90.
13. Charles Williams, *Many Dimensions* (London: Faber and Faber, 1963) p. 261.
14. Williams, *He Came down from Heaven*, p. 97.
15. Charles Williams, *War in Heaven* (London: Faber and Faber, 1962) pp. 253–4.
16. Respectively Williams, *All Hallows' Eve*, p. 76; *The Greater Trumps* (London: Faber and Faber, 1964) pp. 55–6; *The Place of the Lion*, pp. 196–7.
17. Williams, *All Hallows' Eve*, p. 147.
18. C. S. Lewis, *Perelandra* (London: John Lane, 1943) p. 168.
19. Williams, *The Greater Trumps*, pp. 53–4, 111.
20. Williams, *War in Heaven*, pp. 75, 76.
21. Williams, 'The Cross', in *The Image of the City*, p. 138. See also Robert C. Holder, 'Art and the Artist in the Fiction of Charles Williams', *Renascence*, 27 (Winter, 1975) 81–7.
22. Williams, *All Hallows' Eve*, p. 232. Further page references (to edition cited in note 10) in text.
23. On the city in Williams' thought see *He Came down from Heaven*, pp. 95–103; and *The Image of the City*, pp. 92–130.
24. Charles Williams, *Descent into Hell* (London: Faber and Faber, 1949) p. 80. On the patterning in Williams' style see also Gunnar Urang, *Shadows of Heaven: Religion and Fantasy in the Fiction of C. S. Lewis, Charles Williams and J. R. R. Tolkien* (London: SCM Press, 1971) pp. 77–80; Manlove, *The Impulse of Fantasy Literature*, pp. 26–8.
25. On these see Williams, 'The Theology of Romantic Love', in *He Came down from Heaven*, pp. 62–81; *The Figure of Beatrice: A Study in Dante* (London: Faber and Faber, 1943); 'The Index of the Body' (1942), repr. in *The Image of the City*, pp. 80–7; and above, note 23.
26. This aphorism, frequently used by Williams, summarises his espousal of the 'Affirmative Way': it appears in *He Came down from Heaven*, pp. 25, 102–3; *War in Heaven*, p. 137; *Collected Plays*, pp. 160–1.
27. Williams, *All Hallows' Eve*, pp. 167–8.
28. For example, *The Masque of the Manuscript* (1927) and *The Masque of Perusal* (1929), composed for a group of friends at Oxford University Press. For an account see Alice Hadfield, *An Introduction to Charles Williams* (London: Robert Hale, 1959) pp. 67–76.
29. On this see Manlove, *The Impulse of Fantasy Literature*, pp. 26–8.
30. Williams, *The Greater Trumps*, p. 135.
31. On this see Colin Manlove, 'The Liturgical Novels of Charles Williams', *Mosaic*, 12 (1979–80) 161–81.
32. Williams, *All Hallows' Eve*, p. 76.
33. Glen Cavaliero, *Charles Williams, Poet of Theology* (London: Macmillan, 1983) p. 117.
34. Charles Williams, *Taliessin through Logres* (London: Oxford University

Press, 1938) p. 44 ('Bors to Elayne'); *Thomas Cranmer, Collected Plays*, p. 34.

35. Williams, 'The Figure of Arthur', in *Arthurian Torso: Containing the Posthumous Fragment of 'The Figure of Arthur' by Charles Williams and a Commentary on the Arthurian Poems of Charles Williams by C. S. Lewis* (London: Oxford University Press, 1948) p. 80.

CHAPTER 17   C. S. LEWIS

1. C. S. Lewis, *Surprised by Joy: The Shape of my Early Life* (London: Geoffrey Bles, 1955), pp. 169–71.
2. C. S. Lewis, 'On Science Fiction' (1955), repr. in *Of Other Worlds: Essays and Stories* (London: Geoffrey Bles, 1966) p. 68.
3. Luke 24. 6.
4. Lewis, 'On Stories', *Of Other Worlds*, p. 12.
5. Lewis, 'On Science Fiction', ibid., p. 69.
6. C. S. Lewis, *The Pilgrim's Regress*, 3rd edn (London: Geoffrey Bles, 1943) pp. 9–10.
7. C. S. Lewis, 'The Weight of Glory', *'Transposition' and Other Addresses* (London: Geoffrey Bles, 1949) p. 24.
8. See also Lewis, *The Pilgrim's Regress*, pp. 7–10.
9. Lewis, 'The Weight of Glory', *Transposition*, p. 25.
10. Lewis was indebted to Otto's concept of the numinous and the 'other' in his *The Problem of Pain* (London: Centenary Press, 1940) pp. 4–5.
11. J. R. R. Tolkien, 'On Fairy Stories', *Tree and Leaf* (London: Allen and Unwin, 1964) pp. 53–4; Lewis, 'On Science Fiction', *Of Other Worlds*, p. 67.
12. In *'De Descriptione Temporum'*, his inaugural lecture as Professor of Medieval and Renaissance English Literature at Cambridge in 1954, Lewis described himself as one of the few remaining 'Old Western Men', those whose cultural affinities were with pre-industrial civilisation and traditional values: C. S. Lewis, *They Asked for a Paper: Papers and Addresses* (London: Geoffrey Bles, 1962) pp. 23–5.
13. C. S. Lewis, *Perelandra* (London: John Lane, 1943) p. 232. Further page references in text.
14. Greville MacDonald, *George MacDonald and his Wife* (London: George Allen and Unwin, 1924) p. 524.
15. George MacDonald, *'Phantastes' and 'Lilith'* (London: Victor Gollancz, 1962) p. 225.
16. George MacDonald, *The Hope of the Gospel* (London: Ward, Lock, Bowden, 1892) p. 37.
17. Tolkien, *Tree and Leaf*, p. 63. This is the import of his story 'Leaf by Niggle' (1947), repr. in *Tree and Leaf*.
18. Lewis, *Perelandra*, p. 115. See also C. S. Lewis, 'Myth Became Fact' (1944), repr. in *Undeceptions*, ed. W. Hooper (London: Geoffrey Bles, 1971); *Miracles: A Preliminary Study* (London: Geoffrey Bles, 1947) pp. 135–40, 161n., 191–2; *Reflections on the Psalms* (London: Geoffrey

Bles, 1958) chs 10–12; *The Pilgrim's Regress*, pp. 151–61, 170–1; C. N. Manlove, *Modern Fantasy: Five Studies* (Cambridge: Cambridge University Press, 1975) pp. 111–13.

19. In C. S. Lewis, *Out of the Silent Planet* (London: John Lane, 1938) pp. 101–4, 114; *Perelandra*, p. 49; 'Forms of Things Unknown', *Of Other Worlds*, pp. 119–26.

20. Lewis uses this phrase from Wordsworth's 'Immortality Ode' in *Perelandra*, p. 165.

21. C. S. Lewis (ed.), *George MacDonald: An Anthology* (London: Geoffrey Bles, 1946) pp. 16–17.

22. For a fuller account see C. N. Manlove, *C. S. Lewis: His Literary Achievement* (London: Macmillan, 1987) ch. 3, pp. 25–44.

23. Lewis, *The Pilgrim's Regress*, p. 24.

24. C. S. Lewis, *The Great Divorce: A Dream* (London: Geoffrey Bles, 1946) p. 113.

25. On development towards 'otherness' in all Lewis's fiction see also Manlove, *C. S. Lewis*.

26. Lewis, *Surprised by Joy*, p. 170. This was actually said of MacDonald's *Phantastes* by Lewis.

27. For fuller accounts see C. N. Manlove, *Modern Fantasy: Five Studies* (Cambridge: Cambridge University Press, 1975) pp. 140–7, and *C. S. Lewis*, pp. 64–70.

28. Lewis, 'On Stories', *Of Other Worlds*, pp. 20–1.

29. Lewis, 'It All Began with a Picture' (1960), ibid., p. 42.

30. Lewis, 'Sometimes Fairy Stories May Say Best What's to Be Said' (1956), ibid., p. 36.

31. Lewis, 'Unreal Estates' (recording, 1962), ibid. p. 87.

32. C. S. Lewis, *That Hideous Strength: A Modern Fairy-Tale for Grown-Ups* (London: John Lane, 1945) pp. 369–70.

33. Lewis, *Out of the Silent Planet*, p. 177.

34. Lewis, 'Sometimes Fairy Stories May Say Best What's to Be Said', *Of Other Worlds*, p. 37.

35. Lewis, *Surprised by Joy*, p. 207.

36. Lewis has considerable difficulty in imagining the fusion of soul and body that existed before the fall, and this is seen in some of his problems with the account of primal innocence in *Perelandra*. See Manlove, *Modern Fantasy*, pp. 146–51.

37. Lewis, *Letters to Malcolm: Chiefly on Prayer* (London: Fontana, 1966) pp. 103–6: 'I do not know and can't imagine what the disciples understood Our Lord to mean when, His body still unbroken and His blood unshed, He handed them the bread and wine, saying *they* were His body and blood.' But Lewis assigns this to his mortality, and wills himself to silent acceptance: 'Here is big medicine and strong magic. *Favete linguis.*' He has a not dissimilar attitude to the physicality of the image of Christ crucified: see ibid., p. 87.

38. In his 'De Descriptione Temporum': see above, note 12.

39. Lewis, 'Reason', in *Poems*, ed. Walter Hooper (London: Geoffrey Bles, 1964) p. 81.

CHAPTER 18   OTHER WRITERS

1.   'The monsters had been the foes of the gods, the captains of men, and within Time the monsters would win'; 'The worth of defeated valour in this world is deeply felt. As the poet looks back into the past, surveying the history of kings and warriors in the old traditions, he sees that all glory (or as we might say "culture" or "civilisation") ends in night' – J. R. R. Tolkien, '*Beowulf*: The Monsters and the Critics', *Proceedings of the British Academy*, XXII (1936) 264, 265. For a close identification of the outlook of *The Lord of the Rings* with that of *Beowulf*, see Douglass Parker, 'Hwaet We Holbytla . . .', *Hudson Review*, 9 (1956–7) 598–609. On the oblique Christian dimension in *The Lord of the Rings* see *The Letters of J. R. R. Tolkien*, ed. Humphrey Carpenter (London: Allen and Unwin, 1981) pp. 201, 237, 283–7. In a letter of 2 Dec. 1953 Tolkien wrote, '*The Lord of the Rings* is of course a fundamentally religious and Catholic work; unconsciously so at first, but consciously in the revision. That is why I have not put in, or have cut out, practically all references to anything like "religion", to cults and practices, in the imaginary world' (p. 172). Most immediately for Tolkien the book's concern is nearer to *Beowulf's*, with doom, death and hoped-for immortality (p. 246, letter of Apr 1956).

2.   J. R. R. Tolkien, *The Lord of the Rings*, 2nd edn, 3 vols (London: Allen and Unwin, 1966) I, 6. This point recurs in the *Letters*: see pp. 145, 220, 237, 262.

3.   For this and other Christian interpretations of *The Lord of the Rings*, either on its own or in relation to *The Silmarillion* (1977), see for example Gunnar Urang, *Shadows of Heaven: Religion and Fantasy in the Fiction of C. S. Lewis, Charles Williams and J. R. R. Tolkien* (London: SCM Press, 1971) ch. 3, pp. 93–130; Jane Chance Nitzsche, *Tolkien's Art: 'A Mythology for England'* (London: Macmillan, 1979) ch. 5, pp. 97–127; Verlyn Flieger, *Splintered Light: Logos and Language in Tolkien's World* (Grand Rapids, Mich: Eerdmans, 1983) esp. ch. 7, pp. 133–50; Richard L. Purtill, *Tolkien: Myth, Morality, and Religion* (San Francisco: Harper and Row, 1984).

4.   One should recall Tolkien's Christian concept of the 'eucatastrophe' in fairy tale, of which he considered *The Lord of the Rings* to be an example. This concept is outlined in his essay 'On Fairy-Stories' (1939), repr. in *Tree and Leaf* (London: Allen and Unwin, 1964) pp. 60–3. He believes that the story of Christ is essentially in the form of a fairy tale, but one which came true, so that all subsequent fantasies and fairy tales have been hallowed and given a measure of reality by that grand relation. In particular the 'happy ending' of fairy tale, joy coming suddenly out of the midst of seemingly irrecoverable despair, partakes part-sacramentally in the movement in the Gospels from passion and death to resurrection. On this see C. N. Manlove, *Modern Fantasy: Five Studies* (Cambridge: Cambridge University Press, 1975) pp. 162–4. But all this happens without the author overtly intending any Christian meaning.

5. Mikhail Bulgakov, *The Master and Margarita* (London: Fontana, 1979) pp. 408, 155. Further page references in text.
6. J. A. E. Curtis, *Bulgakov's Last Decade: The Writer as Hero* (Cambridge: Cambridge University Press, 1987) pp. 151–7, shows Bulgakov's debt for his demythologised portraits of Jesus and Pilate to D. F. Strauss, A. Drews, F. W. Farrar and Ernest Renan. Curtis observes, 'Bulgakov's interpretations of the figures of Pilate and Iyeshua are ... more than straightforward reworkings of familiar Biblical subjects. He presents them in an unfamiliar mode, with the effect both of suggesting new insights into traditional images and myths, and of creating an entirely new "myth", with repercussions for the larger world of his novel' (p. 153). However, Priscilla Conwell Deck, in 'Thematic Coherence in Bulgakov's *Master and Margarita*' (unpublished PhD dissertation submitted to Brandeis University, 1976) p. 161, sees Bulgakov's deviations from the Gospel accounts as exemplifying the Russian technique of *ostranenie*, or, 'making it strange' – the aim being not to alter our understanding of Christ but to revitalise it.
7. This, as Deck sees it, is the central concern of the novel ('Thematic Coherence', abstract and pp. 229–30). Her account of the issue is, however, rather thin and narrational.
8. On the Gnosticism in the novel see Andrew Barratt, *Between Two Worlds: A Critical Introduction to 'The Master and Margarita'* (Oxford: Clarendon Press, 1987) pp. 171–2, 223, 226, 259, 264, 265, 310, 320–3.
9. Barratt (ibid., pp. 234–40) rejects the usual identification of Satan's ball with a witches' sabbath for this more penetrating interpretation.
10. For instance, the Master himself momentarily takes on the aspect of Christ as he says, 'Farewell, disciple' to Bezdomny at the end (p. 393).
11. For instance Barratt, *Between Two Worlds*, p. 227.
12. David M. Bethea, *The Apocalypse in Modern Russian Fiction* (Princeton: Princeton University Press, 1989).
13. By Bethea, ibid., pp. 110–16.
14. Andrey Biely (*sic*), *St Petersburg*, tr. and intro. John Cournos (London: Weidenfeld and Nicolson, 1960) pp. 133–5, 220–3, 233–5, 244–5.
15. Bethea, *Apocalypse*, p. 143.
16. Ibid., p. 253.
17. T. F. Powys, *Mr Weston's Good Wine* (London: Chatto and Windus, 1927) p. 32. Further page references in text.
18. At p. 200 the narrator tries to extend the point to our own reality: 'A local occurrence of this nature, a divine juggling with time, can happen, so say our modern mathematicians as well as the more learned amongst our Doctors of Divinity, in any place upon the surface of our known world, or, indeed, throughout the whole universe, if God so wills it.'
19. 1 Peter 5. 8; Revelation 20.2–3.
20. On the fusion of 'reality' and the supernatural in the story see H. Coombes, *T. F. Powys* (London: Barrie and Rockliff, 1960) ch. 3, pp. 46–68.
21. This has in fact been suggested, along with parallels with the journeys of

Aeneas and of Bunyan's Christian, by Christopher Booker in *The Seventies: Portrait of a Decade* (London: Allen Lane, 1980) pp. 252–3. A more sceptical view is seen in Christopher Pawling, 'Watership Down: Rolling back the 1960s', in Pawling (ed.), *Popular Fiction and Social Change* (London: Macmillan, 1984) pp. 121–30. In *Shardik*, which might more readily have fitted the prescription for myth, Pawling finds 'the failure of that bizarre fusion of Jung and C. S. Lewis which forms the basis of [the novel]' (p. 233).

22. On this last point see C. N. Manlove, *Science Fiction: Ten Explorations* (London: Macmillan, 1986) ch. 11, pp. 198–216.

23. Gene Wolfe, *The Castle of the Otter* (Willimantic, Conn.: Ziesing Bros, 1982) p. 9.

24. On Wolfe's various intentions see ibid., pp. 7–9.

25. For a full, though uncritical, account see Martha C. Sammons, '*A Better Country*': *The Worlds of Religious Fantasy and Science Fiction* (Westport, Conn.: Greenwood Press, 1988).

26. Stephen Lawhead, *In the Hall of the Dragon King* (Tring, Herts: Lion, 1985) p. 167; see also pp. 168–71.

27. Madeleine L'Engle, *A Wrinkle in Time* (New York: Dell, 1980) p. 60.

28. Roger L. Green and Walter Hooper, *C. S. Lewis: A Biography* (London: Collins, 1974) p. 171.

29. Robert Siegel, *Alpha Centauri* (Westchester, Ill.: Cornerstone Books, 1980) p. 55. Further page references in text. Cf. p. 71: 'Her voice grew dreamlike. "In that world there is no killing. One may live forever in forests where birds are as big as centaurs and trees rise higher than mountains. There one may walk along bright stones on the ocean floor among creatures who sing the tides to sleep."'

30. David Lindsay, *A Voyage to Arcturus* (London: Victor Gollancz, 1968) pp. 58, 82. Further page references in text. Cf. this item from Lindsay's unpublished 'Sketch Notes for a New System of Philosophy' (in the National Library of Scotland, MS accession no. 5616): 'In so far as a living being resembles another, it is dead. The test of real life is originality, and all that part of us that does not create and branch out into unique forms, is already crystallised' – 'Sketch Notes', no. 386, repr. in *Lines Review* (Edinburgh), no. 40 (Mar 1972), a special David Lindsay issue ed. Robin Fulton, p. 26; cf. 'Sketch Notes', no. 483. (Note the word 'crystallised' and compare 'Crystalman': used of a dead condition of being.) Yet it is typical of Lindsay to startle us with an opposed view: 'The nearer a man draws towards perfection in his art, the less inventiveness he displays; because his facility of execution makes all themes of equal value to him. For *surprises* one must look to men who have not yet acquired this self-confidence' (no. 530, p. 27). If the first quotation might seem to support the creative fecundity and inventiveness of imagination displayed in *A Voyage to Arcturus*, the second does not; and yet both visions are present in the novel itself.

31. For accounts of the novel as a *Bildungsroman* in these terms, see for example Colin Wilson, 'Lindsay as Novelist and Mystic', in J. B. Pick, Colin Wilson and E. H. Visiak, *The Strange Genius of David Lindsay*

(London: John Baker, 1970) pp. 46–64; Bernard Sellin, *The Life and Works of David Lindsay*, tr. Kenneth Gunnell (Cambridge: Cambridge University Press, 1981) esp. pp. 138–74; Gary K. Wolfe, *David Lindsay*, Starmont Reader's Guide, 9 (Mercer Island, Wash.: Starmont House, 1982) pp. 14–39; Robert H. Waugh, 'The Drum of *A Voyage to Arcturus*', *Extrapolation*, 26, no. 2 (Summer 1985) 143–51.

32. Cf. 'Real sublimity consists always in active energy. Thus the sea and music are sublime, but mountains and architecture are pseudo-sublime' (Lindsay, 'Sketch Notes', no. 444, in *Lines Review*, no. 40, p. 26; see also 'Sketch Notes', nos 246 (1), 440).

33. E. H. Visiak has strained to fit the novel into a Christian scheme (*The Strange Genius*, pp. 109–11).

34. This is broadly the view of David Ketterer, *Imprisoned in a Tesseract: The Life and Work of James Blish* (Kent, Ohio: Kent State University Press, 1987) ch. 4, pp. 79–104. The novel has been interpreted in Christian terms by Jo Allen Bradham, in 'The Case in James Blish's *A Case of Conscience*', *Extrapolation*, 16 (Dec 1974) 67–80. This interpretation is criticised by Ketterer (*Imprisoned in a Tesseract*, pp. 94–7).

35. James Blish, *'Black Easter' and 'The Day after Judgment'* (London: Arrow Books, 1981) p. 113.

36. John B. Ower, 'Walter M. Miller, Jr.', in E. F. Bleiler (ed.), *Science Fiction Writers: Critical Studies of the Major Authors from the Early Nineteenth Century to the Present Day* (New York: Charles Scribner's Sons, 1982) pp. 445–8. See also Frank David Kievitt, 'Walter M. Miller's *A Canticle for Leibowitz* as a Third Testament', in Robert Reilly (ed.), *The Transcendent Adventure: Studies of Religion in Science Fiction/Fantasy* (Westport, Conn.: Greenwood Press, 1985) pp. 169–75.

37. Walter M. Miller, Jr, *A Canticle for Leibowitz* (London: Corgi, 1970) p. 277.

38. John Wyndham, *The Day of the Triffids* (London: Michael Joseph, 1951) p. 123.

39. By James Blish, in 'Probapossible Prolegomena to Ideareal History' (1978), repr. in Blish, *The Tale that Wags the God*, ed. Cy Chauvin (Chicago: Advent, 1987) pp. 72–82.

40. On this see for example David Ketterer, *New Worlds for Old: The Apocalyptic Imagination, Science Fiction and American Literature* (Garden City, NY: Anchor, 1974); Tom Woodman, 'Science Fiction, Religion and Transcendence', in Patrick Parrinder (ed.), *Science Fiction: A Critical Guide* (London: Longman, 1979) pp. 110–30; Reilly, *The Transcendent Adventure*; Frederick A. Kreuziger, *The Religion of Science Fiction* (Bowling Green, Ohio: Bowling Green State University Popular Press, 1986). Kreuziger's basic argument is 'that science fiction functions today as a religion' (p. 1). (Both Ketterer and Kreuziger consider science fiction from the apocalyptic religious standpoint.) See also Peter Nicholls' invaluable *The Encyclopedia of Science Fiction* (London: Granada, 1981), particularly under 'cosmology' 'eschatology', 'gods and demons', 'messiahs', 'metaphysics', 'mythology' and 'religion', for the huge range of types of 'religious' science fiction.

41. On the alien see Gary K. Wolfe, *The Known and the Unknown: Studies*

in the Iconology of Science Fiction (Kent, Ohio: Kent State University Press, 1979) pp. 184–224; Mark Rose, *Alien Encounters: Anatomy of Science Fiction* (Cambridge, Mass.: Harvard University Press, 1981) pp. 176–95; and the essays by Larry Niven, Clayton Koelb and Colin Greenland in George E. Slusser and Eric S. Rabkin (eds), *Aliens: The Anthropology of Science Fiction* (Carbondale and Edwardsville: Southern Illinois University Press, 1987) pp. 3–12, 157–67, 208–17.

42.　See on this W. Warren Wagar, *Terminal Visions: The Literature of Last Things* (Bloomington: Indiana University Press, 1982) esp. pp. 185–205.

43.　Arthur C. Clarke, *Childhood's End* (London: Pan, 1981) p. 161. Further page references in text.

44.　For an example of how he does this in his *Rendezvous with Rama* (1974) see Manlove, *Science Fiction*, pp. 143–60.

45.　For those written up to 1983 see the checklist in Reilly, *The Transcendent Adventure*, pp. 225–48. Useful collections are Hans Stefan Santesson (ed.), *Gods for Tomorrow* (New York: Award Books, 1967); Mayo Mohs (ed.), *Other Worlds, Other Gods* (New York: Doubleday, 1971); Roger Elwood (ed.), *Strange Gods* (New York: Pocket Books, 1974); and J. S. Ryan (ed.), *Perpetual Light* (New York: Warner Books, 1982).

46.　Ray Bradbury, 'The Man', *The Illustrated Man* (New York: Doubleday, 1976) p. 43. Further page references in text.

47.　Gardner Dozois, 'Disciples', *Penthouse*, Dec 1981, pp. 193–200.

48.　See also Manlove, *Science Fiction*, pp. 122–30, 139–42.

49.　On the influence of Sufism on Lessing see for example Nancy Topping Bazin, 'The Evolution of Doris Lessing's Art from a Mystical Moment to Space Fiction', in Reilly, *The Transcendent Adventure*, pp. 157–67.

50.　See also Douglas A. Mackey, 'Science Fiction and Gnosticism', *Missouri Review*, 7, no. 2 (Feb 1984) 112–20; Robert Galbreath, 'Fantastic Literature as Gnosis', *Extrapolation*, 29, no. 4 (Winter 1988) 330–7. Mackey links Dick and Lindsay as Gnostics, and also draws in Poe's *Eureka* (1848), Olaf Stapledon's *Star Maker* (1937) and J. G. Ballard's *The Unlimited Dream Company* (1979). He remarks, 'In the broad sense, much science fiction may be called gnostic because it so often sounds the theme of the quest for direct experience of reality and for liberation from all constraints, internal or external . . . . Thus gnosticism takes as its starting point man rather than God, and it asserts man's right to take control over the material powers that hold him prisoner. The goals of freedom are deliverance from bondage and ultimately identity with deity. In short, we must become supermen and gods, not merely worship them' (p. 118). Galbreath, considering Gnosticism in terms of 'religious, mythological, or transcendental knowledge', cites among others Dick, Lessing, Clarke and Tolkien. For an account of Gnosticism see Kurt Rudolph, *Gnosis: The Nature and History of Gnosticism* (San Francisco: Harper and Row, 1987).

51.　Patricia S. Warrick, 'Philip K. Dick's Answers to the Eternal Riddles', in Reilly, *The Transcendent Adventure*, p. 110. This essay is in substance reprinted as 'The Search for God and the *Valis* Novels' in Warrick's

Mind in Motion: The Fiction of Philip K. Dick (Carbondale and Edwardsville: Southern Illinois University Press, 1987) pp. 166–85.

52. On the 'real-life' source of *Valis* in certain dreams of February and March 1974 which Dick could see as 'theophanies' see Charles Platt, 'Philip K. Dick', *Dream Makers: Science Fiction and Fantasy Writers at Work* (New York: Ungar, 1987) pp. 155–7. However, Dick was just as ready to interpret them as telepathic communication by Russians: see D. Scott Apel, *Philip K. Dick: The Dream Connection* (San Jose, Calif.: Permanent Press, 1987) pp. 91–110. *Valis* was also the most auto-biographical of Dick's novels, in the 'mundane' sense.

53. That was his preferred title, the novel being the only sequel he had yet written; but the publishers Simon and Schuster changed it 'because they didn't want to get involved in Bantam's promotion of *Valis*' – Gregg Rickman, *Philip K. Dick: In His Own Words*, 2nd edn (Long Beach, Calif.: Fragments West/Valentine Press, 1988) p. 190.

54. Apel, *Dick*, p. 284; Rickman, *Dick*, pp. 188–9, 238, 242. Rickman writes, 'It [*The Divine Invasion*] was at once a sequel to the earlier book and an answer to it, for while *Valis* is a work of mitigated despair *The Divine Invasion* is probably the most optimistic volume in Dick's canon' (p. 36).

55. Apel, *Dick*, p. 284; Rickman, *Dick*, pp. 190–2.

56. Rickman, *Dick*, pp. 190, 192. See also ibid., pp. 50–1, where Dick admits the likeness of *The Divine Invasion* to the world view of C. S. Lewis's *That Hideous Strength* (which he owned and had possibly read), and goes on, 'Do you suppose that I've independently rediscovered theism? Thinking to myself, in my artless fashion, that I had stumbled onto a major new concept, and all I'm doing is reinventing traditional orthodox Christianity?'

57. Philip K. Dick, *The Divine Invasion* (London: Corgi, 1982) pp. 202, 203.

58. See for example David Jasper, *The New Testament and the Literary Imagination* (London: Macmillan, 1987) esp. ch. 4. Note, however, Jasper's *caveat* in *The Study of Literature and Religion* (London: Macmillian, 1989) p. 137ff., against 'diluting "religion" to a point where, as the plaything of sociologists, cultural anthropologists, literary critics and many others, it simply becomes vacuous and theologically trivial'; he is concerned 'to recover a sense of the *theological* importance of the enterprise'.

59. Jürgen Moltmann, *Theology Today* (London: SCM Press, 1988). Among literary correlatives for some of these ideas are Nikos Kazantzakis's *Christ Recrucified* (1948) and *The Last Temptation* (1950–1), Walker Percy's *The Second Coming* (1980) and Russell Hoban's *Riddley Walker* (1980). See Jasper, *The New Testament and the Literary Imagination* p. 90; and Robert Detweiler, *Breaking the Fall: Religious Readings of Contemporary Fiction* (London: Macmillan, 1989) chs 3, 6.

Index

Ab Insulis, Alanus, *Anticlaudianus*, 12, 24, 34; *De Planctu Naturae*, forerunner of voyage myth in Dante, the *Commedia*, 307n.12; invention of myth in, 307n.12

Adams, Richard, *Shardik*, 209, 274, 338n.21; Christian parallels in, 274; *Watership Down*, biblical parallel in, 274; influence on Ford, *Quest for the Faradawn*, 275

Alpers, Paul (quoted), 55

Amis, Kingsley,*The Green Man*, 281

Aquinas, St Thomas, 22; *Summa Theologica*, 23, 25; quoted, 8

Ariosto, Ludovico, *Orlando Furioso*, influence on Spenser, *The Faerie Queene*, 50, 71; compared to *The Faerie Queene*, 55, 162

Aristotle, 23, 26

Arnold, Matthew, 158

Arthurian romance, 12–13; Christianised, 12–13

auctores, the, 23

Auden, W. H., 158

Avitus, *Poematum de Mosaicae Historiae Gestis*, 12, 317n.4

Bacon, Sir Francis, 115

Barth, Karl, 157

Bear, Greg, *Eon*, 290; *Eternity*, 290

Beckett, Samuel, 158

belief, Christian, contemporary American, 10, 304n.17; 'post-modernist', 301–2, 327n.13; Victorian, 156–7, 326n.1

Bellow, Saul, 158

Bely, Andrey, *Petersburg*, 267

Beowulf, only part-Christian fantasy, 305n.4

Bergerac, Cyrano de, *L'Autre Monde*, 94, 326n.3

Bernanos, Georges, 6,158; *Sous le Soleil du Satan*, 281

Bernardus Silvestris, *Cosmographia*, 12,34; forerunner of heavenly voyage in Dante, the *Commedia*, 307n.12; invention of new myth in *Cosmographia*, 307–8n.12; emphasis on allegory at expense of literal in narrative, contrasted to Dante, 307–8nn.12, 13

Bernini, Gian Lorenzo, 105

Béroul, 12

Bible, the, as authoritative truth, 1, 7, 8, 21; as Christian fantasy, 1–3, 4, 21; changing views of authority of, 1–2, 144, 147, 155, 156–7, 160–1, 301–2, 326n.3; varying debt of Christian fantasy writers to, 6, 9–10 and *passim*

biblical epic tradition, 102, 317n.4

Blake, William, view of the Bible as myth, 144,156; debt of his work to Dante, the *Commedia*, and Swedenborg, *Heaven and Hell*, 6; influences MacDonald and Lewis, 6; influences Kingsley, *The Water-Babies*, 194, 207
  works:
  'The Chimney–Sweeper', 194
  Jerusalem, 144
  'The Little Black Boy', 5, 144–7, 194; as Christian fantasy, 5; as critique of the use of Christian fable to console, 144–7; contrasted with Blake's *The Marriage of Heaven and Hell*,144; Swedenborgian influence in, 144, 324n.1
  The Marriage of Heaven and Hell, 7, 8, 132, 136, 137,140, 144, 147–55,156, 158, 165, 181, 320n.18 (cited); compared to Swedenborg, *Heaven and Hell*, 132,136,137,140; contrasted to 'The Little Black Boy', 144;